Date Due

TFS	3/12/03	

C   Access:
A Complete Guide to the State and National Parks
for Visitors with Limited Mobility

For information on how to order additional copies of California Parks Access
for yourself and your friends, please turn to page 319.

Cover photo - Antelope Valley California Poppy State Reserve
by Bonita Ballingham, Desert Sand Photography

Cover Design by Thomas Design Studio, Escondido, CA

Special thanks to Kevin Thomas of Thomas Design Studio,
for his artistic guidance and patient creation of the California Parks Access Map

California Parks Access:
A Complete Guide to the State and National Parks
for Visitors with Limited Mobility

By Linda and Allen Mitchell

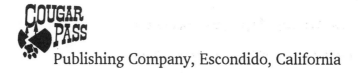
COUGAR PASS Publishing Company, Escondido, California

California Parks Access: A Complete Guide to the State and National Parks for Visitors with Limited Mobility

By Linda and Allen Mitchell

Published by Cougar Pass Publishing Company, PO Box 463060, Escondido, California, 92046-3060

Library of Congress Catalog Card Number: 91-077284

ISBN 0-9630758-3-7

To order additional copies of *California Parks Access*, see page 319

First Edition - 10 9 8 7 6 5 4 3 2 1

To Mom and Dad, who offer us love, consistent encouragement,
and the support we need to meet our personal challenges

Along with his regular duties as Ranger, Mark Wellman is in charge of access for disabled visitors at Yosemite National Park. In 1989, Mark Wellman and his climbing partner, Mike Corbett successfully climbed the 3000-foot face of El Capitan in Yosemite Valley. In the fall of 1991, Mark and Mike scaled Half Dome in the face of unexpected icy winds and inclimate weather.

Foreword

In California we are privileged to live near some of the most unique and varied natural beauty in the United States. Much of it has been preserved in our National and State Parks to be shared by all of us. Until the late 1980's, access for those with physical limitations, was difficult if not impossible. Since then, there has been an increased awareness of the basic access needs of all individuals. Many of the parks now provide improved accessibility and make special arrangements for visitors with disabilities.

As understanding grows about the needs of the disabled population, the State and National Parks systems continue to improve their facilities so that every visitor may create his own outdoor experience. Additional trails are being graded or paved where possible and campsites are being developed with accessible features including restrooms and showers for wheelchair users. Program access is now a prime consideration, so that visitor's of all abilities may participate in park activities. Finally, the parks are working to standardize accessible features so visitors can rely on access being available.

California Parks Access will provide you with the useful access information you'll want for planning a trip to one of California's many beautiful parks. Using the information in the book, you'll be able to choose a destination, get out and "just do it". Remember, on a visit to any of the parks, the most important gear to bring along is a "can-do" attitude. Not all barriers are physical. For some, the fear of the unknown or untried is what keeps them from experiencing the rejuvenation of spirit that comes from being among nature.

A wise man once said that "a journey of a thousand miles begins with the first step". So, take a hike, have a picnic, camp under the stars or rediscover our history at a museum. You will find some destinations more challenging than others, but with the right attitude, you can visit a lot of places you wouldn't have thought to go before. Experience California in whatever way you enjoy, but don't stay home and just read about it.

As a Yosemite National Park Ranger, visitors are constantly asking me for more access information. Having faced many of the same obstacles from my own wheelchair, I am pleased to have contributed to a guidebook that helps to meet the needs of our disabled visitors. *California Parks Access* takes a lot of the guesswork out of a visit to our parks, but the adventure is up to you.

Hope to see you on the trail!

Mark Wellman

Yosemite Park Ranger

Acknowledgements

We thank those whose insight and knowledge propelled us onward:

Patricia Autry — Regional Administration Officer, Frontera District; Chairman, CDPR Disabled Advisory Committee
Mary Beebe — Telephone Pioneers of America
Darrell Bennett — Park Ranger I, Salton Sea District
Dave Bellon — Director, Public Relations, HSN MISTIX
Janet Beutner — Past President, National Handicap Sports, La Habra Chapter
Leslie Blain — Museum Director, Sequoia National Park
Priscilla and Randy Bozarth — Traveling companions, book cover model
Jean Bray — Public Information Officer, Santa Monica Mountains National Recreation Area
Mike Brown — Technical Services Manager, CDPR
Sharon Callahan — Executive Director, Angel Island Association
Phyllis Cangemi — Executive Director, Whole Access, Inc.
Brad Childs — President, The Wilderness Institute
Charles Combs — Park Maintenance Chief I, Anza-Borrego District
Doug Correia — Park Maintenance Chief II, Eel River District
Ann Danko — Personel Services Specialist I, Former Tour Arranger, Hearst San Simeon State Historical Monument
Bobby Del Prete — Interpretive Programs Section, CDPR
Cindy Detwiler — Marketing Manager, Vallejo Red and White Fleet
Costa Dillon — Interpretive Ranger, Santa Monica Mountains National Recreation Area
Dennis Dolinar — Park Maintenance Supervisor, Santa Monica Mountains District
Kathleen Dolinar — State Park Ranger II, Channel Coast District
Kay Ellis — Access Specialist, Redwood National Park
Joseph Engbeck, Jr. — Publications Unit Supervisor, CDPR
Pepi Feinbladt — R.O.A.D., Recreation Outdoor Activities for the Disabled
Alan and Liz Feld — Sportsmobile West, Fresno, California
Linda Frybach — Spokesman, National Handicap Sports, "The Unwreckables" LA Chapter
Nina Gordon — Parks and Recreation Specialist, CDPR
Izell Gunner — State Park Ranger II, Frontera District
Mary Ellen Grigsby — Recreation Director, Shasta Lake Ranger District
Ron Haines — Director, Disabled Student Services, Palomar College, San Marcos, CA
Michael Hargett — Regional Park Supervisor, Castaic Lake Recreation Area
Gary Hathaway — National Park Ranger, Lava Beds National Monument
Bill Heilbronn — Park Maintenance Chief II, Sierra District
Gary Hoshide — Forester, United States Forest Service
Richard Johnson — State Park Ranger I, Eel River District
Don and Ione Larson — Avid park visitors, wheelchair user
Louis Levy — Coordinator, Santa Monica Mountains Conservancy Access Project
LeNae Liebtrau — Wheelchair athlete and camper
Harry Long — Owner, Pacific Mobility, San Marcos, CA
Jeffrey Marks — Administrator, Green Pastures, Inc.
Don Neubacher — Chief of Visitor Services, Point Reyes National Seashore
John Olmstead — President, California Institute of Man in Nature
Dan Poynter — Para Publishing, Inc.
Ann Porch — Wheelchair user, independent traveler
Tom Reed — State Park Ranger I, Klamath District
John Schmill — Staff Services Analyst, CDPR
Doug Seekatz — State Park Ranger I, Mendocino District
William Stewart — State Park Ranger, Klamath District
John Tagg — English Instructor, Palomar College, San Marcos, CA
Bill Truesdell — Chief Naturalist, Joshua Tree National Monument
Steven Wagy — Park Maintenance Chief, Big Sur District
Ray Ann Watson — Manager Recruitment Services Section, CDPR
Mark Wellman — National Park Ranger, Yosemite National Park
Vicki White — Director, Marin Center for Independent Living
Robert Wohl — State Park Ranger II, La Costa District
Clyde Wright — Chairman, Telephone Pioneers of America

TABLE OF CONTENTS

Map of Northern California State and National Parks

LEGEND

NM	NATIONAL MONUMENT
NP	NATIONAL PARK
NRA	NATIONAL RECREATION AREA
NS	NATIONAL SEASHORE
SB	STATE BEACH
SHM	STATE HISTORIC MONUMENT
SHP	STATE HISTORIC PARK
SR	STATE RESERVE
SRA	STATE RECREATION AREA
SP	STATE PARK
SVRA	STATE VEHICULAR RECREATION AREA
WC	WAYSIDE CAMPGROUND

CHAPTER ONE: NORTHERN CALIFORNIA COAST

CHAPTER TWO: NORTHERN CALIFORNIA INLAND

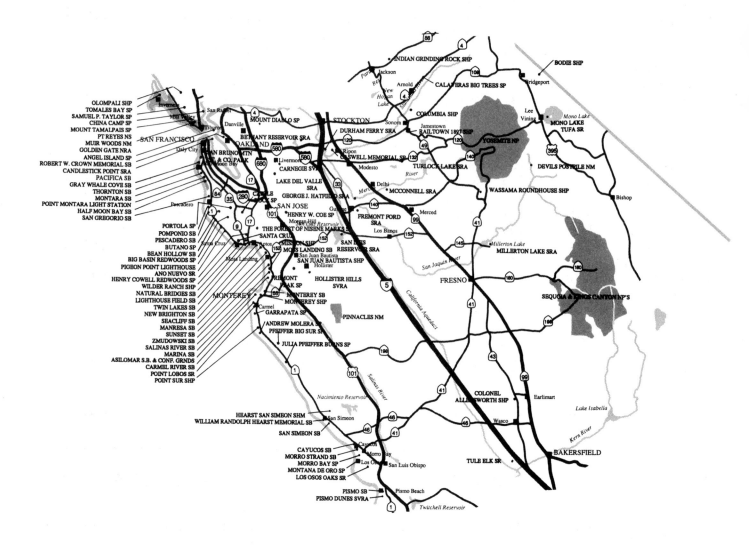

LEGEND

NM	NATIONAL MONUMENT
NP	NATIONAL PARK
NRA	NATIONAL RECREATION AREA
NS	NATIONAL SEASHORE
SB	STATE BEACH
SHM	STATE HISTORIC MONUMENT
SHP	STATE HISTORIC PARK
SR	STATE RESERVE
SRA	STATE RECREATION AREA
SP	STATE PARK
SVRA	STATE VEHICULAR RECREATION AREA
WC	WAYSIDE CAMPGROUND

CHAPTER THREE: CENTRAL CALIFORNIA COAST

CHAPTER FOUR: CENTRAL CALIFORNIA INLAND

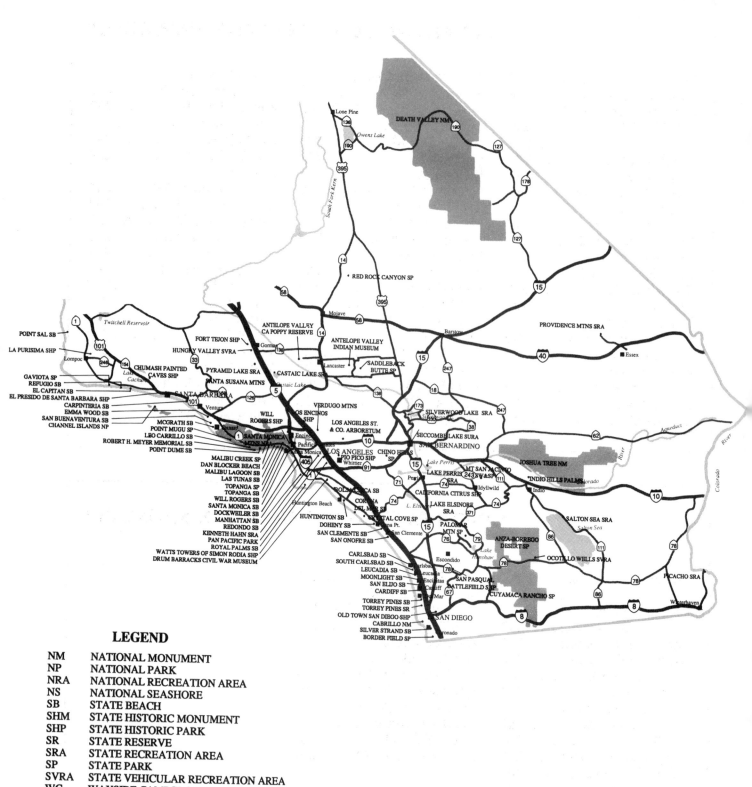

LEGEND

NM	NATIONAL MONUMENT
NP	NATIONAL PARK
NRA	NATIONAL RECREATION AREA
NS	NATIONAL SEASHORE
SB	STATE BEACH
SHM	STATE HISTORIC MONUMENT
SHP	STATE HISTORIC PARK
SR	STATE RESERVE
SRA	STATE RECREATION AREA
SP	STATE PARK
SVRA	STATE VEHICULAR RECREATION AREA
WC	WAYSIDE CAMPGROUND

CHAPTER FIVE: SOUTHERN CALIFORNIA COAST

CHAPTER SIX: SOUTHERN CALIFORNIA INLAND

Preface

Welcome to *California Parks Access*, the first guide book of its kind!

We are so pleased to be able to provide a helpful guide full of information for those with special access needs. California State and National Parks have so much beauty and interesting history to discover, it is a shame that more people are not taking advantage of their many accessible features. If you are already a park-goer, we hope to add more parks to your list of destinations. For those who haven't gotten out to the parks yet, California Parks Access provides you with enough access information to give you the confidence to start visiting California's great wealth of natural and historic preserves.

Our family has enjoyed camping and exploring California's parks for many years. When our son Adam, then 16, suffered a traumatic head injury, we realized that our trips would have to be modified and that there was almost no camping information for people with special access needs. Adam has since recovered, but our experience with adjusting to his mobility limitations made us recognize that we could make a difference for others with similar needs.

There is nothing like first-hand information, so rather than rely on access as reported by rangers or park staff, we personally visited each park in the book. After months of rehab experience, we knew that access needs vary widely from one individual to another. So we decided to gear our research toward wheelchair users, since they are the most limited by space and terrain. We also have taken into account, gradients and textures of traveling surfaces, distances between destinations and the placement of benches or rest areas for those with other kinds of physical limitations. Even Moms and Dads with strollers will find this information helpful.

You will notice that the park information we offer is quite different from the average guide book. General park descriptions are brief so there is room to talk about access considerations. In fact, there is so much access information to discuss, we found that we had run out of room for park maps or other diagrams. Park descriptions often correlate to the wonderful brochures and maps available from each park. If you are planning a trip, supplement *California Parks Access* with a park brochure from your chosen destination. That way you'll have individual park maps to refer to as you read along. (See Introduction for address.)

Not altogether an altruistic project, the research and production of *California Parks Access* has enriched our lives in ways we did not expect. Our experiences have broadened our understanding of the variety of physical and emotional barriers that exist everywhere for the physically disabled. We discovered that discrimination by oversight is the most common reason for access problems. We now understand that the able-bodied community responsible for our public lands and buildings must first become sensitive to the needs of the disabled before the real barriers can truly be eliminated.

The questions we asked when researching for this book undoubtedly increased the awareness of park rangers, maintenance and seasonal staff with whom we have consulted. We thank those who graciously assisted us in our work and we hope that our influence will help encourage some attention to the basic access rights of everyone. With the passage of the Americans with Disabilities Act of 1990, both the California Department of Parks and Recreation and the National Parks System are beginning to make the necessary modifications that will make our parks more accessible. This process will not happen overnight, and will require careful planning and budgeting. So we must be patient, yet persistent in making our needs known.

We applaud the efforts of the many organizations and individual volunteers who have given of their time and expertise to share outdoor experiences with people of all abilities. Those who offered special encouragement and assistance to us are listed in the acknowledgements; the dedicated organizations are listed in Appendix D.

Please write to us in care of Cougar Pass Publishing Co. and let us know about your personal park experience. It is our hope that by the time you visit the parks in our book, access will be even better than we report and that you will inform us about any improvements for our next edition. We welcome your suggestions. You can also help improve our parks by offering constructive suggestions to the park staff where you visit. Most of all, we hope you will use *California Parks Access* as your ticket to get out and partake of the many wonderful sights and attractions at California's State and National Parks.

Happy Traveling!

Allen and Linda Mitchell

Introduction

The authors of *California Parks Access* have filled this book with access information about every State and National Park in California. To more easily find the many valuable information sources, it will be important to understand the basic format of the book. It is arranged in a series of six chapters followed by a bountiful appendix and index.

Each of six chapters describes parks in different geographical regions. Beginning from the north and working southward. The north, central and south regions of the state are described first on the coast then inland. Parks within each chapter are listed as they appear from north to south in their respective region. So, as you read along, parks nearest one another tend to be listed in the same part of the chapter.

A **regional map** precedes each chapter including its location relative to the rest of the state. If you would like a detailed map of a particular park, check the end of each park description. There you'll find the park's address and phone number and a note indicating if a park information folder is available. Highly detailed individual park maps are helpful to have as you read along. In the interest of space, the authors were unable to include park maps in this edition.

In the **Appendix,** the authors have provided a complete reference source for park access information. In Appendix A, you'll find a concise summary of accessibility in each park. MISTIX Camping information follows in Appendices B and C. Appendix D is a listing of organizations that are involved in outdoor access. You may wish to contact them for information about group activities or other interesting points of interest in the parks. There is a glossary of terms used in *California Parks Access,* and a listing of park district offices referred to in the text. Finally, an extensive reference index will help you quickly find specific park information.

(Photo courtesy Whole Access, Inc.)

19

Park Description

California Parks Access includes a brief discussion of every park whether there are accessible features or not. Descriptions of parks that have little or no accessible features are short, thus saving room for detailed information about parks that have better access.

In the opening paragraph(s), you'll find a brief description of main attractions or the historical significance of each park, followed by a thumbnail sketch of its accessibility. For the larger or more accessible parks, appropriate headings announce detailed summaries of features. Major park landmarks described in the text are highlighted in **bold** type. Accessible features or features marked with an international handicap symbol, such as restrooms, parking places, or drinking fountains, are accentuated by using *UNDERLINED ITALICIZED SMALL CAPITALS*. Restroom information is usually toward the end of each descriptive category.

After the park description, a general information section will provide you with the address, phone number, location, and altitude of the park. District office information is available in Appendix E. If a park brochure is available, there will be a note in this section. Unless special instructions are given for obtaining park information, you may receive a park folder by calling the phone number listed (a small fee is usually charged for park folders). Another way to order state publications is to use the Publications Price List, a complete listing of books and pamphlets available for purchase. To receive this list, call or write to:

California Department of Parks and Recreation Office of Publications

1416 9th Street, Room 118
Sacramento, CA 95814
(916) 322-7000

_____

Visitor Centers

Visitor centers, museums, and other interpretive centers are housed in many types of buildings. To add impact to an interpretive display, exhibits are sometimes arranged in historic structures. Though park planners are trying to provide access to every visitor center, many times, the doorways or layout of historic buildings preclude retrofitting for wheelchair access without changing the historic fabric of the building. Therefore, some buildings are not accessible. The State and National Park Services plan to modify as many of these structures as is feasible in the coming years.

Parking

Since parking availability varies so widely from park to park, the authors felt it important to offer at least a general idea of parking surfaces and proximity to park features. Parking places designated for those with handicap-identification placards will be referred to simply as "designated." Designated *PARKING* places are often the same width as standard spaces, but they are usually near the closest access point to a park feature unless otherwise described.

Picnic Areas

Access and accommodations at areas set aside for picnics vary widely. For the most part, picnicking is usually located on natural surfaces. And, unless otherwise mentioned, the tables are standard wooden picnic tables with no modifications for wheelchair access. Sometimes there is room at the end of the table to wheel a chair under, but most standard picnic tables have insufficient knee room for wheelchair access.

Piers

If you can get a wheelchair onto a park pier, it is mentioned in the description. Unfortunately, most piers and fishing bridges are surrounded by high railings that are not modified for fishing access from a seated position. Piers and other fishing locations with special access considerations are noted and described more thoroughly.

Swimming Beaches

The lake and ocean beaches of California's parks are a particularly inviting part of outdoor life here. Unfortunately, too few of the parks provide wheelchair users with a way to get out onto the sand or shoreline. When "beach access" is provided, it is usually a firm temporary surface such as wood plank or rubber matting. At a few parks, permanent paved pathways are provided. Because walkway maintenance becomes increasingly difficult as it nears the water line, stationary access paths usually end well before the high tide level.

Boat Launches

Launching your boat can be a real challenge when there is no way to access the loading dock. The complications double when you face the prospect of parking far from the dock and making your way back to your boat. So that you may plan more easily, descriptions of boat launches include information about loading procedures and parking your boat and trailer.

Restrooms

As with every public facility, restrooms at the parks vary widely even within individual park units. Up to now, there have been no outdoor access guidelines. Newly-built or remodeled restrooms must offer accessible stalls, but the approach to the buildings are not yet regulated. The park description locates all accessible RESTROOMS for you. Those with varying access and approach surfaces are described so you can decide for yourself ahead of time if they fit your needs.

At many parks, restroom doors are left in a open position and remain that way throughout the day. These doors were not tested for resistance. Doors that were particularly heavy to push or pull are noted, but not all doors were tested.

Chemical toilets (known to most as porta-potties) are often provided in primitive or under-developed areas. Sometimes, a wheelchair accessible chemical toilet is also available. Referred to by the authors as an "accessible chemical toilet," these portable units have a ramped doorway and allow for a full-sized wheelchair to enter and close the door behind. Besides primitive areas, accessible chemical toilets are often placed in parks that have no accessible restrooms. If the toilet on a dirt surface, access onto the ramp can be unpredictable and sometimes poses a challenge. This is usually noted, but since these toilets are portable, they may not be in the same location all the time.

Showers

Campers especially appreciate the showers often provided as part of the campground restroom facility. Because most were built before the advent of access standards, shower stalls are usually quite small with only enough room to stand. The doorways, tucked in tight passageways next to the restrooms, are usually narrow and have a lip down into the stall to facilitate drainage. Campers with special access needs will not be able to use them. Gradually, old restrooms and showers are being replaced with new, accessible buildings. Shower stalls having possible access, and new accessible stalls are described in the camping section.

Trails

Most people would consider a hike in the woods out of the question for a person with limited mobility. On the contrary, there are many trails, both short and long, that are very well suited or adaptable for wheelchair users. In fact, some trails have been specially designed to include physically challenged individuals. The authors describe the trail tread and steepness of most trails that would even remotely be feasible for the average wheelchair user. Of course, natural surface trails are subject to change due to weather conditions and other natural occurances, so it is always a good idea to check with a ranger if you are attempting a trail that is new to you.

Several organizations are taking an active role in supervising and building accessible TRAILS in California's parks and wilderness areas. For that reason you will be enjoying easier access to many lovely settings in the woods, along the coast and among desert wildlife. For more information about these access organizations, see Appendix D.

Camping

Getting away from it all for some includes a restful stay in a campground where the cares of everyday life are replaced by the presence of nature and pleasant surroundings. Camping for a wheelchair user can be a very enjoyable experience if you plan ahead. The camping information given will help you decide whether the campground will be appropriate for your needs.

Though campgrounds vary widely in terrain and climate, most of the family campsite improvements are very similar, including a table, a cooking or campfire area, and a place to park. The challenge for most wheelchair users is the uneven terrain conditions and restroom access. Unless special paved sites are provided, camping areas are located in a natural setting with an earthen surface. Usually, a paved road connects the sites, but that too can be steep or rolling. The terrain at every campground is described so you'll know what to expect. Access to restrooms and showers are also discussed toward the end of each campground description.

Where appropriate, the authors suggest campsites or possible alternatives to the handicap site. These campsites are mentioned because they are the most level sites and/or are near an accessible restroom. Whether or not you've made reservations for the campground, the campground staff person or host will often let you drive through to select a site then come back to the kiosk and register for it. Therefore, you may wish to take a look at the suggested sites first.

Most primitive and environmental campgrounds are not included in park descriptions. These sites are largely inaccessible for the average wheelchair user. The sites are unimproved except possibly for a table and fire recepticle, with only a chemical toilet nearby. Environmental campsites are often just a designated area along a trail where camping is allowed. Those with a hardy spirit for adventure can call the park ranger to get more information about access to the primitive areas.

Group Picnics and Camping

If you have a group that is interested in an outing, many parks have accessible group camping or picnicking facilities. Contact the ranger at the individual park you are interested in and he or she will be able to direct you to a suitable spot. Often, group facilities are more accessible than the family camping and picnic areas. Most group campgrounds require a reservation. Since California Parks Access is designed specifically for family outings, most group facilities are not described. For information about State Park group camping and picnic reservations, call MISTIX at (800) 444-PARK and they will send you a complete camping information sheet that includes reservation instructions for group sites. For National Parks, it is best to contact the ranger at the park you are interested in visiting.

Summary

Nearly all the information in California Parks Access was gathered personally by the authors, using an Everest and Jennings Advantage wheelchair, with a 26½" wheel width, foot rests and standard non-pneumatic tires. Since turning radius and clearance needs vary, those with larger chairs or power chairs will need to consider their own chair dimensions when using California Parks Access as a trip planning guide. Sometimes inclines or access routes can only be described in a subjective manner (i.e. "you will need assistance for this path"). In these cases, access was accomplished by a wheelchair user with full upper body capabilities and an able-bodied assistant (when needed).

State Parks

Annual Pass—Frequent day-users of state park facilities may purchase a pass that is permanently affixed to your vehicle. It is good for park entry and boat launch usage for one calendar year. If you use more than one vehicle, you must purchase an additional pass for each. You may purchase this pass at most State Park kiosks or ranger stations. If you visit the parks often, this pass offers a real savings.

Golden Bear Pass—A free pass good for day use and boat launch at park facilities is offered if you are age 62 or older with a limited income. If you receive aid to the blind, disabled or Aid to Families with Dependent Children through the Department of Social Service, you are also eligible. You may obtain your Golden Bear Pass at most State Park kiosks or ranger stations.

Disabled Veterans Pass—If you are an honorably discharged veteran with 70% or more service-connected disability or have a service-connected disability rated 100% for reasons of unemployability, you qualify for the Disabled Veteran's Pass. On payment of a one-time fee, you'll be issued a pass permitting use of most State Park System facilities, including boat launching. Once a pass has been issued, you may make discounted camping reservations through MISTIX, subject to a standard non-refundable reservation charge. For further information, requests must be addressed to: Disabled Veterans Pass Program, Department of Parks and Recreation, PO Box 942896, Sacramento, CA, 94296-0001.

Disabled Discount Pass—If you are permanently disabled, you qualify for a pass which permits a year-round 50% discount of fees for use of State Park System facilities (except Hearst Castle). Once a pass is issued, you may make discounted camping reservations through MISTIX, subject to a standard non-refundable reservation charge and limited to one campsite per pass holder. For further information, requests must be addressed to: Disabled Discount Pass Program, Department of Parks and Recreation, PO Box 942896, Sacramento, CA, 94296-0001.

Senior Citizen Discount—If you're a senior citizen aged 62 or older, you may receive a $2.00 per night campsite fee discount if you request it when making the reservation. When you register at the campground, you'll need to show proof of your eligibility for the discount. This discount is good only for family campsites and must be used by the senior citizen.

National Parks

Golden Eagle Passport—If you're a frequent visitor to the National Parks, you will want to purchase an annual pass. It gives you unlimited entry into any of the National Parks for the calendar year. The Golden Eagle Passport does not provide for a reduced camping fee, and you must renew it annually, but it can be a real savings to avid park-goers.

Golden Age Passport—If you are 62 years of age or older and a citizen of the United States, you qualify for the Golden Age Passport. This FREE LIFETIME PASS will give you free entrance into any federal recreation area that charges fees. It also allows a 50% discount on user fees such as camping fees. When you apply for this pass at any National Park Service area, you must present proof of age.

Golden Access Passport—If you are blind or permanently disabled and a resident of the United States, this FREE LIFETIME PASS

will give you free entrance into any federal recreation area that charges fees. It also allows a 50% discount on user fees such as campground fees. To apply, bring appropriate documentation to any National Park Service area. Persons who lack appropriate documentation may sign a statement attesting to their eligibility to receive the pass.

Camping Reservations

State Parks

Some campgrounds in the state park system are operated by a concessionaire or a government agency other than the State Park System. Instructions for making reservations for these campgrounds will be given in the individual park description. All of the others may be reserved by contacting MISTIX (800) 444-7275. Specific campsites cannot be reserved but are mentioned in the

(Photo courtesy Whole Access, Inc.)

park description to assist you in choosing a site when you arrive at the campground. See the Appendix C for specific MISTIX reservation information listed for each campground.

Unless described otherwise, make your camping reservation with MISTIX no sooner than eight weeks in advance of your visit. If you are calling from a California telephone, contact MISTIX at (800) 444-7275. If you are calling from out of state, call (619) 452-1950. Of course you may also take the chance that there will be an available campsite on the day of arrival, but if you know your schedule ahead of time, it is best to reserve a site early, especially during the busy summer season. If you have a Disabled Discount Pass or are eligible for a Senior Citizen Discount, be sure to so state when making your reservations and a 50% discount on your campground fee will be extended to you. Reservation fees remain the same.

The reservation operator will want to know the dates you wish to reserve, which park you wish to visit and what type of equipment you will be using to camp (tent, RV, camper, etc.). When you make your reservation, be sure that the park, dates, number of days and equipment code are correct. Once you hang up the phone, your reservation is final. If your plans change, you must cancel that reservation, pay a cancellation fee, make a new reservation and pay another reservation fee.

When your reservation is confirmed, you will be given a Reservation Validation Number to register with at the park, along with your driver's license or other picture ID. If you qualified for a disabled discount on your campsite fees, you must also show your Disabled Discount Pass at the campground.

Payment

You may charge your reservation and campsite fees to your VISA, MasterCard, American Express, or Discover Card account or defer payment. Under the deferred payment method, reservations are accepted up to TEN DAYS before your arrival date. Your check or money order for payment in full on all fees must be received by MISTIX within SEVEN DAYS from the date you made your reservation, or your reservation will be automatically canceled. If you have questions about your deferred payment reservation, call MISTIX Customer Service at (619) 452-5956.

Reservation Voucher

When you receive your reservation voucher in the mail, make sure that the park, dates, and equipment codes are correct. If not, call MISTIX Customer Service at (619) 452-5956.

Cancellations and Refunds

You will be refunded the amount you paid for your campsite, less the non-refundable reservation fee and a cancellation fee, if you:

CANCEL BY MAIL—Write a letter and mail it to MISTIX Customer Service, PO Box 85705, San Diego, CA 92138. It must be received at least eight days before your arrival date or you will forfeit the campsite fee for your arrival date.

CANCEL BY PHONE up to eight days before your arrival date. Call MISTIX Customer Service at (619) 452-5956.

You will be refunded a partial amount that you paid for you campsite, if you:

CANCEL BY PHONE from seven days up to 2 p.m. one day before you arrival date. Call MISTIX Customer Service at (619) 452-5956, and you will be refunded the amount you paid for your campsite less the campsite fee for your arrival date, the non-refundable reservation fee and a cancellation fee.

There are no refunds for cancellations made after 2 p.m. on your arrival date. Your reserved campsite will be held by the park until 2 p.m. the day after your arrival date. If you do not appear by then, you will be considered a "No Show", your reservation will be canceled by the park, and no refund will be made.

IF YOU MUST LEAVE THE PARK ONE OR MORE DAYS EARLY, you must check out before 12 noon, and get your copy of the canceled Camp Registration receipt to receive a refund for your unused nights, less a cancellation fee. There are no exchanges and you should keep your voucher until your account has been credited or your refund received, which could take 30 days or more.

———

National Parks

While most camping in the National Parks is provided on a first-come-first-served basis, there are a few popular campgrounds where reservations can be made through MISTIX. The campgrounds that take reservations will be mentioned as part of the individual park description. Reservations may be made no sooner than eight weeks in advance, and up to the day before your planned arrival. Because of the heavy demand at these campgrounds, it is advisable to make your plans early. If you plan to camp during the peak season (as listed in APPENDIX B), you'll need to call exactly eight weeks ahead of the first day of your stay to be sure of getting a campsite. See APPENDIX B for specific campground reservation information about each campground listed with MISTIX.

You may make a reservation **in person** at any park on the reservation system. You may also make your reservation at National Park Service information offices in Washington D.C., Atlanta, Denver, Phoenix, or Agoura Hills, California.

If you wish to reserve **by mail**, pick up or call for a MISTIX brochure, complete the form in the brochure and mail it to MISTIX at the address shown so that it arrives at least three weeks before you plan to start your trip. Be sure to read all the instructions in the MISTIX brochure before filling out your application. You must have your reservation ticket when you check in. The National Park Service or MISTIX does not take responsibility for delays in mail service. While tickets may be purchased at a park if space is available, no tickets for reservations made by mail will be held at a park for pickup on arrival. VISA, MasterCard, personal checks or money orders are accepted for mail orders.

Reservations are available **by telephone** for all National Park campgrounds listed with MISTIX by calling (800) 365-CAMP. VISA, MasterCard, or Discover Card are accepted. Phone reservations made within 10 days of arrival will be held at the campground, all others will be mailed.

The reservation operator will want to know the dates you wish to reserve, which park you wish to visit and what type of equipment you will be using to camp. When you make your reservation, be sure that the park, dates, number of days and equipment code are correct. Once you hang up the phone, your reservation is final. If your plans change, you must cancel that reservation, pay a cancellation fee, make a new reservation and pay another reservation fee.

Reservation Voucher

When you receive your reservation voucher in the mail, make sure that the park, dates, and equipment codes are correct. If not, call MISTIX Customer Service at (619) 452-5956.

Site Selection

Reservations are made for a particular park and campground, but specific campsites cannot be reserved except for the designated sites reserved for holders of a handicap-identification placard. If you arrive early at the campground, most parks will permit you to select a site other than the one assigned as long as it is still vacant and meets the same camping equipment needs. Campsite discussions in each park description are intended to assist you in selecting a site if there is a choice. If campground personnel are not on duty when you arrive, your campsite assignment will be posted on the entry kiosk.

Passport Holders

If you have a Golden Age Passport or a Golden Access Passport you are entitled to a 50% reduction in camping fees. Your Golden Age or Golden Access Passport number must be given to the telephone reservation operator at the time of the reservation to obtain your discount. Be sure to have your Passport with you when you check in at your campground.

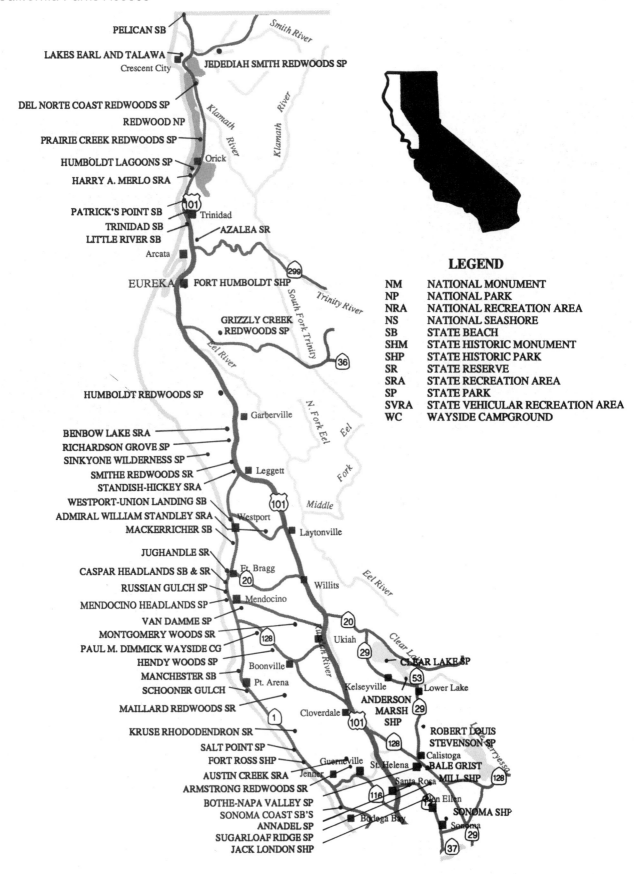

PELICAN SB

LAKES EARL AND TALAWA
Crescent City

JEDEDIAH SMITH REDWOODS SP

Smith River

Klamath River

Klamath River

DEL NORTE COAST REDWOODS SP

REDWOOD NP

PRAIRIE CREEK REDWOODS SP

Klamath River

HUMBOLDT LAGOONS SP — Orick

HARRY A. MERLO SRA

PATRICK'S POINT SB — 101 — Trinidad

TRINIDAD SB

LITTLE RIVER SB — AZALEA SR

Arcata

EUREKA — FORT HUMBOLDT SHP — 299

Trinity River

GRIZZLY CREEK REDWOODS SP

South Fork Trinity

36

HUMBOLDT REDWOODS SP

Eel River

Garberville

N. Fork Eel

BENBOW LAKE SRA

RICHARDSON GROVE SP

SINKYONE WILDERNESS SP

SMITHE REDWOODS SR — Leggett

STANDISH-HICKEY SRA

Fork

WESTPORT-UNION LANDING SB — 101

ADMIRAL WILLIAM STANDLEY SRA — Westport

MACKERRICHER SB — Laytonville

Middle

JUGHANDLE SR

CASPAR HEADLANDS SB & SR — Ft. Bragg — 20

RUSSIAN GULCH SP — Willits

MENDOCINO HEADLANDS SP — Mendocino

Eel River

VAN DAMME SP

MONTGOMERY WOODS SR — 128 — 20

PAUL M. DIMMICK WAYSIDE CG — Ukiah

HENDY WOODS SP — Boonville — 29

MANCHESTER SB — Clear Lake — CLEAR LAKE SP

SCHOONER GULCH — Pt. Arena — 53

Kelseyville — Lower Lake

MAILLARD REDWOODS SR — ANDERSON MARSH SHP — 29

Cloverdale — 101

KRUSE RHODODENDRON SR — ROBERT LOUIS STEVENSON SP

128

SALT POINT SP — Calistoga

FORT ROSS SHP — Guerneville — St. Helena — BALE GRIST MILL SHP — 128

AUSTIN CREEK SRA — Jenner — Santa Rosa

ARMSTRONG REDWOODS SR — 116 — Glen Ellen

BOTHE-NAPA VALLEY SP — SONOMA SHP

SONOMA COAST SB'S — Bodega Bay — Sonoma

ANNADEL SP — 29

SUGARLOAF RIDGE SP

JACK LONDON SHP — 37

1

LEGEND

NM	NATIONAL MONUMENT
NP	NATIONAL PARK
NRA	NATIONAL RECREATION AREA
NS	NATIONAL SEASHORE
SB	STATE BEACH
SHM	STATE HISTORIC MONUMENT
SHP	STATE HISTORIC PARK
SR	STATE RESERVE
SRA	STATE RECREATION AREA
SP	STATE PARK
SVRA	STATE VEHICULAR RECREATION AREA
WC	WAYSIDE CAMPGROUND

Dry Lagoon, Humboldt Bay SP *(Photo courtesy CDPR)*

NORTHERN CALIFORNIA COAST

| Humboldt and Del Norte Counties |

PELICAN STATE BEACH

The northernmost park in the State Park system is Pelican State Beach. This small beach is just a few yards from the Oregon border. You must use a steep bluff trail to reach the secluded beach. Parking is on an unmarked road directly across Highway 101 from the Pelican Beach Motel. There are no other facilities here.

Pelican State Beach
(707) 464-9533 or 458-3310

Location — Twenty-one miles north of Crescent City on U.S. Hwy 101
Elevation — Sea level

LAKES EARL AND TALAWA

Five thousand acres around the mouth of the Smith River provide a natural wetlands for a variety of wildlife at Lakes Earl and Talawa. Presently, this undeveloped area is only for low-impact use. Access to the lakes, river, and ocean is difficult; poorly marked dirt roads in this park lead to unpaved, ungraded walkways.

Environmental campsites are located beyond a locked gate north of Kellogg Road. Each sandy site is secluded in grass-covered dunes that are common to the area. Only chemical toilets are available here. To obtain further information or the gate key, call or stop by the entry kiosk at Del Norte Coast Redwoods State Park.

Lakes Earl and Talawa
c/o Del Norte Coast Redwoods State Park
PO Drawer J
Crescent City, CA 95531
(707) 464-9533 or 458-3310

Location — Approximately ½ mile north of Crescent City off U.S. Hwy 101. Call for further directions.
Elevation — 10 feet

REDWOOD NATIONAL PARK

Thousands of years ago, Giant Redwood forests blanketed much of western North America. Due to dramatic climate changes, redwood survivors now only exist on the California and Oregon coast. In this century, society's insatiable need for lumber products created massive logging efforts that nearly eliminated the last of the species. Twenty-two years ago, a group of forward - thinking conservationists and politicians founded Redwood National Park to preserve and restore what was left of the ancient redwoods. With help from State and National Parks Services and concerned environmentalists, thousand-year-old specimens have managed to outlive their human predators and are joined by new and second-growth trees. With the addition of three State Parks — Jedediah, Del Norte Coast Redwoods, and Prairie Creek — the 28,000-acre redwood ecosystem at Redwood National Park provides a complete habitat that includes watershed protection and coastal access.

The staff of Redwood National Park has given careful attention to the accessibility of its many wonderful features. Turn-outs and picnic areas have accessible RESTROOMS and PICNIC TABLES, and every visitor center or ranger station is accessible. Trails and other dirt surfaces in all of the redwood parks can be muddy and soft during much of the year, so keep that in mind when you plan your visit. If you have questions or suggestions about access to the park, an access coordinator is available at the park headquarters in Crescent City, (707) 464-6101.

Visitor Centers

Hiouchi Ranger Station — The Hiouchi Ranger Station lies at the park's northeast entrance on Hwy 199. Besides park information and exhibits, the VISITOR CENTER sells a fine selection of books, posters, and gift items. In the summer months, park interpreters lead NATURAL HISTORY TALKS and NATURE WALKS in the area and will tailor their presentations to your special needs. If possible, you should call ahead to arrange an enjoyable visit.

Ramps and redwood decking lead from two designated PARKING places to an accessible RESTROOM (pivot-transfer, high toilet, and grab bars) and DRINKING FOUNTAIN. A ramp also leads to the ranger station entrance. Most features inside are low enough to see from a seated position.

Crescent City Park Headquarters — As the park's main visitor center, headquarters is a great place to find what you're looking for in the way of books and informational pamphlets. They have an extensive selection of publications about the redwood region, its history, and its peoples. In addition, park interpreters are available to answer your questions and will help you in any way possible.

Designated PARKING for headquarters is on the street near the main entrance to the building. From the curb cut, a concrete patio leads to the main entrance, which has a heavy door. The restroom in this building is difficult for wheelchair users to manage due to two very sharp turns as you enter the room. The interior is roomy, has a high sink, and diagonal transfer to a high toilet with grab bars.

Crescent Beach Information Center — An old ranch house once belonging to the MacNamara family is home to the Crescent Beach Information Center. The refurbished house has been modified for wheelchair access. Exhibit subjects focus on the coastal environment and on the history of the Indians native to this region. There is a ramp to the front entrance from the designated PARKING; and a nearby RESTROOM is accessible. To find the Macnamara ranch house, take the first narrow road to the left past the Redwoods National Park entrance sign on Enderts Beach Road.

Redwood Information Center — Located near the estuary at the mouth of Redwood Creek is the Redwood Information Center. Besides the information desk and book sales, the center offers a three-dimensional topographic map of the area, a hands-on exhibit low enough for all ages, and an accessible THEATER. A concrete ramp (3%) on the south side of the building will lead you to the entry.

When logging in this region was at its zenith, Redwood Creek estuary was the site of a lumber mill that all but destroyed the natural ecosystem of the wetlands. The estuary is now being restored to its original natural state, and is home again to birds, waterfowl, and river otters. North of the visitor center, seven hundred feet of redwood BOARDWALK will take you on a short tour of the wetlands. Well-marked displays describe the history of the area and tell of further plans for restoration by the Park Service. South of the visitor center, on the

Freshwater Lagoon Spit, the day use area offers a modified _PICNIC_ _TABLE_ and accessible _CHEMICAL_ _TOILET_. The path to the picnic area has a sandy coating that creates some traction problems for wheelchair users.

Picnic and Vista Points

Crescent Beach — Crescent Beach is a popular place to stop for a picnic or a cool coastal pause. There is one designated _PARKING_ spot near an asphalt walkway that leads to a blufftop _PICNIC_ _TABLE_ with extended ends and a nearby accessible _CHEMICAL_ _TOILET_. From there, a gently sloping grassy trail leads to the beach viewing area. To find Crescent Beach, take Enderts Beach Road off Hwy 101 to the picnic area. It is advisable not to pull a trailer beyond this point at Crescent Beach. Further south on Enderts Road, a paved _BEACH_ _OVERLOOK_ could be a great place for whale and bird watching. The beach has no other accessible features besides the overlook.

Vista Point near Demonstration Forest — South of Enderts Beach Road cut-off on U.S. Hwy 101, is a paved turn-out with a bird's-eye view northward to Crescent Beach and Crescent City. Marked wayside exhibits lie along a paved pathway and there is a _PICNIC_ _TABLE_ with extended ends near a designated _PARKING_ place. There are no restrooms here.

Lagoon Creek — Bird-watchers love to linger at Lagoon Creek, where many varieties of wading and field birds make their homes. Near the mouth of the Klamath River, there is a paved _SIDEWALK_ along the northern edge of the lagoon. It leads to an accessible _RESTROOM_ (high toilet, pivot-transfer, and grab bars) and _DRINKING_ _FOUNTAIN_. Not far from the paved designated _PARKING_ is a small accessible _FISHING_ _PIER_ and _TABLE_ with extended ends. You'll have an unobstructed view of the lagoon from here.

Klamath Overlook — From a vantage point high above the mouth of the Klamath River, you'll have a view of the coastline north from Crescent City, south to Patrick's Point, on a clear day. The overlook offers the added convenience of a modified _PICNIC_ _TABLE_ and accessible _CHEMICAL_ _TOILET_. To get here, take Requa Road to Patrick J. Murphy Drive. This paved road is very narrow, steep, and winding, so it is advisable not to drive a long vehicle here.

Coastal Drive — Along this 8-mile coastal scenic route, you'll have yet another great view of the coastline. For a historical slant, markers along the way describe the area as it appeared in the 1940's when it was a radar station. Parts of this road are narrow and unpaved; it is best not to drive an RV or trailer here.

High Bluffs Picnic Area — This spectacular overlook is the site of an old quarry. Of all the viewpoints at Redwood National Park, be sure not to miss this one. On a clear day, the coastline seems to run forever. You will spot bird rookeries nearby, and seasonal whale watching is exceptional. A paved _PATHWAY_ from the parking lot leads to the overlook. Here you'll find a modified _PICNIC_ _TABLE_ and an accessible _CHEMICAL_ _TOILET_. To get to High Bluffs, take the Coastal Drive to a point just north of the western terminus of Alder Camp Road.

The redwoods are a beautiful sight any time of the day.

(Photo courtesy CDPR)

County Fish Hatchery—Across a level bridge from the fish hatchery, a modified *PICNIC TABLE* sits in the shade near a creek. If you linger on the bridge in the fall, you'll be able to spot steelhead trout and salmon as they make their annual spawning journey upstream. The pathway to the picnic area is hard-packed dirt. There is no restroom yet, but there are plans to improve access in this area.

Lost Man Creek—This secluded stream-side picnic spot and trail-head offers picnic tables in a shady redwood grove. The forest floor surfaces are sometimes soft. You may need some help getting across a bed of wood chips to the accessible *CHEMICAL TOILET*. To find this picnic area located on the east side of Hwy 101, make a quick turn onto the dirt road across from the Caltrans field office. The road is south of the fish hatchery and north of Davison/Fern Canyon Road.

Redwood Creek Overlook—On Bald Hills Road, beyond Lady Bird Johnson Grove, is a new picnic area with accessible features. From designated *PARKING*, there is a paved *PATHWAY* to a modified *PICNIC TABLE* and accessible *CHEMICAL TOILET*. A paved overlook will provide you with a splendid view of the Prairie Creek drainage area. From there you can watch the fog approach, engulfing the coastline daily as it brings essential moisture for the coastal redwoods. Interpretive displays illustrate the on-going efforts to rehabilitate this region once ravaged by large-scale logging of the early 1900's.

Trails

Redwood Creek Trail—Along Redwood Creek Trail you'll find examples of old- and new-growth forests merging to repair themselves. The trail begins at the picnic area and trailer turn-around off the right fork of Bald Hills Road. It runs for 8½ miles, but only the first ½ mile is accessible for some wheelchair users. The beginning of the level trail is a hard-packed, uneven dirt surface, but exposed roots and twigs can present obstacles. At the trailhead, there are picnic tables under the trees, but there is no potable water and only a standard chemical toilet.

Lady Bird Johnson Grove—Named for the first lady at the time of the park's dedication, Lady Bird Johnson Grove is a quiet respite from the more well-traveled areas of the park. Take the left fork of Bald Hills Road where it divides shortly after leaving U.S. Hwy 101. The road becomes steep and narrow as you approach the grove. There is an accessible *CHEMICAL TOILET* at the trailhead parking area.

A written guide for the *ONE-MILE LOOP TRAIL* through the forest is available at the trailhead. The trail begins at a bridge that has an uneven transition at its beginning and exposed roots on a steep incline on the other side. If you have help, the first part of the trail as far as exhibit #9 is accessible.

Yurok Trail—At Lagoon Creek's Yurok Trail, marked exhibits of the wet6lands plant and animal life line the first paved portion of the Yurok Trail. It begins a short distance from the traffic circle at the end of the parking area. A brochure is available at the trailhead. Where the paving ends, the trail becomes hard-packed dirt and extends beyond a bridge and out into a river bed meadow. At the first overlook on the dirt section, there is a 15% grade for a short distance. Beyond this point, the trail becomes more unpredictable depending on rain, water level, and foot traffic.

Lodging

Though Redwood National Park provides only day use facilities, there are accessible campgrounds in each of the three state parks within its boundaries. (See park listings for Jedediah Smith Redwoods, Prairie Creek Redwoods, and Del Norte Coast Redwoods State Parks). In addition, the **De-Martin House** near Lagoon Creek, operated by American Youth Hostels, Inc., offers accessible dorm-like lodging at reasonable rates. For further information write for a brochure: American Youth Hostels, 425 Divisadero #306, San Francisco, CA 94117, (415) 863-9939.

Redwood National Park
1111 Second Street
Crescent City, CA 95531
(707) 464-6101

Park Folder—Redwood Map and Guide; Access Guide to Redwood National Park, 1991 publication; Visitor Guide—Redwood National Park (newspaper); The Coast Redwood folder.
Location—Along U.S. Hwy 101 from Orick to just north of Crescent City
Elevation—0-1,000 feet

Families enjoy the beach at the Smith River, Jedediah Smith Redwoods SP.

(Photo courtesy CDPR)

JEDEDIAH SMITH REDWOODS STATE PARK

Jedediah Smith State Park, known for its stately coast redwoods, is also famous for its record-breaking steelhead catches at the Smith River. The Smith is the last major river in California without a dam. From October to February, fishermen converge on the area looking for their own record-breaker.

The park was named for wilderness explorer Jedediah Smith. Smith, the first American to cross the Sierra Nevada. He was also the first to traverse California by land from San Diego to the Columbia River. This park contains an unusual variety of coastal and inland shrubs and trees and has several stands of old-growth redwoods; one of which encompasses more than 5,000 acres. Then there is Stout Grove, home to one of the world's largest coast redwoods, with a diameter of 20 feet! Besides the diverse plant life, the park contains deer, squirrels, an occasional black bear, and many raccoons who sometimes show up to scavenge a meal at the campground.

Families enjoy this park for its beauty and mild summer weather. Because it is an inland park, there is less summer fog and mist common to other coastal redwood areas. Paved roads service the park; the *VISITOR CENTER* and *CAMPFIRE CENTER* are accessible. The campground has some accessible features, and there are trails that can be managed with assistance.

Visitor Center

The visitor center features exhibits low enough to be seen from a seated position and offers many hands-on displays for all ages. In addition, you can view a film about the redwoods. And if you're looking for that "just right" book, you are likely to find it here.

The visitor center and *AMPHITHEATER* are in the middle of the campground. A continuous redwood *BOARDWALK* (max 10%)

leads from designated _PARKING_ to the visitor center. To reach the amphitheater, follow the boardwalk a little further to an area for wheelchair users behind the main seating.

Picnics

Near the Smith River at the end of the park road is an inviting forested picnic area with nearby parking on asphalt or gravel. Unfortunately, all the tables lie on the soft duff of the forest floor. There is an uphill slope from the parking places to the picnic area. You'll find an accessible _RESTROOM_ nearby that has a shallow stall with grab bars, low toilet, and an electrical outlet.

Visitors of all ages favor this beach for swimming and sun bathing in the summer. Most people get to the river through the picnic area. The parking lot overlooks the river and swimmers below. To get to the coarse beach sand at the water's edge, you must cross a rough slope of river rocks.

Trails

Self-Guided Nature Trail— This is a lovely trail that loops through the forest and along the sparkling Smith River. Much of the trail is broad, smooth forest floor but part way along there are several sets of steps leading to the river below the campground. Some wheelchair users may be able to explore either end of the nature trail, but probably will require some assistance. Don't forget to pick up a trail guide at the visitor center.

The trail begins and ends near a parking area along the road above the picnic grounds. For a short scenic hike along the river, look for the wooden trail marker near the parking area. The beginning of the trail has a 10% grade. To avoid it, you can cut through the picnic grounds and meet the trail at river level. Enjoy the scenery as far as marker #5 (900 feet), where stairs lead to a lower portion of the trail. The trail surface can be difficult to traverse in certain areas due to fallen leaves and twigs, soft spongy forest floor, and roots or rocks. If you start your hike at the trail's end, you can explore the forest and surrounding area. Markers #21 through #14 lead you through the trees and eventually to the campground near site #21. Beyond that point the trail becomes more steep and rocky and you soon encounter several sets of stairs.

Stout Grove—Frank D. Stout Memorial Grove features a massive redwood tree, measuring 20 feet in diameter. You'll have a ½-mile loop on a smooth path of dirt and duff to follow through this lush forest of virgin coast redwoods, thick with ferns and saplings. As you pass among the tall giants, they seem to absorb all noise and reverberate with only stillness and solitude.

Just outside the east park entrance off Hwy 199, take South Fork Road south, then turn right on Douglas Park Road (Howland Hill Road). This drive takes you through a grove of virgin redwoods. Be sure to allow plenty of travel time. This is a rough gravel road. It has many potholes and is paved for only one of the three miles to Stout Grove. (No trailers or motorhomes are allowed on this road). The road continues through Jedediah Smith Redwoods State Park. Pavement begins ten miles south of the park at Humboldt Road, where it meets U.S. Hwy 101. When you get to the smooth asphalt parking lot at Stout Grove, a gated asphalt road leads down a 17% grade for 300 feet to the grove. If you get the key from the ranger in the main park, you may avoid walking down this steep grade. You may drive instead to the level part of the grove. Otherwise, there is a gate bypass for foot traffic. Chemical toilets in the parking area are not accessible.

Camping

Filtered sunlight, through a mixture of hemlock, fir, cedar, and redwoods lights this lovely campground. Each site has a packed gravel pull-in, table, fire ring, food storage, and BBQ. Designated _CAMPSITE_ #28 is level and only 50 feet from an accessible _RESTROOM_, but there are no other accessible features. Site #26 is not designated but may be an alternate choice because it is similar to #28. The _RESTROOM_ nearby has a forest floor approach and a shallow stall with a high toilet and grab bars. The _SHOWER_ has a 32-inch doorway; controls are 50 inches from the floor, and grab bars are in place. There is no seat in the shower but there is a seat outside the stall in the dressing area. There is an RV dump station near the entrance station.

Jedediah Smith Redwoods State Park

4241 Kings Valley Road
Crescent City, CA 95531
(707) 464-9533 or 458-3310

Park Folder Available
Location—_Nine miles east of Crescent City on Highway 199_
Elevation—_150 feet_

DEL NORTE COAST REDWOODS STATE PARK

Del Norte Coast Redwood State Park is a mix of old- and new-growth redwoods that seem to march from the hillsides down to the sea. Much of the park is virgin forest; however, the campground area was once the site of a logging center. Now, the scars of clear cutting are healing over, and the lush forest is filled with second-growth redwoods. Many trails meander through the park; most are narrow, and many are steep. A hiking guide is available along with other pamphlets and literature at the entry kiosk (2½ miles east of Hwy 101). Paved roads wind into the forested campground and along the Wilson Beach turn-out. The campground is open April through October and has designated SITES, accessible RESTROOMS and an RV dump station.

Camping

Mill Creek—Few old-growth redwoods remain in this area, which was the center of a logging operation in the 1920's. Large stumps and undergrowth offer privacy between campsites, while there is plenty of shade from young redwoods and red alder. An asphalt roadway leads through the campground to each pull-in of packed dirt and gravel. You can reach the amphitheater from the roadway by way of a 30-foot gravel path. Campsites include a table, fire ring, and food storage on the forest floor. Of the two loops, the southern loop is more level. Two level designated CAMPSITES (#2 and #28) are near accessible REST-ROOMS but have no other access modifications. Site #125 may be a suitable alternative.

The RESTROOM near site #2 has a parking space and asphalt approach. The stall is shallow, with a high toilet and grab bars. There are grab bars at the high sink and an electrical outlet. The shower has a 31-inch doorway with a 1-inch lip down into the stall (29" by 48"). There is a bench outside the stall, no seat inside, and the controls are 46 inches from the floor. There is parking and an asphalt approach at the RESTROOM near site #90. The accessible stall has a high toilet with grab bars. The restroom near site #125 has an accessible stall with no other modifications.

Del Norte Coast Redwoods State Park

4241 Kings Valley Road
Crescent City, CA 95531
(707) 464-9533

Location—Seven miles south of Crescent City on U.S. Hwy 101
Elevation—670 feet

PRAIRIE CREEK REDWOODS STATE PARK

The most diverse of the northern redwood parks, Prairie Creek Redwoods State Park offers a variety of natural settings from lush fern canyons to large meadowlands. Dense summer fog and about 100 inches of annual rainfall insure a rich coastal redwood growth and an abundance of wildlife. Raccoons and bears sometimes show up near the campgrounds and along the trails. Majestic Roosevelt Elk herds roam the forests and open grasslands and often graze in the meadows at Gold Bluffs Beach. Surf fishing for red-tail perch is also a popular pastime on the shore.

Most visitor facilities are located near Elk Prairie Campground. A paved path connects the CAMPFIRE and VISITOR CENTERS. A paved NATURE TRAIL south of the visitor center will lead you through an interesting redwood exhibit. The Elk Prairie Campground offers a designated SITE near an accessible RESTROOM and SHOWER.

Visitor Center

All of the exhibits at this accessible visitor center can be viewed from a seated position. Hands-on displays allow you to touch and feel some natural artifacts of the area. In the adjacent BOOKSTORE, you'll find an assortment of books and postcards about the redwoods region. Across from the access ramp to the building is one designated PARKING space; a low TELEPHONE stands in the grass nearby.

Trails

If you've come to the park for only a brief visit, then the **Five-Minute Nature Loop** is for you. It features, among other natural exhibits, the "Chimney Tree," a large hollowed-out redwood tree trunk that a family used as their home in the 1930's. Well-marked exhibits line the flat, smooth trail. This self-guided asphalt-paved trail begins at the west end of the visitor center. To get to this point, follow the wooden veranda around to the back side of the building.

The majestic Roosevelt Elk   *(Photo courtesy CDPR)*

The **Revelation Trail** guides you through the cool shade of the redwood forest, on a level trail, in walking distance from the visitor center or campground. Blind visitors may use a guide rope at the side of the trail, and you may borrow a tape or a braille trail guide at the visitor center. The guide describes the foliage and natural history you'll encounter along the way. Though the trail is level, the forest floor surface and heavy tree debris make it very soft in some areas. You may require help to traverse the difficult spots. A hemlock tree provides shade at a lovely rest area along the trail with a modified *PICNIC TABLE*. You can reach the trail from the Five-Minute Nature Loop or at the trailhead located near the parking area just down the road from the visitor center.

Picnic

Roosevelt Elk often come to browse in the tall grasses near the picnic area. The best time to see elk is early morning or late afternoon. Standard picnic tables sit on the grass at the edge of the meadow. There is no designated parking nearby. The closest accessible *RESTROOM* is near the campfire center parking area. There is a slight incline to the doorway from the designated *PARKING* nearby. The shallow stall has a high toilet and grab bars.

Campground

Elk Prairie Campground lies on the outskirts of the large elk meadow. Some camping sites are down in a shady grove of "big trees"; others have virtually no shade, but a view of the meadow. The designated *SITE* (#14) is across from the meadow. It is the closest site to an accessible *RESTROOM* with *SHOWERS* and has a double-width, flat asphalt pull-in. The picnic table and fire ring are on the grass next to the parking place.

A gently-sloping concrete ramp leads from nearby parking to the accessible *RESTROOM*. The stall has a wide door with standard fixtures and grab bars. The accessible *SHOWER* has a 31-inch doorway, a seat in the changing area, and a retractable seat in the 40" by 35" shower. There is a low shower head, grab bars on the wall, and the control lever is 36 inches from the floor.

Campsites in the lower shady section are flat and have asphalt pull-ins. Sites #24 and #25 are near the restroom. From the forest floor approach, there are no barriers at the restroom doorway, but the wide stall has no access modifications, and there is no shower.

A smooth asphalt trail will take you to the *CAMPFIRE CENTER*. It begins at the parking lot located 500 feet past the entry kiosk. Take the left fork of the trail for 150 feet (max 7% for 30 feet), then take the second left fork another 100 feet along a paved access route. This route has handrails.

Gold Bluffs Beach

Sheer bluffs form a picturesque backdrop for Gold Bluffs Beach. There is a good chance that Roosevelt Elk will be grazing on the grassy dunes at the side of the road. To reach the beach from Highway 101, take the Fern Canyon turn-off onto Davison Road, three miles north of Orick. Three miles of narrow, steep, winding road lead to the beach, picnic area, campground, and Fern Canyon trailhead. (Vehicles over 20 feet long are prohibited. The road may be closed in rainy weather.)

Fern Canyon Trail begins at the end of the road. Two bridges at the beginning of the trail are not wide enough for a wheelchair. The rest of the trail is a leisurely level hike on coarse sand and pebbles leading through the lush 50-foot fern-covered canyon walls.

Picnic tables in the dunes along the road can only be accessed along a sandy path. There are no accessible restrooms or other features at the beach.

Camping at Gold Bluffs (FCFS) is primitive. All of the sites lie in grassy dunes about 150 feet from the shore and have sandy surfaces. Some have wind blocks, but there is no shade. The restroom has a 5-inch step at the doorway; neither the restroom nor the outdoor shower are accessible.

Other Park Trails

The Big Tree exhibit with its 68-foot circumference is an excellent example of the massiveness of these threatened redwood beauties. The paved **Big Tree Trail** leads into the forest area for about 750 feet. Forest debris cover most surfaces, so the trail can be slick. The trailhead is located north of the Elk Prairie Visitor Center on Hwy 101. There is one designated *PARKING* place next to the asphalt access ramp leading over the curb to the trailhead.

Other trails branch out from Big Tree. Portions of each trail may be accessible with help, but before you start out, check with the ranger about current trail conditions. The **Cathedral Trees Trail** (0.9 mi.) is broad and smooth, but can be muddy in places. The **Foothill Trail** is a wide gravel trail with some incline and tree roots. It leads to the **Circle Trail** which has a very uneven forest floor surface.

The **Cal-Barrel Road** climbs 1,000 feet above its starting point ¼-mile north of park headquarters. It is a narrow, winding dirt road that passes through some magnificent redwood groves. In the spring, pink and red azalea and rhododendron blossoms color the sunny spots among the trees. This 3½-mile road is open from 9 a.m. to 5 p.m. except in bad weather. No trailers or motorhomes are allowed on this road.

**Prairie Creek Redwoods
State Park**
Orick, CA 95555
(707) 488-2171
Park Folder Available
Location—Fifty miles north of Eureka on U.S. Hwy 101
Elevation—0-1,000 feet

HUMBOLDT LAGOONS STATE PARK and HARRY A. MERLO STATE RECREATION AREA

Three lagoons contained in this 1,825-acre park and recreation area offer an excellent place for fishing, boating, windsurfing, and beachcombing. Constantly changing with the rain, surf, and tides, the lagoons are a mixture of salt and fresh water, creating an environment that supports an interesting blend of wildlife and scenery.

Besides a ramp entrance to the visitor center and its accessible *RESTROOM*, there are no other considerations for visitors with limited mobility. The visitor center on U.S. Hwy 101 has a rough dirt parking area with a ramp access of 17% to the door. There is an accessible *RESTROOM* down a short path on the south side of the visitor center. To find it, go around to the opposite side of the building from the parking area. At **Stone Lagoon**, there are 25 sites of primitive camping. All of the surfaces are sand-covered, and chemical toilets are not accessible. There is also a simple sand ramp boat launch at Stone Lagoon campground. **Dry Lagoon** picnic area has multiple barriers; tables stand in sand and the chemical toilet is not accessible.

**Humboldt Lagoons
State Park
Harry A. Merlo
State Recreation Area**
Contact Prairie Creek Redwoods State Park
(707) 488-2171
Location—32 miles north of Eureka on U.S. Hwy 101
Elevation—Sea level

PATRICK'S POINT STATE PARK

Perched atop a picturesque headland, Patrick's Point State Park abounds with the natural beauty of the California coast. Some visitors spend hours watching sea otters, seals, whales, and birds from the bluffs overlooking the ocean. Others enjoy the lush springtime wildflowers in the meadows and bountiful growth of summer berries throughout the park. Black-tailed deer are a common sight as they graze on tender stalks along the bluffs and grasslands. For hundreds of years, the abundance of life at Patrick's Point attracted the Yurok Indians, who spent their summers here.

Wheelchair users may explore both the inland and coastal areas on firm dirt or paved trails. All roads through the park and campground are paved. There are designated *CAMPSITES* and accessible restrooms. The park staff is sensitive to the special needs of visitors with limited mobility and are always working to enhance everyone's park experience.

Visitor Center

Currently, the park staff is building an accessible visitor center near park headquarters. Until it is completed sometime in 1992, the park museum, housed in a historic hand-hewn log building, serves as the visitor center. The museum contains exhibits of the natural history and artifacts of the Yurok Indians who were native to this area. There are two steps up to the narrow doorway (under 27")

at the entrance. An authentic recreation of a **Yurok Village**, next to the museum, depicts the living conditions of the Yuroks in their summer encampments. A packed dirt path leads to the grass surface where the exhibits stand. For wheelchair users, small, low entries limit the view into the village structures.

Picnic

The picnic tables at **Mussel Rock** are nestled in a forested area surrounded by a thicket of green foliage. There is designated *PARKING*, a curb cut to picnic tables on grass, and an accessible *UNISEX RESTROOM.*

At **Palmer's Point** picnic area, you'll get a view of the coast south of Patrick's Point from another prospective. Tables are under the trees on the forest floor, and there is an accessible *CHEMICAL TOILET* in the parking lot.

Trails

Patrick's Point Trail — Don't miss the beautiful view from the headlands at Patrick's Point. The spring and fall, when there is less coastal fog, are the best times for viewing. Even from the designated *PARKING* at the trailhead, you'll have a nice coastal view. An asphalt trail leads 550 feet through a shady vine-covered path to the **Wedding Rock** overlook. From this spot, you can see California Gray whales migrating nearly year round. Sea lions and seals commonly play in the waves and on the rocks below. Much of the trail is level, except for two short segments that have a 13%

grade. A railing at 41 inches surrounds the overlook and may block some of your view from a seated position.

The *RESTROOM* for this area is located near Look-out Rock, along the road beyond the parking lot for Patrick's Point. It has a smooth concrete approach with no barriers, pivot-transfer stall with grab bars, and low toilet.

Self-guided Nature Trail — For an informative look at the flora and fauna of the area, you may follow a smooth asphalt path for a pleasant ½-mile stroll through the woods. From the campfire center, the trail loops through the tree-covered portion of the park, and ends at the campground. There is a hand rail along portions of this path and exhibit markers are labeled in braille.

Agate Beach Vista Point provides a view from the north-facing shore of the park to the black sand beach below. An asphalt walkway leads from designated *PARKING*, past a restroom that is not accessible, gently downhill another 100 feet to the overlook, which has a railing at 41 inches. The steep, narrow Agate Beach Trail begins here and is not accessible.

Camping

Abalone Campground is nestled in a shady tree-filled spot close to the ocean. A lush undergrowth of ferns and bushes provides privacy for most of the sites. You'll find three designated *CAMPSITES* (#65, #68, #69) near an accessible *RESTROOM*. Each is level and covered with smooth asphalt paving under the table, and

A beautiful view of Agate Beach from the overlook at Patrick's Point SP   *(Photo courtesy CDPR)*

around the BBQ and food storage. There is also an accessible *WATER SPIGOT* nearby.

You may park near the *RESTROOM* and take the smooth concrete approach to the door. It has a lever door handle, pivot-transfer stall with grab bars, and high toilet. The *SHOWER* has a wide access with no barriers, and the control for the shower is 50" from the floor, but there is no seat in the 28" by 50" stall.

You can reach the *CAMPFIRE CENTER* along a gently sloping asphalt trail, 350 feet from the designated *CAMPSITES*, or from a parking lot nearby. The trail from the campsites crosses a wood plank bridge (6% grade) and has handrails. Wheelchair users may be seated in

a paved, open seating area at the rear of the amphitheater.

Agate Campground, open year round, is the only one open in the winter. Site #91 is flat and near the restroom; however, most sites in this campground are not level. Near Campsite #91, is a fully accessible *UNISEX RESTROOM/SHOWER* combination. You may obtain the key to the restroom at the ranger kiosk. There are no designated sites in this campground.

Patrick's Point State Park

4150 Patrick's Point Drive
Trinidad, CA 95570
(707) 677-3570

Park Folder Available
Location — Twenty-five miles north of Eureka on U.S. Hwy 101
Elevation — 200 feet

TRINIDAD STATE BEACH

Trinidad State Beach is hidden beneath a bluff in the picturesque historical town of the same name. The area was once a bustling fishing and shipping port and is now a quaint tourist town and marina.

On a bluff overlooking the beach, an asphalt parking and picnic area offer great views of the shoreline. Tables are in the middle of a grassy knoll. A steep bluff trail leads down to the beach. The restroom is not accessible, and there are no other accessible features.

Trinidad State Beach

Contact Patrick's Point State Park
(707) 677-3570

Location — Nineteen miles north of Eureka off U.S. Hwy 101
Elevation — 50 feet

LITTLE RIVER STATE BEACH

Located at the mouth of the Little River, the broad, smooth sand and low dunes of Little River State Beach encompass 112 acres of untouched coastline. The park is not developed for public access; there are no facilities or parking.

Little River State Beach

Contact Patrick's Point State Park
(707) 677-3570

Location — Thirteen miles north of Eureka on U.S. Hwy 101
Elevation — Sea level

AZALEA STATE RESERVE

A profusion of azaleas and assorted berry bushes drink in the sunshine and flourish here at Azalea State Reserve. Thirty acres of timberland at this park have been removed and kept clear so that the flowers can continue to thrive. To view blossoms at their best, be here at the peak blooming season in May and June.

In recent years, the trails have become overgrown, making a hike through the park difficult even for the able-bodied. The self-guided nature trail described in the park folder no longer exists. There is a standard chemical toilet in the dirt parking lot.

Azalea State Reserve

Contact Patrick's Point State Park
(707) 677-3570

Park Folder Available
Location — On Highway 200 (North Bank Road) near U.S. Highways 199 and 101, north of the Mad River
Elevation — 150 feet

FORT HUMBOLDT STATE HISTORIC PARK

During the mining boom in the Trinity River country, shipping routes along the Sacramento River Delta and the San Francisco Bay were crowded and changing tides made passage unpredictable. To help avoid delays in moving supplies to the mining towns, entrepreneurs from the mining companies established a settlement at Humboldt Bay.

As the Humboldt area developed into a thriving trade center, the resident Indian tribes were squeezed out of their homeland. They began to resist the encroachment with violence. So the settlers appealed to the government for protection from the Indians. In 1853, construction of Fort Humboldt began. Fort Humboldt State Historic Park preserves the refurbished ruins of parts of the army outpost, including the post hospital which now serves as the park museum.

Of special interest is the *LOGGING MUSEUM* and *OUTDOOR DISPLAY* of 19th-century equipment and techniques used in the timber industry. An accessible *SELF-GUIDED TRAIL* will transport you back in time to recall the rugged lifestyle of the redwood loggers. You can PARK in a designated space near the park office. From there, an asphalt walk leads to an accessible *UNISEX RESTROOM* with a large lateral-transfer stall. The door is very heavy; the toilet is low and has grab bars.

Logging Museum

Pictures and exhibits in the museum tell the story of the remark-able men who labored to harvest redwood timber. An asphalt path that is rough in places leads you to the logging museum and outdoor display. You may need some help with the door to the museum, but once inside there are no barriers. Most of the exhibits are visible from a seated position.

A paved 850-foot *LOOP TRAIL* leads through an outdoor timber display. Along the path, you'll get to inspect a collection of tools and equipment that was used in the days when loggers cut timber weighing up to 21 tons without the use of power tools. Steam engines called "steam donkeys" dragged the logs through the forest to awaiting trains. You'll see several types of steam donkeys, two restored and functional locomotives used at the time, and a recreation of a typical logger's shack.

Fort

A few of the 14 original fort structures have been refurbished or recreated in their original positions overlooking Humboldt Bay. On weekends, park volunteers open the hospital and surgeon's quarters for tours. The volunteers continue to collect and develop displays of settler and fort history for the museum that is housed in the hospital building. As time and money permits, restoration and development of the fort structures will proceed. From the picnic area, located in the middle of the grassy fort enclave, you'll have a fine view of Humboldt Bay.

You can stroll through the grounds on a rough asphalt service road, or, with a handicap-identification placard, you may take your vehicle onto the road for closer access to the buildings. The access ramp to the hospital is 100 feet from the road along a rough dirt path. The surgeon's quarters, 150 feet beyond, are also accessible by ramp from the path. Other buildings, labeled and listed in the park folder, are in various states of rehabilitation.

Fort Humboldt
State Historic Park

3431 Fort Avenue
Eureka, CA 95501
(707) 455-6567
Elevation—50 feet

GRIZZLY CREEK REDWOODS STATE PARK

Situated at the confluence of the Van Duzen River and Grizzly Creek, this lovely inland redwood park is off the beaten path for most travelers. A small but lush grove of coastal redwoods sur-

rounds the visitor's area, making it seem secluded and private. Take a few short steps into the virgin redwoods of Cheatham Grove, and you are entering a forest as it has existed for thousands of years. Since Grizzly Creek has fewer visitors than the other redwood parks, you may prefer the solitude this 390-acre park has to offer.

The staff at Grizzly Creek Redwoods State Park is sensitive to the special needs of disabled visitors and continues to find new ways to improve everyone's outdoor experience. Currently, there is an accessible *CAMPING SITE, RESTROOM/SHOWER* and access to the small *VISITOR CENTER*. The park ranger also has plans to improve access to the forest walk through Cheatham Grove.

Visitor Center

Park headquarters serves as the entrance to the campground and day use areas. A boardwalk winds around the side of the building for access to the visitor center. Most

displays and wildlife exhibits are low so that everyone may enjoy them. The hands-on nature display is a favorite of every age and appeals to all the senses. An arrangement of animal pelts, antlers, pine cones, and flowers sits on a low table for you to touch and smell. You may wish to purchase a book, map, or souvenir tee shirt while you're here.

Day Use

The best times for steelhead and salmon fishing at Grizzly Creek are the rainy fall and winter months. However, at this time of year, the high waters of the creek make access difficult. And in summer, the way to the creek is a steep gravelly path.

There is a cluster of tables and BBQ's at the day use area on the broad grassy banks of Grizzly Creek. In the late spring, after high waters of the creek have subsided, the ground is saturated with water and very spongy. Access is best in the drier summer months.

Trails

Hiker's Trail, **Nature Trail** and **Grizzly Creek Trail** all begin across Highway 63 from the park entrance. The beginning section of these trails is flat for a short distance and parallels the highway. To get to the trail after you cross the highway, you must descend a short, steep path that is slick with fallen debris. Watch out for logging trucks as you cross the highway! The trail extends 600 feet to the north or south before becoming narrow and impassable. Use caution when hiking in this area; poison oak can be a problem along the perimeter of the path.

(Photo courtesy CDPR)

Cheatham Grove is a marvelous example of an unspoiled, virgin redwood forest. Presently, wheel-chair users will find access very difficult to this lush trail.

Parking for the trail at Cheatham Grove is approximately three miles west of the park office. Before the second bridge across the Van Duzen River, there is a small, sloping dirt lot. The entrance to the trail is behind a fence, near a display of log segments. Check with the park ranger to see if he has made the access changes at the trailhead.

Most of the 26-inch-wide trail threads through a carpet of clover-like redwood sorrel. The smooth forest floor has a layer of duff that can be very messy or soft after a rain. Volunteers and park staff groom the trail once a year in the spring; as the year progresses the debris becomes thicker.

The trail makes a figure-8 loop through the forest. For the longest uninterrupted walk, take the trail fork to the right. There are some short inclines and root gnarls, and, one point, a fallen log with a cut through it crosses the trail, creating a small 3-inch step. It may be best to bypass the last half of the last loop and return by the same trail from which you began.

Camping

An intimate campground rests on the banks of Grizzly Creek. One PAVED CAMPSITE has a picnic table with an extended end, BBQ, fire ring, storage box, and an accessible DRINKING FOUNTAIN. A concrete path leads to the nearby accessible RESTROOM. Other sites in the campground are flat, have asphalt pull-ins, and are shaded by trees or ramadas. Each site has a table, BBQ, fire ring, and food storage.

At the rear of the RESTROOM building is an accessible unisex facility with lateral transfer, grab bars and a high toilet. A small concrete ramp at the shower leads to a 29-inch-wide access door. The SHOWER has grab bars, but there is no seat in the stall, and the control lever is 50 inches from the floor. Even if you are not camping here, you may obtain the key to use the restroom from the ranger at the kiosk.

Grizzly Creek Redwoods State Park

16949 Highway 36
Carlotta, CA 95528
(707) 777-3683

Location—Eighteen miles east of U.S. Hwy 101 on Highway 36. Vehicles pulling trailers should not approach from the east.
Elevation—375 feet

HUMBOLDT REDWOODS STATE PARK

The world's most impressive grove of old-growth redwoods stands along Highway 101 about 45 miles south of Eureka. Within the 50,000 acres of Humboldt Redwoods State Park, a 10,000-acre parcel called the Rockefeller Grove represents nearly 1/8 of California's remaining old-growth redwoods. **The Avenue of the Giants** winds through this peerless grove and parallels Hwy 101 for five miles. Millions of awe-struck travelers have marveled at the magnificence of these enormous trees from their vehicles. But the best way to appreciate these beauties is to walk among them and feel their towering presence. It is hard to believe that you are seeing 2,000-year-old trees in a 20-million-year-old forest!

Whether you visit for an hour or a few days, Humboldt Redwoods State Park offers nature-lovers an excellent outdoor experience. The park has many CAMPSITES at Burlington campground suitable for wheelchair users. With help, the VISITOR CENTER and CAMPFIRE CENTER are accessible, as is the SELF-GUIDED NATURE TRAIL at Founder's Grove. A PARK FOLDER IS A HELPFUL GUIDE TO THIS PARK.

Visitor Center

Included at the visitor center is the park headquarters and CAMPFIRE CENTER. Because this area is heavily-traveled, the park has paved most of the surfaces. There is one designated PARKING place near the CAMPFIRE CENTER and visitor center building. A ramp with a 13% grade and grab bars leads to the visitor center entry door, which has a 2-inch sill.

Most exhibits and photos in the visitor center are low enough for easy viewing from a seated position. Throughout the day, you can watch a video presentation and slide show of the natural history of the region. To further enhance your redwood visit, books and maps are available for purchase at the information counter. There are no barriers at the information booth, but the telephone in the building is too high to reach from a seated position.

The visitor center and campground share the _RESTROOM_ that is just inside the adjacent campground entrance. A paved path leads from the visitor center to the accessible _UNISEX RESTROOM_ that has grab bars and a low toilet.

Picnic

Federation Grove—An unhurried drive down Bull Creek Flats Road offers a much more personal feel for the huge dimensions of the giant redwood forest. Though the picnic area in the grove is not accessible, the drive is worth a sightseeing side-trip.

Williams Grove—A dirt trail leads to tables on the grassy forest floor of Williams Grove picnic area. There are no curb cuts in the paved parking area, and the restroom is not accessible. The park's RV dump station is located at this turn-out.

Franklin K. Lane Grove—If its a cozy picnic you want, the pull-out at Franklin K. Lane Grove is a nice spot. Tables are secluded close to the road under the trees. Unfortunately, you will have to cross a dirt surface to get there and the restroom is not accessible.

Garden Club of America Grove—With features similar to Franklin K. Lane Grove, this serene forested area makes a lovely backdrop for a redwood photograph.

Trails

Founder's Grove Nature Trail—At Founder's Grove, a smooth, broad, dirt trail makes a 1/3-mile loop among enormous old-growth redwoods. Founder's Tree, dedicated to the conservationists who established the Save-the-Redwoods League, is the centerpiece of the trail. You can inspect it up close on a _BOARDWALK_ that leads directly to its base. There may be a few roots in the trail along the way, and there are no benches, but access to most of the trail is good and exhibits are well-marked.

The trail begins near the parking lot entrance. Designated _PARKING_ at this very popular and often

Roots and fallen debris on the forest trails often create challenges for wheelchair users. *(Photo courtesy CDPR)*

crowded self-guided trail is across from the fully accessible *UNISEX RESTROOM*. The restroom has a high toilet, grab bars, high sink, and a *DRINKING FOUNTAIN* outside.

Big Tree Trail—Big Tree Trail makes a beautiful 1/5-mile loop through hundreds of tall giants. However, the path leading from designated *PARKING* to the access bridge at the trailhead is rocky and steep (15%). One end of the bridge has two steps that render the trail inaccessible.

Rockefeller Loop Trail — Similar to Big Tree Trail in accessibility, a portion of the Rockefeller Loop Trail leads down along a creek bed and is rocky and steep.

Visitor Center Nature Loop—Across the avenue from the visitor center is a pleasant ¼-mile loop among redwoods where you'll experience the quiet grandeur of the forest. This broad undulating trail has rapid grade changes, so some wheelchair users will require an extra push or two. As with most other forest trails, fallen twigs and exposed roots also present obstacles along the route.

Camping

Hidden Springs Campground—The hillside campground at Hidden Springs is five miles south of park headquarters on Highway 254. Roads through the area are steep. Few sites have a table on the same level as the parking; the parking is often off-camber. Though two sites in this campground are designated (#3 and #79), the campground is not convenient for wheelchair users.

The *RESTROOM* across from campsite #8 has a concrete approach

and a large lateral-transfer stall. The controls in the shower are high and there is no seat. A dirt path leads to the amphitheater from a parking area near another restroom. The restroom is not accessible, but there is a low *TELEPHONE* on a dirt surface.

Avenue of the Giants *(Photo courtesy CDPR)*

Burlington Campground— Next to park headquarters and the visitor center, this campground is at the hub of park activity. Burlington Campground lies in a gently sloping, shady grove of second-growth redwoods. It is the campground preferred by wheelchair users. Each forest floor site has a table, fire ring, and food storage, with pull-in parking on packed or gravel-embedded forest floor. Though there are no designated campsites, #17, #18, and #43 are level and near an accessible *RESTROOM*.

The *RESTROOM* across from sites #17 and #18 has no doorway barriers, a shallow stall with grab bars, low toilet and an electrical

outlet. The accessible *SHOWER* has a large entry, grab bars, and controls 48 inches from the floor, but no seat inside. The *RESTROOM* near site #43 is just inside the campground entrance. A smooth concrete approach leads to the unisex unit with grab bars and a low toilet.

Albee Creek Campground— This campground is off the beaten path, two miles north of Weott and five miles west of Hwy 101 on Bull Creek Flats Road. There are no designated sites, and the restrooms are not accessible. Since the campground is located on the side of a hill, the asphalt road through this area is steep. Campsite parking is usually on a different level than the table making camping difficult for wheelchair users.

Humboldt Redwoods State Park

Contact Eel River District Office
(707) 946-2311

Park Folder Available
Location—Forty-five miles south of Eureka on U.S. Hwy 101 and Highway 254 (Avenue of the Giants)
Elevation—150 feet

BENBOW LAKE STATE RECREATION AREA

Benbow Lake is a small seasonal lake occupying about one mile of the South Fork of the Eel River. The lake is created by a dam that is placed on the river in May and removed in September. Picnickers, sun-bathers, and beginning canoeists enjoy relaxing here in the summer. A concessionaire rents canoes and paddleboats on the

Picnickers have a view of Benbow Lake.   (Photo courtesy CDPR)

Benbow Lake State Recreation Area

Contact Eel River District Office
(707) 946-2311
*Location—Two miles south of
    Garberville off U.S. Hwy 101*
Elevation—400 feet

lake shore. The day use area is closed during the winter high-water months. For overnight camping, there is a designated *CAMPSITE* in the campground across the river.

Picnic

The day use area contains a huge lawn and tree-shaded picnic tables overlooking the lake. *PARKING* is in large asphalt lots adjacent to the grass. The lawn slopes from the parking lot level, stretching 200 feet down to the beach at a 10% grade. There are no paved pathways or walkways at the lake. You'll find a number of restroom buildings adjacent to the parking areas, with designated *PARKING* provided near each. To reach one of the restrooms, you'll have to cross a bit of lawn then go up a 10-foot access ramp (10%). The narrow doorway and tight turns make wheelchair maneuvering difficult. The small stall has grab bars and a low toilet. The main day use area around Benbow Lake is west of U.s. Hwy 101.

At the dock on the beach, a concessionaire rents canoes and paddleboats. On regularly scheduled days, a ranger-led "*CANOE HIKE*" leaves from here to explore the lake shore. You can make prior arrangements for the concessionaire to assist you into a boat either from the dock or the shore so that you and a companion can join in the canoe trip or set out to explore on your own.

Camping

Oak trees protect the flat lands and offer shade to the campground, which is located above the Eel River west of U.S. Hwy 101. Designated *CAMPSITE* #8 is completely paved around the modified picnic table, fire ring and food storage. An asphalt path leads from the site to a nearby accessible *UNISEX* *RESTROOM*. All other sites have a table, fire ring, and food storage on dirt surfaces, and most are level. A paved road leads through the campground, and there is a designated *PARKING* place at the *RESTROOM* for those that have chosen an alternate site.

RICHARDSON GROVE STATE PARK

Follow Hwy 101 along the South Fork of the Eel River in south Humboldt County and it will bring you to the dense coastal redwoods of Richardson Grove State Park. Named for California's 25th Governor, "The Grove," as it is affectionately called, currently hosts over half a million visitors a year. Peaceful silence surrounds you as you hike through the thick growth of tall trees and lush forest vegetation. Many return here year after year to renew their spirits in this tranquil setting. During the winter months of high river water, the Eel draws fishermen to the park for a try at king salmon and steelhead trout.

Of the park's three forested campgrounds, Madrone offers a designated *CAMPSITE* and accessible *RESTROOM* and *SHOWER*. Near the accessible *VISITOR* *CENTER* and *CAMP STORE*, you will also be able to take a short hike on a smooth *NATURE WALK* among the trees.

Visitor Center

Built originally in 1928 as a hunting lodge, the visitor center is open only in the summer months. Inside, you'll see displays about the Indian life in this region as well as a variety of natural history exhibits, curios, film, and book sales. Pavement leads from designated *PARKING* at the lodge to a ramp access onto the veranda at the *VISITOR CENTER* and *CAMP STORE*.

The entrance to the cluttered *CAMP STORE* has a small lip at the door; the aisles are narrow and difficult to manage. There are a few picnic tables on the wood-planked veranda outside. An accessible *UNISEX RESTROOM* with a high toilet is just outside the camp store along an asphalt pathway. The telephone nearby is too high to reach from a seated position.

Trails

For a pleasant, short (1/8-mile) trip on a well-marked *SELF-GUIDED NATURE TRAIL*, try the trail just to the south of the lodge. The smooth forest floor gently undulates through marked exhibits of the plant life native to this region. Parts of the trail can be soft after a rain, and there is one steep (19%) 15-foot segment.

Many other trails in the park are broad and fairly smooth but most are too steep for wheelchair users to manage without help.

Camping

A profusion of plant life and tall trees shade the campgrounds at the park. Asphalt roads lead to paved campsite pull-ins; each includes a table, BBQ and food storage locker. The *CAMPFIRE CENTER* is centrally located near the visitor center. You get to the amphitheater by taking a 70-foot asphalt path (7% max.) uphill from the

designated *PARKING* place at the foot of the path.

Huckleberry Campground — Hidden in a dense redwood forest, this campground has the most private campsites in the park. The restroom near campsite #5 has parking nearby and the stall is wide enough for a wheelchair. But there are no access modifications in the restroom or showers.

Madrone Campground — Many campsites in this heavily forested area are fairly level and smooth. At designated *SITE* #74 there is pavement under the table and BBQ. A gently sloping (4%) asphalt path leads to the accessible *RESTROOM* nearby. Even though it is not paved, site #75 may be a good alternate choice.

The *RESTROOM* has a high toilet and grab bars, but the sinks are not accessible. The ample shower has a retractable seat in the stall (48" by 84"), low controls (37") and a lower and upper shower head.

Oak Flat Campground — Across the Eel River is the rolling hillside campground at Oak Flat. Shaded by an abundance of oak trees, the grounds are more open and sunny than the redwood forested campgrounds. Most of the roads and campsites are not level, and there are no accessible restrooms.

Richardson Grove State Park
  1600 U.S. Hwy 101
  Garberville, CA 95440-0069
  (707) 247-3318
Park Folder Available
Location — Eight miles south of Garberville on U.S. Hwy 101
Elevation — 450 feet

Mendocino County

SMITHE REDWOODS STATE RESERVE

This small grove of redwoods, donated by the Smithe family, is a good place for a quick roadside rest stop. A concrete *WALKWAY* leads from the parking area to an accessible *UNISEX RESTROOM* with a lever door handle, lateral transfer to a high toilet, and grab bars.

Trails lead to the south fork of the Eel River and to a 60-foot waterfall. Soon after leaving the parking area, the tree-lined trail is deep with twigs and pine needles. Beyond 100 feet it is not passable for wheelchair users. Picnic tables that rest on the thick forest duff are difficult to access.

Smithe Redwoods State Reserve
  Contact Eel River District Office
  (707) 946-2311
Location — Four miles north of Leggett on U.S. Hwy 101
Elevation — 750 feet

STANDISH-HICKEY STATE RECREATION AREA

Once a privately-owned logging area, Standish-Hickey State Recreation Area is now a forest of second-growth redwoods and a variety of oaks. The park is named after two men. Edward Hickey's family donated the first acreage to the state, and A.M. Standish also donated land. Standish was a direct descendent of Captain Miles Standish from the historic Mayflower sailing ship. The trees in the park date from the 1940's when a disastrous fire began in a section of clearcut and spread through the area. A few virgin coast redwoods remain. Most notable is the Captain Miles Standish Tree, the only remaining redwood of its size in the park.

The park offers hiking, picnicking, swimming, and fishing and is not as heavily visited as some of the more famous redwood parks. There is a designated *CAMPSITE* with accessible *RESTROOM*, but trails and other accommodations will present a challenge for some.

Picnic

At the end of Hickey campground loop is the *CAMPFIRE CENTER* and picnic grounds. Hard-packed dirt leads to the *CAMPFIRE CENTER* and to picnic tables clustered in a stand of oak trees. The restrooms here are not accessible.

Trails

The park lies within the canyon of the South Fork of the Eel River. All of the trails are steep foot paths on the hillsides near the river, or very narrow hiking trails through the forest.

Camping

A fine forest of oak and redwood create a shady canopy for the campgrounds at Standish-Hickey State Recreation Area. All the roads and parking in the campgrounds are paved, and each site has a table, fire ring, and food storage box.

Hickey—Most sites at Hickey Campground are flat and shady. *CAMPSITE* #79 is designated; it has a large parking area and an accessible *WATER SPIGOT*. The table and BBQ at each site rests on a dirt surface. Sites #61 (pull-thru), #77, and #78 are close by and very similar to the designated site. Not far from these sites is a fully accessible *UNISEX REST-ROOM/SHOWER* combination with a retractable seat in the shower.
Be sure to obtain the key to the restroom at the kiosk when you enter.

Rock Creek—There are no designated campsites at Rock Creek Campground, but site #27 is flat and near the *RESTROOM*, which has a shallow stall with grab bars. The shower is not accessible.

Redwood—Parts of this campground skirt the banks of the Eel River. There are no designated sites nor are there any accessible restrooms. Campsite parking is not always on the same level as the rest of the site. There is also day use parking overlooking the river, but a rocky river bank prohibits easy access to the water. Closed in winter, Redwood Campground is not appropriate for trailers and motorhomes because of its steep winding access roads.

**Standish-Hickey
State Recreation Area**
PO Box 208
Leggett, CA 95455
(707) 925-6482
Park Folder Available
Location—One mile north of Leggett on U.S. Hwy 101
Elevation—800 feet

SINKYONE WILDERNESS STATE PARK

The only State Park with "wilderness" as part of its name, Sinkyone Wilderness State Park occupies one of the few places that is not accessible by highway. The Lost Coast region has changed little since the days of the Sinkyone Indians, the area's earliest known inhabitants. Forest, prairies, bluffs, beaches, and tide pools offer hikers and horsemen a surreal environment for exploration. A herd of Roosevelt Elk, transplanted from Prairie Creek Redwoods State Park, also resides on the park's steep hillsides.

County Road 435 makes its way down a steep, narrow grade from Redway, winding 30 miles to the coast at Sinkyone Wilderness State Park. After a rain, this road is very slippery. An old ranch house doubles as a park office with limited lodging upstairs, but is not accessible. You can reach a primitive campground at the southern boundary of the park by taking County Road 431 from Hwy 1 at Leggett. Campsites in this area have a table, fire ring, and a nearby chemical toilet. Before traveling into the park, you should obtain a good road map of the area. Most visitors to the wilderness are either backpackers or horsemen; wheelchair users find this beautiful park inhospitable.

Sinkyone Wilderness State Park
PO Box 245
Whitehorn, CA 95489
(707) 986-7711
Park Folder Available
Location—Thirty miles west of Redway on County Road 435, or 50 miles north of Ft. Bragg off Hwy 1
Elevation—100 feet

WESTPORT-UNION LANDING STATE BEACH

Seven separate primitive camping lots along two miles of coastal windswept bluffs overlook the scenic, rugged coast at Westport-Union Landing State Beach. Surf fishing and tide pool exploration is popular on the beach below. Meanwhile, folks on the cliffs have a spectacular ocean view as they set up camp or arrange a picnic. The view of sunset is especially nice from the bluff.

Picnic

Day Use areas at each end of the park have BBQ's and tables on flat grassy surfaces. You get to the beach from there on a 100-foot *BOARDWALK* that leads directly onto the coarse sand.

Camping

Each of seven dirt camping lots at Westport-Union Landing are situated on the bluff overlooking the ocean. Fire rings and tables line the bluff in the general area of the camp sites and drinking water is available at each lot. Pit toilets have 35-inch doors and a slight lip at the doorway, but no access features inside. Stairs or narrow paths lead from the bluff to the beach below. (FCFS)

Westport-Union Landing State Beach

Contact Mendocino District Office
(707) 937-5804

Location—Two miles north of Westport off Highway 1
Elevation—Sea level

ADMIRAL WILLIAM STANDLEY STATE RECREATION AREA

This small 45-acre park near the south fork of the Eel River is open to hikers and picnickers who enjoy exploring back roads. The lovely grove of redwoods at Admiral William Standley SRA is so isolated, however, that it receives few visitors and is not accessible.

Admiral William Standley State Recreation Area

Contact Eel River District Office
(707) 946-2311

Location—Fourteen miles west of Laytonville on Branscomb Road
Elevation—1,700 feet

MacKERRICHER STATE BEACH

MacKerricher State Park contains a potpourri of nature with a variety of thriving ecosystems. Waves crash turbulently against the sheer black sand beaches to the north while a resident population of harbor seals plays in the surf of the rocky headlands at Laguna Point. Inland, sand dunes covered in tall grasses and wildflowers give way to a pine forest replete with berry bushes and Stellar's Jays. The park also contains two lakes encircled by a hearty growth of willows and cattails.

MacKerricher offers some choice opportunities for wheelchair users to enjoy its many faces. Seven miles of abandoned road, used now for pedestrians and bicycles, wind through the park. Two *BOARDWALKS* bring you closer to the

abundant life at this coastal oasis. *CAMPING* here is also accessible.

Picnic

Formerly a tidal lagoon, the now freshwater **Lake Cleone** offers a pleasant setting for a picnic lunch and a stroll on the accessible *BOARDWALK* leading along the water's edge among willows and cattails. The lake is stocked regularly with rainbow trout for fishing enthusiasts. Motorless boats can launch at the northeast end of the lake at the primitive ramp near the parking lot. There is a curb cut near a designated *PARKING* place to nearby picnic tables and concrete BBQ's in the grass. The restrooms for this area are not retrofitted for wheelchair access.

Trails

One of the most popular areas of the park, **Laguna Point**, is the playground for a resident group of harbor seals. A 0.3-mile *BOARDWALK* will take you over the sand to a rocky prominence overlooking the surf. The coastal view from the end of the path also makes for great whale watching from late November to January.

The *BOARDWALK*, built by the Telephone Pioneers of America, begins at the beach parking lot. Designated *PARKING* is illogically placed at the north end of the parking lot, while the trailhead for the boardwalk is at the southern end. Except for a 4% incline at the beginning of the boardwalk, most if the way is level. You'll find is seating half-way along the boardwalk and at the seal-watching station on the point.

Another redwood boardwalk at Lake Cleone leads you through reeds and cattails for a pleasant lake view stroll. The trail begins not far from a paved parking place and makes its way along a level course for about 1,500 feet.

Camping

Camp sites at MacKerricher State Park are either tucked into pockets of sand dunes surrounded by tall grasses, or shaded by pine and fir trees in the midst of berry bushes. Most of the four camping sections are resonably flat, and all have asphalt paved roads and campsite pull-ins, a table, fire ring, and food storage box. An RV dump station is just beyond the ranger station at the campground entrance.

West Pinewood — Pine trees shade the designated *CAMPSITE* (#73) at West Pinewood. The site is paved under the table and around the BBQ, and has a *WATER SPIGOT* with a lever control. An accessible *RESTROOM* and *SHOWER* is nearby. Other sites in this vicinity are not paved, but may be desirable alternates if site #73 is occupied.

The *RESTROOM* has fully accessible features including a lateral-transfer stall with high toilet, high sink with push water control, and an accessible *DRINKING FOUNTAIN*. The *SHOWER* has a wide doorway, retractable seat in the stall, and grab bars. The control lever is 45 inches from the floor, which gradually slopes into the shower stall.

East Pinewood, Cleone — The surroundings at both of these campgrounds are similar. Sites at East Pinewood are shaded by pines and dotted with berry bushes, while the sites at Cleone get more sunlight and are closer to Lake Cleone. There are no designated campsites nor accessible restrooms in either campground.

Surfwood — On the southern edge of Lake Cleone, brush provides more privacy between level sites at this campground. The restroom is not accessible.

MacKerricher State Park

Contact Mendocino District Office
(707) 937-5804

Location — On the outskirts of Cleone, three miles north of Fort Bragg on Highway 1
Elevation — 50 feet

The boardwalk to Laguna Point at MacKerricher State Park

(Photo courtesy Telephone Pioneers of America)

JUGHANDLE STATE RESERVE

The main attraction at Jughandle State Reserve is a self-guided, 5-mile-round-trip nature trail. The trail follows five terraces of wave-cut sediment through geologic history dating back 500,000 years. It ends at a pygmy forest, similar to the forest at Van Damme State Park. There is no wheelchair access to the forest at Jughandle, and only portions of the trail are accessible with help.

The north section of the lower trail loop leads out onto the headlands for a nice view of Jughandle Bay. It begins at an asphalt parking lot off Hwy 1. A combination of grass and dirt creates a lumpy surface on which to travel. Picnic tables are located in an uneven grassy area at the trailhead. Chemical toilets nearby are not accessible.

Adjacent to Jughandle State Reserve, the California Institute of Man in Nature operates an accessible 100-year-old farm including a hostel and education center, library and gardens. For more information about the farm, call CIMIN at (707) 964-4630.

Jughandle State Reserve
Contact Mendocino District Office
(707) 937-5804
Park Folder Available
Location—One mile north of Caspar on Hwy 1
Elevation—97 feet

CASPAR HEADLANDS STATE BEACH AND RESERVE

Sheltered in a small sandy cove of a bay, the three-acre beach at Caspar Headlands State Beach is a beachcomber's delight. A sandy path leads from a gravel parking lot to the beach, but there are no accessible facilities.

Caspar Headlands State Reserve is a three-acre parcel of rugged coastline adjacent to the beach. Visitors must have an entry permit for the Reserve, which is kept in its natural state.

Caspar Headlands State Beach and Reserve
Contact Mendocino District Office
(707) 937-5804
Location—Four miles north of Mendocino off Hwy 1, west on Point Cabrillo Drive
Elevation—30 feet

RUSSIAN GULCH STATE PARK

Ten miles south of Fort Bragg, Russian Gulch is yet another of the scenic coastal parks in the Mendocino area, offering all types of interesting outdoor exploration. Headland bluffs provide terrific views of the gulch and of its many rock formations. Skin divers and sun-bathers enjoy the sandy cove at the mouth of Russian Gulch Creek. For a secluded accessible get-away, you can *CAMP* in a snug little valley surrounded by lush second-growth redwoods. A disused park road now provides a scenic *BIKE PATH* to a 36-foot waterfall. Other trails meander through a wide variety of trees and shade-loving undergrowth that fills the park.

Birds-watchers and nature-lovers will be amazed by the number of animals and winged species that live along the coast and in the inland canyons. At various times campers have spotted raccoons, rabbits, chipmunks, deer, skunks, and an occasional bobcat or fox in the campground and in surrounding hills. Stellar's jays, quail, red-tailed hawks, and ravens live inland, while osprey, king-fishermen, and great blue heron make their home with the other ocean birds on the coast.

Picnic and Day Use

The main picnic area sits atop a bluff where you have an impressive view of Russian Gulch Creek and its scenic beach. You get to this day use area across a broad, sloping grassy lawn from a gravel parking area. One of the many picturesque bridges of Hwy 1 crosses the canyon at Russian Gulch Creek, framing its quaint beach. Photographers love this vantage point and have taken thousands of photographs of the Hwy 1 bridge that frames the quaint beach at the mouth of Russian Gulch creek. Most wheelchair users will require some help to get to the shady picnic tables on the lawn. Unfortunately, the restroom in this day use are has not been retrofitted for access.

The beach parking lot is under the Hwy 1 bridge. Access onto the small sandy cove is limited; curbing surrounds the paved parking area. There is no designated parking, and the restroom here is not accessible.

Trails

Fern Canyon Trail—At the end of the campground road, an abandoned paved road winds its way up the moist, forested valley that is

A view of Russian Gulch Bridge from the picnic area
(Photo courtesy CDPR)

lined by thick, fern-covered walls. It leads 2½ miles along a creek to a 36-foot waterfall. This is an uphill push on rough pavement that becomes dirt before you arrive at the waterfall. But if you have a willing assistant to help you uphill, or you are using a power chair, you'll enjoy this hike.

Devil's Punch Bowl — Devil's Punch Bowl piques the interest of many visitors to Russian Gulch. This blow-hole occurred when a sea-cut tunnel about 200 feet long collapsed at its inland end, forming a huge hole 100 feet across and 60 feet deep. Looking into it, you can see the waves roll in underneath you, but the blowing effect only happens during heavy seas. The trail to the overlook is 200 feet from the end of the gravel picnic area parking lot. Take care to avoid the poison oak along this level, narrow dirt path. To get to the trailhead, you must climb a short 12% incline from the parking area.

Camping

In the woods near the mouth of the gulch, forested hillsides protect the campground, giving it a feeling of seclusion. The flat campsites have a table, concrete BBQ, and food storage on a dirt surface. A profusion of trees in the valley offers shade at most sites.

Designated *CAMPSITE* #21 enjoys a nice shady spot immediately across from an accessible *RESTROOM*. It has a wide parking area with paving around the table and BBQ. A 20-foot (9% grade) ramp leads from designated *PARKING* in front of the building, to the nearby accessible *UNISEX RESTROOM*. Other restrooms in the campground are not retrofitted for access. However, they have no doorway barriers, and the stall doors will accommodate a wheelchair.

Russian Gulch State Park

Hwy 1
Mendocino, CA 95460
(707) 937-5804

Location — Two miles north of Mendocino on Hwy 1
Elevation — 0-100 feet

MENDOCINO HEADLANDS STATE PARK

The Mendocino coastline is famous for dramatic rocky bluffs and crashing surf well-represented at Mendocino Headlands State Park. A grassy meadow carpets the flat lands and surrounds the picturesque village of Mendocino. For a view of the entire coastline, you can enjoy a drive along the perimeter of the meadow.

This is a day use park, popular for its hiking, diving, and picnicking. In town, the historic *VISITOR CENTER* is accessible and worth a visit. Accessible *RESTROOMS* are provided at two locations.

Day Use

Along Heesler Road, on the north-facing portion of the headlands is a rest stop and viewpoint of the coastline north of Mendocino. From late November through January, this is a good place for whale-watching. Near designated *PARKING* in the lot, an accessible *RESTROOM* has a shallow stall, low toilet, and accessible fixtures including a *DRINKING FOUNTAIN.*

Visitor Center

Located on the south-facing portion of the headlands, the historic Ford House in old downtown Mendocino is now home to the *VISITOR CENTER* and *MUSEUM.* Here you'll see displays and a film about Mendocino's human and natural history. At various times of the year, the town of Mendocino holds festivals and art exhibitions on the lawn around the house.

The only parking for the visitor center is at the curb of the narrow downtown street. There is no designated parking, but there is a curb cut near the walkway to an accessible *RESTROOM.* From here, a series of ramps leads to the veranda at the Ford House. At the threshold, there is a 1- to 2-inch lip and some passageways in the museum are narrow. From the veranda, you'll have a great view of the coastline south of Mendocino.

Mendocino Headlands State Park

Contact Mendocino District Office
(707) 937-5804

Location — On Hwy 1 surrounding the town of Mendocino
Elevation — 40 feet

VAN DAMME STATE PARK

Abounding with a variety of natural wonders, Van Damme State Park centers around the Little River Canyon. The canyon lies peaceful and lush, with a dense fern growth on its walls and floor. A picturesque beach languishes at the mouth of the river, sheltered by rocky outcroppings. Further inland, a raised *BOARDWALK* takes you on a personal visit to a pygmy forest, where mature cypress and pine trees stand full grown at heights of 6 inches to 5 feet. You'll also want to visit the newly-remodeled accessible *VISITOR CENTER.*

Visitor Center

A historic log structure, recently converted by the Telephone Pioneers of America in cooperation with the Mendocino Area Parks Association, serves as the Van Damme visitor center. There are a variety of videos to watch and publications for sale at the center.

Visit a pygmy forest on the Discovery Trail, built by the Telephone Pioneers of America.

(Photo courtesy Telephone Pioneers of America)

But the star of the show is the unique diorama that chronicles humankind's interdepedence with the ocean, in the special "Living with the Sea" exhibit. Since access is the first priority of the Pioneers during their remodeling projects, they have built a ramp access near designated *PARKING*, and the interior of the visitor center is barrier-free.

Beach

Best known as Mendocino's finest abalone diving spot, the beach at Van Damme is tucked in a small cove at the mouth of the Little River. On any given day during abalone season, it's common to see divers organizing their gear in the parking lot and swimming out to rocky sea beds where the shellfish thrive.

In the beach parking lot, you'll find paved designated *PARKING* near an accessible *UNISEX COMPOSTING TOILET* that has grab bars and a low seat. To get there, follow the gently inclining wooden ramp at the end of the parking lot. For access to the beach sand, look for the curb cut directly next to the outdoor shower.

Trails

Pygmy Forest Discovery Trail — Due to the continued upheaval of lands in the Mendocino region, the miniature forest here resulted from a soil devoid of nutrients. The impoverished vegetation survives in some the most acidic soil in the world. Marked exhibits along *SELF-GUIDED BOARDWALK NATURE TRAIL*, built by the Telephone Pioneers of America, tell the story of the Pygmy Forest.

The 1/3-mile boardwalk loop begins at the edge of a paved parking lot. From the parking lot, you must cross a short stretch of packed dirt and manage a 1½-inch transition onto the foot of the boardwalk. There are benches and a railing at 32 inches along the trail. When you get to the fork in the boardwalk, you'll find a trail guide in a wooden box positioned just above the handrail. To get to the trail from Hwy 1, take Little River Airport Road south of the campground entrance. Look for the sign at approximately 2¾ miles.

Fern Canyon Trail — The creek-fed canyon at Van Damme is rich in second-growth redwood and alder. Its walls are literally overflowing with a dense blanket of ferns. A gated asphalt road in various states of repair begins at the campground and follows the verdant canyon along a mostly gentle 2-mile route. But in some sections the road has an 8% incline. Though rough and pot-holed in places, the road is suitable for bikes, strollers, and wheelchairs. Beyond the pavement, the road turns to dirt and continues to the Pygmy Forest for a total distance of about 5 miles.

If you plan to hike this distance, bring along a willing friend to help; your trip will be much more enjoyable. If you have a handicap-identification placard, you can obtain a *SPECIAL USE PERMIT* at the district office that will allow you to drive up the road beyond the locked gate for a close-up experience with the lush jungle-like environment. When you are driving on the road, be on the look-out for pedestrians who won't be expecting to see a car. (See appendix for district office address.)

Camping

Protected by the trees and walls of the canyon, most campsites in the lower portion of the main campground are shady and level. Each includes a table, fire ring, and food storage. There are no designated sites, but those in the vicinity of campsite #11 may be suitable. Sites #31 through #74 do not have an accessible restroom nearby.

An accessible *UNISEX RESTROOM/ SHOWER* with a parking place out front is near site #11. The *RESTROOM* has grab bars, high toilet and high sink. The *SHOWER* has a retractable seat in the stall; the controls are 35 inches from the floor. Asphalt paving leads to another *RESTROOM* near site #20. It has a small lip at the door; the stall is shallow, has grab bars,, and the toilet is low. Accessible *DRINKING FOUNTAINS* are located at each restroom.

At the camp *AMPHITHEATER*, a paved access ramp lead from nearby parking to the rear of the seating area where there is space for wheelchairs. *ENROUTE CAMPERS* can use the beach parking lot. The RV dump station is near the entry kiosk.

Van Damme State Park
Contact Mendocino District Office
(707) 937-5804
Location — Three miles south of Mendocino on Hwy 1
Elevation — 0-450 feet

MONTGOMERY WOODS STATE RESERVE

In the heart of the coast range, this remote park contains a two-mile self-guided nature trail that passes through five stands of old-growth redwoods. The trail begins with a steep incline over a hill and continues on a rough, steep descent into the redwood groves. By contacting the district office, disabled visitors may obtain a *SPECIAL USE PERMIT* to drive on the service road into the park. There are no restrooms or other facilities at the Reserve.

Montgomery Wood State Reserve
Contact Mendocino District Office
(707) 937-5804

Location — Eleven miles northwest of Ukiah on Compatche Road (Orr Springs Road) near Orr Springs
Elevation — 1,500 feet

PAUL M. DIMMICK WAYSIDE CAMPGROUND

Giant redwoods watch over Hwy 128 as it winds six miles east of Hwy 1 on its way to a shady primitive campground located along the Navarro River. Set among the redwoods on a packed forest floor, 28 level campsites have a table, fire ring, and food storage on a dirt surface (FCFS). The restroom is not accessible, and there is no shower. Twelve miles of frontage along the Navarro River and 650 acres of redwoods and mixed forest are preserved here in their natural state. Trails through the park are narrow, rough and unimproved.

Paul M. Dimmick
Wayside Campground

Contact Mendocino District Office
(707) 937-5804

Location — Six miles east of Hwy 1 on Hwy 128
Elevation — 45 feet

Hendy Woods SP   *(Photo courtesy CDPR)*

HENDY WOODS STATE PARK

As scenic Highway 128 finds its way from Cloverdale to the coast, you'll snake along the Navarro River through a heavily-wooded area that includes Hendy Woods State Park. Resting on the northern slope of the Greenwood Range, the park contains one of the last stands of redwoods in the Anderson Valley wine district. Campers and tourists alike enjoy the milder climate of the wooded hillsides and redwood groves at Hendy Woods. You'll like the secluded forest camping that is close enough to the wine country for a day trip. The campground has

several designated *CAMPSITES*, each with electrical hook-ups. Visitors with limited mobility will also appreciate the *"ALL-ACCESS" TRAIL* that leads into one of two old-growth forests.

Picnic

At the end of the park road, an inviting sunny meadow dotted with giant oaks opens onto the Navarro River. Picnic tables and BBQ's seek the shade of the trees in this level, but rough grassy expanse. The paved day use PARKING lot has a designated place. A pit toilet in the grass nearby is labeled with an access symbol. It has a short ramp, grab bars, low toilet, and a wide entry door that only opens inward, making it impossible for wheelchair users to close the door behind them. This parking area also serves the trailhead of the All-Access Trail.

Trails

Gentle Giant All-Access Trail — Built by the Telephone Pioneers of America, the All-Access Trail is a level ¼-mile path that is free of debris and exposed roots. It wanders through the last sizeable virgin redwood grove in the region. Marked exhibits along the way are described in the trail guide available at the entry station or the trailhead. Three plank bridges cross difficult areas, and, depending on conditions, there may be a 1- to 1½-inch transition at each end of these bridges.

You'll find the trailhead near the picnic area. The first 100 feet of the trail is packed gravel. If you use a wheelchair, you may need a friend to help you cross the gravel, and, you will definitely need to have someone reach the trail guides. You'll find them in a box, high on a sign post at the beginning of the trail.

The **Discovery Trail** cuts off from the All-Access Trail and undulates in a 1½-mile loop further into the woods. It is broad and well-maintained but several root gnarls and fallen debris will create barriers for wheelchair users.

Camping

Cloaked in a profusion of oaks, fir, and redwoods, **Wildcat Campground** provides a relaxing atmosphere to drink in the sights, sounds, and smells of nature. Each campsite offers a table, fire ring, food storage, and a dirt parking place off the paved road. For those with chair batteries to charge or other special needs, electrical hook-ups are provided at each of the designated *CAMPSITES* (#5, #37, #40, and #41). These sites are roomy; concrete paving encompasses the accessible table, food storage, and fire ring. Parking, however, is located on an uneven gravelly surface. There is plenty of shade and most of the other sites in the area are flat.

Concrete pathways lead from each designated site to an accessible *RESTROOM*. The fixtures are modified to include lateral transfer to a low toilet with grab bars, and a high sink. The *SHOWER* is a long, wide room with a fixed seat in the changing area and one in the stall; controls are 35 inches from the floor. Accessible *WATER SPIGOTS* are located along the path to the restroom, and there is an RV dump station at the campground entrance.

Scenic picnic and camping sites at Manchester State Beach are rustic and difficult to access.

(Photo courtesy CDPR)

Hendy Woods State Park

Contact Mendocino District Office
(707) 937-5804

Location — Eight miles northwest of Booneville and ½ mile south of Hwy 128 on Philo Greenwood Road
Elevation — 200 feet

MAILLARD REDWOODS STATE RESERVE

Preserving 242 acres of old- and second-growth redwoods, this park is mostly undeveloped. The park is located west of Hwy 128, at the end of a 3½-mile gravel road. The road continues onto Hwy 1 near Anchor Bay. One picnic table and a small gravel parking lot are the only improvements here.

Maillard Redwoods State Reserve

Contact Mendocino District Office
(707) 937-5804

Location — Twenty miles northwest of Cloverdale on Fish Rock Road, 3½ miles west of Hwy 128
Elevation — 1,000 feet

MANCHESTER STATE BEACH

Depending on the time of year, the 4½ miles of shoreline at Manchester State Beach can be bathed in sun or whipped by ocean winds. Located directly on the San Andreas Fault, the beach is divided by two creeks that empty at the shore, creating a natural wetlands. Here the endangered mountain beaver makes his home along with a myriad of waterfowl. The beach a fine place to bird watch; and those who like to surf fish can cast their lines for surf perch at the shore.

There are no accommodations at Manchester State Beach for wheelchair users. There is a view of the beach from the day use parking lot, but restrooms are in the middle of the sand. The primitive campground at Manchester is dotted with Monterey cypress and covered in dune grasses. Forty-eight sunny campsite pull-ins are gravel coated, mostly level, and offer a table on grass. Pit toilets in the area are not accessible.

Manchester State Beach

Contact Mendocino District Office
(707) 937-5804

Location — Seven miles north of Point Arena on Hwy 1. Enter 1/2 mile north of the town of Manchester.
Elevation — Sea level

SCHOONER GULCH

Seventy acres of beach and sheer headlands characterize the Schooner Gulch area. From its high bluffs, this undeveloped park offers stunning views of the coastline and evening sunsets. There are no other facilities.

Schooner Gulch

Contact Mendocino District Office
(707) 937-5804

Location — Five miles south of Point Arena at the north side of the bridge on Hwy 1 at milepost 11.25
Elevation — 100 feet

> **Clear Lake Area**

CLEAR LAKE STATE PARK

Clear Lake is California's largest natural body of water located entirely within the state. Since two miles of lake shoreline serve as a portion of the park boundary, it is understandable that water spots are the focus of park activities. Besides fishing for crappie, blue gill, catfish, perch, and black bass, visitors also enjoy swimming and water skiing in the lake's crystal blue waters. Wheelchair users can enjoy activities with friends and family; asphalt paving is provided

in popular areas and most features are accessible.

Visitor Center

In the northwest portion of the park, a large parking lot serves the visitor center, boat launch, and day use areas. In June and July, blackberry bushes, laden with ripe fruit ready for the picking, line the parking lot. At the south end of the lot, the district office and ranger station share a building with the visitor center that houses displays of regional natural history and stories of the native Pomo Indians. For access to the veranda that encircles the visitor center, you'll take a gently sloping ramp that begins near an accessible *DRINKING FOUNTAIN* and *TELEPHONE*. An RV dump station is provided in the parking lot.

Boat Launch

The boat ramp is located at the opposite end of the visitor center parking lot. Steel ramps (15%) lead to the launching area and a *very* steep ramp (50%) with handrails drops to the loading dock. A designated *PARKING* place for car and trailer are nearby. There is a restroom in the parking lot with a doorway that is wide enough for wheelchair access, but there are no modified fixtures inside. The only curb cut for this restroom from the parking area is near the visitor center, 300 feet away.

Picnic and Swimming

You'll have a lovely view of Cole Creek and the boat launch from the family picnic area. Ducks and other waterfowl hunt for insects and preen themselves on the creek

bank near picnic tables on the lawn. A Chinese-style footbridge arches over Cole Creek, adding to the charm of this shady spot. Plenty of day use *PARKING* (one designated place) is provided in a lot nearby. At the foot of the parking lot, a concrete walkway leads to an accessible *RESTROOM*, that offers a large lateral-transfer stall with a high toilet and grab bars. An paved path leads to the park *AMPHITHEATER* 350 feet beyond; the last 20 feet is steep (10%).

Swimming Area — Just north of Dorn Cove at Soda Bay, a small swimming area attracts sunbathers and waders. Lifeguards are on duty in season, and, since fishing and boats are not allowed in the swimming area, visitors are assured of a safe place to enjoy the water. From the dirt parking lot, an uneven dirt surface leads to the gravel beach where a few picnic tables have shade ramadas. There is also a dirt approach to the restroom at the parking lot, and a 1½-inch transition onto a concrete slab near the doorway. The toilet is low and has grab bars, but there are no other access modifications.

Parasailing

While you're visiting Clear Lake, you won't want to miss an opportunity to go parasailing. Strapped securely to a colorful parachute, you'll be effortlessly lifted high in the air from the back of a speeding off-shore boat. After your ride around the lake, you'll land back on the boat with the assistance of an experienced crew member. The folks at "On the Waterfront," a watersport rental company, invite visitors of all ages and abilities to

Near the picnic area at Cole Creek, Clear Lake State Park

(Photo courtesy CDPR)

take this ride of a lifetime. Try it once, and you'll be back for more. "On the Waterfront" is located about 20 minutes from the Clear Lake entry gate in nearby Lakeport. Call them for more information at (707) 263-6789.

Trails

Kelsey Creek Trail—Since much of the park terrain away from the lake is very hilly, the trails are narrow dirt paths that wander among the trees. The only level path is along Kelsey Creek as it parallels the road to Kelsey Creek campground and follows the contour of the creek to the lake shore. Parts of the trail are narrow and off-camber, and though it is flat, this short trip among cattails will require help.

Camping

Four campgrounds in the park offer a variety of camping opportunities. One is in a parklike setting; another is level and near the lake; while two overlook the water from a hillside. Kelsey Creek Campground is preferred by boaters and those who wish to be near the lake. Because it is flat and has accessible restrooms and showers, Kelsey Creek is also the campground of choice for wheelchair users.

Cole Creek—A lovely meadow in the shade of tall oaks and cottonwoods provides cool summer camping at Cole Creek Campground. Here, campers have a choice of pitching their tents under the trees or on an open lawn. Most of the campground is level,

but the restrooms are not accessible. Each site along the asphalt-paved loop has a table, BBQ, and food storage, and paved pull-in parking.

Kelsey Creek—Located on the north-facing lake shore, Kelsey Creek Campground is comprised of four small camping loops connected by smooth asphalt road. Sites have paved pull-ins and some bushes between them that offer a bit of privacy. Designated sites #49 and #50 have extra-wide asphalt parking, and paving under a modified table and around a fire ring.

Most sites in the campground are level and have limited shade. All are near the centrally located *RESTROOMS*. A few select sites, hidden among the trees and bushes at

55

the lake's edge, are particularly popular. The dirt beach at these sites is only a few feet wide, so the lake is at the doorstep of each waterfront campsite, allowing campers to beach a boat or canoe on shore. You'll need to reserve one of these premium spots well in advance.

Fully accessible UNISEX RESTROOMS and SHOWERS are located between pairs of camping loops. You can reach them by way of smooth asphalt from designated PARKING, or from the campsites. The accessible SHOWERS have a retractable seat in the stall and the control is 35 inches from the floor.

Upper and Lower Bayview —Oak trees cover the hillside overlooking Soda Bay at the Bayview campgrounds. Due to the hilly terrain, tables, parking, and tent sites are usually on different levels, and the restrooms at these campgrounds are not accessible.

Clear Lake State Park
5300 Soda Bay Road
Kelseyville, CA 95451
(707) 279-4293
Park Folder Available
Location—Three and a half miles northeast of Kelseyville on Soda Bay Drive
Elevation—1,400 feet

ANDERSON MARSH STATE HISTORIC PARK

The Pomo Indians native to this region thrived on the rich resources of the wetlands for thousands of years. Each summer season, park volunteers construct a Pomo Indian village on a knoll in the grasslands that surround the ranch. Park visitors may hike to the village for an experience with Pomo history or browse through the old Anderson Ranch House that contains artifacts and historic displays of the ranch. Every winter, bald eagles use this region as a wintering ground, making the park a favored destination for birdwatchers. Though the walk to see the village is easy, the footpath is uneven and narrow.

There are no accommodations for wheelchair users at the park. The ranch house does not have ramp access, and there are no accessible restrooms on the grounds. Because this day use park has limited hours, it is best to call ahead before making plans to visit.

Anderson Marsh State Historic Park
Contact Clear Lake District Office
(707) 994-0688
Park Folder Available
Location—On Hwy 53 between Lower Lake and Clear Lake
Elevation—1,320 feet

Napa Valley/ Inland Sonoma County

ROBERT LOUIS STEVENSON STATE PARK

Primarily used by hikers, Robert Louis Stevenson State Park features a five-mile hiking trail to the 4,240-foot summit of Mount Saint Helena. Beginning in dense woods, the trail climbs to the open mountainside where there are magnificent views of the Sierra Nevada Range, Mount Shasta, Lassen Peak, and Napa Valley. There are no accessible facilities at this day use park.

Robert Louis Stevenson State Park
Contact Napa District Office
(707) 942-4575
Location—Seven miles north of Calistoga on Hwy 29
Elevation—2,200 feet

BOTHE-NAPA VALLEY STATE PARK

Bothe-Napa Valley State Park, rich in ancient Indian heritage, was a huge private estate in its colorful recent past. For thousands of years the Napa Valley provided plentiful food and shelter for the Wappo Indians. During the Mexican era in the 1840's, 18,000 acres of this fertile land was acquired by entrepreneur Dr. Edward T. Bale. In the 1930's, Reinhold Bothe purchased a part of the land to build the Paradise Park Resort, which fell on hard times after World War II and was later purchased by the state.

A secluded area on the edge of the wine country, most of the park lies on a shallow rolling hillside overlooking the fertile Napa Valley. CAMPING is conveniently retrofitted, and many features of the park are accessible. Accessible TELEPHONES are located at the entry kiosk and the day use PARKING lot.

Visitor Center

At the visitor center, displays recounting the natural and social history of the Napa Valley line the walls. In addition, a large horizontal relief map of the region lies in the center of the room, but is difficult to see from a seated position. Book sales and an information station will help you with questions and trip planning.

The visitor center is located near the park entrance. A set of stairs leads to the main entrance. If you cannot manage stairs, you may access the main floor at the rear entrance. Park on the asphalt in front of the building and follow a sloping uphill paved path around to the back door, which has a 1½-inch door sill. If someone has not already noticed you on your way to the rear entry, rap on the door.

Picnic

At the end of the park road that parallels Hwy 29, tables under shady oaks invite you for a picnic. The grassy forest floor here is uneven and often covered in oak leaves. A gently sloping asphalt path leads to a _RESTROOM_ that has two short ramps at the doorway,

and an accessible stall with grab bars and standard fixtures. Parking throughout the picnic area is on dirt.

There are fewer obstacles and a paved designated _PARKING_ place at the picnic area near the pool and campfire center. You can reach the _CAMPFIRE CENTER_ in the day use area by way of a flat dirt trail across from the designated _PARKING_ space. Just off the pavement in the dirt near the campfire center, you'll find an accessible _TELEPHONE._

Swimming

For a refreshing break from traveling and sightseeing on a hot summer day, you can take a dip in the swimming pool at the day use area. The pool deck and pathway are paved, and a lifeguard is on duty in the summer season. There is no one to assist you in and out of the pool, so if you need help, be sure to bring a friend. Pool hours in the summer are 10:30 a.m. to 7:00 p.m. There is an additional charge to use the pool.

Trails

Most of the trails in the park are well-traveled and broad but are steep, rough, and not recommended for wheelchair use.

History Trail — A short loop trail (0.1 mile) will take the more adventurous to a pioneer cemetery dating to the late 1800's. Some of the region's early settlers and developers are buried here. The trail begins near the picnic area and is broad and level for 150 feet. The next 250 feet leading to the cemetery are steeper (10%) and narrower. Once at the cemetery, the terrain among the tombstones is very uneven. The trail continues on from here to Bale Grist Mill, but is not passable for wheelchair users.

Camping

Richie Creek — The campground is a perfect home base from which to plan a wine-tasting tour of the Napa Valley. Set in an assortment of oak and manrose trees, most of the campsites have some slope, but many have a table on the same level as the dirt pull-in. Each provides a table, BBQ, and food storage.

DESIGNATED CAMPSITE #9 is level and near an accessible _RESTROOM_, but the pull-in parking at the site has a slight slope. There is no paving around the table, but a table extension is available at the kiosk upon request. Sites #12 or

Camping at Bothe-Napa Valley SP is shady and flat.

(Photo courtesy CDPR)

#14 are fairly level and are adequate alternatives if the designated site is taken.

Both *RESTROOMS* in the campground are accessible. Paved designated *PARKING* is provided at each unisex unit (lateral transfer, grab bars, low toilet). A diverter head, which can be attached to a fixture on the wall, is available at the kiosk for the *SHOWER* near site #9. There are seats in the shower stall and the changing area. The shower head control is 48 inches from the floor.

**Bothe-Napa Valley
State Park**

3801 St. Helena Highway North
Calistoga, CA 94515
(707) 942-4575

Park Folder Available
*Location—Four miles north of St.
    Helena on Hwy 29*
Elevation—360 feet

BALE GRIST MILL
STATE HISTORIC PARK

In the mid-19th century, farmers that settled the fertile Napa Valley chose grain as their main crop. Edward Bale, an enterprising physician with a checkered past, had married into the Vallejo family and, in so doing, received a large parcel of land as his dowry. Not wishing to farm, he sold off enough land to build a water-powered grist mill to process the harvest for the other settlers in the valley. He also traded some land so he could build and operate a sawmill. Ultimately, Dr. Bale sold his mills and sought his fortune in the gold rush. The grist mill still

stands in working order at Bale Grist Mill State Historic Park.

The mill remained in use until the early 1900's. Today the park Ranger/Miller operates the grist mill with its 36-foot water wheel on Saturdays and by special request. Call ahead for the operation schedule so you don't miss the rare opportunity to watch a piece of living history. Most of the mill is accessible for viewing. When the mill is not running, park docents show a video in the museum that describes the mill's function. The ranger or park volunteers are available to answer questions.

To get to the mill, located adjacent to Bothe-Napa State Park, *PARK* in one of the designated spaces in the paved lot, then take a concrete access trail with handrails (max grade 10%) that leads 850 feet down a forested bank to the mill. Midway in the trail is the park's accessible *UNISEX RESTROOM* with grab bars and a low toilet.

**Bale Grist Mill
State Historic Park**

Contact Napa District Office
(707) 942-4575 or 963-2236
Park Folder Available
*Location—Three miles north of Street
    Helena on Hwy 28*
Elevation—60 feet

ANNADEL STATE PARK

Thirty-five miles of trails and fire roads weave among the rolling hills, meadows, and woods of Annadel State Park, making it a favorite for hikers, bikers, and horseback riders. Cobblestone quarries in this area once provided

paving for San Francisco after the 1906 earthquake; stones were hauled out of the hills on a narrow gauge railway. There are no paved roads nor any developed facilities at this day use park.

Annadel State Park

6201 Channel Drive
Santa Rosa, CA 95409
(707) 539-3911

Park Folder Available
*Location—East of Santa Rosa and
    south of Hwy 12. Take Mission
    Boulevard south, Montgomery
    Boulevard east, then right on
    Channel Drive.*
Elevation—300-1,800 feet

SUGARLOAF RIDGE
STATE PARK

Perched in the Mayacamas Mountains between the Sonoma and Napa Valleys, Sugarloaf Ridge State Park is a popular hiking, riding, and rock-climbing park. Twenty-five miles of trail wind through a creek-fed forest, open meadows, and chaparral-covered mountains on their way to three summits. Summer temperatures on the ridge range in the 90's, so most visitors prefer to come to the park in the spring and fall. Camping and day use areas are not accessible, but the *VISITOR CENTER* is modified for access if you'd like to come up for a picnic on the veranda.

Visitor Center

Access to the newly refurbished visitor center includes a wooden veranda overlooking Sonoma Creek, an accessible *TELEPHONE*, book sales, and displays of the

Jack London's House of Happy Walls   *(Photo courtesy CDPR)*

park's natural history and trail guides. You may *PARK* in a designated space on pavement and enter the building by a ramp nearby.

Camping and Picnic

Campsites dot the perimeter of an open meadow surrounded by a forest of oak and fir trees. A table and fire ring on a grass and dirt surface are adjacent to each site's dirt pull-in. The tiny nearby restrooms are not accessible.

Day Use picnic tables are situated in a grassy spot beyond the campground. There are no accessible restrooms nor modified tables.

Sugarloaf Ridge State Park

2605 Adobe Canyon Road
Kenwood, CA 95452-9004
(707) 833-5712
Park Folder Available
Location—Seven miles east of Santa Rosa on Hwy 12, then north 3 miles on Adobe Canyon Road. A narrow road meanders through a residential section on the way to the park.
Elevation—1,100 feet

JACK LONDON STATE HISTORIC PARK

In tribute to her husband, Charmain London wished that Jack London's 800-acre ranch and homes be set aside so that others would remember him for his prolific creativity and love of life. He called his main home the **House of Happy Walls**. In it is preserved a great deal of London memorabilia and furnishings, including a portion of his extensive library. Much of the literature displayed here has been transferred from his cottage near the ranch where he did much of his writing. The furnishings you see in the museum were specially designed and built for the London's dream castle, The **Wolf House**. Unfortunately, the castle was destroyed by fire before they could occupy it.

You can visit the House of Happy Walls and take a tour of the rest of the ranch with the help of the volunteer organization at the park. Along with a visit to the House of Happy Walls, you'll see the remains of the Wolf House and pass by the cottage at the ranch where London spent much of his time.

Visitor Center

The **House of Happy Walls** stands on a hill overlooking the London ranchland and serves as the park museum. A set of stairs blocks access to the main entry, so a *WHEELCHAIR LIFT* is provided at the side of the museum building, allowing access to the lower floor of the house. Though some of the displays are high, the flavor of the London lifestyle is very apparent in the rich decorations and accessories. The park ranger's office and a book sales area are also located on this floor.

Two designated *PARKING* places are located in a paved lot down the hill from the house. To get to the museum from there, take the broad asphalt road uphill (11.5% grade) for 350 feet. An accessible *RESTROOM* (grab bars and a pivot-transfer stall) is 150 feet from the parking places down a separate asphalt path; fifty feet of this path has a 15% grade.

Special Access

On weekends from noon to 4 p.m., park volunteers shuttle visitors from the parking lot to the museum in an electric cart. Most of the trails and pathways in the upper portion of the park are much too rocky and steep for wheelchair users, but you may also call ahead to the park office and make arrangements for a golf cart tour of Wolf House, Jack London's grave site, and other ranch features that would ordinarily be accessible only to the able-bodied. For more details, contact the Valley of the Moon Natural History Association at the park.

Jack London
State Historic Park

2400 London Ranch Road
Glen Ellen, CA 95442
(707) 938-5216
Park Folder Available
Location — Twenty minutes north of Sonoma off Hwy 12 on London Ranch Road
Elevation — 650 feet

SONOMA
STATE HISTORIC PARK

In the early 1800's, Sonoma was the site of the most northerly Franciscan Mission in California. Threatened by the power of the church and driven by the desire to make his influence felt, the Mexican governor was determined to undermine the mission system. It was governor Figueroa's intent to locate the Mexican provincial

headquarters at the doorstep of the Northern Frontier and install Mariano Guadalupe Vallejo as his Director of Colonization. So, in 1834, he sent Vallejo to secularize the recently established mission settlement of Sonoma, free the Indian workers, and disperse the mission assets among the population.

Not long thereafter, California became a republic and then a state. In the ensuing years, the buildings around the original town square changed hands many times and were used for diverse purposes. Many of the original structures have been preserved and still stand near the central plaza at Sonoma State Historic Park. You can visit two hotels and the army barracks where Vallejo's men were stationed. The restored mission chapel still stands nearby; the living quarters at the mission is the oldest building in Sonoma. There are a number of other original buildings and sites around the plaza as well. For an informative brochure and map of the town, call

the park office and ask for the park folder, or pick one up at the mission.

Parking

A public *PARKING* lot with two designated places is located behind the barracks building north on First East past Spain Street. Beyond the curb cut to the historic buildings is a fully accessible *RESTROOM* with a short ramp at the doorway. The grounds in this area are firm decomposed granite.

Historical Buildings

Sonoma Barracks — Originally built to house Vallejo's Mexican army, the barracks building now hosts a museum of local military history. Lighted displays are visible from a seated position. The only barrier to the building is the rough, worn wooden door sill at the entry.

Mission San Francisco Solano de Sonoma — What remains of the original living quarters and reconstructed chapel is open daily for visitation. Twenty feet of brick paving form a pathway (16%) to the entrance. If not propped open, the mission doors are heavy; some of the floors are brick and many displays are high on tables making them difficult to see from a seated position. The mission is on the corner opposite

Sonoma Barracks, Sonoma SHP

(Photo courtesy CDPR)

the barracks; there are curb cuts at each corner.

Toscano Hotel – This building has been used for many purposes throughout the years. Presently, it is furnished in the turn-of-the-century decor of its most recent inhabitant, the Toscano Hotel. There are two alcoves off the sidewalk, each with a 1-inch transition, from which to peer inside the parlor. Tours inside the hotel are given on Saturdays, Sundays, and Mondays, but only the lower floor is accessible.

Vallejo Home – The well-manicured grounds of the Vallejo home are lush and inviting, but difficult for wheelchair users to access. Two steps precede the 4-inch front porch door sill, and much of the pathways have a gravel covering. The home is open for viewing during park hours, but you will need someone to help you up the steps to the first floor. The home has been preserved inside as though no one had left. The dining room table is set, and you feel as if General Vallejo himself will appear at any moment.

A gravel-covered path leads to a small visitor center and information station outside the house. The paved parking lot is level, but the restrooms are not accessible.

Sonoma State Historic Park
20 East Spain Street
Sonoma, CA 95476
(707) 938-2588 or 938-1215
Park Folder Available
Location – Downtown Sonoma on
*   Spain and Third Streets. Vallejo*
*   Home located north on Third West*
*   from West Spain.*
Elevation – 90 feet

You can view inside the downstairs rooms at Petaluma Adobe SHP.   *(Photo courtesy CDPR)*

PETALUMA ADOBE STATE HISTORIC PARK

General Vallejo managed his huge agricultural empire from a two-story building high on a knoll, where he had a view of his 66,000 acres of prime production land. Each of the adobe's refurbished rooms contain artifacts, equipment, and furniture of the period and descriptive information about each exhibit.

Begin your *SELF-GUIDED TOUR* of the grounds at the visitor center. It is open from 10 a.m. to 5 p.m., and contains the story of ranch life of the 1840's. Stories about the Indians, vaqueros, and the all-important hide and tallow trade will orient you to the workings of the ranch. Books and park folders are also available here.

The adobe is located at the end of a paved walkway (8%) 400 feet from designated *PARKING*. Firm packed dirt covers the courtyard and surrounds the building. Door-ways on both floors are open so you may view the displays inside, but the upstairs rooms are not accessible. Of particular interest is the outdoor hide tanning exhibit in back of the adobe that describes the tanning process in series of displays.

A *PICNIC AREA* and the only restroom at the park is located off the paved parking lot. There is a curb cut next to a designated *PARKING* place to make it easier get to the picnic area and the path leading to the adobe. Picnic tables are distributed on the dirt surfaces around the parking lot in the shade of oak trees. The restroom is not modified for access.

**Petaluma Adobe
State Historic Park**
3325 Adobe Road
Petaluma, CA 94952
(707) 762-4871
Park Folder Available
Location – Seven-tenths of a mile east
*   of Petaluma on Hwy 116, then 2*
*   miles north on Casa Grande Road*
Elevation – 150 feet

Sonoma Coast

KRUSE RHODODENDRON STATE RESERVE

Sun-loving rhododendrons thrive in their preserve at Kruse Rhododendron State Reserve. Several varieties of the flowering bush took a foothold at the site of an old forest fire where the shade trees were eliminated, allowing a flood of sunlight to encourage their growth.

To find the park, take Kruse Ranch Road from Hwy 1 at the northern edge of Salt Point State Park. Drive on the dirt road for one mile to a pull-out at the end. There is no space to turn around a motor-home or trailer, so don't bring them down this road. A series of stairs lead up to the trail which meanders through the reserve; the trail is not accessible.

Kruse Rhododendron State Reserve

Contact Salt Point State Park
(707) 847-3221

Park Folder Available
Location — Twenty-two miles north of Jenner off Hwy 1
Elevation — 500 feet

SALT POINT STATE PARK

Salt Point State Park ranges along six miles of coastline and stretches two miles inland. This 6,000 acres encompasses a broad diversity of natural habitats, making it an interesting destination for nature-lovers. The park is home to all kinds of animals. Along the shore, you'll spot seals, sea lions, and shore birds. Between December and May, migrating California Gray whale sightings are common. Inland, animal life is abundant in the forest and prairie. Blacktail deer, coyotes, wild pigs and raccoons make their home here and sometimes visit the campground.

SCUBA divers will want to explore one of California's first underwater parks, **Gerstle Cove Marine Reserve**. The rich marine life in the cove is protected, so divers may visit and observe but may not disturb the plants or animals. Fishing is allowed anywhere outside of the reserve.

You can take a scenic _PAVED_ _TRAIL_ to Salt Point. There you'll have a bird's eye view of the cove and the rugged northern California coastline. If you decide to stay overnight, two designated _CAMPSITES_ are nestled in a lovely wooded hillside across Hwy 1 at Woodside Campground.

Picnic

Gerstle Cove — At the end of the park road at Gerstle Cove picnic tables on a bluff overlook the rocky coastline. The view from here is quite nice making it a pleasant place for a picnic lunch. But, parking and tables are located on a sloping, uneven dirt surface, and there is only a standard chemical toilet nearby.

Stump Beach Cove — Parking for Stump Beach Cove is in a sloping dirt lot with a standard chemical toilet nearby. Next to the parking, there is a shady picnic table, but it has no ocean view. The dirt trail leading to the beach is steep and includes a set of stairs.

Fisk Mill Cove — This is also a beach access point. A steep, narrow trail leads to Fisk Mill Cove from the paved parking lot on the highway level. Picnic tables on the dirt surrounding the parking lot do not have an ocean view, but there is an accessible shasta toilet at this turn-out.

Trails

Salt Point Trail — For the best vantage point of the Underwater Reserve at Gerstle Cove and the coastline beyond, take a short trip to the end of Salt Point Trail. Because the waters southeast of the point are protected, an abundance of sea mammals and birds frequent this area and nature-watching is excellent. Between December and May, you may spot California Gray whales from the point, on their migratory journey between the warm waters of Baja California and the chilly Bering Sea.

The Salt Point Trail begins at Gerstle Cove parking lot with a short 50-foot asphalt grade (10%). From there, the remainder of the 700-foot trail to Salt Point is smooth and gently sloping. The parking lot is paved with lattice paving blocks and there is a designated _PARKING_ place. The _RESTROOM_ here has an accessible _DRINKING_ _FOUNTAIN_ and an accessible stall with grab bars and otherwise standard fixtures. There is a crude boat ramp at the cove for launching small boats. Check with the ranger for launching information.

Camping

Woodside — In the shelter of a mixed forest of Douglas fir, bishop pine, tan oak, and second-growth redwoods, campsites at Woodside are distributed along two asphalt loops in the gently sloping hillside east of Hwy 1. Due to the terrain, tables, food storage, and fire rings are not usually on the same level as the paved pull-ins. At the campground entrance, you'll find a telephone that is too high to use from a seated position and an RV dump station.

Woodside Campground has two designated *CAMPSITES*, #56 and #98. Site #58 provides a table and food storage box on a hard-packed, dirt surface that is level with the parking. There is parking and an asphalt approach in front of the nearby *UNISEX SHASTA TOILET*, which has a heavy door, grab bars, and standard fixtures.

Campsite #98 has double-wide paved parking, but due to the cramped camping area, access to the picnic table is limited. The *RESTROOM* has the same features as the one near site #58, but it is downhill from this site. Site #100, also uphill from the restroom, may be preferable because it is flatter and more roomy than #98.

Gerstle Cove (formerly Moonrock) — A drive through the rocky moonscape of Gerstle Cove Campground explains why it was originally named Moonrock. Nearer to the ocean than Woodside, the rolling terrain and soft surfaces throughout this area do not afford an ideal camping situation.

There are no designated sites in this campground, however, sites #11 and #17 are close to a restroom and are fairly level. A hardened dirt path leads to an accessible *RESTROOM* across from site #12. It has an accessible sink,

Fort Ross Chapel   *(Photo courtesy CDPR)*

grab bars in the stall, and a low toilet. An RV dump station is provided at the entrance, and *ENROUTE CAMPING* is also available.

Salt Point State Park

25050 Coast Hwy 1
Jenner, CA 95450
(707) 847-3221
Park Folder Available
Location — Twenty miles north of Jenner on Hwy 1
Elevation — 100 feet

FORT ROSS
STATE HISTORIC PARK

In 1812 an envoy of Russians and Aleuts landed on the Sonoma Coast seeking their fortune in sea otter pelts. Otters were plentiful, as was the wildlife on shore, making this an ideal base of operation for their quest. They immediately built a stockade at this location, in what was Spanish territory in an attempt to establish a claim to the area. Once fortified and protected,

they set about the business of harvesting the sea otter populatio to near extinction.

At Fort Ross State Historic Park, a careful reconstruction of Fort Ross stockade structures stand on their original site on a scenic ocean bluff. Some of the buildings have ramp entrances providing access to the various artifacts displayed in each exhibit.

Living history celebrations are given here at various times during the year. Docents re-enact the life of the Russian and Alaskan pioneers. Many Russians know about this bit of history, but very few Americans realize that the Russian flag once flew over California.

The *VISITOR CENTER* is accessible, but access to the fort is challenging, so bring along a friend to help you over some of the rough and sometimes steep surfaces.

Visitor Center

Through words, pictures and exhibits, the visitor center presents the interesting story of Russian history in early California. Most of the exhibits and the film presentation are visible from a seated position. The Fort Ross Interpretive Association has docents on hand to answer your questions. If you're looking for more information about Russian history in California, they will be glad to help you find just the right book among their large collection to purchase.

Four designated _PARKING_ places are provided 150 feet from the entrance where there is an accessible _TELEPHONE_ and _DRINKING FOUNTAIN_. The _RESTROOMS_ inside the building are fully accessible, but you may need help with the heavy doors at the entry and restroom.

Fort Ross

Within the hand-hewn redwood walls of the fort, some of the original fort buildings have been reproduced with ramp access and are open for inspection. With some imagination, you might envision Princess Helena, the last commandant's wife, entertained her guests in the _COMMANDANT'S QUARTERS_. Behind the house in the _OFFICIAL'S QUARTERS_, along with sample bunks and military artifacts, you'll get a rare look at several applications of the tinsmith's and woodworker's trades displayed in the alcoves. The lower floor of the supply house is crammed with crates and goods, but there is a step up to the exhibit area. The supply house is ramped to the back door, which opens onto the upper floor where large items were stored. The Russian Orthodox wooden chapel is not open for visitors, but you can see into the interior from the doorway.

(Photo courtesy CDPR)

There are two ways to access the fort from the visitor center. One is by a walkway that begins at the back door. It takes you down a ramp (max. 13% grade) with a handrail to a ¼-mile asphalt path that leads to the fort. Benches are provided along the way. Another way to access the fort if you have a disabled placard is by driving down the service vehicle road at the end of the visitor parking lot. On the ocean side of the fort, there is a roadside designated _PARKING_ place. From there, follow a sloping paved path 225 feet to a fort entrance. You may also park on the dirt at the lower fort gate where the dirt and grass surface slope uphill to an opening in the fort walls.

The grounds of the fort are mainly uneven grass and dirt that gently slope in the direction of the ocean. Traveling over the lumpy surface will be the most challenging part of your visit to the fort. Pit toilets on the grounds have a 1-inch lip at the doorway, grab bars, and standard fixtures. There are no paved walkways within the fort.

Camping

Primitive camping can be found two miles south of the fort in a shallow canyon. All sites and the road through the campground are uneven dirt surfaces. Low, flush toilets are located a step up on a concrete slab. They have wide doorways and grab bars.

Fort Ross
  State Historic Park
  19005 Coast Highway
  Jenner, CA 95450
  (707) 847-3286
  Park Folder Available
  Location — Twelve miles north of Jenner on Hwy 1
  Elevation — 90 feet

SONOMA COAST STATE BEACHES

The Sonoma Coast State Beaches feature the premier coastline of Sonoma County. For many travelers, this stretch of coast is the most memorable part of the scenic drive up Hwy 1. High coastal bluffs, rocky promontories, and sandy beaches remind us why the California coast is the subject of countless photographs.

The mouth of the Russian River is the fascinating scene of wildlife activities. Harbor seals come here to socialize and birth their pups. From the scenic day use area at **Whale Point**, you will spot them frolicking in the waves and lying among the rocky outcroppings. Seabirds of many varieties scud along the tide pools as the waves break against the rocks.

Sunset is a lovely time to appreciate the beauty of the **Goat Rock** area. The paved parking lot is flat, and there is an accessible _RESTROOM_ with a low shasta toilet in a shallow stall with grab bars. Picnic tables are located on a sandy surface at the perimeter of the parking lot. If you don't care to leave the car, roll down your windows and fill your senses with the sweet aroma of the sea breeze and the blush of the setting sun as it fades to darkness. To find Goat Rock, take the Whale Point turn-off just south of the Russian River bridge and follow it to the end.

Along the coast route north of the State Park headquarters located at **Salmon Creek**, a number of pull-outs offers you a chance to stop and enjoy the magnificent views of the rugged Sonoma Coast. At most of these stops there are only steep cliff trails to the beach or rocks below, and few have a restroom. **Duncan's Landing** has designated _PARKING_ near a dirt path that slopes uphill to a low accessible _UNISEX SHASTA TOILET_ with lateral transfer and grab bars. There are a couple of picnic tables overlooking the water and a small primitive boat launch.

Bodega Head is the southernmost point of the park. On a clear day, from this high promontory the coastal view sweeps all the way south to Point Reyes, making this a prime whale watching position in season. All parking areas on the Head are on uneven dirt, and there are no other facilities.

Camping

Bodega Dunes—Snug in the dunes north of Bodega Bay, each site in Bodega Dunes Campground is bounded by acacias and conifers, providing cozy privacy for beach campers. The asphalt paved roads and pull-ins are mostly level. Sites include a table, food storage, BBQ, and/or fire ring. The telephone at the entrance is not accessible. An RV dump station is provided.

Four designated _SITES_ (#16, #29, #80, and #92) have pavement completely covering the surfaces around a modified table, storage box, tent site, and BBQ, and/or elevated fire ring. Site #29 is preferable if _RESTROOM_ access is a priority; the access ramp here is not as steep as the others.

Each of the _RESTROOMS_ has a shallow stall with a low toilet and grab bars; all other fixtures are standard. Ramp access to the restrooms near sites #80 and #92 is steep (13-15%). _SHOWERS_ in each restroom building have no barriers, controls are 40 inches from the floor, and each has a bench in the changing area. The _SHOWER_ near site #16 has an additional retractable bench inside the stall. These heavily used restroom facilities are often in disrepair.

You can reach a _BEACH OBSERVATION DECK_ by an accessible 425-foot _BOARDWALK_ that begins at the paved beach parking lot. Designated _PARKING_ is near the start of the boardwalk where there is also an accessible _PIT TOILET_ with a sloping door sill. A series of stairs from the observation deck precludes access to the beach.

Wright's Beach—Just north of Ocean View, a narrow access road leads down to water level from the highway. Surrounded on three sides by tall bushes and ocean bluff, campsites are separated from one another by bushes and are clustered on a flat sandy surface. Each site has a fire ring, table and storage box. Several of the sites are bordered by the beach.

The day use picnic area lies at the entrance of the campground where tables and fire rings are scattered in the sandy dirt. Designated _PARKING_ is provided at the accessible campground _RESTROOM_ and _TELEPHONE_. The _RESTROOM_ has a stall with lateral transfer to a high toilet with grab bars.

Sonoma Coast State Beach

Bodega Bay, CA 94923
(707) 875-3483
Park Folder Available
Location — Between Jenner and Bodega Bay on Hwy 1
Elevation — Sea level

ARMSTRONG REDWOODS STATE RESERVE and AUSTIN CREEK STATE RECREATION AREA

In the 1870's, a foresighted lumberman, Col. James Armstrong, recognizing the beauty and importance of the ancient giants he harvested, set aside a 600-acre parcel of land as a botanical garden. Thanks to Colonel Armstrong, a visit to this park is reminiscent of the times when the entire northern coastline of California was covered with three hundred-foot redwoods.

Armstrong Redwoods State Reserve includes the famous **Colonel Armstrong Tree**, a 1,400-year-old redwood that dominates an accessible _FOREST PATH_. For picnickers, designated sites are provided in the _PICNIC AREA_ near fully accessible _RESTROOMS_. The rangers give programs in the redwood forest theater which can be accessed with assistance.

65

Austin Creek State Recreation Area and Armstrong Redwoods State Park share a mutual boundary. You must pass through Armstrong Redwoods to reach Austin Creek. If you continue on the park road beyond the picnic area at Armstrong Redwoods, it narrows to one lane where it then enters Austin Creek SRA. No trailers or vehicles longer than 20 feet are allowed beyond this point. At the end of the road, a shady campground provides a good base camp for hikers and horsemen. This 4,200-acre park of rolling grassy hills and oak groves is a wonderful wildlife habitat, but there are no accessible features here.

Visitor Center

At the kiosk entry for Armstrong Redwoods and Austin Creek, a ramp access leads to a modular building that serves as the visitor center. You must cross a 4-inch door sill to enter the small information area where you'll find various books and pamphlets about the region and displays describing its natural history. A paved ramp access from designated _PARKING_ leads to a accessible _UNISEX_ _RESTROOM_ with grab bars and an accessible _DRINKING FOUNTAIN_.

Picnic

A very pleasant picnic area awaits among the trees and forest undergrowth 0.7 miles up the park road. Two well-marked designated _PICNIC SITES_ are conveniently located near a fully accessible _UNISEX RESTROOM_. To find the designated sites, make a left at the first road you come to in the picnic area and drive to the end. Sites are paved under the table, have an extra wide paved parking area and an accessible _WATER SPIGOT_. An asphalt pathway leads to the restroom where there is additional designated _PARKING_. These sites cannot be reserved, but are usually the last picnic areas to be occupied.

The popular Armstrong Redwoods State Reserve

(Photo courtesy CDPR)

Trails

The **Pioneer Trail** begins at the 310-foot Parson Jones Tree and winds through the forest to the Armstrong Tree. The main parking is at the entry kiosk and is about 600 feet from the trail head. There is a small _PARKING_ area near the Armstrong Tree and one designated _PARKING_ place at Burbank Circle. Either of these parking spots is close to the trail and is preferable for those with special access needs. The park is very busy in the summer vacation season, so finding a parking place then will be difficult.

The **Colonel Armstrong Trail** is a wide level path that is relatively smooth, with a maximum 7% grade. Most of the trail is kept clear, but fallen pine needles and tree bark create a problem with tire traction in some spots. A _SELF-GUIDED NATURE TRAIL_ begins at the Armstrong Tree. Boardwalks cover the heavy surface roots around some of the huge trees so wheelchair users can get right up next to the tree bark. For blind visitors, there is braille signage along the trail.

The portion of the trail from Armstrong Tree to the rest area at Burbank Circle, 1,000 feet away, is the most accessible section of the park trail system. On the east side of Fife Creek the trail becomes steep (up to 17% in places) and has more forest debris and exposed roots.

Camping

Bullfrog Pond (FCFS) — At Austin Creek State Recreation Area, a steep, narrow, rough road winds its way to a hilltop that is covered in oaks and pines. Hidden among the trees, the campsites with dirt pull-ins are on uneven surfaces; many sites have tables on different levels than the parking. The restroom has a flush toilet with grab bars and no other access modifications. There are no designated campsites, and the telephone is not accessible.

**Armstrong Redwoods
State Reserve and
Austin Creek State Recreation Area**

17000 Armstrong Woods Road
Guerneville, CA 95446
Armstrong Redwoods SR
(707) 869-2015
Austin Creek SRA — (707) 865-3483
Park Folder Available
_Location — Two miles north of
    Guerneville on Armstrong Woods
    Road_
Elevation — 170-1,940 feet

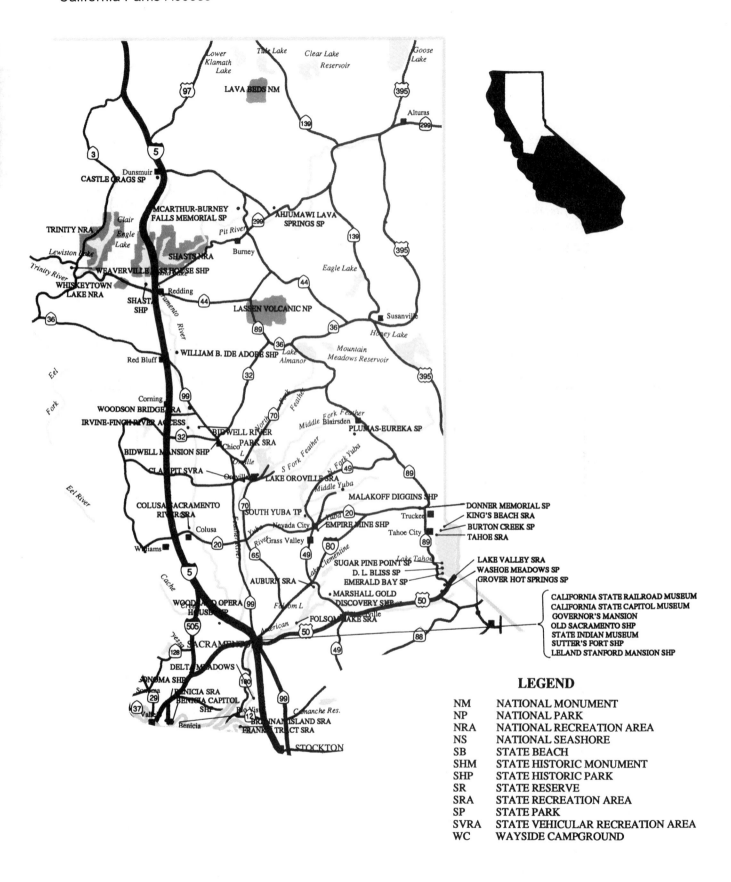

LEGEND

NM	NATIONAL MONUMENT
NP	NATIONAL PARK
NRA	NATIONAL RECREATION AREA
NS	NATIONAL SEASHORE
SB	STATE BEACH
SHM	STATE HISTORIC MONUMENT
SHP	STATE HISTORIC PARK
SR	STATE RESERVE
SRA	STATE RECREATION AREA
SP	STATE PARK
SVRA	STATE VEHICULAR RECREATION AREA
WC	WAYSIDE CAMPGROUND

Though seemingly desolate, Lava Beds National Monument holds hidden natural treasures.   *(Photo courtesy NPS)*

2

NORTHERN CALIFORNIA INLAND

Redding Region

LAVA BEDS
NATIONAL MONUMENT

The State of California precariously rests on the edges of major tectonic plates. When the earth's crust shifts, much of the state feels the effects. For millions of years, molten lava and steaming ground water has found its way through cracks in the earth and developed into volcanos and other eruptions along the full length of the state. Throughout Lava Beds National Monument you will see evidence of many facets of volcanic activity. The park lies in the southern Cascade Range at the northern base of the Medicine Lake Volcano. The topography here is a result of the eruptions and vents of this volcano, which has been active for at least a million years. Spatter cones and cinder cones dot the landscape of lava and ash. A popular attraction at the park is the lava tube caves, formed when the outer edges of swiftly-moving lava flows cooled and hardened.

Along with its violent geological history, the land within the park was also the scene of human suffering. For thousands of years, the Modoc Indian culture thrived at the site of what once was the huge Tule Lake. The Indians gathered grasses and harvested the bounty of the land until the 19th century brought immigrants to California who claimed it as United States territory. To forever control this region, the government instructed the U.S. Army to collect the In-

69

dians remaining on the land and transport them to a reservation in Oklahoma. The Modocs resisted, resulting in the bloody Modoc War of 1872. At its conclusion, the army took 155 Modoc prisoners of war and returned them to the reservation.

On your journey through Lava Beds National Monument, the park road will take you past many lava tube caves, volcanic formations, and historical sites. Ladders, stairs, or steep sandy paths present obstacles at most of the volcanic features listed on the park map. Steep dirt paths lead to many historical sites. However, the rangers at the visitor center have a variety of information and travel tips for visitors with special needs. Check with them before planning your stops. With prior arrangements, you may take a trip down into a lava tube cave, or a ranger-led _NATURE WALK_ designed with your needs in mind. In addition, a designated _CAMPSITE_ is available in a campground near the visitor center.

Prepare yourself for a wide range of temperatures at Lava Beds. In the summer, temperatures can soar to over 100°, and winter night mercury can drop to a chilly 20°. As with most desert areas, the most desirable seasons to visit are fall and spring, when the weather is milder.

Visitor Center

The _VISITOR CENTER_ and _RESTROOM_ facilities are fully accessible. From designated _PARKING_, a smooth asphalt walk leads to the visitor center entrance and 75 feet beyond to a completely accessible unisex _RESTROOM_ and _DRINKING FOUNTAIN_.

A small display of native plant life flanks the walkway.

Rangers are available at the _VISITOR CENTER_ to answer questions and arrange tours of the park. While you're there, have a look at the displays, book sales, and historical artifacts. The park staff wishes to make each individual's visit as full and interesting as possible and will suggest scenic destinations based on your abilities. They also will loan you flashlights and hard hats to take along on your cave explorations. If you are not going spelunking or want a preview of your adventure, the interpretive staff has compiled a photo album of the lava tubes that you can flip through. The visitor center is open daily except Thanksgiving and Christmas.

Park Features

Mush Pot Cave — Just across the parking lot from the visitor center, Mush Pot Cave is the only lighted lava tube cave in the park; it is also the most visited. For those who cannot descend a steep, narrow flight of stairs, you don't need to stay topside. The park staff has devised a "stair chair" to carry you into the cave. If you have at least two willing assistants to carry the chair, one front and one back, you can arrange to borrow it when you arrive. Or make arrangements ahead of time and the staff will have it waiting for you. Once inside, the cave's flat walking surface is firm and damp.

Valentine Cave — A very narrow trail leads to several rock steps at the mouth of Valentine Cave (the first cave along Hwy 139 from the south entrance of the park). In-

side, the flat, sandy cave floor runs for 1,000 feet under the lava beds. While not everyone will be able to explore this cave, those who have help and a healthy spirit of adventure shouldn't miss this unique opportunity.

Fleener Chimneys — Globs of molten lava piled on top of each other form the spatter cones at Fleener's Chimneys. The various shapes and textures provide a picturesque backdrop for the picnic area. A packed lava chip trail leads for 75 feet from a gravel parking area to a standard picnic table on pavement. A chemical toilet nearby is not accessible, and there is no shade, nor is water available.

Captain Jack's Stronghold — By 1840, the steady stream of westward-bound settlers had created a very strained existence for the Modoc Indians in the Klamath Basin. United States government administrators persuaded the Modocs to move their home north with the Klamath Indians. Neither tribe was able to live in harmony with the other, so the Modocs returned to their homeland. In 1872, the government ordered the American military to collect the Modoc Indians and deliver them to a reservation in Oklahoma. Determined to stand their ground, the Modocs, under the direction of Captain Jack (Kientpoos), fought back in a succession of bloody battles.

A series of exhibit markers on a self-guided trail will direct you through the sequence of events culminating in the eventual submission of the few surviving Modocs. Located approximately 3 miles west of the northeast park entrance, the initial asphalt path to the ½-mile loop is steep (17%). Parts of the rolling trail tread are loose ground lava and would require assistance. Rocks or other obstacles also may block your way. Tables and pit toilets at the trailhead are not accessible.

Camping

Indian Well—Across the highway from the Visitor Center, Indian Well Campground is open year round. A _CAMPSITE_ is reserved until 4 p.m. each day for visitors with a handicap-identification placard. Most sites are flat; each has an asphalt pull-in, with a table, BBQ, and fire ring on hard-packed sand. Foliage is sparse with the limited shade provided by an occasional juniper.

Designated _SITE_ #87 in loop A has extra wide asphalt parking, a picnic table with an extended end, and some shade. An asphalt roadway (8%) leads from the site to an accessible _RESTROOM_ with an electrical outlet and lateral transfer to a low toilet with grab bars. The _AMPHITHEATER_ is 350 feet beyond the restroom along an asphalt path. You'll encounter one steep (17%) section along the way. The restroom in Loop B is not accessible.

Lava Beds National Monument
PO Box 867
Tulelake, CA 96134
(916) 667-2282
Park Folder Available
Location—Five miles south of Tulelake on Hwy 139
Elevation—4,000-5,700 feet

The formations for which Castle Crags SP was named   _(Photo courtesy CDPR)_

CASTLE CRAGS STATE PARK

Three major geologic formations pierce the skyline and stand like sentries around Castle Crags State Park. Granitic material forced slowly upward from under the earth's surface forms the spectacular Castle Crags that command the northern horizon. Appearing prominently in the east is the volcanic Mount Shasta. In the southwest, you will see a different formation, where Grey Rocks form the crest of Flume Creek Ridge.

The park has a long mild summer season and is very convenient to I-5. Camping and hiking are challenging, however, because there are no facilities for the disabled.

Picnic

Soda Springs—Fishers and water lovers appreciate the shady oak picnic grounds along the bank of the Sacramento River, east of I-5. Each site here has a stone BBQ and a table. The restroom is not accessible, however, and a steep bank is the only access to the river.

Vista Point—If you have a strong assistant to push you up a very steep path, your efforts will be rewarded with an awesome view of the crags and Mount Shasta. A hard-packed path leads to an observation area atop a ridge at the end of the park road. You should not attempt this long (350'), steep (16%) climb without help. A vault

71

toilet in the asphalt parking lot below the view point is not accessible.

Trails

River Trail — Gates at either end of an asphalt road leading from the campground to the river and picnic area make this trail inaccessible to visitors using wheelchairs (max grade 12%).

Root Creek Trail — If the climb up to the Vista Point isn't for you, perhaps you'd like to take a trip through a cool mountain forest. Look for the trailhead marker on the road just before you get to the Vista Point parking lot. From there, a smooth hard-packed dirt trail with few obstacles winds for ½ mile among Jeffrey pine and weeping spruce trees. Beyond the ½-mile point, a small foot bridge and other obstacles make the trail very difficult to negotiate without help. Though there are no views from the trail, you'll enjoy the peacefulness of a stroll among the trees.

Camping

There are several level campsites along the hilly asphalt road, ¾ mile from the park entrance. Each asphalt pull-in has a table, food storage, and a concrete BBQ on a dirt surface. The campground is close to I-5, so you can expect some traffic noise, especially at night. Restrooms at the south loop have a 2-inch lip at the doorway and no retrofitted stalls. _SHOWERS_ in this building are large (48" by 48") and have no barriers; controls are 42 inches from the floor, and there are no seats in-

side. A steep, narrow dirt path leads from the Pacific Crest Trail parking area to the campfire center and is not accessible.

Castle Crags State Park

PO Box 80
Castella, CA 96017-0080
(916) 235-2684
Park Folder Available
Location — Six miles south of Dunsmuir on I-5
Elevation — 2,000 feet

AHJUMAWI LAVA SPRINGS STATE PARK

Ahjumawi Lava Springs State Park preserves one of the largest systems of natural springs in the world. Several miles of interconnected waterways and springs interspersed with lava flows and marshes support a variety of plant life and abundant water fowl. Hardy explorers also will find traces of the native American societies that flourished here. Of course, all artifacts and natural resources at the park are protected and may not be collected. Few visitors are able to appreciate the 6,000 pristine acres of canoeing and nature-watching pleasure because access to the park is only possible by boat.

Ahjumawi Lava Springs State Park

Contact McArthur-Burney Falls
Memorial State Park
(916) 335-2777
Location — Three and a half miles north of the town of McArthur (Hwy 299E)
Elevation — 3,000 feet

MC ARTHUR-BURNEY FALLS MEMORIAL STATE PARK

Located about half way between Mount Shasta and Lassen Peak, the McArthur-Burney Memorial State Park encompasses huge lava flows and beautiful evergreen forests on the Modoc plateau. Thousands of outdoor lovers annually come to the park to enjoy its scenic beauty and recreational opportunities. The most spectacular feature within the park is Burney Falls, an awesome waterfall that flows all year. President Roosevelt once called the falls "the eighth wonder of the world."

Though there are some accessible day use features, the best parts of the park are not modified for access. Paved roads serve the park, and there is a hardened trail to the visitor center and amphitheater. Access to both picnic areas and the swimming beach will require assistance. The only accessible restroom in the park is near the falls trail. Visitors crowd the park from June until late September, seeking refreshment in the cool waters of Lake Britton or in the misty canyons surrounding the falls.

Picnic and Day Use

The main picnic area, campfire center, and park museum are near the camp store and Burney Falls overlook. An accessible _RESTROOM_ with designated _PARKING_ is on the falls side of the road. The _RESTROOM_ has a shallow stall, grab bars, and a low toilet. You can get there by way of a gently-sloping ramp.

Across the road, a broad, smooth path reinforced with soil cement leads to the _CAMPFIRE CENTER_, park

of the parking lot at the end of the park road, a sandy path drops onto a very popular deep-sand swimming beach. Picnic tables sit nearby on the forest floor among tall trees, and a boat launch provides access to the lake for fishing or paddling. Sand sometimes covers the walkway to the accessible *LOADING DOCK* at the launch. Boat rentals are also available here, but the office is located in the middle of deep sand.

Trails

The centerpiece of the park is the year round majesty of Burney Falls. You can see the falls from a paved observation area across the road from the picnic grounds. But, if you're a wheelchair user, a railing may partially block your view. The one-mile loop trail down to the base of the falls on either side of Burney Creek is steep (up to 13% grade) and not accessible. You must negotiate a set of steps at the bottom of the paved trail on the east side of the creek. The dirt trail on the west side of the creek is more primitive.

Camping

Both the **Rim** and **Pioneer Campgrounds** are well-used areas with scattered shade and very little undergrowth for privacy between campsites. The dirt sites are mostly level but uneven; each has a table, food storage, fire ring, and rock BBQ. The restrooms central to each campground have a 1-inch lip through a 26-inch doorway and have no accessible stalls; the showers also are not accessible. An RV dump station and *ENROUTE CAMPING* are available in the campgrounds.

McArthur-Burney Falls

(Photo courtesy CDPR)

MUSEUM, and accessible *DRINKING FOUNTAIN*. The museum (short ramp entrance of 13% grade) features pioneer and Indian history displays along with information about the falls. The campfire center is just beyond the museum along the same path (150 feet from parking). If you decide to spread your picnic lunch out at a picnic table in the open space nearby, prepare to cross some very uneven forest floor surfaces.

The northern portion of the park borders Lake Britton. To the north

Store/Snack Bar

If you need a snack or a souvenir, there is an accessible *GIFT SHOP*, *MARKET,* and *SNACK BAR* just inside the park entrance past the park office. Since there is such heavy foot traffic in this area, smooth asphalt covers most of the surfaces around the building. The outdoor snack bar on the side of the building has a 40-inch counter top and a small paved decking. Visitors with a handicap-identification placard may *PARK* in a designated spot near the building where there is also an accessible *TELEPHONE*.

McArthur-Burney Falls Memorial State Park

Route 1, Box 1260
Burney, CA 96013
(916) 335-2777
Park Folder Available
Location—Six miles north of Hwy 299
on Hwy 89 near the town of Burney
Elevation—3,000 feet

WHISKEYTOWN SHASTA — TRINITY NATIONAL RECREATION AREAS

In 1965 the National Park System established this 203,587-acre National Recreation Area comprised of three separate units within the National Forest. The boundaries of Shasta Lake and Clair Engle (Trinity)—Lewiston Lakes Units, administered by the U.S. Forest Service, lie within the Shasta Trinity National Forest. The National Park System directs activities at Whiskeytown Lake Unit. Water sports enthusiasts throughout the state are familiar with all three parks. Houseboaters especially like the seclusion in along the convoluted lake shores at Shasta and Trinity. Fishers enjoy all three lakes.

Due to the recent drought of several years, the water levels at both Shasta and Trinity Lakes are well below capacity. This condition has left most of the water-related facilities high and dry. Access to boat launch areas and marina docks is largely down very steep, make-shift ramps on the lake bed. Often, a wooden plank is the only access to boat docks. On the other hand, Whiskeytown Lake is a water storage lake and is usually full. Check with the Visitor Information Station before planning a trip to Shasta or Trinity Lakes.

Shasta Lake National Recreation Area

1935 marked the first year of construction on the tallest concrete dam of its kind in the United States. When it was filled in 1948, Shasta Lake became the largest man-made lake in California. The dam impounds three rivers, the Pit, McCloud, and Sacramento. These three main arms of the lake are outlined by 370 miles of ragged shoreline to explore. The features listed below correspond with those on the park map issued by the U.S. Forest Service. You can obtain a map and other park flyers at the Information Center or by calling the park office at (916) 275-1587.

Visitor Centers

Shasta Lake Information Center—The U.S. Water and Power Resources Service operates the Shasta Dam Information Center. Besides the usual maps, brochures, and general park information, it offers a complete pictorial history of Shasta Lake and the Central Valley Project. You can watch a film about the dam construction in an accessible *THEATER*. In the lobby, a *SNACK BAR* serves hot and cold food and beverages.

You'll find two designated *PARKING* places near the entrance. The *SNACK BAR* just inside is accessible but does not have accessible tables. An outdoor shaded concrete patio at the end of the building has tables that are more accessible for wheelchair users. The *RESTROOM* stall has a high toilet with grab bars, pivot transfer and accessible sinks. A nearby *TELEPHONE* is also accessible. From a Vista Point close by, you'll have a panoramic view of the dam, the lake, and Mount Shasta. To find the dam, take Shasta Dam Blvd. west from I-5. For dam information, call (916) 275-4463.

Mountain Gate Information Center—The Mountain Gate facility is your main source for Shasta Lake recreation information. In the lobby, you'll find itemized lists of the camping, fishing, and boating opportunities that are available at the lake. Rangers will advise you of current water conditions and closure notices. The Forest Service also publishes a flyer that points out accessible park features. The following text outlines each of these features. An accessible *TELEPHONE* is just inside the building entrance. A heavy door here opens into a small *RESTROOM* that has a shallow stall with grab bars and a low toilet. The Mountain Gate Information Station is south of Shasta Lake off I-5 at Mountain Gate/Wonderland

Blvd. Designated *PARKING* is provided. For park information, call (916) 275-1589.

Lakehead Area

Interstate 5 follows the Sacramento River arm of Shasta Lake. This area is a favorite among short- and long-term campers and boaters. **Antlers Campground** is the popular camping location in the Lakehead area. Dotted with oak and madrone trees, the grounds are mostly flat, hard-packed dirt surfaces connected with asphalt roads and paved campsite pull-ins. There is designated *PARKING* and a curb cut near the *AMPHITHEATER*. Asphalt pavement connects the parking place with the paved seating area.

Designated *CAMPSITE* #3 is next to an accessible *RESTROOM* across from the campground host. Its only access modification is a table with extended ends. Most of the other dirt campsites are similar but they do not have an accessible table.

The *RESTROOM* has a small lip at the doorway, and a shallow pivot-transfer stall with a low toilet and grab bars.

Gilman Road Area

Each campsite at **Hirz Bay Campground** has asphalt parking near a table and tent site on an uneven dirt surface. A stall in the *RESTROOM* here is wide enough for wheelchair access, but no other accessible modifications. To get to the doorway, you must cross a rough dirt surface.

O'Brien Area

Bailey Cove—When the lake level is up, the oaken knoll at Bailey Cove is a lovely day use area and a pretty place to camp. In the day use area, a paved asphalt walkway leads from two designated *PARKING* places to an accessible *RESTROOM*. If you continue to follow the path, it will take you to two *PICNIC TABLES* that have table-level BBQ's and extended ends. When the lake water

level returns to normal, the campground at Bailey Cove will reopen. Plans for 1992 include an accessible *RESTROOM* at the campground. Because the campground is perched on a hillside, steep roads connect the restroom and the lake to the campsites.

Lake Shasta Caverns are further along Shasta Caverns Road. A concessionaire offers daily tours of the caverns. Unfortunately, due to the many stairways in and around the caverns, the tours are not appropriate for those with limited mobility.

For a convenience stop on I-15, the **O'Brien Rest Area** is fully accessible. Paving and curb cuts provide access from designated *PARKING* to accessible *RESTROOMS*. Pavement also leads to several *PICNIC TABLES* with shade ramadas.

Jones Valley Area

The dirt *LAUNCHING RAMP* (14% grade) at Jones Valley has designated *PARKING*. Set in a rolling oak forest, campsites at the nearby **Upper Jones Valley Campground** overlook the water. Each has a dirt pull-in, table, and fire ring. There are no accessible restrooms in the Jones Valley Area. Due to the difficult wheeling conditions, this area is recommended only for the stout-hearted.

Shasta Dam   (Photo courtesy U.S.D.A.)

Shasta Dam Area

There are two day use areas on Lake Drive east of the Shasta Dam Information Center. Steep shores surround the confluence of the Pit and Sacramento Rivers at **Fishermen's Point**. This quiet picnic area has a great view of the dam. Shaded tables and accessible *RESTROOMS* (lateral transfer, high toilet, grab bars, high sink) are not far from designated *PARKING*. You can get to both the tables and the restroom by way of asphalt paving.

There is room for three vehicles with trailers to *PARK* in the designated spaces next to the *LAUNCHING RAMP* (12%+). Smooth pavement leads to an accessible *UNISEX RESTROOM* in the upper parking area.

Shasta Lake
National Recreation Area

6543 Holiday Drive
Redding, CA 96003
(916) 275-1587

Information Available—Park Map, Camping Guide, Trails Guide, Fishing Guide, Handicap Facilities Guide, Commercial Services List
Location—Fifteen miles north of Redding on Interstate 5
Elevation—1,100 feet

Clair Engle (Trinity)/ Lewiston Lakes National Recreation Area

Rugged, granite peaks of the Trinity Alps Wilderness provide a picturesque backdrop to Engle and Lewiston Lakes. This area is more commonly known as the Trinity Unit of Whiskeytown—Shasta—Trinity National Recreation Area. The uncrowded and mostly undeveloped shoreline of Trinity Lake attracts boaters and hikers while Lewiston Lake is a favorite for campers and fishermen. There are few considerations at Trinity for visitors with limited mobility.

Private resort and houseboat rental companies are based in the marinas near Trinity Center or at the west arm of Trinity Lake. Some have boats that will occommodate a wheelchair. But when the water level in the lake is low, you have to pick your way through rocks down steep inclines to get to the docks.

Highlights of the campgrounds, resorts, picnic areas, and marinas around the lakes are listed below as they appear on the park map from the southern tip of Lewiston Lake to the northern portion of Trinity Lake at Trinity Center. You can obtain a map by calling (916) 623-2121.

Mary Smith—Sloping walk-in campground; dirt pull-ins, concrete BBQ's, shade, and flush toilets.

Cooper Gulch—Campground on Lewiston Lake with primitive campsites, vault toilets, concrete BBQ's, and some shade.

Lakeview Terrace—Run by concessionaire; cabins, a pool, and trailer sites.

Pine Cove—Run by concessionaire; trailer park, boat marina and rental, vault toilet.

Tunnel Rock — Walk-in hillside campsites.

Ackerman — Campground with few trees, dirt parking, fire rings or BBQ's, and a table. Flush restrooms and an RV dump station.

Trinity Alps Marina—Coffee shop, accessible *TELEPHONE*, accessible *FOOD STORE*, parking in gravel.

Fairview—Boat launch.

Tannery Gulch—The only campground at Trinity Lake with some access. Camping is arranged in a series of forested loops with a central restroom in each. Asphalt roads connect each loop and cover the pull-in at each campsite. Some sites are level, each has a table and fire ring. The most desirable site, #45, is flat and near a *RESTROOM*. Like all the other restrooms in Tannery Gulch Campground, gravel embedded in the forest floor surrounds this building. There are no other barriers at the doorway. The accessible stall has a high toilet and grab bars.

Tan Bark—Hike in to a picnic area overlooking the lake (when it is full). The narrow, ill-kept trail begins with a steep drop-off.

Stuart Fork—Boat launch.

Stoney Point — Picnic tables around the perimeter of a dirt parking lot. Walk-in campsites with tables and concrete BBQ's.

Stoney Creek—Swimming area not in use when water level is low. Restrooms and changing facilities are not accessible.

Pinewood Cove — Run by a concessionaire; campground, camp store, laundromat, amusement room, and RV dump station. No accessible features.

Cedar Stock Resort—Concessionaire-operated marina with a store, boat rentals, snack bar, gas, and restaurant/bar. Open seasonally. No accessible features.

Minersville—Rough steep walk-in campground sites.

Clark Springs—Campground in ill-repair with no accessible restroom. The _BOAT LAUNCH_ is newer and has designated _PARKING_ and an accessible _DRINKING FOUNTAIN_.

Estrellita—A tree-shaded picnic area on rough surfaces overlooks the marina at Estrellita. There is a step at the general store entrance.

Hayward Flat — Forest floor camping with an asphalt road and parking. Each site has a table, some shade, and a fire ring. The restroom is not accessible.

Alpine View—Rolling campsites with a lake view through trees. Each site has parking on packed dirt, a concrete BBQ, and a table. Restrooms are not accessible.

Trinity Center—Access to the lake through the town of Trinity Center. The town has all the regular services of a small town. Limited access to the marina, no accessible restrooms.

Whiskeytown—Shasta—Trinity National Recreation Area

Contact Weaverville Ranger District
PO Box 1190
Weaverville, CA 96093-1190
(916) 623-2121
Park Folder Available
Location—West from Redding on
Hwy 299 to Weaverville, then east
on Hwy 3
Elevation—2,370 feet

A quiet fishing spot at Whiskeytown Lake
(Photo courtesy NPS)

Whiskeytown Lake National Recreation Area

Formed by damming Clear Creek, six miles west of Redding, Whiskeytown Lake serves as a storage lake for water traveling to the Sacramento River. Unlike Trinity and Shasta Lakes, the Park Service usually keeps the water level stable at Whiskeytown Lake. Thousands of local residents and vacationers arrive at Whiskeytown every year to enjoy the developed swimming beaches and reliable fishing spots at the lake.

Brandy Creek Area

Swimming Beach—The Brandy Creek area is a favorite cooling off spot among the local residents of nearby Redding and surrounding areas. A gently sloping asphalt walkway leads from designated _PARKING_ to an accessible _RESTROOM_ and to the beach area beyond.

The _RESTROOM_ has a lip at the door and a shallow stall with grab bars. A changing room having no special fixtures adjoins the restroom.

Along the walkway (10% grade) beyond the restroom are an accessible _DRINKING FOUNTAIN_ and a _SNACK BAR_ with a 44-inch counter. Purchase a quick lunch or bring your picnic to one of several oak-shaded tables on the firm, but uneven lake shore. Assistance may be required to negotiate some soft spots on the dirt surface.

You'll find additional parking at **Davis Gulch**. Arranged on flat beach dirt, the picnic area here is about 300 feet down a steep (14%) asphalt road from designated _PARKING_. A dirt path leads from there for another 300 feet to the _SNACK BAR_. Restrooms in this area are not accessible.

Marina—A large lot near the boat launch has two designated _PARKING_ spaces for trailers and tow vehicles. Both the _LAUNCH_ and _DOCK_ are gently sloping and accessible with assistance. The RESTROOM in the parking area has a large lateral transfer stall with grab bars and a low toilet. Accessible TELEPHONES are located outside the restroom. The nearby CAMP STORE sells fishing supplies and is also accessible.

Camping—There is no restroom in the camping lot for self-contained RV's that is located on a hill above the lake. The paved surface is flat and an RV dump station is available.

Oak Bottom Area

Judge Francis Carr Power-house—At the tip of the lake's western arm, the powerhouse produces electricity from water traveling through a tunnel from Lewiston Dam at Trinity Lake. From a grassy rest area nearby, you have a view of Whiskeytown Lake with a different perspective. An asphalt walkway skirts the perimeter of the lawn where you can relax on benches provided at scenic points along the way. In early summer, berry bushes along the roadway abound with ripe fruit just waiting to be picked.

There is an accessible WATER SPIGOT and DRINKING FOUNTAIN outside the restroom near a designated PARKING space. A stall in each restroom is 30 inches wide but has no other accessible conveniences.

Marina and Dock — A large PARKING area with many designated places serves both the marina, accessible FISHING PLATFORM, and nearby amphitheater. A paved path leads to the AMPHITHEATER; a steep (16%) ramp along the path turns toward the restroom, which

has a low toilet, grab bars, and pivot transfer.

A system of concrete ramps gradually (less than 6%) descends to the boat dock and rental headquarters. There is a 3-inch drop from the gangway to the dock. The experienced staff at **Oak Bottom Marina** has served many wheelchair users and is happy to help you wih your special needs. They rent several types of boats, and sell fishing gear, fuel, and food. It is advisable to call ahead, discuss your needs, and arrange a rental, (916) 359-2269.

Fishing Platform—An asphalt path leads from designated PARKING at the end of the marina parking lot to a specially designed fishing platform. The curbed platform has a lowered section of railing for easy fishing access from a wheelchair. Half way along the path to the platform, you'll find a modified PICNIC TABLE surrounded with pavement. Depending on the time of day, there may not be any shade in this area, so bring along a hat.

Boat Launch—The boat launch, at the head of the marina parking lot, has a gentle slope to the water and an asphalt drive to an accessible DOCK. Designated PARKING is nearby.

Swim Beach—The swim beach at **Oak Bottom** is a pleasant sandy cove and very popular on warm summer days when temperatures range in the 90's. Wheelchair users will find this area particularly enjoyable because not only is the restroom and refreshment area paved, there is also a paved access path to the beach.

From designated PARKING, pavement leads to a patio area bounded on one side by a SNACK BAR (42-inch counter) and shaded tables. On the other side is an accessible RESTROOM (shallow stall, grab bars, low toilet) and outdoor showers (control 46 inches high). There is also an accessible TELEPHONE and DRINKING FOUNTAIN nearby. From there, a 300-foot asphalt PATH leads through coarse sand to a partially shaded portion of the beach at the water's edge.

Camping—The campground is walk-in style and has no accessible features. ENROUTE CAMPING is also available in the parking lot. A set of stairs and a very narrow access path render the camp store in the main parking lot inaccessible.

Whiskey Creek Area

Fishing and boating is a bit more peaceful at Whiskey Creek, where it feeds into the northeast arm of Whiskeytown Lake. A BOAT LAUNCH and FISHING PLATFORM are accessible, as are the restrooms nearby. On the road to Whiskey Creek a STORE and POST OFFICE are also accessible with assistance.

A well-marked accessible FISHING PLATFORM with lowered railing has an accessible DRINKING FOUNTAIN and two designated PARKING places nearby. A gently-sloping path leads 150 feet to the lake shore and 150 feet more to a picnic area where you'll find shaded tables on a dirt surface.

There is also a gentle slope at the BOAT LAUNCH and the DOCK is accessible from an asphalt drive. Designated PARKING is provided for your boat trailer and tow vehicle. On the southeast side of the parking area, a steep-ramped asphalt approach leads to the _RESTROOM_. The accessible stall has a pivot transfer with one grab bar and a low toilet.

Whiskeytown Lake
National Recreation Area

PO Box 188
Whiskeytown, CA 96095-0188
(916) 241-6584

Park Brochure Available
Location — Six miles west of Redding on
Hwy 299
Elevation — 1,210 feet

_____

WEAVERVILLE JOSS HOUSE STATE HISTORIC PARK

As the oldest continuously used Chinese temple in California, the Joss House is steeped in rich cultural history. Weaverville Joss House overflows with ornate furnishings and symbols of Taoist worship. This long-preserved tradition is still recognized by worshippers today.

In the summer months, tours of the temple are given every half hour. In the off-season, you can arrange a tour. The rangers regularly lead tours with wheelchair users and will prepare a special route of access to the interior. A short, arched, wooden bridge (15% grade), one step of 5 inches onto a wooden veranda, and one

step of 4 inches into the temple will require assistance.

You will be able to see all of the displays in the _VISITOR CENTER_ from a seated position. Though there is no designated parking in the lot nearby, a curb cut and paved walk leads to the entrance. Unfortunately, the public restroom in the patio area is not retrofitted for access.

Weaverville Joss House
State Historic Park

PO Box 1217
Weaverville, CA 96093-1217
(916) 623-5284

Park Folder Available
Location — On the south side of Hwy
299 in downtown Weaverville
Elevation — 2,000 feet

_____

SHASTA STATE HISTORIC PARK

Once the "Queen City" of California's Goldrush era, Shasta City now is only a shell of its former bustling self. Most of the remaining structures in town are mere masonry ruins. With a hearty imagination and some help from the _Brief History and Tour Guide_, the character of the Goldrush era can still be experienced — even from your car. If you send for a park brochure before your visit, the town map will direct you to each key building site and fill you in on the historic details of the town.

The old Masonic Hall at Shasta SHP is still in use today.

(Photo courtesy CDPR)

The old Shasta County Courthouse is the centerpiece of Shasta State Historic Park. Restored to its 1861 appearance, it houses a large collection of historical exhibits, paintings, and artifacts. Your time will be well spent browsing among memorabilia that rekindles the spirit of this now-defunct town.

Most of the historic structures in the park front on Hwy 299. The two-lane highway can be a very busy in the summer. Parking is difficult, streets are not level, and there is no designated street parking. The walkway to the *MUSEUM* is the only pedestrian area off the highway besides a few footpaths.

If you are going to visit the *MUSEUM*, try to find a place to park nearby, on the same side of the street. At the *MUSEUM*, the ranger will open another entrance for wheelchair users and place a portable ramp at the doorway. There are no accessible restrooms in town.

Shasta State Historic Park

PO Box 2430
Shasta, CA 90687
(916) 243-8194
Park Folder Available
Location—Six miles west of Redding on Hwy 299
Altitude—1,000 feet

LASSEN VOLCANIC NATIONAL PARK

Humanity has long been in awe of the power of volcanic eruptions. As recently as 1921, Lassen Peak was calming down from almost seven years of geologic tumult. You will see signs of volcanic activity throughout the park along the roadside and trails. The mountain continues to be a subject of geothermal testing and study. Meanwhile, Lassen Volcanic National Park is host to over 500,000 visitors a year. People come from everywhere to enjoy the lakes and meadows, play in the snow, and partake of the park's awesome beauty.

A view of cauldrons and fumeroles at Lassen Volcanic NP

(Photo courtesy CDPR)

The main park road loops around three sides of Lassen Peak. Plan on an unhurried scenic drive through the park; the speed limit is 35 MPH. If you want to take a closer look at the surroundings, use the turn-outs that are provided along the way. Roadside markers indicate some of the most notable park features. You'll find descriptions of each point of interest in a booklet entitled, *A Road Guide to Lassen National Park*. You can purchase a guide at any entrance station or information center, or by contacting the Loomis Museum Association at (916) 595-4444.

As you make your way through the park, follow along in the road guide for interesting stories about each stop. Most of the points of interest in the road guide (except campgrounds) are listed below in order of their appearance. Our tour begins at the south entrance station and follows the park road north to the visitor center near the junction of Hwys 44 and 89. If traveling from north to south, simply begin reading the descriptions in reverse order. Have your binoculars and cameras ready. You won't want to miss the scenic detail of Lassen National Park.

Park Features

Lassen Chalet and Southwest Information Booth — The Lassen Chalet is used primarily in the winter. A coffee shop and gift store are located upstairs. At ground level, the *DRINKING FOUNTAIN* and *RESTROOMS* are completely accessible, but the telephone is too high to reach from a seated position. At the information booth on the edge of the paved parking lot,

a park naturalist will help you with your questions. You can also ask about suggested side trips or current campground and trail conditions. You may also choose from a fine selection of books and pamphlets about the park and surrounding area. The booth is not accessible, but the ranger will leave the booth to accommodate disabled visitors.

Sulphur Works — A bubbling mud cauldron and steaming fumaroles at Sulphur Works are thought to be the main vent for Lassen Peak's volcanic activity. You can see this phenomenon from a railed overlook point. A short paved trail (350 feet) leads from a designated *PARKING* space across the highway. On the same side of the road as the parking, a steep (12%) boardwalk will take you 250 feet to a cluster of steaming pots. Due to the varying elevations of the pots and railing that lines the boardwalk, you may not get a full view of the area.

Bumpass Hell — Though you'll have a good view of Bumpass Hell from the parking lot, the self-guided nature trail that winds through this diverse hydrothermal area is not accessible for most wheelchair users. There is an accessible *CHEMICAL TOILET* near a designated asphalt *PARKING* space.

Lake Helen Picnic Area — At an elevation of 8,164 feet, the deep blue waters of Lake Helen are frozen most of the year. Carved by glacial ice, the region around Lake Helen is devoid of trees. Picnic sites south of the lake lie in a barren spot just off the highway. Pic-

nicking is level but the dirt surfaces are very rough.

Lassen Peak Trailhead — Hikers attempting the steep 2,000-foot ascent to Lassen Peak can park in a paved lot at the foot of the well-traveled Lassen Peak trail. From here, hikers look like ants as they thread their way up the south-facing slope. There is an accessible *CHEMICAL TOILET* near a designated *PARKING* space.

King's Creek — From your picnic table on the fringes of King's Creek Meadow, you will want to keep an eye out for deer foraging in nearby grasses. Tables and fire rings are snuggled under a canopy of fir trees on a packed forest floor. If you decide to stop here, park at the side of the road and follow an asphalt walkway to the picnic area and an accessible *RESTROOM*.

Summit Lake — This is the half-way point in an auto tour of Lassen National Park. At lunch time, the picnic area at the edge of Summit Lake can be crowded. Nevertheless, a shady lake view picnic is quite pleasant here. Tables on the forest floor are near a dirt parking area. The accessible *RESTROOM* across the road has a rough asphalt approach.

Devastated Area — On May 30, 1914, Lassen Peak began to erupt. For several years it continued to spew steam, boulders, mud, and lava toward the Sacramento Valley. At the devastated area, you will see evidence of Nature's slow recovery from this phenomena.

You can now visit the paved, wheelchair accessible, self-guided

Devastation Trail. As you progress along the ¼-mile path, interpretive markers retell the story of the eruption and its consequences. Lassen Peak looming ominously to the south reminds us that Nature continues to be a most powerful force in our lives. The trail is north of **Hat Lake**, at the Devastated Area pull-out near **Immigrant Pass**. Though a short segment of the trail is 12%, most is less than 3% and very smooth.

Loomis Museum—Park staff and volunteers have begun restoring the historic Loomis Museum, so it is not open at this time.

Reflection Lake—Most of the uneven trail around Reflection Lake is level, but the steep initial access from the road is difficult for wheelchair users.

Manzanita Lake—Manzanita Lake was formed by an avalanche about 1,200 years ago and further enhanced by a small earthen dam on its southwestern shore. It is stocked with brown and rainbow trout; fishermen cast their lines from small boats or off the shore.

Picnic tables among the trees are a stone's throw from the lake. Parking is close by also, but curbing interferes with access in the most popular area. Some dirt surfaces are too steep to cross safely without help. Slopes are more gradual on the east side of the lake near the primitive boat launch. To get there, drive to the end of the road. You can park near the dirt trail that leads back along the lake shore.

Most campground services are near the entrance. The *FOOD STORE*, laundromat, and *SHOWERS* are accessible, but the restroom here is not. Designated *PARKING*, behind the restroom building is near an accessible *TELEPHONE* and an accessible *WATER SPIGOT*.

The *SHOWERS* have accessible stalls with lateral transfer to a shower bench. Controls are 41 inches from the floor. There is a steep approach from the front of the shower building to the men's shower. It is preferable to park or have someone drop you off in the rear of the shower building if you are using the men's shower.

Visitor Center—With Lassen Peak in clear view, **Manzanita Lake Entrance Station** and visitor center is your first introduction to Lassen National Monument if you are a southbound visitor. Ramps (8%) lead from an asphalt parking lot to both the restroom and information station buildings. *RESTROOMS* are fully accessible (shallow stall) and there is an accessible *DRINKING FOUNTAIN* outside.

In the summer months, photographic displays line the veranda of the visitor center. Inside, representatives of both the National Parks Service and the National Forest Service offer information about the region. You can also purchase books, maps and posters.

Camping

Southwest—Narrow dirt footpaths branch off of a steep asphalt trail that leads downhill to each walk-in site at the Southwest Campground. Near the parking lot, asphalt paving leads to a *RESTROOM* that is retrofitted with a high toilet, pivot transfer, accessible sink, and electrical outlet.

Summit Lake—Engulfed in red fir and pine, two campgrounds at Summit Lake flank its north and south shores. Asphalt roads wind through the trees to a paved pull-in or pull-thru at each forest floor site, with a table and fire ring.

South—On Loop D, closest to the shore of Summit Lake, there is a gently sloping 50-foot trail to the water. An accessible *CHEMICAL TOILET* is on a paved path, central to the campsites.

North—Campsites on the north shore of Summit Lake are more level than on the south. Rough asphalt pavement near the picnic area leads to an accessible *RESTROOM* with pivot transfer to a high toilet with grab bars and an accessible sink. The restroom on Loop B is not accessible.

A dirt and gravel forest trail winds 800 feet along the lake between the North and South Campgrounds to the *AMPHITHEATER*. Some segments of the trail are steep (more than 10%) and may be soft due to fallen pine needles and other forest debris.

Crags—When other campgrounds are full, Crags opens for the overflow. Though it is flat, there are no access modifications at Crags.

Manzanita Lake—A mixed forest of fir, pine, manzanita, and cedar offer shade and privacy to a series of six loops near Manzanita Lake. Most have paved parking, and all have a table and fire ring.

There are two designated *CAMPSITES* (C37 and D36), and an RV dump station at the entrance.

Site C37, next to an accessible *RESTROOM*, has a shady pull-thru on smooth asphalt, with a modified table close by on the forest floor. Site D36 is also close to an accessible *RESTROOM*. Rough asphalt paving covers the parking place, and extends under a modified table and around a fire ring. This site has no shade. Both *RESTROOMS* are totally accessible by way of a ramp (11%) with handrails. There is an accessible *WATER SPIGOT* and *DRINKING FOUNTAIN* at each. Other flat sites that are near accessible restrooms but have no other accessible features are: C36, D9 (pull-thru), D10, D11, E16, and E17.

With some help, you can get to the *CAMPFIRE CENTER* by way of a 450-foot asphalt walkway (max 13% grade) from designated *PARKING* near the *CAMP STORE* and gas station. Space in the rear of the seating area is provided for wheelchair users.

Lassen Volcanic National Park
PO Box 100
Mineral, CA 96063-0100
(916) 595-4444
Park Folder and seasonal Lassen Park Guide Available A list of Lassen Volcanic National Park publications is available by writing to Loomis Museum Association, c/o the Park.
Location—Southern entrance on Hwy 89, 8 miles north of Mineral. Northern entrance at the junction of Hwys 89 and 44, 45 miles east of Redding.
Elevation—Up to 7,000 feet at Summit Lake

Sacramento Valley

WILLIAM B. IDE ADOBE STATE HISTORIC PARK

When West Coast settlers petitioned to become a United States territory in the 1840's, William B. Ide was a notable advocate of California statehood. As the first and only official president of the California Republic, he played a major role in the colorful history of the Wild West. His adobe home and grounds have been restored to remind us of the contributions he made to the development of state government and civilized behavior in the Redding area.

The restored buildings and artifacts of Ide's homestead create a scene typical of his day. Due to its historic nature, there is no paving or special accessibility for wheelchair users; doorways have either a porch or large sill. Most of the surfaces are packed dirt with gradual grade changes. A designated *PARKING* place is near the homestead, but the nearby restrooms are too narrow for wheelchair access.

William B. Ide Adobe State Park
21659 Adobe Road
Red Bluff, CA 96080
(916) 527-5927
Park Folder Available
Location—Two miles northeast of Red Bluff. From Northbound I-5, take Main Street through town north of Adobe, then east to the park. From Southbound I-5, take Wilcox Golf Road east to Adobe.
Elevation—275 feet

WOODSON BRIDGE STATE RECREATION AREA

Woodson Bridge State Recreation Area borders the Sacramento River on a main flyway between Canada and Mexico. In the spring and fall, the park becomes a prime bird watching location. Fishing is always a popular pastime on the Sacramento River. Meanwhile, a dense oak forest provides shelter and a cool respite at the campground.

Several dirt trails lead from the cozy campground to the swiftly moving Sacramento River. Access down its steep banks is difficult for even the sure-footed. Most campsites are level in both the oak-covered northern loop and the southern loop, which has more grass and open area. In the southern loop, extra long asphalt pull-ins lead across grass to tables and fire rings in the shade. Restrooms at both loops have small steps at the doorways, and there are no accessible stalls. An accessible *TELEPHONE* and an RV dump station are near the entry kiosk.

Woodson Bridge State Recreation Area
25340 South Avenue
Corning, CA 96021-0616
(916) 839-2112
Location—Six miles south of Corning and I-5 on South Avenue
Elevation—200 feet

BIDWELL RIVER PARK and IRVINE-FINCH RIVER ACCESS

Bidwell River Park, with its nearly four miles of water frontage, is a well-kept secret in the Chico area. Along a slough of the Sacramento River, this quiet waterway is used mainly by local fishermen. At its southern end, a rocky beach at Big Chico Creek, called "the washout," is a destination place for river rafters and inner tube floaters.

Five miles up river from the washout is the Irvine-Finch River Access. This park was developed as a launching area for river floaters and small boats. A concessionaire rents all types of floating devices. You can rent here and float to the pick-up station down river at **Big Chico Creek** in Bidwell River Park. The five mile trip takes approximately 2½ hours, so bring a hat and something to drink.

The raft rental company is sensitized to floaters with special needs. For rafters with lower body disabilities, they suggest renting a "dirtbag," a large bag of Styrofoam that supports the lower body and allows the rider to sit up. It comes with a kayak paddle and life jacket. Bring along an extra person to drop you off and pick you up at either end of the trip. Call for further information and reservation of a raft, (916) 894-RAFT.

Nut trees shade the parking area at the river access. You'll find designated _PARKING_ near the rental booth. An accessible _CHEMICAL TOILET_ is also close by. A paved ramp will take to an accessible _PICNIC TABLE_ and _DRINKING FOUNTAIN_ that overlooks the launching area. All these are paved surfaces.

On the other hand, facilities at Big Chico Creek are primitive. The shore is gently sloping but covered in river rock. You are allowed to drive your vehicle directly to the water for raft retrieval. The bumpy gravel road to Big Chico Creek can be found by taking River Road south from West Sacramento Road. Other day use pull-outs (mostly for fishermen) along River Road have a table or two on grass or uneven dirt surfaces and usually a primitive boat launch. **Indian Fishery Day Use Area** also has an accessible _CHEMICAL TOILET_ on an uneven dirt surface.

Bidwell River Park Project/ Irvine Finch River Access

12105 River Road
Chico, CA 95926-4819
(916) 342-5185
Location — The southwest corner of the Hwy 32 river bridge between I-5 and Chico
Elevation — 195 feet

(Photo courtesy CDPR)

BIDWELL MANSION STATE HISTORIC PARK

John Bidwell and his wife Annie were a most respected couple in California's early years. As pioneers, social activists, and agriculturalists, Congressman and Annie Bidwell entertained a multitude of notable guests in their 10,000 square foot mansion located by California State University at Chico. Even the massive trees in the park-like front yard do not overshadow this impressive structure.

Members of the Bidwell Mansion Association give hourly tours of the home. The Association has done a lovely job in preserving the memory of the Bidwell family. Displays in the foyer are most informative, and the mansion decor has been well-maintained. Much of the lower floor is accessible. A slide presentation detailing the rest of the house is offered to those who cannot climb a flight of stairs. For lasting memories, you can also purchase a video tape of the mansion.

There is a 15-foot ramp access (15%) to the front porch at the far end of the circular drive from a designated _PARKING_ place. The main doorway has a 2-inch lip and small door sill. Due to the tall interior dimensions of the mansion, much of the decor is high on the walls. Restrooms in the mansion are not retrofitted for wheelchair use. Don't miss seeing the Bidwell's personal transportation display in the _CARRIAGE HOUSE_ behind the mansion. To find it, take the paved path around the side of the mansion.

Bidwell Mansion State Historic Park

525 The Esplanade
Chico, CA 95926-3995
(916) 895-6144
Park Folder Available
Location — From Hwy 99 take First Avenue to The Esplanade south to the mansion
Elevation — 195 feet

COLUSA-SACRAMENTO RIVER STATE RECREATION AREA

Once the site of an unpleasant city dump, this small park at a crook of the Sacramento River has been completely transformed into a cozy base camp for fishermen in their quest for steelhead, king salmon, rainbow trout and striped bass. Bird and wildlife watching is a pleasant pastime from the cottonwood-shaded banks of the river.

Though designated parking and camping arrangements are not provided, you may find that the _RESTROOM_ and campsites are appropriate for your needs. _ENROUTE CAMPING_ is also available.

Picnic and Day Use

An opening in the curbing at the easternmost corner of the day use parking lot provides access to the picnic area. Cottonwoods and willows offer shade to this river-view picnic area set on a grassy knoll. Standard tables are also available along the perimeter of the parking lot.

Anglers at this part of the river have their best luck from a boat. You can launch your boat at the end of the day use parking area from a primitive ramp into a quiet estuary of the river.

Camping

A shady lawn surrounds the parking-lot-style campground. At each campsite, there is a picnic table, storage box, and BBQ. An asphalt path near sites #5, #6, and #7 leads to a _RESTROOM_ with an accessible stall that has grab bars

and standard fixtures. There are no barriers to an adjacent shower. It has a 29-inch doorway, 47" by 47" interior, and the control is 43 inches from the floor.

Colusa-Sacramento River State Recreation Area

PO Box 207
Colusa, CA 95932-0207
(916) 458-4927
Park Folder Available
Location—Nine miles east of I-5 off Hwy 20 in Colusa
Elevation—60 feet

WOODLAND OPERA HOUSE STATE HISTORIC PARK

After almost eighty years of closure and seven years of painstaking restoration, this turn-of-the-century Opera House has recently reopened. Visitors can enjoy live, year-round, family entertainment ranging from musical concerts and dance performances, to period comedies and melodramas.

The park staff and volunteers have taken great care in the detailed reproduction of the theater furnishings and decor. Modern conveniences, including wheelchair _ELEVATOR_ access have also been added. There is room for up to six wheelchairs in the seating area. _RESTROOMS_ on this floor have a pivot-transfer stall with grab bars, but there is no knee room under the sinks. You can get to the third floor _MEETING ROOMS_ and intermission area by elevator.

Designated _PARKING_ is provided in a small lot on Dead Cat Alley, 50

feet from the theater entrance. The elevator to the left of the main entrance is available for use during daily business hours and productions. You can obtain a seasonal production schedule by calling the Opera House office.

Woodland Opera House State Historic Park

340 Second Street
PO Box 1425
Woodland, CA 95695
(916) 666-9617
Brochure available from the park office
Location—In the central downtown district of the town of Woodland
Elevation—30 feet

| Gold Country/ Sierra Foothills |

PLUMAS-EUREKA STATE PARK

Once the site of a huge gold mining operation that lasted from the 1850's until World War II, Eureka Peak in Plumas-Eureka State Park is now a favorite with hikers and especially four-wheel drive explorers. Mines and tunnels still lace the granite mountainsides at elevations as high as 8,000 feet, where steep roads offer dramatic views of the greenery below.

The park furnishes a comfortable _CAMPING SITE_ with accessible _RESTROOM_, and a spacious _PICNIC AREA_ with a river view and excellent accessibility. You can pick up road maps and details about the outlying mining areas at the accessible _VISITOR CENTER_, which contains artifacts and information unique to this region.

Visitor Center

Asphalt paving leads from a designated _PARKING_ place to a wood-planked veranda and 1-inch door sill at the entrance. The information station, some exhibits, and a designated _RESTROOM_ are on the main floor. Some visitors may find the _RESTROOM_ difficult to use. There are grab bars, but the toilet is low, the sink is not accessible, and the pull chain flush is 50 inches high.

Several restored buildings from the Plumas-Eureka mining days are on display, surrounded by a sloping lawn across the parking lot from the visitor center. A gravel path will take you for a closer look.

Picnic

The **Jameson Creek Picnic Area** offers a pleasant change from the dense forest and the stark granite peaks. This section of the park, on the banks of Jameson Creek is open and sunny for those who sometimes feel hemmed in by the dense forest around them. You will find the picnic area just off the park road before you arrive at the visitor center.

At the end of the dirt picnic access road, you'll be surprised to find a completely accessible _PICNIC AREA_ alongside the gurgling creek, where in spring the mountain run-off fairly rushes through this gulch. All of the surfaces in the parking area, under the table and BBQ, and at the creek overlook are paved in concrete. A concrete walk also leads to an accessible _UNISEX RESTROOM_ with a high toilet, grab bars, and push-type faucet controls.

Camping

The campground is nestled in a profusion of evergreen trees about 1½ mile from the park entrance. An undulating trail (not suitable for wheelchairs) also winds through the forest from the visitor center to the campground, crossing small rivulets along the way.

Each campsite furnishes a table, fire ring, and food storage box near an asphalt pull-in. There is a restroom in each camping loop.

Designated _SITE_ #8 is near the only accessible campground _RESTROOM_ and _DRINKING FOUNTAIN_. The entire camping area around site #8 is paved for accessibility, but the table is standard. The _RESTROOM_ nearby has a designated _PARKING_ spot, a sloping (7%) asphalt approach, and fully accessible fixtures. In the adjoining shower, there are no barriers, to the stationary seat in the stall; the control is 50 inches from the floor.

Other sites on the #6-21 loop are flat and may be suitable for your camping needs. All of the other tables and fire rings are on the forest floor. For your convenience, there is an RV dump station at the campground entrance.

Plumas-Eureka State Park

310 Johnsonville Road
Blairsden, CA 96103
(916) 836-2380

Location — Five miles west of Blairsden on Johnsonville Road (County Road A-14)

Elevation — 5,175-8,000 feet

_____

LAKE OROVILLE STATE RECREATION AREA

In the northern belt of the Mother Lode Country, impounded by the tallest earthen dam in the United States, Lake Oroville is a shining example of the cooperative efforts of water control and public recreation. As the largest reservoir of the State Water Project, the lake is a pleasure for outdoor enthusiasts because it is seldom crowded. Though wheelchair access has not been specifically considered at the picnic areas, some visitors may find them suitable. If you're just here for the day, don't miss the day use facilities at Thermalito North Forebay. For a longer stay, each of the two campgrounds has some accessible features and may be just what you're looking for in a pleasurable vacation spot.

Boating and fishing are the sports most enjoyed at the lake; there are several launching ramps on the lake shore. Anglers try their luck from their boats, off the face of the dam, or near the spillway boat launch. Fishers bring in blue gill, crappie, bass, silver salmon, lake trout, brown trout, and sturgeon.

Visitor Center

The California Water Project designed the Lake Oroville visitor center to be used by everyone. A collection of photographs in the exhibit hall chronicles the history and progress of the dam construction in the late 1960's. You also may be interested in one of several brief films on subjects that cover the region's gold dredging history, the local Chinese cultural story, or the ghost towns of the area.

Plumas-Eureka in the early days

(Historic photo courtesy CDPR)

A paved ramp (9%) from designated *PARKING* leads to the complex, where there is an accessible *RESTROOM* and *DRINKING FOUNTAIN*, visitor information, and a *PICNIC AREA* on a concrete patio overlooking the lake. A telephone nearby is too high to reach from a seated position. The *RESTROOM* is fully accessible (high toilet, pivot transfer, high sink, and low hand dryer) but the door is very heavy and may require help to open.

Picnic and Day Use

Loafer Creek—When the lake level is up, the park staff distributes tables and BBQ's on a grassy knoll beside the water at Loafer Creek. From here you have a lake view and gentle access to the lake. There is a designated *PARKING* place in a nearby lot. The descent to the picnic area along a steep (13%) 50-foot asphalt path will require assistance. Fifty yards from the base of the path, concrete paving leads to a *RESTROOM* and changing facilities. The dressing room is one large area in the restroom that has a high pivot-transfer toilet, high sink, and accessible hand dryer. When the lake level is low, visitors don't often use this area.

Bidwell Canyon Marina—A concessionaire rents houseboats, patio boats, fishing boats, and other water paraphernalia at Bidwell Marina. A store and ski shop are also on the dock. There is a 3-inch transition onto the dock from the gangway. When the water level is low, access to the marina and *BOAT LAUNCH* can only be accomplished on a long steep (20%) ramp. Designated *PARKING* and an accessible *RESTROOM* are at the top of the ramp, well above water level.

The staff at the marina are very willing to help disabled visitors with their boat rental needs. The largest of the rental *HOUSEBOATS* has plenty of room for a wheelchair. The concessionaire will arrange access to the restroom and captain's chair. A wheelchair will also fit on the *PATIO BOATS*, but the chair would first have to be lifted over a railing. You may contact the marina for reservations or questions, (800) 589-3152.

Bidwell Canyon Picnic Area —A cozy picnic area awaits you across the historic **Bidwell River Bar Toll Bridge** that was reconstructed at this site. A hard-packed dirt trail leads over the wooden bridge. On the other side is a small, heavily-shaded island with picnic tables and BBQ's on uneven, hard-packed dirt. When the lake level is up, this is a lovely setting for a cool picnic with view of the water. You probably will need help to manage some lumpy surfaces on the island.

Dam Spillway—You'll have a breathtaking view of the Sacramento Valley from the road that winds up the back side and across the top of the 770-foot high dam, before descending to the spillway on the other side. If you'd like to get out to fish or to have a better look at the scenery, there is a pedestrian walkway along the crest of the mile-long dam. At the spillway area, park staff has devised a temporary boat launch to allow for the lower water level. Ordinarily, the rocky boat launch is a good fishing area, but it is not accessible.

Thermalito North Forebay— Thermalito North Forebay serves as a water storage area for regulating water flow used to generate power. You'll find this area three miles north of Oroville, off Hwy 70 on Garden. A park-like setting with grass and young trees surrounds the shoreline of the forebay where non-powered boating, swimming, and fishing are accessible to all. At the west end of the park, there are a few accessible PICNIC SITES with shade ramadas near an accessible CHEMICAL TOILET and DRINKING FOUNTAIN. Nearby, at the accessible FISHING PIER, rainbow trout is the catch of the day. The railing on this paved pier has been lowered for easy access.

Camping

Bidwell Canyon — Two RV camping loops occupy opposite sides of the day use parking lot for the Bidwell Canyon Marina. Paved roads through the campground are more level on the eastern loop. Though there is less privacy and shade, this loop would be preferable for accessibility. All of the asphalt pull-in sites have hook-ups. Campsites encircle an accessible

RESTROOM, DRINKING FOUNTAIN and SHOWER at each loop. You may park near each fully accessible RESTROOM (pivot transfer, grab bars, high toilet). The shower stalls are very roomy, but do not have a seat inside.

Loafer Creek — An oak forest shelters many level campsites at Loafer Creek Campground. Each site has an asphalt pull-in, table, and fire ring on an uneven dirt surface. Designated SITE #3 has the added advantage of asphalt pavement around a modified table and is close to an accessible restroom.

The RESTROOM/shower building is central to Loafer Creek Campground and is the closest restroom to the designated campsite, 150 yards away. The telephone here is too high to access from a seated position. From the parking lot, a concrete approach (12%) runs for a short distance to the restroom entrance and accessible DRINKING FOUNTAIN. The accessible stall has a high toilet with lateral transfer

and grab bars. The designated shower stall has a 28-inch entry, 1½-inch lip down to the stall (29" by 33"), a high control knob, and no seat.

The campfire center rests in a natural hillside amphitheater across from the campground entrance, where there is an RV dump station. Along its 130 yards, the broad, lighted trail that leads there can be very steep in places. The last few feet of pavement drops into the campfire center and onto a dirt surface at a very steep 20%.

Dam Spillway (FCFS) — For spillway fishermen, there is self-contained RV CAMPING near the dam spillway on a flat asphalt parking surface covered with gravel. Only chemical toilets are provided here.

Lake Oroville State Recreation Area

400 Glen Drive
Oroville, CA 95966
(916) 538-2200
Visitor Center — **(916) 538-2219**
North Forebay — **(916) 538-2221**

*Park Folder Available — Park Information
Newspaper, The Dam News,
available from the park office or
ranger kiosks, or by calling the
Bidwell Bar Association at (916)
538-2219*
*Location — Seven miles east of Oroville
via Hwy 162*
Elevation — 900 feet

Unlike the one in the photo, an accessible picnic ramada at the forebay has paving.

(Photo courtesy CDPR)

CLAY PIT STATE VEHICULAR RECREATION AREA

The clay used to build the mammoth earthen dam at Lake Oroville came from an area three miles west of the town of Oroville. Years of mining created the great depression that is now Clay Pit State Vehicular Recreation Area. Beginning off-roaders try out their ATV's here on the rolling terrain. For shooting enthusiasts, there is a rifle range in one corner of the park. This undeveloped area has a chemical toilet in the dirt parking lot; all access points have rough dirt surfaces.

Clay Pit State
Vehicular Recreation Area

Contact Lake Oroville State
Recreation Area
(916) 538-2200

Location — Two and a half miles south
of Hwy 162 on Larkin Road
Elevation — 135 feet

MALAKOFF DIGGINS STATE HISTORIC PARK

Even in the 1800's, saving the environment was an issue in the hills near Nevada City. While hydraulic mining yielded a multi-million dollar fortune for mine owners, the valley below was deluged by silt and mud run-off. Conflict continued between farmers in the valley and the miners until 1884, when the process of blasting hillsides to

extract minerals with heavy streams of water was declared illegal. Great quarries and scoured mining pits remain in the park as evidence of the richest hydraulic gold mine in the world.

Many mining sites are visible from the car as you travel along the road through the park. On summer weekends, you also may enjoy learning about the colorful history of the mining town of North Bloomfield on a RANGER-LED TOUR. In their experience with disabled visitors, the park rangers are accustomed to dealing with obstacles such as door sills and steps. As always, if you have special needs, it is a good idea to arrange for a tour before you arrive. Much of the town is flat, but there are few paved or smooth surfaces. For those who wish to explore on their own, a self-guided historical tour map of the area is available at the visitor center.

Visitor Center

Filled with artifacts and historical documents of the golden era, the visitor center is a central feature of North Bloomfield. As the restoration and preservation process continues within the park, the visitor center provides visitors with an image of life as it was here in the 1840's.

A very narrow, uneven concrete walkway off the main street leads from the road to a boardwalk at the visitor center. The interior of the museum is accessible, but there is a very steep (20%) 15-foot ramp to a lower level, where additional mining and cultural exhibits of the era are displayed. On Sundays, you can watch a film on the lower level. Next door, at the Ostrom Livery, peek into the stable where you'll see a collection of wagons and other vehicles of the time.

Day Use and Picnic

Picnic — Two grassy areas in town have picnic tables on a grass surface. Across from the visitor center, the lawn is more level and there is parking nearby. On the west side of the General Store, there are several tables in the shade but the uneven terrain is sloping and difficult to access.

The town of North Bloomfield at Malakoff Diggins SHP

(Photo courtesy CDPR)

Though challenging, a trip through the cemetery is quite a journey into history.

(Photo courtesy CDPR)

Cemetery—To find the North Bloomfield Community Cemetery, take the short dirt road behind the school house. Grave markers dating from the mid-1800's remind us of the real-life people who lived, worked, and died here in the northern Sierras. A lattice of rutted dirt paths weaves among the headstone in the small, gently sloping area that is surrounded by a gated cyclone fence that is kept unlocked.

Restroom—In the downtown North Bloomfield section, a public restroom is located behind the General Store. The accessible UNISEX RESTROOM has a high sink, low toilet and grab bars. It is best to drive as close a possible to the doorway to avoid the gravel in the parking lot.

Blair Lake—Bring a willing pusher with you when you climb the 350 feet of steep (10%) hard-packed trail to Blair Lake. You'll be glad you made the effort when you arrive at this charming little reservoir. Some picnic tables at

Blair Lake are within access to the trail along the firm, yet uneven tree-lined shore. If you like to fish, you may want to drop a line for blue gill, black bass or catfish while enjoying the serene lake.

Camping

Chute Hill — Low-hanging branches of the hillside forest shade a narrow, winding, ½-mile road to the campground overlooking the town of North Bloomfield. Each campsite has a table, fire ring, and food storage. Most are uneven, but there are several sites (#11, #13, #14, #15) with tables on the same level as the dirt and gravel pull-in parking. Asphalt paving surrounds a large accessible UNISEX RESTROOM (grab bars, low toilet) nearby. There is a slight incline from the dirt and gravel parking nearby.

Carter Cabins—Three rustic cabins in the middle of the town of North Bloomfield can be reserved through the park office. Bunk beds, a wood stove, and a table

take up much of the floor space inside, leaving little room for a wheelchair. You may park near the cabins on the grass, but there are two steps up to the front porch. The restroom for cabins is down a gravel path and is not accessible. Instead, you may use the restroom behind the General Store.

Malakoff Diggins State Historic Park

23579 N. Bloomfield Road
Nevada City, CA 95959
(916) 265-2740

Park Folder Available
Location—From Nevada City, the best access is north on Hwy 49 to Tyler-Foote Crossing. Cut off on Lake City Road (dirt) to North Bloomfield Road for a total of 27 miles.
Elevation—3,300 feet

SOUTH YUBA RIVER PROJECT

California State Parks and Sequoya Challenge (a non-profit organization) in cooperation with several other organizations, are creating the nation's first wheelchair wilderness trail, the **South Yuba Independence Trail**. Perched on the south bank of Yuba Canyon, the trail follows the gentle contours of abandoned gold mining canals, called flumes, and is never more than a 5% grade. Thus far, Sequoya Challenge and others have completed more than three miles of the backpack trail with camping and fishing facilities. They have set the year 2000 as the target date for the eventual completion of nine miles of trail. Whether day hiking or overnight camping, you'll enjoy this forest encounter that includes scenic views of the river canyon.

There are designated *PARKING* places at the trailhead. You'll find the trailhead on an asphalt pull-out approximately 6 miles north of Nevada City on Hwy 49. The pull-out area is easy to miss, so look for the blue parking signs on the east side of the highway. The trail is wide, smooth, and mostly hard-packed, but after a rain it can be muddy. It is best to call ahead for trail conditions. The trail currently runs to the east for 0.8 miles and to the west for 2.3 miles. For westbound blind hikers, 0.6 miles of a tap board line the trail. Beyond that, the trail is in the flat flume bottom bounded on either side by hillside or berm.

Eastbound hiking takes you ½ mile to an overlook with a view of the highway and the river. There are benches here if you need to take a rest. One-tenth of a mile beyond, the flume forms a tunnel under a rock. Be careful beyond this point, the trail does not have protective railings, and it's a long way down. At the 0.8 mile point, a 400-foot bridge spans the river. You may camp on the other side of the river with a special permit from the Sequoya Challenge. You also can reach this point of the trail by a four-wheel drive road from Nevada City. Call Sequoya Challenge for more information, (916) 272-3823.

Westbound, the trail leads under a low bridge at the highway; you'll have to duck if you're walking. The first river overlook at 0.4 miles has accessible *TABLES*, benches, and an emergency telephone in a covered gazebo. An accessible *PIT TOILET* is 0.1-mile beyond. At the one-mile point where the flume crosses Rush Creek, you'll get a great view of a waterfall. Here, fishermen have a

chance to try their luck from a 400-foot *FISHING RAMP LANDING*. Just beyond the fishing ramp, a *PICNIC DECK* overlooks the creek. Campers often use this as an overnight stop. (Campers should check in with the Sequoya Challenge if planning an overnight trip along the trail.) The trail is only periodically maintained for the next 1¼ miles beyond this point, and may be difficult to pass without assistance.

As funds become available, the trail will continue to grow and develop. For current trail conditions and any new accessible features, contact Sequoya Challenge: (916) 272-3823 or 272-3459. YOU SHOULD NOT MISS THIS UNIQUE OUTDOOR EXPERIENCE.

South Yuba River Project
17660 Pleasant Valley Road
Penn Valley, CA 95946
(916) 432-2546
Park Information flyer available from Sequoya Challenge
(916)272-3823
Location—Six miles north of Nevada City on Hwy 49
Elevation—1,400 feet

William Bourne's Empire Cottage   *(Photo courtesy CDPR)*

EMPIRE MINE STATE HISTORIC PARK

In 1850, not too long after the discovery of gold at Sutter's Mill, news spread about the discovery of a huge vein of gold in Grass Valley. Miners and prospectors flocked to the town, and small claims sprang up all around. Gold-diggers, lacking the skill to draw the gold efficiently from the quartz hills, gradually sold their claims to a single operation. After many owners, the mine seemed doomed to close down operation.

A California-raised man educated in England was to save the mine from closure. William Bourn brought modern hard rock mining techniques from England to modernize the mine. Soon production soared, as did profits. His Empire Mine became known as the largest, most efficient gold mine in California. Mr. Bourne built one of his family mansions on the grounds of the mine, **Empire Cottage**, from which to direct the daily workings of his enterprises.

Gravel surrounding many remaining structures of the mining operation makes wheelchair access challenging. Unfortunately, the mine shaft is not visible from a seated position in the viewing area. With advance notice, the park ranger will let you drive through the exhibit area on park service roads where you can see most of the grounds from your car.

You may wish to take the flat footpath of packed dirt alongside the historic homes and well-manicured gardens of the park. Call the park ahead of your visit and the ranger will place an access ramp at the lower floor doorway of Empire Cottage.

Visitor Center

Mr. Bourne's original carriage house and groom's quarters house the visitor center. It serves as park headquarters and entrance to the grounds of the mining operation. A short ramp leads to the doorway of the visitor center where you'll learn the story of Grass Valley and its mining history. Also on display is a real gold nugget from the historic mine. Another ramp leads to the park exhibits and to the theater that occupies one of Mr. Bourn's garages. You may drop off passengers near the doorway before *PARKING* in designated places in a dirt and gravel parking lot. An accessible *RESTROOM* in the parking lot has a 1½-inch lip at the doorway.

Empire Mine State Historic Park

10791 East Empire Street
Grass Valley, CA 95945
(916) 273-8522

Park Folder Available—Ask for a
calendar of events
Location—One mile east of Hwy 49 on
Empire Street
Elevation—2,650 feet

AUBURN STATE RECREATION AREA

At the American River, wild waters that tumble from the high regions of the Sierras create a thrilling raft or kayak ride and provide a back country setting for fishing opportunities. Thirty-thousand acres of Auburn State Recreation Area encompass a portion of the North and Middle Forks of the American River. The state purchased this land to reserve as the proposed reservoir for the Auburn Dam.

Primitive campgrounds with chemical toilets border the river at four locations. Each is accessible by steep, rocky four-wheel-drive roads, and is most often used by rafters and fishermen. There are no facilities in the park for wheelchair users, but the views are breathtaking from the Forest Hill bridge and along the North Fork of the American River.

A multitude of rafting outfitters makes regular runs on the American River. If you're interested in running the river before it is dammed forever, Environmental Traveling Companions (ETC) offers summer river raft trips for visitors of all abilities. Call or write to ETC for more specific information. ETC, Fort Mason Building C, San Francisco, CA 94123, (415) 474-7662.

Auburn State Recreation Area

PO Box 3266
Auburn, CA 95604
(916) 885-4527

Park newspaper available
Location—Park Headquarters located
about 2 miles east of Hwy 80 on Hwy
49
Elevation—500 feet

MARSHALL GOLD DISCOVERY STATE HISTORIC PARK

Among his other entrepreneurial endeavors, John Sutter wanted to cash in on the growing lumber industry. It was his intent to build a water-powered sawmill at the South Fork of the American River. When Mr. Sutter commissioned James Marshall to build the mill, he could never have dreamed that the tiny gold flecks Marshall found would lead to "The Goldrush." The nearby town of Coloma became instantly famous and attention immediately turned from milling to mining.

The Marshall Gold Discovery State Historic Park encompasses the original town site. Many structures here date from the 1840's and 50's and still stand along pathways or at the side of the road. When you come to the park, be sure to stop at the visitor center. From there you can plan a walking or driving tour of the historical town sites or relax in the shady picnic area. In the summer months, the all-volunteer Gold Discovery Park Association gives "living history" demonstrations using a working model of the original Sutter's Mill.

Visitor Center

Exhibits and movies at the visitor center retell the story of John Sutter, James Marshall's gold discovery, and the 1840's Goldrush. This is a good place to begin a park visit or purchase pamphlets, books, and other information. You can reach the building on a concrete ramp from a paved designated *PARKING* place in the south lot.

Nearby is an accessible _TELEPHONE_ and a _RESTROOM_ with pivot transfer to a high toilet, grab bars, and an accessible sink.

Picnic and Day Use

North of the visitor center, several picnic tables stand in a grassy area under large oak and maple trees. Most of the grounds are uneven, but near the crosswalk from the main parking lot, you will find an accessible _PICNIC TABLE_ and _DRINKING_

A reproduction of Sutter's Mill at Marshall Gold Discovery SHP   *(Photo courtesy CDPR)*

FOUNTAIN in a shady spot. In the middle of the lawn, surrounded by asphalt, is an accessible _RESTROOM_ with a shallow stall, low toilet, and grab bars.

North Beach Picnic Area — The South Fork of the American River runs through the park to the east of Hwy 49. Here picnickers may try their hand at gold panning in the cool river water, but there is no access to the river for wheelchair users. All of the picnic tables are on an uneven sloping lawn. A concrete walkway at the north end

of the parking lot leads to an accessible _TELEPHONE_ and a _RESTROOM_ with lateral transfer, grab bars, and a low toilet.

The **Beer Garden Picnic Area** is not wheelchair accessible.

Trails

The park brochure outlines four different walking tours; two are wheelchair accessible. After exploring the visitor center area on the two walking tours, take a driving tour of the remainder of the town. As it winds through the old town, the road will take you into the hills to the south. It passes the James Marshall Monument, an old church, and several original building sites. The drive is pleasant, and the tour offers an easy way to view the historic sites of the old town. Keep in mind that the picnic area and restroom at the top of the hill are not accessible.

The **Discovery Tour** leads from the visitor center across the street to the Sutter Sawmill replica and

gold discovery sites. Along the path you'll find the well-labeled remains of the old mining structures. Much of the wide, packed dirt path is rutted in places. There is little shade on the east side of Hwy 49, so bring along a hat. The Gold Discovery site is about 300 yards from the parking lot near the sawmill replica.

The **Town Tour** takes you along an asphalt paved road to view some old buildings of Coloma that still stand along the roadside. Most are not approachable by wheelchair.

Marshall Gold Discovery State Historic Park

PO Box 265
Coloma, CA 95613
(916) 622-3470
Park Folder Available
Location — Twenty miles east of Hwy 80 on Hwy 49
Elevation — 750 feet

FOLSOM LAKE STATE RECREATION AREA

Folsom Lake has plenty of good fishing, up to 75 miles of shoreline, and it is only 25 miles from Sacramento. No wonder Folsom Lake draws over four million visitors a year. Swimming beaches, picnic areas, and a network of hiking, horseback riding, and biking trails add to the attraction for outdoor-lovers.

On the western shore, most of the developed day use areas provide accessible _RESTROOMS_ and _PICNIC FA-CILITIES_. _CAMPGROUNDS_ have designated sites, but may offer

A view from the picnic area at Folsom Lake

(Photo courtesy CDPR)

challenges for restroom access. A *BIKE PATH* leads from Beal's Point south to Nimbus Dam and beyond the park for 35 miles to Old Sacramento. Though it is hilly, the paving is very smooth. Wheelchair atheletes use the path for a great workout.

The western lake shore includes three main developed areas: Granite Bay, Beal's Point, and Negro Bar. Other locations have limited access and will be listed individually. Many park facilities may be closed or in limited use due to drought conditions and subsequent lowered water levels. During these times, you may be able to drive directly on the beach to

the water in some places. Check with a ranger for current lake access conditions.

Granite Bay

Near the busy *BOAT LAUNCH* at the south portion of Granite Bay, pavement from designated *PARKING* leads to a *SNACK BAR* and restroom (27-inch stalls with no doors or grab bars). Picnic tables are shaded on the nearby lawn. Another *RESTROOM* just north of there is accessible (low toilet, grab bars).

At the northern section of the bay, you'll find designated *PARKING* near

a packed dirt path that leads to tables on a grassy knoll. A concrete walkway with handrails (34") takes you to an accessible *RESTROOM* (lateral transfer, grab bars) and seasonal *SNACK BAR*. An asphalt trail (8%) with handrails leads to a coarse sandy beach below. Depending on the lake level, the beach may extend as far as 200 yards to the water line from the base of the trail.

Beal's Point

Day Use

A large parking lot overlooking the lake provides ample space for this obviously popular picnic area

In some locations at Folsom Lake, boaters launch from the beach.   *(Photo courtesy CDPR)*

nor is the restroom near the boat launch.

Camping

Campsites line the periphery of an asphalt parking lot surrounded by continuous curbing. A pathway leads from the curbing to each site, but there is no ramp access over the curb to the two designated *CAMPSITES*. An accessible *UNISEX RESTROOM* in the parking lot is central to the campsites and an RV dump station is near the day use entry.

Picnic tables under young shade trees or ramadas, border the lot. At the south end of the lot, an asphalt ramp (6%) leads to an accessible *RESTROOM* (low toilet, grab bars) and *DRINKING FOUNTAIN*. Near Beal's Point swim beach to the north, pavement leads from designated *PARKING* to a patio area. Accessible features here include *UNISEX RESTROOMS*, *TELEPHONE*, *DRINKING FOUNTAIN*, *SNACK BAR* and picnic tables with a view overlooking the sunbathers on the shore (when the lake level is up). Asphalt paved walkways follow the shoreline along the entire day use area.

Camping

Beal's Point Campground is located on a hilly section of the park near the many accessible facilities at Beal's Bar. Most of the shady pull-in or walk-in campsites are not level; each has a table and fire ring. At the campground, the designated *SITES* #11 and #19 are close to a fully accessible *UNISEX RESTROOM* that has a shower with a heavy door and no seat. The in-

side dimensions are 32" by 54" and the control is 54 inches from the floor. Site #11 is uphill from the restroom. It has pavement under the table and has a dirt tent site. Site #19 is similar but is downhill from the restroom. You may be able to find a suitable site in the lower camping loop if the designated sites are occupied. Keep in mind that the restroom will be uphill from these sites.

Negro Bar

Day Use

An asphalt walkway encircles the entire day use section at Negro Bar. At the picnic area you'll find accessible *PICNIC TABLES* on concrete under a ramada. A short packed dirt path (9%) connects the picnic area to a fully accessible *RESTROOM* with designated *PARKING*. From the parking area below the campground, a packed 300-foot dirt path leads to the beach and to a very shady lawn. A chemical toilet near the beach is not accessible

Other Features

Folsom Powerhouse — Since 1895, Folsom Powerhouse has generated power for the city of Sacramento from a dam here on the American River. Of course, a new hydro-electric plant and dam have since been built, but the original powerhouse still stands and is open for tours.

With a handicap-identification placard, you may drive down the access road from the main parking lot to a flat dirt picnic area near the powerhouse. There is a gate at the head of the road. If you let the docents know when you plan to arrive, they will open the gate for you.

The turbine and generator rooms are accessible and visibility is quite good from a seated position. Park volunteers give accessible *TOURS* at regular intervals Wednesday through Sunday in the afternoons. You may be able to arrange a special tour for another time by calling the park volunteers at the park number.

Nimbus Dam—From this overlook, you'll have an unobstructed view of Nimbus Dam. There also is an accessible _RESTROOM_ in the parking area.

Dyke 8—At the end of a small point of land at Dyke 8 there is an accessible _PICNIC TABLE_ on concrete with a lake view and an accessible _CHEMICAL TOILET_ nearby. Oaks shade most of the other tables on an uneven dirt surface. The sign for Dyke 8 is small and easy to miss, so keep an eye out.

Folsom Lake Marina—This concessionaire-run marina has no accessible features.

Peninsula Campground—A long, narrow, winding road (partially dirt) leads from Hwy 49, 15 miles to the peninsula area that includes a campground, boat launch, and _PICNIC_ facilities. The campground, with a view of Granite Bay, clings to a hillside; there is no paving, and all roads, campsites, and restroom approaches are sloping. There is, however, a shady accessible _PICNIC TABLE_ and _DRINKING FOUNTAIN_ in the day use area overlooking the lake.

Rattlesnake Bar—This is an undeveloped boat launch area with chemical toilets only.

Folsom Lake
State Recreation Area
7806 Folsom-Auburn Road
Folsom, CA 95630-1797
(916) 988-0205
Park Folders Available—_Folsom Lake SRA, Folsom Powerhouse_
Location—_Twenty-five miles east of Sacramento on Folsom-Auburn Road between Auburn and Folsom off Hwy 80 or Hwy 50_
Elevation—_456 feet_

Lake Tahoe Region

Donner Party Memorial Statue
(Photo courtesy CDPR)

DONNER MEMORIAL STATE PARK

Donner Memorial State Park commemorates the infamous plight of the Donner Party, a pioneer group stranded in a blizzard at this mountain pass in 1846. Displays at the _IMMIGRANT TRAIL MUSEUM_ recount this and other stories about the westward movement of the pioneers. You also will discover interesting information about the natural history of the region.

Donner Lake offers accessible _CAMPING_ and _PICNICKING_. Though the fishing here is not exceptional, the park is a good base camp for fishing elsewhere. A _TELEPHONE_ at the entry kiosk is accessible.

Visitor Center

Among the many exhibits in the accessible Immigrant Trail Museum, are stories of how rugged railroad men built the Central Pacific Railroad through this forbidding territory, and of the human tragedy suffered at the hand of Mother Nature. A 12% ramp from designated _PARKING_ leads to the entrance of the museum and adjacent accessible _RESTROOM_ (heavy door, low toilet, grab bars and pivot transfer). Outside the museum, a flat gravel-embedded pathway leads a short distance to the **Donner Memorial Statue** built in remembrance of the sacrifices of California's pioneer ancestors.

Picnic

Follow the tree-lined picnic road along the southern lake shore to the end. There you'll find a picturesque picnic spot overlooking the lake, with standard tables and a stone BBQ. Asphalt covers all surfaces in the parking area, under the tables, and extends on to an accessible _DRINKING FOUNTAIN, WATER SPIGOT,_ and _RESTROOM_ (lateral transfer, low toilet, grab bars).

Camping

Three campground loops wind their way through a forest of fir, lodgepole, and Jeffrey pine, offering a rustic mountain atmosphere to each secluded campsite. There are two designated _SITES_ in **Split-rock Campground**. At both Site #116 and #153, there is paving under a table and around a fire ring and food storage. The pavement continues down a path to an accessible _RESTROOM_. Of the two campsites, #153 is more private, but the _RESTROOM_ near #116 has an accessible _SHOWER_ with retractable seat (control is 53 inches from the floor). Both _RESTROOMS_ have parking in front, pivot transfer, low toilet, and grab bars.

Donner Lake is a lovely backdrop to a special State Park.

(Photo courtesy CDPR)

Donner Memorial State Park

PO Box 9210
Truckee, CA 95737
(916) 587-3841

*Location—On Donner Pass Road, 2
 miles west of Truckee*
Elevation—5,950 feet

KING'S BEACH
STATE RECREATION AREA

A broad white-sand stretch of
beach is the attraction at this
small but popular and remarkably
picturesque park located on northwest Lake Tahoe. Pavement ex-

tends the length of the park, and
you can *PARK* in a designated space
near an accessible *RESTROOM* (low
toilet, grab bars). Unfortunately,
three steps descend to the sand,
and the picnic areas are surrounded by curbing, making access difficult. North Tahoe Public
Utility District operates King's
Beach State Recreation Area.

King's Beach
  State Recreation Area

  Contact Sierra District Office
  (916) 525-7232

*Location—On Hwy 28, on the northwest
 shore of Lake Tahoe, 12 miles
 northeast of Tahoe City*
Elevation—6,250 feet

TAHOE STATE
RECREATION AREA
and BURTON CREEK
STATE PARK

Tahoe State Recreation Area is a
tiny 13-acre park on the outskirts
of Tahoe City. Though it is a
quaint place to camp or stroll near
Lake Tahoe, the park offers little
in the way of accessibility. The
shady campground has dirt or
wood chip parking at each sloping
grassy campsite. The restroom is
not accessible. Hillside tent camping across Hwy 28 is steeper yet.

Burton Creek State Park covers
2,000 acres of undeveloped for-

97

ested land directly northeast of Tahoe State Recreation Area.

A half-mile west at the Truckee River outlet to Lake Tahoe is **Gatekeeper's Museum**. Originally, the gatekeeper's job was to watch the water flow from the lake to the Truckee River and to assure that there was enough water to send logs along their way. Today a museum occupies a reproduction of the old gatekeeper's home. Inside, there is a display in words, pictures and artifacts that describes the history of the logging industry in the Tahoe area.

You'll find the museum tucked behind a restaurant just south of the junction of Hwys 28 and 89. For wheelchair access, _PARK_ in the designated place on a dirt and gravel parking lot and follow an asphalt pathway to the rear of the house. An asphalt walkway leads also to an accessible _RESTROOM_ in front of the house and to nearby lake-view picnic tables on a packed dirt surface. The museum is open Wednesday through Sunday. For more information, you can phone the museum at (916) 583-1762.

Tahoe State Recreation Area

PO Box 583
Tahoe City, CA 95730
(916) 583-3074

Location — East of Tahoe City on
_ Hwy 28_
Elevation — 6,250 feet

Sadly, there is no wheelchair access to the lovely Hellman-Ehrman Mansion at Sugar Pine Point SP.

(Photo courtesy CDPR)

SUGAR PINE POINT STATE PARK

In 1860, a Kentucky frontiersman named "General" William Phipps chose this scenic promontory of the west Lake Tahoe shoreline to homestead and later build his mansion. His Pine Lodge (known also as the Hellman-Ehrman Mansion) stands on a beautiful forested point overlooking Lake Tahoe and now houses a museum. When you take a walk along the paved _SHORELINE TRAIL_ below the mansion, it is no surprise why General Phipps found this area so irresistible.

Other historic buildings are on display along an asphalt path, but visitors are not allowed inside. Accessible _RESTROOMS_ are available at both the day use visitor center area and the campground. There are no designated campsites at this mostly level campground.

Visitor Center

Begin your visit to Sugar Pine Point State Park at the day use area around the Hellman-Ehrman Mansion. A **Nature Center** displaying the wildlife and plants of the region is closest to the gravel day use parking lot. Wheelchair users should enter by way of the "back door" on a dirt and asphalt walkway. A ranger is usually on hand here to answer questions about the park.

Other paved walks will take you by the maid's quarters and other out-buildings. Unfortunately, the museum at General Phipp's mansion is not accessible due to a series of flagstone steps to its veranda entrance. An accessible _RESTROOM_ located along the walkway has a high toilet with pivot transfer and an electrical outlet.

Trails

For views of the forested lake shores that are hard to beat, take the accessible _PAVED TRAIL_ along the lake shore. With a handicap-identification placard, you may _PARK_ in a special lot down the hill from the mansion. The mostly level trail that starts here has a maxi-

mum grade of 8%. It follows the waterline south for ½ mile near the old caretaker's house, the pump house, and a 400-foot accessible pier that has no railings.

Several packed dirt paths lead from the museum area to the lake shore. They are steep, and some are too narrow for wheelchair passage. Other trails north of General Creek lead through a natural preserve. These trails are not strenuous but are rough and uneven.

Camping

General Creek — On the west side of Hwy 89, a stately forest of pine and fir stands watch over 175 campsites. A rough, paved road loops among the trees, connecting paved campsite parking. Most shady sites are level or gently sloping and furnish a table, BBQ, and food storage on the forest floor.

The shower, restroom building, and an RV dump station are near the entrance to the last camping loop. Smooth asphalt surrounds the _RESTROOM_ where the accessible stall has a low toilet and grab bars; showers are not accessible. A flat forest floor path leads from a dirt parking area to the _CAMPFIRE CENTER_, just inside the entrance to the campground. There is an accessible _TELEPHONE_ on a concrete slab in the dirt nearby.

Sugar Pine Point State Park
PO Box 266
Tahoma, CA 95733
(916) 525-7982
Location — Ten miles south of Tahoe City on Hwy 89
Elevation — 6,250 feet

D. L. BLISS STATE PARK

D.L. Bliss State Park showcases one of the more scenic parts of Lake Tahoe — the Emerald Bay area. Six miles of captivating shoreline extend from this park south to Emerald Bay State Park, offering visitors one of the finest beaches at Lake Tahoe. Since the park is very popular in the summer, most visitors arrive in the morning to find a place to park near the beach.

There are accessible _RESTROOMS_ at the campgrounds and in the picnic area near the beach. Though there are no designated campsites, you may find that many are suitable for your needs. For wheelchair users with help, picnicking may be possible at Lester Beach.

Picnic and Day Use

In the summer months, panoramas from Lester Beach and Colowee Cove draw large numbers of sunbathers and hikers to the lake shore. To find a place to park in the small lots near these areas, you may need to be here before 10 a.m. _PARKING_ overlooking Colowee Cove Beach offers two designated spots near an accessible _RESTROOM_. Trails leading to the beach from this area are very steep and narrow. Access to Lester Beach is more level, but the restroom nearby has a very steep approach. Tables are either on the beach or in the shade of pine trees on the forest floor.

Camping

Three camping loops wind through a wooded hillside along a 1½ mile asphalt road that descends from the park entrance to

the lake shore. Many campsites are level. Each has a dirt pull-in, table, fire ring, and food storage; some have BBQ's. Central to each camping loop is an accessible _RESTROOM_ with a high toilet, pivot transfer, and grab bars. Except for the first camping loop, the approach to each restroom is sloping forest floor. Adjacent accessible _UNISEX SHOWERS_ include a retractable interior bench and lever controls 42 inches from the floor.

You will have to cross a sloping forest floor trail to reach the _CAMPFIRE CENTER_. No special wheelchair access is provided. At the entry kiosk, the only park telephone is too high to reach from a seated position; an RV dump station is nearby.

D.L. Bliss State Park
PO Box 266
Tahoma, CA 95733
(916) 525-7277
Park Folder Available
Location — Just north of Emerald Bay on Hwy 89
Elevation — 6,920 feet

EMERALD BAY STATE PARK

Think of the beauty of Lake Tahoe, and chances are a picture of Emerald Bay comes to mind. As one of the most photographed places in California, nature has outdone itself in creating its visual splendor. Emerald Bay State Park encompasses a thickly forested hillside that tumbles to the lake shore. Though picturesque, the grounds are steep, and there are no facilities for visitors with limited mobility. You may enjoy the alpine scenery from one of several road-side pull-outs.

Vikingsholm is a striking Scandinavia reproduction of a Norse fortress, built in 1928 by a wealthy woman from Santa Barbara. Her stately home stands on land she purchased at the head of Emerald Bay. It is a favorite destination of park visitors, but can only be reached by way of a rugged one-mile trail. Difficult even for the able-bodied, the trail to Vikingsholm is not accessible.

Camping

Campsites skirt the main park road that descends from the highway to the trailhead for Vikingsholm. The sites are sloping and the asphalt parking is not on the same level as the table, BBQ, and food storage. Restrooms have a 2- to 4-inch step at the doorway and do not have retrofitted stalls.

Emerald Bay State Park

Contact Sierra District Office
(916) 541-3030
Park Folder Available
Location—Twenty-two miles south of Tahoe City on Hwy 89
Elevation—6,800 feet

LAKE VALLEY STATE RECREATION AREA and WASHOE MEADOWS STATE PARK

The meadows at Lake Valley State Recreation Area double as the Lake Tahoe Golf Course in summer and a great snowmobile and cross-country skiing area in winter. Next to the golf course, an undeveloped meadow and woodland area encompass the 620 acres of Washoe Meadows State Park. There are no accessible facilities at either location.

Lake Valley State Recreation Area
Washoe Meadows State Park

(916) 544-1583
Location—Three and a half miles southwest of South Lake Tahoe on Hwy 50
Elevation—6,300 feet

Lake Tahoe is one of the most photographed spots in California.

(Photo courtesy CDPR)

GROVER HOT SPRINGS STATE PARK

Grover Hot Springs State Park is a natural jewel hidden in the high country south of Lake Tahoe. The park is surrounded in Hot Springs Valley on three sides by rugged 10,000-foot granite peaks. Hot Springs Creek, a warm water stream that runs year round, threads through the beautiful valley meadow. On its fringe, campsites have been carefully placed among a large grove of evergreen trees.

Man and Nature have combined their efforts to create hot and cold pools at the park. Runoff from six mineral hot springs feeds a small concrete pool with 102° to 105° mineral water. The hot pool is accessible and open year round for your enjoyment. Meadow nature trails are easy hikes, but not recommended for wheelchair users. Because of the peaceful beauty of the surrounding forest and meadows, and the accessible campground facilities and hot spring pool, Grover Hot Springs State Park is a wonderful get-away.

Pools

Hot Springs Road passes the park entrance station and ends at the hot springs pool and cold swimming pool. The pool gate is on the north side of the fenced area, near asphalt parking. A short ramp at the entrance takes you to the same level as the unheated pool and dressing rooms. Unlike the able-bodied visitor, if you are disabled, you may take a floating device with you into either pool. There is no special access into either pool, so bring along someone to help you if you need to.

To get to the hot pool on the upper level, you must climb a short ramp (15%, handrails) from the swimming pool deck. Paving surrounds both pools but is a bit off-camber around the hot pool.

Inside the dressing room, there is a shallow toilet stall with standard

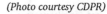

A view from the campground at Grover Hot Springs SP   *(Photo courtesy CDPR)*

fixtures and no grab bars. There are grab bars in the large shower; controls are 52 inches from the floor. Unfortunately, there are no seats in either the shower, or in the ample changing area nearby. Check with the park ranger for current pool hours.

Picnic

You'll find the picnic area and campfire center located just past the park entrance station. This spot also doubles as the park's winter campground. The picnic grounds are mostly hilly. Each site has an asphalt pull-in and a table. In the restroom building, the stall is wide enough (no grab bars, low toilet), but there is a 3-inch lip at the doorway. The approach to the nearby campfire center is over a sloping forest floor surface and will require help.

Camping

Valley meadows embrace a small campground that winds through a stand of conifers near Hot Springs Creek. Nature-watching in the morning and evening hours is especially rewarding from the campsites that border open spaces. Two of the best sites at the park are designated. Pavement covers both sites #25 and #26 under a table, BBQ, and fire ring. An accessible _RESTROOM_ is close to the campsites. When you check in, pick up a key to the fully accessible _UNISEX_ _RESTROOM/SHOWER_ from the ranger.

Grover Hot Springs State Park

PO Box 188
Markleeville, CA 96120
(916) 694-2248
Park Folder Available
Location — Three miles west of
  Markleeville on Hot Springs Road
Elevation — 5,840 feet

There's always something happening at Old Sacramento SHP. _(Photo courtesy CDPR)_

Sacramento Area

OLD SACRAMENTO STATE HISTORIC PARK

The original 19th century town of Sacramento still thrives with shops, restaurants, and historical exhibits at Old Sacramento State Historic Park. Period buildings have been restored or carefully recreated to closely resemble the boom town of the Goldrush era. Once you get to town, let your imagination transport you back in time when the railroad was king and the river boat was queen. Within the park's 14 acres along the Sacramento River, you can shop for all sorts of goodies, explore some original merchant buildings, or board a river boat for a cruise. Fascination with trains brings many visitors to Old Sacramento. An authentic recreation of a steam train depot awaits its passengers near the dock, reminding you to visit the world-renowned State Railroad Museum near park headquarters on I Street. The museum alone is worth the trip.

Tours

The Old Sacramento Walking Tour Docents offer accessible guided tours of the town by prior arrangement. Or, you can pick up instructions for a _SELF-GUIDED_ _TOUR_ at the Railroad Museum or at the visitor center near the Delta King. All of the sidewalks in town are boardwalks. Most provide ramp transitions to asphalt roads and crosswalks. In keeping with the original building design, many, but not all, of the store fronts have 4-inch to 6-inch door sills. Call the Docents at (916) 324-0040 for tour information.

Parking

Automobile traffic on the roads in Old Sacramento is light. You can use the parking structure on the edge of town, or there are designated _PARKING_ places at the foot of "I" Street and near the corner of Capitol and 2nd. In addition, you will find designated parallel *PARKING* in town.

Riverfront

A stroll along the river is a pleasant contrast to the hustle-bustle of town activity. A railroad tie boardwalk runs along the Sacramento River waterfront. It can be quite uneven, and you must cross a set of countersunk railroad tracks to get there. From an overlook, you can watch river boats patiently wait while the "I" Street Bridge rotates to allow them passage, or admire the restored 1920's river boat, *Delta King*, as it adds romantic charm to the docks below.

If you feel inspired to take a river trip, the paddleboat *Spirit of Sacramento* offers lunch, dinner, or narrated sightseeing cruises on the Sacramento River. Boarding ramps lead directly to the accessible restaurant deck where the crew is eager to help you on board. An accessible *RESTROOM* is available on the boat. For information, call (916) 552-2933.

Restroom

The only accessible *RESTROOM* in town is at the train depot. It has a lateral-transfer stall with grab bars. The entry door is heavy, and the handle is high, so you may need help to open it.

Old Sacramento
State Historic Park

Contact Sacramento District Office
(916) 445-7387

Location — On the Sacramento River at the foot of "I" Street

Don't miss the California Railroad Museum   *(Photo courtesy CDPR)*

CALIFORNIA STATE RAILROAD MUSEUM

The California State Railroad Museum, at the northern edge of Old Sacramento State Historic Park, offers the finest displays of railroading anywhere. The Museum of Railroad History houses a collection of locomotives and rail cars dating from 1862. The well-designed and artfully arranged museum, creates an eye-appealing look at this most important form of 19th-century transportation. A reconstructed passenger station and freight depot is a block away, near the riverfront. It contains more engines and rail cars and is a center for steam-train excursions in the summer, but the trains here are not accessible for wheelchair users.

Of the twenty-one beautifully restored railroad engines and cars on display in the museum, five have stairs up to the doorway for a closer look inside each car. Of these, three have a self-serve *WHEELCHAIR LIFT*. A peek into the passenger car windows (40 inches high) would be difficult from a seated position, but the *REFRIGERATOR CAR* and *POST OFFICE CAR* are readily accessible. Don't miss the *POST OFFICE CAR*, it is very interesting!

Though the surfaces vary from wood planking to carpet or pebble-embedded concrete, all of the interior walkways of the museum are accessible, having slopes of less than 5%. An *ELEVATOR* or a ramp leads you to the theater on the mezzanine level where there are more exhibits. There are handrails (34 inches) at all elevation changes. Unfortunately, a railing at the 40- to 50-inch level blocks your view from the balcony overlooking the main exhibit floor. That is a minor drawback to an otherwise wonderful experience.

If someone in your party would like to borrow a wheelchair, ask the attendant at the lobby counter. Conveniently located *RESTROOMS* are accessible (lateral transfer, grab bars, low toilet) except that the door handles are high. If you need a *TELEPHONE*, you'll find it near the elevator on the lower floor.

California State Railroad Museum

Contact Sacramento District Office
(916) 445-7387 or 323-9280

Folder—A guide to The Museum of Railroad History, available at the museum, shows wheelchair accessible features of the exhibit area.

Location—On the Sacramento River at the foot of "I" Street in Old Sacramento

---

SUTTER'S FORT
STATE HISTORIC PARK

In his ambitious drive towards wealth and power, Swiss immigrant John Sutter came to California in the early 1840's. It didn't take long for him to establish himself as a land baron and military commander. He was cooperative with the Mexican government. They rewarded him with 150,000 acres of land and a title of major general of the California militia. With the discovery of gold on his land at the American River, workers at his ranch left to seek out their own fortunes. The agricultural empire developed by Sutter was abandoned. Later, during California's struggle for statehood, the new leadership ignored his military title because of his sympathies with Mexico. After years of squandering his acquired wealth, John Sutter was a broken old man. In 1865 he and his wife moved to Washington, D.C. to try and reclaim his confiscated land from the U.S. government. They never returned.

John Sutter based his operation at Sutter's Fort. By the 1850's, only the central building remained. Today, the restored fort is in 1846 condition and is open daily. To make your visit more interesting, try to arrive on special demonstration days or when volunteers reenact a "living history" program on given days throughout the year. Ask the park staff or district office for the seasonal newspaper, *Sacramento State Historic Parks Guide.*

Demonstration Days are listed in the Special Events Calendar.

Your users fee includes a recorded *SELF-GUIDED TOUR* of the fort with an account of John Sutter's life in Sacramento. The tour begins at the front entry. You may need help to wheel on the uneven dirt surfaces within the walls of the fort. Most of the exhibits are in rooms along the perimeter of the central courtyard where some 28-inch doorways have small door sills. At the east end of the fort, a heavy door opens to an accessible *UNISEX RESTROOM* that has grab bars and a low toilet. The most convenient parking is on "L" Street near the entrance to the fort. From a designated *PARKING* spot near a curb cut, a sandy packed dirt path (8%) leads 50 feet to the gate. All other curbside parking is metered and there is no off-street parking.

Sutter's Fort State Historic Park

Contact Sacramento District Office
(916) 445-4422

Location—In the city of Sacramento at 2701 "L" Street

Doorways open to many excellent historical displays at Sutter's Fort SHP.

(Photo courtesy CDPR)

STATE INDIAN MUSEUM

California's heritage begins with the North American Indian. Through the generations, ceremonial and family objects that have survived, contribute to our understanding of native California's rich traditions.

Carefully chosen artifacts and personal photographs displayed in the State Indian Museum represent over 150 tribes and countless generations of Indian people.

Located on the same block with Sutter's Fort, a packed dirt path leads to the entrance near "K" Street from a walkway that encircles both parks. There are no curb cuts nearby except at the street corners. Once you get there, there are no barriers inside the museum. An accessible _RESTROOM_ with a shallow stall, high toilet, and grab bars stands in a small building east of the museum on "K" Street.

State Indian Museum

Contact Sacramento District Office
(916) 324-0971

Location—In the city of Sacramento at 2618 "K" Street

GOVERNOR'S MANSION

Though it has not housed a governor since 1967, the Governor's Mansion is preserved in downtown Sacramento. It is now a museum dedicated to the elegant and varied lives of 13 California governors since 1903. Docents give tours of the house hourly from 10 a.m. to 5 p.m. They share stories about the furnishings and personal items left by its many occupants and offer a brief history of the mansion's Victorian beginnings.

Exhibits in glass cases line the walls and fill the exhibit area and can be seen from a seated position.

(Photo courtesy CDPR)

Due to a steep flight of stairs at the entry, wheelchair users cannot access the mansion. Future plans for the mansion include a ramp access to the back door.

The carriage house, 100 feet up a concrete driveway from "H" Street curbside parking, contains a small visitor center. Here, you can view a slide show tour, spiced with interesting tidbits of the historical mansion background. Behind the carriage house, a small accessible _RESTROOM_ has a high toilet with grab bars and a high sink.

Governor's Mansion

Contact Sacramento District Office
(916) 323-3047

*Location— On the corner of 16th and
"H" Streets*

CALIFORNIA STATE CAPITOL MUSEUM

Unlike most museums that collect artifacts and evidence of past societies or historical events, the California State Capitol Museum is the embodiment of history in the making. Exhibit rooms in the basement and first floor of the Capitol display interesting items that date from the political beginnings of California's government. Several offices are restored to their original appearance and best viewed on one of the free daily tours.

Meanwhile, the real action occurs on the floors of the House and Senate when the legislature is in session. From the gallery, you may watch lawmakers deliberate over the fate of future California law.

Forty acres of beautifully landscaped greenbelt surround the State Capitol with trees from around the world. Countless benches line concrete walkways that crisscross the park. This is a cool place to spend some time during warm Sacramento summer days. At the east end of the park, the **California Vietnam Veteran's Memorial** stands in tribute to Californians who sacrificed their lives in service of their country.

Docents offer _TOURS_ of the Capitol Building daily on the hour from 9 a.m. to 5 p.m. in the summer months. The rest of the year, weekday tour hours are the same,

California is proud of its State Capitol. *(Photo courtesy CDPR)*

but tours on the weekends begin at 10 a.m. All tours are accessible and tour guides are sensitized to the needs of wheelchair users. There is ramp access to exhibits on the main floor. Elevators provide access to the gallery areas upstairs and the basement exhibits.

Accessible entrances to the Capitol Building are located off "L" and "N" Streets. Designated street _PARKING_ is available 200 feet from the entry. Accessible _RESTROOMS_ throughout the building offer lateral transfer and grab bars, but most have low toilets and heavy doors.

California State Capitol Museum

Contact Sacramento District Office
(916) 324-0333

Location—In downtown Sacramento at 10th and "L" Streets

LELAND STANFORD MANSION STATE HISTORIC PARK

In 1861, Leland Stanford, a founder of the Central Pacific Railroad and later governor of California, purchased this impressive two-story brick home. Later he remodeled and expanded it into the three-story house that stands today in the midst of tall office buildings. While the Stanford House is being restored, docents give occasional tours by reservation. Stairs and undesirable paving surfaces make the house inaccessible at this time.

Leland Stanford Mansion State Historic Park

Contact Sacramento District Office
(916) 324-0575

Location—In Sacramento at 8th and "N" Streets

The preceding parks are part of the Sacramento Historic District. The district office publishes an annual newspaper that thoroughly describes features and activities in each park. *Sacramento State Historic Parks Guide* is available at each park or by calling the district office.

Sacramento Historic District

101 "J" Street
Old Sacramento, CA 95814
(916) 445-7373

Elevation—30 feet

| Delta Area |

BRANNAN ISLAND and FRANK'S TRACT STATE RECREATION AREAS and DELTA MEADOWS

The maze of waterways through the Sacramento-San Joaquin Delta has formed countless islands, marshes, lakes, and other wetlands. Besides providing prime habitat for wildlife and waterfowl, the delta is a highly desirable recreation area for water-loving park visitors. **Brannan Island State Recreation Area** offers accessible camping, picnic, and boat launch facilities. To reach the good fishing and waterfowl hunting at **Frank's Tract State Recreation Area** to the southeast, you'll have to take the waterways. If you travel farther upriver, you'll come to quiet waters of the tule marshland at **Delta Meadows**. Behind the historic town of Locke near an old Pacific Railroad right-of-way, you can anchor for up to 15 days in "Railroad Slough." You can also reach Delta Meadows on land by way of a dirt road just north of the Cross Delta Canal. Delta Meadows is undeveloped.

Brannan Island State Recreation Area

Spring and summer bring out fishermen stalking the striped bass at the delta, as well as vacationers seeking other water sport activities. Water-skiers, hunters, and bird watchers favor the waters around Brannan Island and Frank's Tract. Plan ahead for a trip to Brannan Island State Recreation Area, and make your reservations well in advance. The park is open year round. It receives heavy use in the spring and summer, but usually is not as busy in fall and winter.

Brannan Island is a square-shaped island bounded on two sides by the Jackson and Three Mile Sloughs and on the other two by the Sacramento River. The State Recreation Area lies on the southwest finger of the island in a grassy, open section sprinkled with pine trees and low shrubbery. A levee borders the campground along Three Mile Slough and extends to the boat ramps and berthing area. Beyond the boat ramps, the park road swings north to a swimming beach and picnic area located on the smaller Seven Mile Slough. The park offers designated *CAMPING* and *PICNIC SITES* along with reserved *PARKING* at the boat launch near accessible *RESTROOMS*. There is an RV dump station at the park entrance.

Visitor Center

Just inside the park entrance a small modular structure houses the visitor and information center. Many of the natural history displays and book sales are visible from a seated position. A 20-foot ramp (10%) leads from parking in an adjacent dirt lot to the doorway (1-inch sill). Access for a wheelchair user is not ideal and will require assistance.

Picnic and Day Use

Swimming Area—The beach at Seven Mile Slough is bordered by a lawn area containing several picnic tables. At the nearby parking lot, there is designated *PARKING*. Midway in the parking lot, an smooth asphalt path leads toward the beach and a paved area with a MODIFIED PICNIC TABLE and a view of the activities below. From that point, the beach is down a grassy knoll and would not be considered accessible. The restroom in this area was destroyed by fire in 1990; it will be replaced by a fully accessible unit by 1992.

Boat Launch—Loading docks meet flush with the gently sloping launching ramp. Four designated PARKING places are provided for your vehicle and trailer. On a concrete patio next to the parking, you will find tables with ramadas, an accessible TELEPHONE, an accessible DRINKING FOUNTAIN and a RESTROOM/shower. The shallow stall in the restroom has only one grab bar and standard fixtures; the 36" by 40" shower has a 26-inch doorway, grab bars, and no seat; the control is 48 inches from the floor.

Camping

The **Willow** and **Cottonwood Campgrounds** loop parallel Three Mile Slough on level ground alongside the levee. Each site has an asphalt or dirt pull-in with a table, food storage, and fire ring on grass or dirt. In the summer months, rangers lead a program twice a week at the CAMPFIRE CENTER. To get there, follow the asphalt path that leads between camping loops.

Designated SITES #44, #55, and #57 have the added convenience of pavement under the table and around the fire ring and additional BBQ. There are plans to replace the existing RESTROOM with a fully accessible unisex unit. Currently, the accessible stall has grab bars. All other features are standard and

the approach to the restroom is rough asphalt.

Boat-in Camping slips can be rented at the berthing area near the boat launch. Camp sites for this area atop the levee overlook the slips. To get there from the water you must climb a 300-foot walkway of 14%. The main barrier here, however, is the gangway to the dock. One-and-a-half-inch wooden cross slats on the aluminum ramp make the climb difficult even for a walking person.

Brannan Island
State Recreation Area

17645 Hwy 160
Rio Vista, CA 95471
(916) 777-6671

Park Folder Available
Location—Three miles south of Rio Vista on Hwy 160
Elevation—25 feet

Frank's Tract

Contact Brannon Island SRA
(916) 777-6671

Park Folder Available
Location—Accessible only by boat five miles southeast of Brannan Island
Elevation—11 feet

Delta Meadow

Contact Brannan Island SRA
(916) 777-6671

Location—One mile east of the town of Locke on a dirt road just north of Cross Delta Canal, one hundred yards south of Locke

---

BENICIA CAPITOL
STATE HISTORIC PARK

Before Sacramento became the permanent State Capitol, the hub of government resided in San Jose, Vallejo, and Benicia. Of the pre-

Sacramento capitols, the only surviving structure is the Benicia State Capitol building. Many of the original building fixtures were used to carefully restore every detail of the building to its original state.

Unfortunately, the only entrance to the building is a long brick staircase. The grounds are paved in rough brick, and there are no curb cuts from the parallel street parking.

Benicia Capitol State Historic Park

PO Box 5
Benicia, CA 94510
(707) 745-3385

Park Folder Available
Location—First and G Streets in Benicia
Elevation—20 feet

BENICIA
STATE RECREATION AREA

Reaching across the Carquinez Strait between San Pablo Bay and Suisan Bay, Dillon Point cradles a cove of grassy marshland and rocky beaches that are preserved at Benicia State Recreation Area. Roller-skaters and joggers use the two-and-a-half miles of asphalt road that border the wetlands for a scenic workout. Picnic areas overlook the water from hillsides where tables and restrooms are accessible for some.

An asphalt road follows the contour of the park along the grassy marshland then up onto the higher ground overlooking the water. The marsh road begins near the Military West off-ramp of I-780 and continues to the main entrance of the park on its way to the picnic area on the hill. Designated *PARKING* and access to the park from Military West is free, but there are no restrooms here. At the main gate, a toll machine accepts dollar bills or a pass card available only to local residents.

A series of parking lots and picnic areas line the road through the upper portion of the park. Each lot has designated *PARKING* and varying access to standard picnic tables with great views of the strait and wetlands. Tables are usually on uneven or sloping dirt surfaces. There is an abundance of pine trees around the tables so the ground can be slick with needles. At the end of the park road, a designated *PARKING* place is provided near an asphalt ramp to a table and BBQ on rough asphalt.

There are restrooms at the first and last picnic areas. The approach to the first is by way of a 10% grade dirt and gravel path; you will reach the restroom at the end of the park road by way of an asphalt walkway. Both restrooms, while converted inside, have a 1-inch lip at the door (shallow stall, grab bars, high toilet, and a high sink).

Benicia State Recreation Area

(707) 648-1911
Location—One-and-a-half miles west of Benicia at the Columbus Avenue off-ramp of I-780
Elevation—0 feet

109

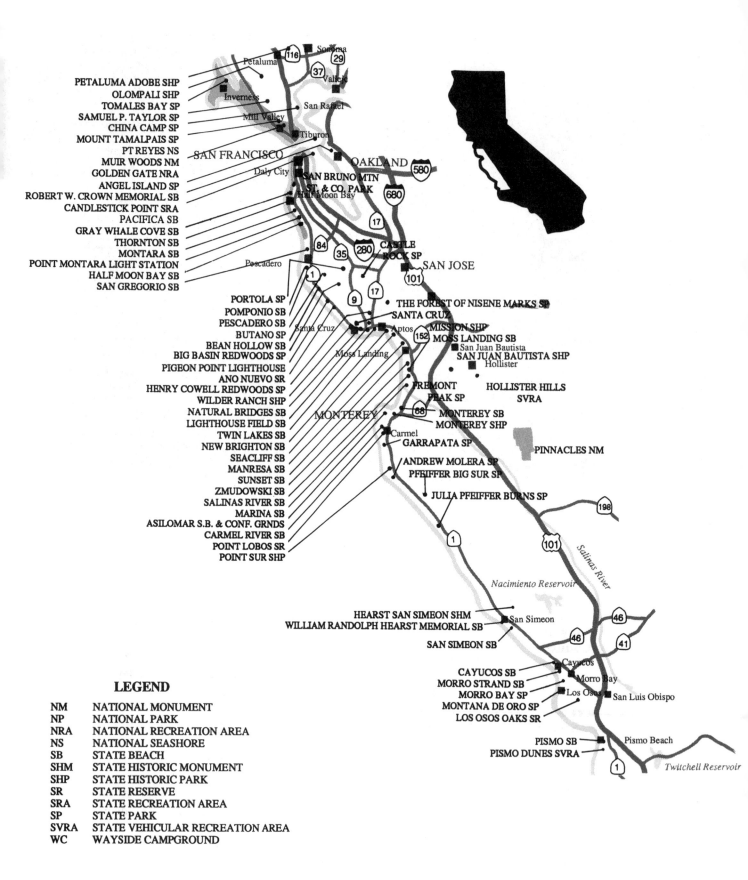

PETALUMA ADOBE SHP
OLOMPALI SHP
TOMALES BAY SP
SAMUEL P. TAYLOR SP
CHINA CAMP SP
MOUNT TAMALPAIS SP
PT REYES NS
MUIR WOODS NM
GOLDEN GATE NRA
ANGEL ISLAND SP
ROBERT W. CROWN MEMORIAL SB
CANDLESTICK POINT SRA
PACIFICA SB
GRAY WHALE COVE SB
THORNTON SB
MONTARA SB
POINT MONTARA LIGHT STATION
HALF MOON BAY SB
SAN GREGORIO SB

PORTOLA SP
POMPONIO SB
PESCADERO SB
BUTANO SP
BEAN HOLLOW SB
BIG BASIN REDWOODS SP
PIGEON POINT LIGHTHOUSE
ANO NUEVO SR
HENRY COWELL REDWOODS SP
WILDER RANCH SHP
NATURAL BRIDGES SB
LIGHTHOUSE FIELD SB
TWIN LAKES SB
NEW BRIGHTON SB
SEACLIFF SB
MANRESA SB
SUNSET SB
ZMUDOWSKI SB
SALINAS RIVER SB
MARINA SB
ASILOMAR S.B. & CONF. GRNDS
CARMEL RIVER SB
POINT LOBOS SR
POINT SUR SHP

SONOMA
Petaluma
Inverness
San Rafael
Mill Valley
Tiburon
SAN FRANCISCO
Daly City
SAN BRUNO MTN ST. & CO. PARK
Half Moon Bay
Pescadero
OAKLAND
CASTLE ROCK SP
SAN JOSE
THE FOREST OF NISENE MARKS SP
SANTA CRUZ
Santa Cruz
Aptos
MISSION SHP
MOSS LANDING SB
Moss Landing
San Juan Bautista
SAN JUAN BAUTISTA SHP
Hollister
FREMONT PEAK SP
HOLLISTER HILLS SVRA
MONTEREY
Carmel
MONTEREY SB
MONTEREY SHP
GARRAPATA SP
PINNACLES NM
ANDREW MOLERA SP
PFEIFFER BIG SUR SP
JULIA PFEIFFER BURNS SP
Nacimiento Reservoir
Salinas River
HEARST SAN SIMEON SHM
WILLIAM RANDOLPH HEARST MEMORIAL SB
San Simeon
SAN SIMEON SB
CAYUCOS SB
Cayucos
MORRO STRAND SB
Morro Bay
MORRO BAY SP
Los Osos
San Luis Obispo
MONTANA DE ORO SP
LOS OSOS OAKS SR
PISMO SB
Pismo Beach
PISMO DUNES SVRA
Twitchell Reservoir

LEGEND

NM   NATIONAL MONUMENT
NP   NATIONAL PARK
NRA   NATIONAL RECREATION AREA
NS   NATIONAL SEASHORE
SB   STATE BEACH
SHM   STATE HISTORIC MONUMENT
SHP   STATE HISTORIC PARK
SR   STATE RESERVE
SRA   STATE RECREATION AREA
SP   STATE PARK
SVRA   STATE VEHICULAR RECREATION AREA
WC   WAYSIDE CAMPGROUND

Ayala Cove, Angel Island State Park   *(Photo courtesy CDPR)*

CENTRAL CALIFORNIA COAST

San Francisco Bay Area and Marin County

POINT REYES NATIONAL SEASHORE

The Point Reyes Peninsula has long been of interest to geologists for its diverse land formations atypical to the region. Scientists believe that this portion of land was once a part of the coastline 310 miles to the south. Through constant shifting of the earth's plates, it now rests north of San Francisco Bay. The 65,303 acre park is bounded on the east by a rift created by the San Andreas Fault, forming the 16-mile long Tomales Bay. The Inverness Ridge paralleling the fault fends off dense fog that often shrouds the steep granite cliffs of the Point Reyes headlands.

Bear Valley Visitor Center is a good place to begin your visit to the Seashore. Access to the visitor center and surrounding grounds is excellent. Because the Inverness Ridge shelters Bear Valley from the coastline, it can be sunny and beautiful here while fog, wind, or rain engulfs other parts of the park. It is a good idea to get weather information at Bear Valley before continuing your visit. Other developed places at the Seashore have varying degrees of accessibility, but many provide an accessible restroom.

111

Bear Valley Area

Visitor Center

Bear Valley Visitor Center is completely accessible. A series of gently sloping amps guides visitors through the multi-level interior where exceptional displays of animal and plant life native to the area are mounted in colorful dioramas. All exhibits and a movie are arranged at a level visible from a seated position. You'll find a fully accessible *RESTROOM* and *TELEPHONE* near the entrance. There is designated *PARKING* in a lot alongside the building; the approach is smooth and gently sloping. If someone in your party would like to borrow a wheelchair to use at the park, ask for it at the visitor center.

Morgan Horse Ranch

Named after its single foundation sire, the Morgan horse is the first true American breed. You may visit the ranch that actively breeds, raises, and trains Morgan horses that are employed in the National Park System. With a handicap-identification placard, you may take the maintenance road up the hill above the visitor center to a small parking lot near the stable. Some days are quiet at the various ranch buildings. On other days, you are welcome to watch horse shoeing, veterinary work, or training in progress. You may observe an informative riding demonstration in the arena by making arrangements through the visitor center. Most of the grounds are gently sloping and have smooth asphalt paths. While you're there, stop at the accessible *BARNS* to see interesting horse-related displays.

Trails

Earthquake Trail — Across from the visitor center lies the epicenter of the 1909 San Francisco earthquake. A rolling asphalt *TRAIL* (0.6 mile) meanders through the area where the earth split apart. Interpretive signs along the path mark earthquake activity and describe the movement of geologic plates of the western region. It is at this very location that you encounter the North American Plate sitting side-by-side with the Pacific Plate that originated in Southern California. Seeing this will remind you of the tremendous force and massive shifting that progresses inch by inch over millions of years. Most of the trail slopes gently with grades of less than 6%. A *RESTROOM* at the trailhead near a designated dirt *PARKING* space has a shallow stall, high toilet seat, grab bars, and standard sinks.

Bear Valley Trail — Though rough and a bit rocky at the beginning, most of the first 1.6 miles of the 4.6-mile Bear Valley Trail is broad, well-packed dirt fire road, shaded by a thick canopy of Douglas fir and Bishop pine. The trail begins near earthquake trail parking lot and leads over a hill to the ocean at Arch Rock. The first part is uphill and can be a bit dusty. Unless you have an electric wheelchair, you probably willneed someone to help push part of the time. Your efforts will be rewarded at the top at **Divide Meadow**, where you'll share the open spaces with birds and other animals that gather to enjoy the grasses and creek waters. Early morning light and evening shadows bring out deer. The pit toilet at Divide Meadow is not accessible. Beyond

the meadow, the trail continues down a winding path to the ocean. Because the trail becomes steeper at this point, most wheelchair users who make this trip usually head back to the trailhead from here.

Miwok Trail — East of the visitor center, the dirt trail to the Coast Miwok Cultural Exhibit at the top of the hill is very steep and would require assistance. Once at the village, loose dirt surrounds the exhibits and there are no accessible restrooms.

Point Reyes Area

The tip of Point Reyes, at the end of Sir Francis Drake Highway, is 20 miles from the Bear Valley Visitor Center. Along the way, roads branch off northward to the pounding surf at Point Reyes North and South Beaches, and southward to the protected wading area at Drakes Beach. Everywhere you look, the ocean has had a powerful effect on the landscape.

Great Beach

Beachcombing is excellent on the windswept beaches northwest of Point Reyes. There is, however, no wheelchair access to the sand. Each parking lot at North and South Beaches has an accessible *RESTROOM* and several designated *PARKING* places. The shallow *RESTROOM* stall has grab bars and a low toilet seat; the sinks have foot controls and are not accessible.

Drakes Beach

Beach access is difficult at Drakes Beach, but there are some accessible facilities here. The **Kenneth**

C. Patrick Visitor Center offers an accessible, newly refurbished display area, _RESTROOMS_, _SHOWER_, and _SNACK BAR_ with a wooden veranda and an ocean view. The _VISITOR CENTER_ is open on Saturdays, Sundays and holidays. It features informative displays and a marine aquarium with underwater life from the **Gulf of Farallon National Marine Sanctuary** that lies to the southwest.

Accessible _RESTROOMS_ offer ample lateral-transfer stalls with a high toilet and grab bars, push faucets, and a low hand drier. In the shower room, there is a large changing area that has no walls or doors. The _SHOWER_ has a bench inside, grab bars and low fixtures. An accessible _TELEPHONE_ is near the restroom. You can get to the building complex by way of a ramp (8%) from designated spaces in the large asphalt _PARKING_ lot.

Point Reyes Lighthouse

At the end of Sir Francis Drake Boulevard an unlocked gate blocks the access road to the visitor center and lighthouse. You need not park in the lot outside the gate if you have a handicap-identification placard. Instead you may open the gate and drive further up the road. (Be sure to close the gate behind you.) If it is not convenient to get out of your vehicle, you can call ahead to the lighthouse visitor center and arrange to have the gate opened for you when you arrive. There is a designated _PARKING_ area at the bottom of a smooth asphalt road, 700 feet (10% incline) from the visitor center. Or, if you wish, you may drop passengers off at the visitor center and park below.

Visitor Center

The visitor center is open Thursday through Monday, weather permitting. Newly-renovated accessible _RESTROOMS_ are just outside the entrance. A few hundred feet from there, a paved walkway leads to an accessible _OBSERVATION PLATFORM_. You'll have a spectacular view perched atop the rocky cliffs 300 feet above the hazardous waters that have taken many a ship to its watery grave. From there, a long staircase descends to the lighthouse. On the platform, you'll have an impressive view of the lighthouse or the seasonal migration of California Gray whales. Known for being the windiest point on the Pacific coast from Canada to Mexico, Point Reyes has highly unpredictable weather. Prepare for cold wet winds or chilly fog any time of the year.

Tomales Point Area

Pierce Point Ranch

West of Bear Valley Visitor Center, Pierce Point Road ends in the midst of the Tule Elk range on Tomales Point beyond the turn-off for Tomales Bay State Park. Once, huge herds of Tule Elk roamed the point, but they have just recently been reintroduced after 100 years of absence. During the previous century, the point was a cattle ranch. Rolling packed soil cemented paths of no more than 8% slope wander through the remaining structures of Pierce Point Ranch. Parking for the ranch and for the Tomales Point Trail has a dirt surface. Just below the ranch parking area, the road branches off to the McClure's Beach trailhead. There is an accessible _TELEPHONE_ in the dirt parking lot here, but the trail to the beach is steep and narrow.

The **Tomales Point Trail** begins at the ranch and leads to the end of Tomales Point. The wildlife that abounds on the point is quite evident as you make your way along the trail. All sorts of animal foot prints cross the dirt and dried mud. If you look carefully, you'll spot Tule Elk grazing in the ravines or sunning themselves on the surrounding hillsides. If you don't see any elk, you'll surely be able to see their hoof prints on the sandy beach below the bluffs. The natural beauty of the coastline and the peacefulness of the area make this challenging trail a very appealing outing and worth the extra effort required to get onto the trail. Most of the trail has mild grades, but some sections are as steep as 8%. The most difficult trail surfaces encountered are near the ranch, where you may need help to get by root gnarls and some soft sandy spots.

Other Areas

Limantour Beach

Limantour Beach is a year-round haven for wildlife. Springtime is particularly active. Mother seals come here to have their pups, and waterfowl make their nests in the marshlands. Besides the many bird species, deer and antelope are attracted to the marsh. A short paved path meanders through the marsh, offering fine wildlife watching opportunities. You will not be able to view the shoreline activities, because the asphalt path to the beach ends just before the crest of a dune. While the path surfaces are smooth, overgrowth is not always cut back and can create a barrier for wheelchair users. A pit toilet along the path has a 4-inch step at the door and no grab bars. Designated _PARKING_ is provided for the beach and marsh access. From the parking place there is a steep 75-foot drop to the marsh level path. From there the level pavement extends for about 1,000 feet.

Point Reyes Hostel

In a wooded valley, two miles from Limantour Beach, an old ranch house and an adjacent redwood bunkhouse have been modified to accommodate up to three wheelchair users for an overnight stay.

For more information, call (415) 663-8811 between 7:30 and 9:30 a.m. or 4:30 and 9:00 p.m.

Point Reyes National Seashore

Point Reyes Station, CA 94956
Bear Valley Visitor Center
(Access Coordinator)
(415) 663-1092
Lighthouse Visitor Center
(415) 669-1534
Drake's Beach Visitor Center
(415) 669-1250

Park Information Available — Park Folder; Point Reyes National Seashore seasonal newspaper; Morgan Horse Ranch flyer
Location — 46 miles north of San Francisco on Point Reyes Peninsula
Elevation — 0-1,200 feet

TOMALES BAY STATE PARK

A million years ago, the Pacific and North American tectonic plates shifted, moving over 300 miles to create the Point Reyes Peninsula. Tomales Bay formed at a rift of the San Andreas Fault on its eastern edge. Protected from winds and severe weather by the high Inverness Ridge to the west, Tomales Bay State Park is home to a variety of waterfowl, a marvelous grove of virgin Bishop Pine and secluded sandy beaches.

Heart's Desire Beach is the most visited and accessible of the coarse sand beaches at the park. Its gentle shoreline and convenient

A paved path leads all the way to the sand at Heart's Desire Beach, Tomales Bay SP.   *(Photo courtesy CDPR)*

facilities make it a popular family destination. Bounded on either side by prominent rock formations, you can access the cove from the lower parking lot. Asphalt paving leads 150 feet from designated *PARKING* to an accessible *RESTROOM* with lateral transfer to a low toilet. The path then continues to within 50 feet of the water's edge. At the parking lot entrance, you'll find picnic tables on an asphalt surface not far from the restroom. The walkways are no steeper than 5%.

Several trails explore the diverse landscape of the area, but none are accessible to wheelchair users. At the upper *PARKING* lot, a space is designated along a rugged asphalt path. The path leads to a *RESTROOM* that has a shallow stall with a low toilet and grab bars. The steep, narrow trails from here to the beach are impassable by wheelchair.

Tomales Bay State Park

Star Route
Inverness, CA 94937
(415) 669-1140

Park Folder Available
Location—Four miles north of Inverness
on Sir Francis Drake Boulevard, then
north on Pierce Point Road
Elevation—86 feet

SAMUEL P. TAYLOR STATE PARK

In the 1870's and '80's, Samuel P. Taylor developed this area as one of the nation's first camping resorts and appropriately named it Taylorville. Recreation was only a sideline to his primary businesses. His paper mill busily recycled

The old Taylorville papermill   *(Photo courtesy CDPR)*

scrap paper and rags into newsprint and paper bags. He also ran a mill that manufactured black powder for ammunition. But it ultimately exploded in 1874. Today, nothing remains of Mr. Taylor's endeavors except Samuel P. Taylor State Park, a popular place for picnickers and campers.

Sir Francis Drake Highway follows the contours of **Papermill Creek** as it snakes through the southern portion of the park. Redwoods and ferns fill the canyon bottom. Midway on the park road at the camping and picnic areas, *RESTROOMS* have been modified for access and there is designated *CAMPING*. Paved roads serve the campground and picnic areas. There is an accessible *TELEPHONE* at the entry kiosk and an RV dump station near the campground.

Picnic

The main picnic area is just inside the park entry kiosk. Tables and rock BBQ's fringe a shady parking loop on the forest floor near Papermill Creek. Though access to the creek is down a steep embankment, it is pleasant to picnic and hear the water splashing nearby. The *RESTROOM* at the west end of the loop is retrofitted for access. After ascending a short ramp at the doorway, you'll find a shallow pivot-transfer stall with grab bars and a low toilet.

Trails

Bicycle/Horse Trail—Once the railroad was established into this valley, Mr. Taylor built his resort and expanded his mills. A paved road paralleling the west side of Papermill Creek will take you by the old mill sites. It runs for three forested miles on the old Northwest Pacific Railroad right of way to a gate near the northern park boundary.

In late November and December, salmon and steelhead make their annual journey upstream in Papermill Creek. Because fish have become scarce due to overfishing and lowered water levels, fishing is prohibited in this creek.

Across the creek and opposite the picnic area to the south, the pavement ends, and a gently sloping dirt access road parallels the creek for ½ mile. Tanoak and fir trees shade the well-packed road as it ascends to overlook the creek below. It then descends to a creek crossing and the end of the accessible portion of the trail.

Ox Trail and **North Creek Trail** undulate along either bank of the creek. Poison oak abounds in this area, threatening even the most cautious hiker with certain discomfort. Be especially careful when hiking on the narrow portions of the trail.

Camping

Redwoods engulf both the upper and lower campgrounds. Each flat, shady campsite has a table, rock BBQ, food storage, and fire ring. Of the 60 developed _SITES_, two (#21 and #58) are designated. They offer the additional convenience of an asphalt paved campsite, a lowered BBQ and an accessible picnic table. Each is located near an accessible _RESTROOM_.

On the lower loop, a level concrete approach leads to the _RESTROOM_ and _SHOWER_ from campsite #21. The stall has a pivot transfer to a low toilet with grab bars. The adjacent shower has a 1-inch lip at the doorway, a small seat in the dressing room, one hand rail, and the shower control knob at 40 inches from the floor. There is no parking near this building. On the upper loop, site #58 is next to a

On a clear day, there is a tremendous view from Mount Tam.　　　*(Photo courtesy CDPR)*

modified _RESTROOM_ with a shallow stall and standard fixtures. Two 2-inch steps precede the shower stall where the control for the high shower head is 40 inches from the floor; there are grab bars on two walls, but no seat. You may park near this restroom.

The _CAMPFIRE CENTER_ is hidden between the two loops and is best accessed from the upper loop near site #58. Most wheelchair users will need some help to climb the 13% smooth asphalt grade to the campfire center, about 200 feet away.

Samuel P. Taylor State Park

PO Box 251
Lagunitas, CA 94938
(415) 488-9897
Park Folder Available
Location—Fifteen miles west of San Rafael on Sir Francis Drake Boulevard
Elevation—150 feet

_____

MOUNT TAMALPAIS STATE PARK

San Francisco residents have long known of the great views and natural beauty at Mount Tamalpais. 6,300 acres of Mount Tamalpais State Park surround dense old-growth redwoods at Muir Woods National Monument. Parts of Golden Gate National Recreation Area lie at the park boundaries in the heart of Marin County north of the Golden Gate.

For the hiker or horseman, Mount Tamalpais State Park has a tangle of scenic trails that pass through oak covered knolls and open grasslands then drop to dense forests of Douglas fir or redwoods carpeted with fern. For the sightseer, no view of the bay area is more magnificent than the one from the east peak of Mount "Tam."

Mount Tamalpais is primarily a day use park, but there is a walk-in campground and enroute camping with limited accessibility at Pantoll Ranger Station. Accessible _RESTROOMS_ are provided at the ranger station and at the summit. There is also an accessible _PIT TOILET_ across from the group camp entrance gate near Mountain Home Inn. An asphalt walkway with handrails will take you to the entrance at the end of a downhill slope.

East Peak

From your 2,571 foot-high vantage point atop Mount Tamalpais you have a 360° panoramic view of urban and natural scenery below. Spread before you is all of the metropolitan Bay Area to the south and east, and the Farallon Islands to the west. On a clear day, you'll even get a glimpse of the Sierra Nevada mountain range beyond East Bay.

For views to the south and east unrestricted by trees or shrubbery, take the **Verna Dunshee Trail Loop**, a smooth paved trail that encircles the peak. From designated _PARKING_, the trail takes you 500 feet to the most eastern lookout point where it becomes more steep and rough. Eventually the trail leads to stairs on the north side of the peak. Parts of the trail are off-camber, sloping to the downhill side. Since little of the trail has guard railing, it's important to be cautious at all times and to take your time around the corners. It also is a good idea to take along a hat. There is very little shade along the trail, but the views are worth the effort.

Designated _PARKING_ at the peak is located in a special area next to an accessible _RESTROOM_. The restroom has a long pivot-transfer stall, high toilet, and high sink. An accessible _TELEPHONE_ can be found here as well.

Picnic

Neither **Boot Jack** nor **Rock Springs Picnic Areas** is desirable for wheelchair users. Most of the features are on sloping ground with stairs or very steep inclines for access.

Camping

Pantoll Walk-in Campground has shady sites on a very steep (16%) hillside. With limited level camping space, these sites would not be considered accessible. _ENROUTE CAMPING_ is available in the parking lot near the ranger station. An accessible _DRINKING FOUNTAIN_ and _UNISEX RESTROOM_ serve both the enroute and walk-in camping areas. A telephone in the vicinity is too high to reach from a seated position. (FCFS)

Mount Tamalpais State Park

801 Panoramic Highway
Mill Valley, CA 94941
(415) 388-2070

Park Folder Available
Location — Six miles west of Mill Valley
on Panoramic Highway
Elevation — 200-2,571 feet

Suzette Widergren leading a nature tour of Muir Woods NM.   *(Photo courtesy NPS)*

MUIR WOODS NATIONAL MONUMENT

Muir Woods National Monument is hidden in a deep valley, surrounded by Mount Tamalpais State Park. Foreboding hillsides and the narrow canyon pass probably saved the redwoods here from certain harvest by 19th century loggers. In 1908, this 295-acre parcel was given to the U.S. government and set aside as a national monument named in honor of the conservationist John Muir.

Though small, most of its 1.2 million visitors a year find the park very accessible. Muir Woods is quite a popular sightseeing stop for tour busses. A smooth paved asphalt walkway takes you into the midst of the thick, lush forest. So dense, that food for wildlife is scarce. You'll not see or hear much animal activity except for an occasional Stellar's jay scolding from a tree branch. Bring a jacket for this ½-mile round trip; this much shade can be chilly even in the summer.

There are several reserved PARKING places at the park entrance. If you don't have a handicap-identification placard, you may pick up a temporary PARKING permit at the office. An accessible TELEPHONE and accessible RESTROOMS are located in the parking lot. The restroom has double-wide, lateral-transfer stall with a high toilet and a high sink.

The walkway through the park has a very gradual slope. You can listen to the quiet from benches and turn-outs at regular intervals along the way. The VISITOR CENTER at the kiosk is full of books and pamphlets about the redwoods and bay area. A ranger is usually on hand to answer any questions you may have. Behind the visitor center, is a SNACK BAR and GIFT SHOP you can get to by way of a 13% ramp with a hand rail at 31 inches. You'll also find an accessible DRINKING FOUNTAIN near here.

Muir Woods National Monument
  Mill Valley, CA 94941
  (415) 388-2595
  Park Folder Available
  Location—Twelve miles north of the Golden Gate Bridge via U.S. 101 and Hwy 1
  Elevation—250 feet

GOLDEN GATE NATIONAL RECREATION AREA

Golden Gate National Recreation Area begins at the narrow mouth of the San Francisco Bay and follows the Pacific shoreline to the north and south, creating a vast coastal preserve. Features of the park are as varied as the city it surrounds. At Marin Headlands, vast expanses of windswept hillsides protect deep forested valleys and offer breath-taking views of San Francisco to the south. Secluded beaches dot the shoreline, and urban trails wander in and out of heavily visited tourist attractions on the San Francisco Peninsula. City dwellers pass right by historical sites or museums on the waterfront without a second thought, not realizing how much of San Francisco's history is preserved at the National Recreation Area.

There are so many features in Golden Gate National Recreation Area, that you should get a map ahead of time. It will help you understand the following text.

Marin Headlands

The natural beauty of windswept ridges, wooded valleys, and sandy beaches at Marin Headlands is just a bridge span away from the city lights of San Francisco, yet miles different in atmosphere. After crossing the Golden Gate Bridge from the City, the view back across the channel from vista points along the narrow hillside roads is a distant reminder that millions of people live and work just across the bay. Now the terrain changes from rows of streets and high rises

to wide open valleys and shrub-covered ridges. Gun emplacement batteries and Nike missile sites evidence past military presence. They can be viewed from pull-offs in the road. For beach enthusiasts, Stinson, Muir, or Kirby Cove Beach may be a destination. Whatever your interest, a day at the headlands will give you a new perspective on the San Francisco area.

For a sweeping view of the city skyline, a common tourist stop is the cliff-top overlook at **Juan Manuel de Ayala Vista Point**. The well-marked turn-out is just northeast of the bridge and is usually crowded with tour busses and families. However, the twelve designated PARKING spaces are rarely full. Unfortunately, a stone wall surrounds much of the lookout area, blocking the view from a seated position. There is one section where you'll find a wooden rail fence, and the view from here is only slightly restricted. Near the accessible RESTROOMS in the center of the parking lot, is a large display map and other information about the Golden Gate Bridge. The RESTROOM has a high toilet seat, grab bars, and a high sink.

Lime Point

Locals and people in the know seek out quieter places in the headlands from which to enjoy the sight of San Francisco. One of these is beneath the Ayala Vista Point. This spot offers a special unrestricted look at the City, and an accessible FISHING PIER along the way at Horseshoe Bay. In addition, a path leads directly under the Golden Gate Bridge at Lime Point for an uncommon perspective of this remarkable landmark.

A glorious view of the Golden Gate Bridge from Marin Headlands   *(Photo courtesy CDPR)*

To find Lime Point, take the Alexander exit from U.S. Hwy 101 east to East Road. Follow it south to the gravel-covered parking lot at the end. You will pass the pier and an accessible *CHEMICAL TOILET*. From the parking lot, a ramp with handrails leads uphill to the decomposed granite path. You may have this little-known path all to yourself. It takes you under the bridge to a spot with a fine Pacific Ocean view.

Conzelman Road

Dynamic bridge and city panoramas await you along a narrow, winding drive that roughly follows the hilly coastline of the Marin Headlands. As you drive through what was once a prime defensive military installation, the skeletal remains of military batteries are still visible from the road. For closer inspection, dirt paths lead from roadside parking to many of these. Every bend in the road reveals a new and better perspective of the San Francisco Peninsula. You'll be glad you took the time to explore the coastal headlands. North of the bridge, take Alexander Road to Conzelman Road.

Visitor Center

Maps and natural history displays fill the old Fort Barry Chapel near Rodeo Lagoon that serves as the **Marin Visitor Center**. In addition, dioramas and models will help you understand the significance of the headlands to the history of San Francisco. The National Park Service operates the center; a park attendant is on duty during the day and there are books, postcards and gift items available for purchase. Take the dirt road around to the north side of the chapel where there is designated *PARKING*, an access ramp, and an accessible *CHEMICAL TOILET*.

Rodeo Beach and Lagoon

The coarse sand at Rodeo Beach is an inviting place to watch the crashing waves break onshore. An accessible *CHEMICAL TOILET* and designated *PARKING* places are provided near the north end of the

119

beach parking. A few picnic tables with BBQ's and an accessible *DRINKING FOUNTAIN* have been placed on asphalt up the road from a beach access point that is short and steep. From the southern parking lot, an accessible *BRIDGE* spans the narrowest portion of Rodeo Lagoon. There is wider observation area on the bridge where nature-watchers lingering to get a glimpse of a variety of waterfowl that includes tufted and harlequin ducks. At the other end of the bridge the coarse sand beach continues.

Muir Beach and Muir Beach Overlook

Further up the coast, you'll find Muir Beach off Hwy 1 (Shoreline Highway). Two designated *PARK-ING* places are marked in a dirt lot near an accessible telephone. A packed dirt pathway leads to a modified picnic table nearby, but there is little shade in this area. The path continues toward the beach for another 150 feet then turns to beach sand 200 feet from the shoreline. On a bluff north of the beach, the **Muir Beach Overlook** offers fine vistas of the rugged coastline. The ocean scenery is great from the picnic area near the parking where there is an accessible *TABLE* and *CHEMICAL TOILET*. For those on foot, a walkway extends out onto the bluff for an even better vantage point where there are stairs with handrails.

Stinson Beach

A busy summer destination, Stinson Beach has every accommodation for an all-day stay. If you're hungry, the town of Stinson Beach is not far away, or there is a snack bar open seasonally on the beach.

The snack bar is not accessible. Swimming is allowed here and a lifeguard is on duty in the summer months. Designated *PARKING* is provided in each of several lots. Between the lots, picnic tables and BBQ's occupy the shade on grassy strips. Curb cuts provide access to both the picnic and the restroom areas. Each *RESTROOM* has a large stall with lateral transfer, grab bars and a changing bench inside. The beach sand starts directly from the concrete slab of the restroom and continues 150 feet to the water's edge. Stinson Beach is located at the intersection of Hwy 1 and Panoramic Highway.

San Francisco Waterfront

From Hyde Street Pier to Fort Point, the San Francisco Bay waterfront bustles with tourists, noontime joggers and commuters on the busy streets of the City. A prominent feature of Golden Gate National Recreation Area is Fort Mason. Military structures, part of what was once a major port of embarkation during World War II, are being renovated to offer a full spectrum of cultural, educational, and recreational programs. With Fort Mason as backdrop and the changeable bay to the north, the Aquatic Park and Hyde Street Pier are home to the Maritime Museum and several historic ships.

Golden Gate Promenade

Designed for joggers, walkers, and sightseers, the Golden Gate Promenade extends for 3½ miles from the Fort Point parking lot to the foot of the Hyde Street Pier. Parts of the Promenade are accessible.

At **Fort Point**, parking is in a paved lot with an accessible

CHEMICAL TOILET and two designated *PARKING* places. To access the paved promenade at the National Park Service administration building east of the fort, you can *PARK* in a designated place near an accessible *TELEPHONE* and *RESTROOM* (pivot transfer, low toilet, grab bars). Beyond the fishing pier next to the administration building, the Promenade trail tread becomes rough hard-packed gravel as far as the **Coast Guard Station**.

Traveling further to the east, you encounter the grassy waterfront of **Crissy Field**, where windsurfers favor the strong bay breezes. There is parking here. The trail is smooth and long until a set of six 4-inch steps at the **St. Francis Yacht Club** interrupts the continuity of wheelchair access.

From the east entrance of the **Presidio** east to Fort Mason, the promenade is a broad, concrete sidewalk stretching along the bay side of the level lawns at **Marina Green Park**. Fly a kite or sunbathe here in the sunny open spaces where everyone is busy doing something they enjoy. Restrooms at either end of Marina Green have marginal accessibility. Both the restroom near the **Harbor Master's Office** and the one at the eastern edge of the Green have stalls that are wide enough, but are not modified for wheelchair access.

The Promenade continues through Fort Mason where its surface changes to loose crushed gravel and climbs steeply into the wide-openness of **The Great Meadow**. Passing near the youth hostel, it then follows a steep (8%) asphalt roadway back downhill to meet the foot of the **Municipal Pier**. From there it is a pleasant flat stroll around the perimeter of the **Aquatic Park** and the ever-crowded beachfront to **Hyde Street Pier**.

Fort Mason

Formerly a very busy military transferring station, Fort Mason is a complex of military housing, office buildings, warehouses, and piers. Most of the paved roads through the fort are hilly. Park headquarters is located at the corner of Polk and McArthur. A ramp will take you from three designated parking places to the back door. Office hours at the headquarters are 7:30 a.m. to 5 p.m. on weekdays only.

Stores, offices, and a theater occupy dockside warehouses near the Fort Mason Piers 1, 2, and 3; most are not accessible. Paved designated *PARKING* is provided in several locations near ramps to the former loading docks. People often fish from these piers. The *Liberty Ship Jeremiah O'Brien* is open for tours at Pier 3, but is not accessible for wheelchair users. All sorts of programs, entertainment and other events are scheduled throughout the year in the various fort facilities. Ask for a calendar of events and accessibility information by phone at (415) 556-0560, or when you visit the park office.

Youth Hostel

A Civil War-era Army barracks at Fort Mason is home to the **San Francisco International Hostel** where accessible dormitory accommodations are available. A long ramp leads to the upper floor of the barracks dorm. The *RESTROOM* here offers lateral transfer to a high toilet and an accessible sink. A large *SHOWER* has grab bars but no seat in the stall. Due to a flight of stairs, the kitchen and dining room downstairs are not accessible. To get hostel information or make reservations call (415) 771-7277.

National Maritime Museum

If you visit the Fisherman's Wharf area, you can't miss noticing a side-wheeler and an assortment of historic merchant vessels docked beside the Hyde Street Pier. As part of the National Maritime Museum exhibits, the ships are vivid evidence of early West Coast maritime commerce. Also docked at the waterfront is the World War II submarine *Pampanito* berthed at Pier 45, and the *Liberty Ship Jeremiah O'Brien* at Fort Mason's

Hyde Street Pier, Golden Gate National Recreation Area *(Photo courtesy CDPR)*

Pier 3. At Pier 43, the *Balclutha*, a square-rigged Cape Horn sailing ship circa 1886, is also part of the collection. Of the eight ships displayed, four can be boarded for close inspection; two are partially accessible.

In her day, the side-wheeler *Eureka*, built in 1890, was the world's largest passenger ferry. Hauling as many as 2,300 passengers and 120 autos, she was the workhorse that connected the city to other points across the bay. Park staff and volunteers give daily tours. Wheelchair users can manage the lower auto deck; plans are being made for upper deck access.

You'll have a gorgeous view of the bay from the main deck of the *Balclutha,* located about one thousand feet from the pier entrance. But you'll need an assistant to help you up the steep (10%) gangway that takes you on board above decks and for a peek into the deck below.

Disabled school children from the bay area participate in hands-on overnight camping experiences on board these sailing ships. Soon, physically challenged adults also will be included. These and other programs are directed by Marine Programs, 2905 Hyde Street, San Francisco, CA, 94123, (415) 556-8370.

A nominal admission fee is charged to visit the Hyde Street Pier. Books, park folders, and other park-related information can be obtained at the accessible *BOOK-STORE* at the foot of the pier by way of a rear access ramp. In addition, an accessible *CHEMICAL TOILET* is provided near the pier entrance. Designated street *PARKING* is on Jefferson near the pier and on Beach

Street at the entrance to the Maritime Museum.

The **Maritime Museum** building west of Hyde Street Pier houses hundreds of artifacts, photographs, and documents charting the seafaring history of the West Coast. New exhibits are developed and displayed regularly in the Harmon Gallery. Wheelchair users must access the museum's first floor through the Senior Center at the east end of the building. The *RESTROOM* on the main floor is fully accessible.

Aquatic Park

Open lawns, a sandy shoreline, and calm waters of the lagoon are often in a hubbub of activity. Sloping concrete sidewalks lead down through the Aquatic Park from Beach Street. The most gradual sidewalks are the westernmost path at the foot of Van Ness (near two designated *PARKING* places) or the Hyde Street sidewalk below the cable car turnaround.

Municipal Pier

Follow the flat concrete walkway that leads from Jefferson Street around the Aquatic Park Beach to the Municipal Pier. By traveling down the middle of the pier to its end, you'll have a magnificent view beyond the lagoon, up to Ghirardelli Square, the Cannery, and the City on the hills above. A concrete wall running the distance of the pier blocks any downward views and has no lowered sections for fishing from a wheelchair. The **Van Ness Pier** to the west has lower guard rails, but lacks the lagoon view of the Aquatic Park.

Best known for its role as a federal penitentiary from 1934 to 1963, Alcatraz Island was home to famous convicts such as The Birdman and Al Capone. As early as 1850, the island's strategic location in the San Francisco Bay made it an important defensive outpost. During the Civil War, it was a heavily armed fort. Between 1969 and 1971 the island was the site of a Native American demonstration and occupation. Many buildings at Alcatraz are in disrepair, but the main cellblock remains much like it was when the last prisoner left the island in 1963. Self-guided walking tours aided by either cassette tape or a trail map take you on a historical journey into the colorful past of "the island of no escape."

A trip to Alcatraz Island offers you a rare opportunity to visit the most famous of the federal prisons. Here you'll see first hand how the inmates lived. A visit to this distinctive part of Golden Gate National Recreation Area is well worth the planning and physical effort required.

Ferries run regular daily trips to the island from San Francisco. The ferry departs from Pier 39 near Fisherman's Wharf at regular intervals. Make your reservations for the ferry trip to Alcatraz Island at least a day in advance by calling Harbor Carriers, (415) 546-2700. You may return from the island any time, but be sure that you're at the dock at least 10 minutes before scheduled departure. To pick up tickets or for last-minute purchases, an all-weather ramp at the rear of the ticket building will take you to the ticket window. For other questions about the ferry ride, you may phone the office, (415) 546-2805.

The ferry boarding ramp is very steep, but the Red and White Fleet cruise line is accustomed to assisting visitors who have physical limitations. They will help you on board ahead of the other passengers. Once on board, plenty of windows afford visibility from the lower deck of the ferry. The brief boat ride seems even shorter as you try to take in all the sights of the harbor on your way to Alcatraz.

When you arrive at Alcatraz Island, a park ranger will give a short orientation at the dock. There are accessible CHEMICAL TOILETS in this area, but the regular restroom is not accessible. Pick up a self-guided tour booklet near the dock and be sure not to miss the slide presentation at the VISITOR CENTER located 50 yards up the road. An 8% ramp connects the BOOKSTORE to the adjoining small theaters. Just outside the bookstore, you begin your SELF-GUIDED TOUR.

Walkways on the island are a hodgepodge of concrete pavement with rough transitions but are manageable with assistance, so, bring a capable companion. The ¼-mile walking tour up to the cell block, will take you on a hike that is the uphill equivalent of a thirteen story building. So plan on some serious uphill pushing. There are level rest areas at intervals, so you and your friend can catch your breath. You'll need it for some of the steep switchbacks.

Most of the prison is accessible to wheelchair users except the upstairs infirmary. A clearly marked access ramp to the main cellblock

is located at the south end of the building. This is also the place to go if you wish to rent an audio tour tape. Accessible CHEMICAL TOILETS are near the ramped entrance to the cellhouse.

Golden Gate
and West Peninsula

From the Golden Gate Bridge south to Fort Funston, Golden Gate National Recreation Area encompasses miles of coastline preserving windswept sandy beaches and historic military sites. You can explore a bunker with a surprise hidden cannon, take a long walk along the beach, watch while hang gliders soar out over the ocean, or take home a lasting memory of the City-by-the-Bay as seen from the Golden Gate.

Golden Gate Bridge

For a look at the Golden Gate Bridge from a pedestrian's point of view. Park near the south bridge entrance and wheel onto the causeway. The panoramic view of the bay is magnificent from midspan. The guard railing is 48 inches high, however, so from a seated position, you must peer through spaces between the vertical posts of the railing.

The parking lot at the foot of the bridge is undersized for the traffic it must bear. There are two designated PARKING places; one near an accessible RESTROOM and one close to the bridge viewing area. It is best to get there in the morning, because by 11:00 a.m., the lot fills with tourists and tour busses jockeying for a parking spot. From a paved viewing area about 100 yards up a 6% incline from the parking, you'll have an unre-

stricted view of the entire length of the Golden Gate Bridge. A GIFT SHOP on this level is also accessible. Beyond that, the pavement becomes steeper and leads directly onto the pedestrian walkway of the bridge itself. It is often windy and cold here, so bring along a jacket. For a look at the underpinnings of the bridge, take a short trip to Fort Point.

Fort Point

By the mid-19th century, San Francisco Bay was of great strategic military and commercial importance. To protect the bay area, the U.S. Army Corps of Engineers constructed the massive Fort Point giving it the capability of handling 126 muzzle-loaded cannons and 500 troops. Located under the Golden Gate Bridge, the fort, with all its fire power, became outmoded during the Civil War and was retired, never having used its cannons for defense. Today, power of a different sort takes shape in the Golden Gate Bridge looming overhead. The power of creativity is exemplified in the intricate latticework of I-beams and steel cables that form the rust-red bridge infrastructure.

The information center in the fort is open daily (except Christmas and New Year's) when docents are on hand to conduct tours and answer questions. There is a paved parking lot with a nearby accessible CHEMICAL TOILET and TELEPHONE. From designated PARKING, the narrow entry (28") door with a 3-inch sill is preceded by a 1- to 3-inch transition to a concrete slab. Notice the thick walls of solid brick when you pass through the narrow (28") arched doorways. The building contains living quarters, powder magazine, hospital, kitchen, jail, and storerooms, each with interpretive signs describing different aspects of fort life. Books, pamphlets, and souvenirs are for sale in the gift shop. People often fish in the cold waters of the bay from the edge of the parking lot at Fort Point.

Baker Beach

From this west-facing beach you have a view of the Marin Headlands and the mouth of the bay. A flat walkway leads from the north end of the parking lot to **Battery Chamberlain**, a military museum open to the public. On weekends, weather permitting, the "disappearing gun," a 95,000-pound 1904 cannon, is cranked from the battery to its firing position. You'll be able to see the gun from the parking area. An accessible _CHEMICAL TOILET_ and _DRINKING FOUNTAIN_ are available at the northwest portion of the parking lot near a ramp that leads to the beach. At the southeast end of the lot, near another accessible _CHEMICAL TOILET_ and _DRINKING FOUNTAIN_, an asphalt walkway takes you 100 feet inland to a picnic area protected by a forested hillside. A picnic table among the grouping has an extended end and a lowered BBQ. Designated _PARKING_ is provided at either end of the parking lot.

China Beach

Nestled into the steep shoreline south of Baker Beach, China Beach is one of few swimming beaches in San Francisco. A small sandy strip with gentle water, the shore is an excellent place for an outing for families with small children. A beach house at the foot of the

access road provides restrooms, changing rooms, showers, and a telephone, but none of these facilities are accessible. From the beach house, a paved ramp leads directly onto the moist sand no more than 20 feet from the water. There is an accessible _PICNIC TABLE_ on pavement nearby, but unfortunately it lies behind a 48-inch seawall that blocks the ocean view. Though the regular parking lot on the cliff above is paved, the asphalt walkway is steep from there to the beach level. With a handicap-identification placard you may park in a space provided at the bottom of the road. Call (415) 556-8371 or (415) 556-7894 for further information about China Beach. The lifeguard station is open April 15 to October 15.

Land's End

Early city dwellers and tourists had great fun taking a steam train from town to Seal Rock House, at a point of land south and west of the bridge. They would have a meal and watch the seals play in the rocks offshore. Parts of the old train route are now a coastal trail for hikers who enjoy the relative tranquility of the open space on the point.

Combined with old military roads, residential sidewalks, and beaches, over nine miles of trail has been created to offer foot travelers outstanding views of Point Reyes, Marin Headlands, and the Farallon Islands. A portion of the trail can be accessed at 32nd and El Camino del Mar. Not far from the roadside parking, wheelchair users can access an _OBSERVATION DECK_ on packed, uneven dirt. On a clear day, there is a wonderful view of the northern coastline.

Cliff House

Today the Cliff House Visitor Center is still a major tourist stop. Besides the information station on the lower level of the building, gift shops, a restaurant and a _MUSEUM_ are popular attractions. Many people bring binoculars to watch the large sea lion and marine bird population at Seal Rock from the visitor center _PATIO_. With luck, a designated _PARKING_ place near the Cliff House will be available. From there, access to the overlook area can be reached by way of 1,000 feet of concrete paved walkways. Follow the pavement downhill (7%) around the south end of the buildings to the lower level. Two openings in the solid concrete wall offer a full view across the water of activities on the rocks.

There are no accessible restrooms in this area. The closest one is near the **USS San Francisco Memorial** in West Fort Miley (at the end of El Camino del Mar). This is a shady rest stop with designated _PARKING_ and an accessible _CHEMICAL TOILET_. Another accessible _CHEMICAL TOILET_ is in the **Sutro Heights Park** parking lot above the Cliff House on Point Lobos and El Camino del Mar.

Ocean Beach

Ocean Beach stretches for four miles along the Great Highway, from the Cliff House to south Fort Funston. The **Esplanade**, a path for joggers and beach walkers, parallels the highway for two miles, beginning at Lincoln Way and ending at Sloat Boulevard. Though a sea wall blocks much of the ocean view from a seated position, the fresh sea air and constant activity on the Esplanade make it a good place for an athletic wheel-

China Camp State Park

(Photo courtesy CDPR)

chair user. Three _RESTROOMS_ along the way have accessible stalls, but there is no ramp access to the beach. Transitions on the highway crossing from street parking on the other side at Lincoln and Sloat are the major challenge of accessing Ocean Beach Esplanade. Sometimes sand builds up at the curb cut areas making it difficult to maneuver onto the sidewalk.

Fort Funston

Once the site of **Battery Davis**, built in 1939 for Naval gunnery defense, only remnants of the subterranean concrete structure exist today. Now a pleasant one-mile asphalt loop trail winds through the dunes at the battery, affording great views as far north as Point Reyes. The portion of the walkway loop nearest the water slopes more gently and is preferable.

For some reason, Fort Funston has also become a very well-used dog-walking area. At any given time there may be 10-20 dogs either on- or off-leash prowling through the ground cover on the dunes.

Strong winds and high cliffs here are a perfect combination for hang gliding. A _BOARDWALK_ with a maximum slope of 9% leads out 200 feet from designated _PARKING_ to a viewing platform that will allow you to watch the flyers as they take off for the sky and return to land close by. Large gaps between the boards of the walkway could cause a problem for your front casters, so be alert.

Golden Gate
National Recreation Area

Fort Mason
San Francisco, CA 94123
Headquarters — (415) 556-0560
Marin Headlands Information
(415) 331-1540
Muir and Stinson Beaches
(415) 868-0942
Maritime Museum — (415) 556-2904
Fort Point — (415) 556-1693

Park Literature Available — Golden Gate and National Maritime Museum Park Folders; San Francisco Maritime National Historical Park flyer; The Maritime Museum flyer; Park Events, quarterly newspaper
Location — The coastline in and around the mouth of San Francisco Bay
Elevation — 0-1,500 feet

CHINA CAMP STATE PARK

Located on the southwest shore of San Pablo Bay, China Camp was one of twenty or thirty fishing villages established in the bay area during the Goldrush days. Initially, the promise of wealth lured the Chinese to the San Francisco area. But as gold fever waned, the new immigrants ultimately profiting from the abundant harvests they fished from the bay. Drawing on skills they had learned in China.

A small cluster of weather-beaten buildings is all that remains of this 1880's community that was home to approximately 500 people. Preserved historic structures house a _VISITOR CENTER_ and _MUSEUM_. Words and pictures interpret the life of the Chinese fisher. Packed dirt with a sandy top layer covers the surfaces in the village area. A boardwalk leads to the entrance of the museum where there is a small door sill. Rangers give history talks at the museum each Saturday and Sunday, May through October.

A small coarse-sand _SWIMMING BEACH_ is near the village and shares the same dirt parking lot. Since there are no waves, kayakers and windsurfers launch from the shore, that waders and small children also enjoy. The best approach to the beach is down a packed dirt path from the restroom. _RESTROOMS_ near the swimming beach are fully accessible, but there is a 1-inch transition onto the concrete slab near the entry. The building also contains an accessible _DRESSING ROOM_ with a bench and a grab bar. An old-fashioned _CONCESSION STAND_ near the fishing pier sells bait and food and is open only on weekends. Hours vary at the museum, so it is best to call ahead for the schedule.

Picnic

From the picnic areas along the road west of the village, you have wonderful views of the bay and tidal marshlands as they change with the tide. Each is on a point of land overlooking the water. Picnic tables and BBQ's are provided on uneven dirt or grass surfaces. Accessible _CHEMICAL TOILETS_ are available at **Buckeye Point**, **Weber Point** and **Bullhead Flat**, but the dirt approach to each may be difficult.

Camping

Back Ranch Meadows — Thirty walk-in campsites, forested by oaks and laurels, are located 30 to 100 yards away from the parking lot on the edge of a quiet meadow. Each site has a table, fire ring, and food storage. The dirt parking lot is also used for _ENROUTE CAMPING_ and contains an accessible _CHEMICAL TOILET_ and _DRINKING WATER_. For safety, the ranger locks the campground gate in the evening and reopens it in the morning. Call ahead for campground hours.

China Camp State Park
R.R. No. 1 Box 244
San Rafael, CA 94901
(415) 456-0766
Park Folder Available
Location — Three miles north of San Rafael via U.S. 101 and North San Pedro Road
Elevation — Sea level

ANGEL ISLAND STATE PARK

Located in the midst of the San Francisco Bay, Angel Island (once named Isla de los Angeles) has played a major role in the history of the San Francisco region. Before explorers came to develop the area, the island was a haven for Native American hunters and fishermen. Upon the arrival of European explorers, Isla de los Angeles was all too soon considered a strategic location for military defense of the vital harbor. In the early 20th century, the military shared the island with an immigration station; by the first World War, East Garrison became the military's busiest induction center. Even as parts of the island were being dedicated as state park land, the U.S. government was installing a Nike missile base that remained active until 1962.

Now you can visit what remains of the garrisons and encampments on the 740-acre island and to understand its historical significance. Nature lovers come here to enjoy the combination of native and introduced plant life and to bird-watch along the shoreline. Everyone likes to sightsee from here. The hills of San Francisco across the bay are an amazing sight from your vantage point at Angel Island. Don't get too carried away; you must not forget to catch the last ferry off the island.

Dock Area

When your ferry arrives at **Ayala Cove Dock**, you will find that smooth pavement leads ¼ mile to the visitor center. On the way, an accessible _RESTROOM_ (lateral transfer to a high toilet with grab bars) is not far from the disembarking

Wheelchair users and able-bodied join in an invigorating paddle to Angel Island. Trips are sponsored by Environmental Traveling Companions.
(Photo courtesy ETC)

platform. Another 150 feet brings you to an accessible _SNACK BAR_ with a picnic table on pavement. This may be just the place to stop for a view of the cove and to watch the hustle-bustle of the other passengers at the ferry landing.

Visitor Center

Tucked back above the cove, the visitor center presides over a multitude of picnic tables and BBQ's scattered under the trees and on the lawn of a sloping grassy area. A clearly marked wheelchair access route guides you to the rear of the building where there is a 1-inch door sill at the entrance. Inside the small visitor center, displays of local flora and fauna line the walls. The docents also show a 20-minute film in a small theater that describes the diverse history of the island. Books and maps are available for purchase and a docent is on duty to answer your questions. The visitor center is open to coincide with the ferry schedule.

Park Features

Perimeter Road circumnavigates the island in a series of steep climbs and descents. Road conditions alternate from rough asphalt to poorly packed dirt and gravel. Parts of the road are so rough you won't want to travel on them in your wheelchair. For all but the very athletic or those with a well-charged electric wheelchair or a willing friend for auxiliary power, wheeling around the island is prohibitive.

Van Tour — Most park buildings are manned by the Angel Island Association, a volunteer organization devoted to the preservation and interpretation of the island's rich heritage. Sometimes there aren't enough volunteers available to open the buildings on weekdays or during the off-season. At these times, you will not be able to explore the interiors of some historic structures.

The association has a van equipped to handle up to three wheelchairs for a personalized tour around the island. Since there is not always a docent on the island to take you on a tour, it is important to call well ahead of your visit and make arrangements for this service, (415) 435-3522.

If you're lucky enough to arrange a van trip, your driver will be acquainted with the accessible features of the park. Among them you won't want to miss the **Immigration Station** at North Garrison known as the "Ellis Island" of the west. Operated from 1910 to 1940, the government built the station large enough to accommodate expected masses of immigrants from Europe through the Panama Canal. Instead, it became a detention center for Asians anticipating a better life in America. A _WHEELCHAIR LIFT_ will take you to the main floor of the building where you'll get an all-too-tangible impression of what life was like for captive Chinese immigrants. In a building near the Immigration Station, a short ramp leads to the door of an accessible _RESTROOM_ that has a high toilet, grab bars, and a push faucet.

Angel Island Association is host to several groups offering a "comfortable but rustic" camping experience for the disabled at **West Garrison, Camp Reynolds**. Once the site of multiple gun emplacements and army personnel quarters in the early 1900's, the refurbished structures now serve as makeshift dorms for small groups of special visitors. For a real adventure, Environmental Traveling Companions (ETC) sponsors kayak trips for people with special needs. The group leaves from Sausalito in tandem kayaks and arrives on the beach at Camp Reynolds. For information contact ETC, Fort Mason Building C, San Francisco, CA 94123, (415) 474-7662.

Ferry Service

Angel Island can be reached on commercial ferries that leave several times a day from Vallejo, San Francisco and Tiburon, or you can dock your own boat at a slip in Ayala Cove. From Tiburon, the ferry leaves from a dock on Main Street off Tiburon Boulevard (Hwy 131). Look for the sign at 21 Main Street directing you to the ferry landing between the two businesses: Main Treat and Bird 'n Hound. There is one designated _PARKING_ place ½-block west of the landing and more designated _PARKING_ in a lot at the east end of Main Street. The gangway to the ferry is steep and there are wide spaces between the wooden planking, so front casters can easily get caught. The ferry crew is very helpful and will make sure that all passengers get on board safely.

From San Francisco, the boarding procedure is similar to that of the Alcatraz Island Ferry. The boats leave from Pier 43½ at the foot of

Powell Street near the Franciscan Restaurant. There are no public restrooms at this location. You may purchase tickets on board the boat or at the main ticket office at Pier 41. Persons requiring assistance are boarded first. A crew member will direct you to appropriate seating if necessary.

From Vallejo, you leave from the dock on Mare Island Way near the Wharf Restaurant. There is a passenger loading zone in front of the accessible terminal, but curb cuts are conspicuously absent. Instead, you should park in the restaurant parking lot on the west side of the terminal building. From there, access to the building is barrier-free and there is an accessible *RESTROOM* inside. Large catamarans service the route from Vallejo to Angel Island. Unlike the other ferries, these are equipped with accessible *RESTROOMS*. Deck hands are sensitized to the needs of the disabled. When you board, you will be directed to places on the boat that lend a good view during your ride.

For information and sailing times of the ferry service from Tiburon, contact the Angel Island State Park Ferry Co., (415) 435-2131. For maps, schedules, and rates from San Francisco or Vallejo, contact The Red and White Fleet, (415) 546-2815.

Angel Island State Park
  PO Box 318
  Tiburon, CA 94920
  (415) 435-1915
Park Folder Available
Location—A ferry ride away in the San Francisco Bay from Vallejo, Tiburon, or San Francisco
Elevation—0-781 feet

OLOMPALI STATE HISTORIC PARK

Since the 1300's the Olompali tribe of Miwok Indians permanently inhabited the land in this region of the Marin Peninsula. Recently, vast troves of archaeological findings have unlocked many secrets of the Miwok past. Included in the treasures is evidence of contact with English explorers predating Sir Francis Drake. Because of its rich and varied history, the park promises to be a popular destination in the Marin District. At this time it is not developed adequately for public visitation.

Olompali State Historic Park
  PO Box 1016
  Novato, CA 94948
  (415) 892-3383
Location—On U.S. Hwy 101, 3 miles north of Novato

ROBERT W. CROWN MEMORIAL STATE BEACH

Robert W. Crown Memorial State Beach, on the western shore of Alameda is a welcome change from most beaches. The East Bay Regional Park District and the California Coastal Conservancy combined their resources to create a friendly environment for wheelchair users and others with special needs. The result is a multiple day use park with access to an *OBSERVATION PIER*, two miles of *COASTAL WALKWAY*, and a ramp leading directly into the bay at a rocky *TIDAL POOL*. In addition, accessible *RESTROOMS* and designated *PARKING* spaces have been thoughtfully planned for optimum convenience.

Crab Cove

The Crab Cove portion of the park has been designated by the State of California as a marine reserve. Plants and animals are protected and may not be collected, so everyone may observe and enjoy them. An *ALL-WEATHER CONCRETE WALKWAY* with a sturdy grab rail gradually descends into the *OBSERVATION AREA* at the cove. This is an ideal place for wheelchair users to experience the tidal reserve up close. One hundred feet of the *TRAIL* are flat, and during high tide are under 2 to 3 feet of water. At low tide you'll be able to have an intimate encounter with the creatures living in the cracks and crevices of the rocky cove. For the most satisfying experience, plan ahead for low tide when much of the rocky shore is exposed. To find the tidal trail at the foot of McKay Avenue, take the exercise path west for a short distance.

Visitor Center

On weekends from March through November, naturalists at **Crab Cove Visitor Center** offer a number of activities and programs designed to inform and enlighten guests of the San Francisco Bay. Elaborate three-dimensional dioramas representing the underwater world of the bay, and a salt water aquarium alive with creatures native to the area help visitors appreciate the richness of the local marine environment. The visitor center is open Wednesday through Sunday.

A 30-foot access ramp (11%) leads to the McKay Avenue entrance of the Crab Cove Visitor Center. There is one designated *PARKING* space at curbside and two more

At low tide, wheelchair users can explore the rocky shore at Robert W. Crown Memorial State Beach   *(Bob Walker ©)*

north of the building in a small lot near an accessible _RESTROOM_. At the restroom, another 30-foot ramp (5%) provides access to a lateral-transfer stall with grab bars and a low toilet. An additional accessible _RESTROOM_ with a sliding door and lateral transfer to a high toilet with grab bars is near the tidal access path at the foot of McKay.

Picnic Area and Day Use

Covering much of Crown Memorial State Park is a lovely rolling grassy area with paved pathways crisscrossing wide open spaces. Picnic tables and BBQ's on small concrete slabs seek the shade of young trees on grassy knolls and are not particularly accessible for wheelchair users. Nearer to the beach, the terrain is flatter. Some paved paths converge at the bathhouse, where you'll find a seasonal _SNACK BAR_, and an accessible _TELEPHONE_ and _DRINKING FOUNTAIN_. The _CHANGING ROOM_ here is accessible, but the _RESTROOM_ offers only a shallow stall with grab bars. The fine sand of Crown Beach meets the edge of the pavement at the bathhouse.

South of Crab Cove, two freshwater lagoons host ducks and other waterfowl. A raised walkway over the water is a nice place to linger and can be reached by way of a packed dirt path. The grassy turf in this area is more level as it engulfs several clusters of picnic tables on lattice pavement packed with dirt. There is a large _TABLE_ here without benches, and the ends of several others are accessible. There is also an accessible _RESTROOM_ nearby.

The park's main _PARKING_ lot is located on 8th Street at Otis Drive. Designated _PARKING_ places are conveniently situated near a well-marked crosswalk and curb cut. Accessible _RESTROOMS_ are on the second and third tier of the lot.

A smooth, flat _EXERCISE PATH_ follows the shoreline from Crab Cove past the picnic area, to the grassy dunes and marsh overlook at the southern boundary of the park. Of the five _RESTROOMS_ along the path, those at the terminus of Grand, Park, or Broadway are accessible. You'll find additional designated _STREET PARKING_ near the Park and Broadway restrooms as well.

Elsie Roemer Bird Sanctuary and Marsh Overlook

At the southernmost point of the park along Shoreline Drive, the marshy waterfront from Broadway to Park Street is one of the few remaining wetlands on the San Francisco Bay. Now set aside as a bird sanctuary, a large array of waterfowl and shore birds seek haven here in the spring, fall, and winter. At the foot of Broadway, a 100-foot _OBSERVATION PIER_ extends over the marsh so you may quietly watch food-gathering activities in the mud below. Unfortunately, railing blocks part of the view from a seated position, but you'll still see San Francisco glittering across the bay.

Robert W. Crown Memorial State Beach

1252 McKay Avenue
Alameda, CA 94501
(415) 531-9043
Program Reservations
(415) 521-6887
Park Folders Available by calling the park office—An activity schedule for the entire East Bay Regional Parks Department is published monthly.
Location—Off Hwy 880 on 8th Street in Alameda
Elevation—Sea level

The windblown shoreline at Candlestick Point.

(Photo courtesy CDPR)

CANDLESTICK POINT STATE RECREATION AREA

During World War II, Candlestick Point was a landfill created for the Naval Shipyard. As a recent addition to the State Park System, Candlestick Point State Park is evolving into a prime picnic and fishing park. The park currently features two fishing piers with fish cleaning facilities, hiking and biking _TRAILS_, lots of picnic sites, and an exercise course that is popular with seniors. Much of the land north and west of Candlestick Park sports stadium is yet to be developed.

Afternoon winds rush through the Alemany Gap from the ocean to the bay providing prime windsurfing conditions at the south shore of the park. People and cars sometimes line the shore to watch these daring athletes skillfully battle to keep their sails erect as they skid along the whitecaps.

Windscreens shelter many of the picnic tables near the south shore of the point from westerly breezes.

Each has a fire ring and is surrounded in packed decomposed granite. However, at many sites, there is a 1- to 4-inch transition onto the dirt surface. You can reach other tables in grassy areas along one of the many paved or smooth decomposed granite _WALKWAYS_ that lace the park.

At the end of Candlestick Point, a 125-foot _FISHING PIER_ stretches out over the bay. Smooth walkways take you right to its base about 1/3 mile from the parking lot. The pier railing is an inconvenient 44 inches high and there are no lowered sections. Pavement surrounds a _PICNIC TABLE_ near the pier, but it is only accessible at its end.

All of the _RESTROOMS_ in the park are the accessible unisex type and can be reached by way of pavement, except for one at Jack Rabbit picnic area. It has a 1- to 2-inch transition from the surrounding packed dirt surface onto the concrete slab. An accessible _TELEPHONE_ is available at the entry kiosk. You can get a map of the walkways that charts all of the distances between park features by

131

sending a self-addressed stamped envelope to the park, c/o San Francisco District, 1150 Carroll Avenue, San Francisco, CA, 94124.

Candlestick Point State Recreation Area

Contact San Francisco District Office
(415) 557-2539

Location—Just south of Candlestick Park stadium in San Francisco, off U.S. Hwy 101 on the Candlestick exit
Elevation—Sea level

| San Mateo County Coast |

THORNTON STATE BEACH

Thornton State Beach is a small strip of sand at the bottom of a bluff trail off Hwy 35 on Olympic near the northern boundary of San Mateo County. There are no accessible features. For information call the San Francisco District Office at (415) 557-4069.

SAN BRUNO MOUNTAIN STATE AND COUNTY PARK

San Bruno Mountain presides over 2,266 acres of state park land at the northern reaches of the Santa Cruz range on the San Francisco Peninsula. A drive to its summit is rewarded with uncommon views of the bay and the city of San Francisco below. The Santa Cruz range acts as a barrier for fog and wind entering the bay area from the ocean. Some days you can watch from this high perch as

tumbling fog banks flow around to the north and engulf the city.

Along the highway beneath the mountain is a beautiful picnic area on a broad expanse of grass. Paved walkways weave through the rolling terrain where there are two accessible *PICNIC TABLES* on pavement. A nearby *RESTROOM* is fully accessible (low toilet) and there is an accessible *DRINKING FOUNTAIN* and *TELEPHONE* adjacent. Four designated *PARKING* places are conveniently located near these accessible features. The weather is changeable in this area, so prepare for sun, wind, rain, or fog.

The County of San Mateo operates the park, and collects fees on Fridays, Saturdays, and Sundays. To find the park when driving eastbound, take Eastmoor Avenue off I-280 until it becomes East Market (out of Daly City), then follow the signs to Guadalupe Canyon Parkway. Westbound traffic should take Guadalupe Canyon Parkway from Bay Shore Drive.

San Bruno Mountain State Park

Contact Central Coast Region Headquarters
(415) 649-2840 or 363-4020

Location—In Brisbane just south of San Francisco between U.S. Hwy 101 and Interstate 280
Elevation—250-1,314 feet

PACIFICA STATE BEACH

Pacifica State Beach is a very popular surfing area in the City of Pacifica off Hwy 1. It has a small dirt parking lot, an inaccessible restroom, and a narrow steep trail down a bluff to the beach. For

information call the Pacifica City Parks and Recreation Department at (415) 875-7380.

GRAY WHALE COVE STATE BEACH

The ultimate in seclusion and raw beauty, Gray Whale Cove is actually a series of coves dominated by a half-mile of sheer rugged cliffs. Each sandy cove offers a new vantage point from which to watch the surf pound on the shore. A concessionaire administers the park and, if needed, will provide transportation to and from the beach down a steep dirt service road.

With prior notice, an attendant will meet you at the parking lot on the inland side of Hwy 1, (keep an eye out, it's easy to miss), assist you into a park vehicle, and transport you and your gear to the sand below. At a predetermined time, the attendant will pick you up and take you back to your car. Rides are available from 10:30 a.m. to 5 p.m. in the cold months and 9:30 a.m. to sunset during the summer. To arrange a ride to the beach, call the park at (415) 728-5336. You may leave a message after the recorded weather report and your call will be returned. There are no accessible facilities on the beach.

Gray Whale Cove State Beach

Contact San Mateo Coast District
(415) 726-6238

Folder Available for the San Mateo Coast Beaches
Location—Twelve miles north of Half Moon Bay on Hwy 1

MONTARA STATE BEACH

This two-mile-long sandy beach, 8 miles north of Half Moon Bay, can only be accessed by steep sandy paths. There are no accessible features at Montara. For information contact the San Mateo Coast District Office at (415) 726-6238. A park folder is available that describes all the San Mateo Coast beaches.

POINT MONTARA LIGHT STATION

Built in 1875, the picturesque Point Montara Fog Signal and Light Station became a youth hostel in 1980. Today, up to 45 guests can stay at nominal fees, and there are accessible *SLEEPING*, *RESTROOM*, and *SHOWER ACCOMMODATIONS* for wheelchair users. You should make prior arrangements by calling the hostel in the evening or early morning.

**Point Montara Light Station
AYH-Hostel**
  16th Street/Hwy 1
  Montara, CA 94037
  (415) 728-7177
  San Mateo Coast District
  (415) 726-6238
*Park Folder Available from American
  Youth Hostels, 425 Divisadero #306,
  San Francisco, CA 94117*
*Location—Between Montara and Moss
  Beach on Hwy 1*
Elevation—Sea level

HALF MOON BAY STATE BEACH

Twenty-five miles south of San Francisco, a two-mile crescent is scooped out of the sandy shoreline at Half Moon Bay. Here, folks come to play on the beach. Half Moon Bay State Park consists of four different beaches. Francis Beach, at the foot of Hwy 1 from Kelly Avenue, is the most popular and provides accessible day use and camping accommodations. Surfers like the vigorous wave action, but rangerrs discourage swimming here. A dirt road off Hwy 1 leads to the other three; they have no accessible features.

Day Use

Two large parking areas serve Francis Beach. At the south end of the day use lot, there is a designated *PARKING* place. Nearby are picnic tables and BBQ's that must be accessed down a short grassy incline. From this level coarse sand overlook, you'll have a pleasant view of the beach and surf. A *RESTROOM* nearby has a shallow stall with a high toilet, grab bars, and a high sink. There is also a 54" by 30" *CHANGING STALL* with a bench but no grab bars.

Camping

On a bluff overlooking the ocean, the north parking lot at Francis Beach is the overnight camping area. Some sites on the perimeter of the parking area have a grassy spot for a tent. Others are simply RV parking locations. None are shaded. Sites on the south end of the campground lot have better wheelchair access to the surrounding grassy area. There is a concrete BBQ, table, and food storage box at most perimeter sites. The adjacent *RESTROOM* has a shallow stall, a high toilet, and grab bars.

Beach Access

Between the two lots, a concrete ramp (8%) leads down to the beach level. In the summer months, rangers place a sectioned *REDWOOD DECK* at the end of the ramp for easier access to the sand. It extends 60 feet out onto the beach and ends with a 20-foot square *PICNIC PLATFORM*. This allows you to be much closer to the spray of the waves breaking on shore without having to struggle through the sand.

Half Moon Bay State Park
  95 Kelly Avenue
  Half Moon Bay, CA 94109
  (415) 726-6238
*Folder Available for San Mateo Coast
  State Beaches*
*Location—In the City of Half Moon Bay
  off Hwy 1*
Elevation—Sea level

SAN GREGORIO STATE BEACH

In the summer, the tides shove extra sand onshore forming a lagoon at the mouth of San Gregorio Creek. Shell collecting and exploring are great, but there are no accessible features at this beach. Sand trails lead to the shore from a paved parking lot that has standard chemical toilets. For information, contact the San Mateo Coast District at (415) 726-6238. Ask for the folder describing the San Mateo Coast Beaches.

POMPONIO STATE BEACH

Craggy bluffs and a sandy shoreline at Pomponio State Beach offer an inviting setting for a picnic. Tables and BBQ's stand on a sand and grass surface that lines the paved parking lot. A trail of sand leads to the beach and there is a standard chemical toilet nearby. Pomponio is 12 miles south of Half Moon Bay on Hwy 1, just north of Pescadero. For information contact the San Mateo Coast District, (415) 726-6238. A folder is available that describes the San Mateo Coast Beaches.

PESCADERO STATE BEACH

Pescadero State Beach includes a mile-long sandy beach on one side of Hwy 1; on the opposite side is the 500-acre **Pescadero Marsh Natural Preserve**. While there are plans to provide wheelchair access to the marsh for nature walks and spectacular bird-watching, neither the preserve nor the beach currently has accessible features. From the second of three parking lots is a paved vista point with views of the beach to the west and the marsh to the east. All three parking lots have chemical toilets that are not accessible.

Pescadero State Beach
Contact San Mateo Coast
District Office
(415) 726-6238

Folder Available that describes all the San Mateo Coast Beaches
Location — Fourteen and a half miles south of Half Moon Bay

BEAN HOLLOW STATE BEACH

Stairways are the only way down to the small beach at Bean Hollow. There is one designated _PARKING_ place at the beach overlook. Nearby, an accessible _RESTROOM_ in the parking area has a 7% ramp approach, but may be closed due to water shortages. For information, contact the San Mateo Coast District at (415) 726-6238. A park folder is available that describes the San Mateo Coast beaches.

PIGEON POINT LIGHTHOUSE

Pigeon Point lighthouse, built in 1872, is one of the tallest lighthouses in the United States. On Sundays, you can take a _GUIDED TOURS_ of the lighthouse grounds. Most of the _TOUR_ is accessible and includes a boardwalk path to the tip of the point, where there is a marvelous ocean view. Former Coast Guard family residences have been converted to house up to fifty overnight guests. Some rooms are modified for wheelchair access. You can reserve rooms for couples, individuals, and families. The accessible lodging is in great demand, so advance reservations are recommended. For more information or to make reservations call the hostel in the evening or early morning.

Pigeon Point Lighthouse
AYH-Hostel
Pescadero, CA 94060
(415) 879-0633
San Mateo Coast District Office
(415) 726-6238

Park Folder Available from American Youth Hostels, 425 Divisadero #306, San Francisco, CA 94117
Location — Between Half Moon Bay and Santa Cruz, 5 miles south of Pigeon Point Road
Elevation — Sea level

AÑO NUEVO STATE RESERVE

Año Nuevo Island and the adjacent mainland beaches comprise one of the most important seal and sea lion rookeries in Central and Northern California. Año Nuevo State Reserve is best known as the breeding area of the world's largest mainland population of Northern Elephant Seals. These magnificent creatures can reach 16 feet in length and weigh as much as three tons.

Año Nuevo is an extremely fascinating place to visit any season of the year. During the summer, elephant seals lie on the beach as they molt, saving precious energy to grow a new coat. Females and juveniles visit in April and May, "teenage" males in June and July, and the awesome adult males hang around in July and August. Winter is mating season for the elephant seals, so, during this time, human visitors are restricted to the daily guided tours. Whatever time of year you arrive, you'll hear the echoing barks of hundreds of seals and sea lions drift across the water from Año Nuevo Island.

A set of binoculars and a camera are essential on this trip. Occasionally you'll spot a northern fur seal or a sea otter among the

Bull elephant seals at Año Nuevo State Reserve   *(Photo courtesy CDPR)*

throngs of Stellar sea lions, harbor seals, and California seal lions on the island lounging near the abandoned lighthouse. In the winter, California Gray whales, on their way to calf in the warmer Baja California waters, pass close by.

Accessible Boardwalk

Park visitors have the rare privilege of sharing the beach with these imposing mammals. Anyone planning to visit the beach must first get a permit at the kiosk. From the parking lot, there is a 1½ mile walk to the seal observation area. Much of the hike is through very deep soft sand. Visitors using

wheelchairs and those with other mobility limitations can use a boardwalk. It leads from the end of a park service dirt road to a beach overlook. Park docents have a van with a wheelchair lift and will transport you from the parking lot to the head of the boardwalk. From there you travel through the indigenous grassy dunes to a marvelous spot from which to watch the activities on the beach. At certain times of the year, a trip to the end of the boardwalk will bring you face-to-face with a huge bull elephant seal lying along the path. Your naturalist tour guide will be able to point out wildlife and explain

natural phenomena so you won't miss anything.

It is important to call before your visit to Año Nuevo so a park docent will be available to transport you to the boardwalk. You will meet the van in the parking lot beyond the entrance station. An accessible *CHEMICAL* *TOILET* is located at both this parking area and at the head of the boardwalk.

An outing among these unusual creatures may take a little extra planning, but the opportunity to get up close and personal with a full-grown elephant seal or a mom and her pup is well worth the effort. YOU WON'T WANT TO MISS THIS TRIP.

135

Año Nuevo State Park   *(Photo courtesy CDPR)*

Visitor Center

In the late 1800's, dairy ranching was popular in the coastal region of California. One of the old barns that used to be part of the Steele Ranch, now houses the park visitor center. Rough dirt and grass surround the barn. There is an accessible *TELEPHONE* located on the outside of the building near the entrance. A steep board ramp leads to interpretive displays of local wildlife. In the small gift shop, you'll find books and pamphlets about the park's sea lions and information describing other facilities in outlying areas. From picnic tables arranged in front of the visitor center on grass and dirt you'll have a direct view of Año Nuevo Island across the channel, so bring your binoculars.

Gazos Creek Coastal Access

— Off-highway parking and a chemical toilet are provided at the bluff access to Gazos Creek 1½ miles north of the reserve entrance. There are no accessible features at this location.

Año Nuevo State Park

Contact San Mateo County Coast District Office
(415) 879-0595
Park Folder Available
Location — Nineteen miles north of Santa Cruz on Hwy 1
Elevation — Sea level

> ### Santa Cruz Mountains

BUTANO STATE PARK

Butano State Park is secluded on a wooded rise three miles inland above shrub-covered coastal hills. Hiking trails and fire roads wind eastward through the park in a heavily forested area of the Santa Cruz Mountains. While there are no particular accessible trails or other features, you may find the campground enjoyable for an overnight stay. An accessible *TELEPHONE* is available at the park entrance.

Ben Ries Campground loop at the end of the park road offers campsites with plenty of privacy.

Hidden in the redwoods, 20 roomy campsites have a level asphalt pull-in with a table, fire ring, and food storage on the shaded forest floor. There are only a few level sites, but each is very private. Forty walk-in sites have varying degrees of accessibility; most are not desirable. An accessible *RESTROOM* has a sloping asphalt parking place in front and is central to the campsites. Its shallow stall has grab bars and a high toilet.

Butano State Park

PO Box 9
Pescadero, CA 94060
(415) 879-0173
Park Folder Available
Location — Seven miles south of Pescadero, 3 miles east of Hwy 1 on Cloverdale Road
Elevation — 500 feet

PORTOLA STATE PARK

Between two rugged ridges in the northern Santa Cruz Mountains, deep in a canyon, the natural stream basin of Portola State Park invites travelers to "get away from it all." Mixed evergreens, new- and old-growth redwoods, shade Pescadero and Peters Creeks, while oaks and shrubs tolerate the elements in the exposed hillsides. Because this area is within an hour of Redwood City, Palo Alto, or San Jose, Portola, city-dwellers come to revel in the beautiful forests and peaceful streams of the park. Adding to the seclusion, the park road from Highway 35 is very narrow, winding, and rough.

Though the general ambience of the park is inviting, few of its features are accessible. If you have someone to help, you will enjoy picnicking among the trees at Madrone picnic area or camping in the seclusion of the dense forest near Peters Creek. Paved roads connect park features, but there are no accessible trails. There is an accessible _RESTROOM_ in the campground, but you should read the description in the camping section before you use it.

Day Use

You can obtain maps and brochures, view natural history displays, and gather park information at the visitor center. A park ranger or interpreter is usually on duty to help you. The interior of the lodge building is accessible, but there is a 2-inch lip at the doorway. The telephone outside is too high to reach from a seated position.

An asphalt road takes you around the side of the visitor center to a restroom that is not accessible. It then leads downhill to the **Sequoia Nature Trail**, described in the park folder. The trail is rocky and narrow in spots and crosses the creek in two places; it is recommended only for the sure-footed.

Picnic

As you enter the park, before you reach park headquarters, you'll see three picnic areas along the road. Of the three, **Madrone Picnic Area** is the most level. Here, tables with BBQ's seek the shade of a mixed forest of Douglas fir and madrone in a pleasant natural setting. The parking area is encircled by logs. However, if you go to the back section, there are gaps in the logs that are wide enough to allow wheelchair passage. Unfortunately, the restroom in this area is not retrofitted for access.

Camping

Camping is very private and quiet in the thick forest and huckleberry undergrowth of Portola. Campsites are arranged in small clearings between the trees. They have paved pull-ins and a forest floor camping area that includes a table and BBQ. None of the campsites are designated. Campsite #53 may be your best choice even though it has no access modifications because it is near the accessible restroom. A _MODIFIED_ _TABLE_ is available, but you need to arrange ahead of time to have it placed at your campsite. Campsites can be very spongy when wet, so if this is a problem for you, be sure to check ahead with the ranger for campsite conditions.

Though the _RESTROOM_ and _SHOWERS_ near campsite #53 are fully accessible, to get there, you must climb a very steep (16%) concrete approach ramp for a distance of 15 feet from the parking spot below. You'll need an electric chair or assistance up this brief incline. The other restroom and shower in the campground are not modified for access.

Rangers offer campfire programs regularly in the summer months. A dirt footpath leads from the campground road near the group camping area to the amphitheater. There is no parking near there, so plan to travel about ¼ mile or more. The park is open year round. You should make your weekend and summer camping reservations well in advance.

Portola State Park
  Star Route 2
  La Honda, CA 94020
  (415) 948-9098
Park Folder Available
Location—Six miles off Highway 35 (Skyline Drive) on Alpine/State Park Road
Elevation—450 feet

CASTLE ROCK STATE PARK

Castle Rock State Park is a semi-wilderness escape, not far from city stress. Perched on the western ridge of the Santa Cruz Mountains that separates the San Francisco and Monterey Bays, the park is a blend of wild, natural redwood and fir forests, open meadows, and unusual rock formations. This varied backcountry can only be experienced on "foot" or horseback.

Several trails depart from the main parking lot 2½ miles south of Hwy 9 on Hwy 35. One _TRAIL_, marked by a universal access symbol, has been graded and widened for wheelchair use. With slopes no greater than 4%, the four-foot wide gravel-coated path wanders a short distance (225 feet) into the seclusion of the woods. There, a shady modified _PICNIC_ _TABLE_ invites you to stay awhile. There are no restrooms nor water at the trailhead. Due to a gravel-covered uneven approach, access to the trail from designated _PARKING_ can be challenging.

Castle Rock State Park
  15000 Skyline Boulevard
  Los Gatos, CA 95030
  (408) 867-2952
Park Folder Available
Location—Two and a half miles west of SH 9 on SH 35
Elevation—3,215 feet

BIG BASIN REDWOODS STATE PARK

Virgin redwood forests and mixed evergreens blanket much of the Big Basin area 23 miles northeast of Santa Cruz. The trees here have been preserved through the initial efforts of Save-the-Redwoods-League. In the early 1900's, our dwindling redwood forests needed human advocacy if they were to be saved from the saw blade. Through hard work and strong convictions, California's first state park, California Redwood Park was created in 1901. Success at saving this park soon ignited concern over other diminishing red-wood forests. Consequently, more old-growth areas were added to state park lands. Later renamed Big Basin Redwoods State Park, the acreage has expanded to include the chaparral-covered hills to the west, forming a corridor all the way to the ocean at Waddell Beach.

Because of its location, Big Basin Redwoods is a very popular destination for outdoor-lovers from the San Francisco Bay area. Hikers, picnickers, and mountain bikers come for the day to enjoy a needed relief from "civilization," or to camp in the beautiful forest greenery. Miles of hike and bike trails meander through the tree.

Five different campgrounds have something to offer most enthusiasts, including a variety of features for wheelchair users. A camp store and snack bar provide just enough convenience to balance your experience with nature.

Park Headquarters and the main visitor's area are situated in the northeast section of the 16,000-acre park, the only inland portion with paved roads. Rangers are on hand at park headquarters to help you with your needs. You'll be able to arrange for tent camping, pick up the passkey for the _UNISEX_ _RESTROOM_ at Bloom Creek Campground, or obtain other information or pamphlets.

A hike among the redwoods at Big Basin is a treat for everyone.

(Green Pastures, Inc. ©)

Although it is very tempting, please don't feed wild animals.   *(Green Pastures, Inc. ©)*

There is designated *PARKING* on the street near headquarters and across the street by the snack bar and gift shop. Parking along the street can be a bit difficult, especially during the busy summer season. There is one designated *PARKING* place and a 9% ramp to the doorway. A rough asphalt walkway leads behind the building to an accessible *RESTROOM* with a shallow stall, low toilet, and grab bars. An accessible *TELEPHONE* is available at the front of the building.

The *SNACK BAR* and *CAMP STORE* are only open during the summer season. A wooden ramp leads from the parking area to the snack bar entrance (1-inch door sill). The camp store is in the same building. There is a 2-inch transition to that portion of the store. Several tables and benches are available outdoors in the shade, or you can enjoy your meal at a designated *PICNIC AREA* down the road.

Close by, a *NATURE LODGE* offers displays of geological and natural history of the Big Basin and can be accessed by a ramp to the doorway. The park *AMPHITHEATER* is nearby at the end of a flat decomposed granite pathway.

Picnic

Along North Escape Road, north of the snack bar area, picnic tables are scattered at the roadside and on the banks of Opal Creek. Among them is a designated *SITE*; pavement covers the parking area, the path, and under the accessible *PICNIC TABLE*. In addition, there is also an accessible *CHEMICAL TOILET* here.

The kids in the family, both young and old, will be delighted to share their day with the tame deer that walk right up to the tables looking for a hand-out. But please don't feed the wild animals! It is not healthy for them to eat human food.

Beach

A small portion of the park rolls down brush-covered hills to Waddell Beach. While popular with the windsurfing crowd, it is not accessible for wheelchair users.

Trails

The Redwood Trail, a broad, well-maintained, and heavily traveled *SELF-GUIDED NATURE TRAIL*, winds through the redwoods near the park headquarters. Most of the rolling trail tread is comprised of decomposed granite. Some spots are as steep as 10% for up to 75 feet. A trail guide describing the native plant life and historic significance of the forest is available at the park headquarters. The restroom near the trail is not retrofitted for access.

Camping

Bloom Creek — South of park headquarters, hidden in the moist undergrowth of the forest, Bloom Creek Campground, lies dwarfed among massive redwood stands. From the main park road, pavement rolls through the campground and to each pull-in. Designated *SITE* #137 is the only campsite near an accessible *RESTROOM* and *SHOWER*. Concrete covers the surfaces under the parking, table, around the fire ring, and leads to the *RESTROOM*. You may have difficulty with this site because the short parking area slopes abruptly away from the campsite. Several other sites in the vicinity are more level, but only the parking areas are paved. Parking is available near the accessible *UNISEX RESTROOM* and *SHOWER*. The door is normally locked, so you'll need to pick up a passkey from the ranger at park headquarters.

Sempervirens — Off Big Basin Highway at Sempervirens Campground, a narrow asphalt road winds among the *sequoia sempervirens* and mixed evergreen communities. Most of the level sites have a dirt pull-in, table, fire ring and food storage on an uneven forest floor surface. The restrooms here are not retrofitted for access.

Huckleberry — For a comfortable camping experience, you may wish rent a *TENT CABIN*. Just before entering the Huckleberry campground, a concessionaire-run tent cabin loop offers accessible solid-floor cabins nicely spaced among stately redwoods. Each hard-sided tent cabin has two platform double beds, a table, and a wood stove. In addition, there is space to pitch a tent outside near a picnic table and fire ring. If you need to, you can rent a lantern or bed linens. Two cabins (#19 and #40) have a ramp to the doorway from a packed dirt pull-in. Inside, there is just enough room to roll by the beds to the small sitting area beyond. *RESTROOMS* are no more than 75 yards away on an asphalt road and have a pivot-transfer stall with a high toilet and grab bars. For information or a tent camping brochure call (408) 338-4745.

Wastahi and **Jay Trail** — Because both campgrounds are walk-in type, they are not accessible for most wheelchair users.

Big Basin Redwoods State Park

21600 Big Basin Way
Boulder Creek, CA 95006
(408) 338-6132
Park Folder Available
Location — Nine miles northwest of the town of Boulder Creek on Hwy 236
Elevation — 0-1,400 feet

HENRY COWELL REDWOODS STATE PARK

Henry Cowell Redwoods State Park was once part of a huge estate owned by the wealthy Cowell family. It is a tribute to the beauty of majestic redwoods and the pioneer spirit of early California

Trace the centuries on the log segment at Redwood Loop Trail.

(Photo courtesy Ione Larson)

settlers. Just after miners and loggers built a rail system inland, the area became a favorite tourist destination for city folks from nearby Santa Cruz. Today, the park continues to draw visitors who come to enjoy the "great outdoors" among its forests, meadows, and hillsides.

There are two entrances into the park. The main entrance on Hwy 9 south of Felton leads to the picnic area, educational center, nature center, and the popular *REDWOOD LOOP TRAIL*. This is also the location of park and district headquarters. The campground

and additional trailheads are on the opposite side of the park off Graham Hill Road.

Day Use and Picnic

A large paved parking lot services the popular day use area. An asphalt walkway leads from designated *PARKING* spaces to *RESTROOMS*, an educational center, and the picnic area. Tables and BBQ's, shaded by indigenous sycamores and box elders, rest on a hard-packed dirt surface. The *RESTROOMS* nearby have shallow stalls, low toilets, and grab bars.

The **Nature Center** is at the end of the asphalt walk 450 feet from the designated *PARKING*. Redwood ecology, geology, and Indian history are only a few of the topics discussed in the exhibits here. Park volunteers are on hand to answer questions or direct you to brochures or books that you may purchase.

The **Redwood Loop Trail** begins here as well. Pick up a trail brochure and follow the broad, firm path of decomposed granite and forest dirt through a gorgeous stand of coast redwoods. You'll find benches at regular intervals along the 0.8 mile walk, inviting you to linger as long as you wish. At the half-way point is a *RESTROOM* with no barriers but no special fixturization.

Camping

An asphalt road loops through oaks and madrones at the gently rolling campground at Graham Hill. The campground entrance is 3 miles east of the town of Felton on Graham Hill Road. The sites have dirt pull-ins, a table, fire ring and food storage. *RESTROOMS* are high sinks. There is a slight slope down the concrete approach to the restroom near #30. Parking is provided at the restroom near #109. The showers near #23 and #109 have no barriers at the entry and no seat in the stall. The doorways are a slim 28 inches, and the controls are 45 inches from the floor.

Henry Cowell Redwoods State Park

101 North Big Trees Park Road
Felton, CA 95018
(408) 335-4598

Park Folder Available
Location — Five miles north of Santa Cruz on Hwy 9
Elevation — 500 feet

The Redwood Loop Trail at Henry Cowell Redwoods SP   *(Photo courtesy Ione Larson)*

THE FOREST OF NISENE MARKS STATE PARK

Ten thousand acres of previously logged redwood forests are preserved as mostly undeveloped parkland at The Forest of Nisene Marks State Park. Many trails and mountain bike paths explore the park's scenic interior, but there are no facilities for wheelchair users. According to the wishes of the Marks family who donated the land to the state in 1963, most of the park will remain undeveloped. Secluded picnic areas at the roadside are charming, but not accessible; each has a pit toilet and no potable water.

The Forest of Nisene Marks State Park

Contact Santa Cruz Mountains District Office
(408) 335-9145

Park Folder Available
Location — Four miles north of Aptos on Aptos Creek Road
Elevation — 800 feet

central to each of four loops. The designated CAMPSITE #23 is level, has a modified table, and is near an accessible RESTROOM. Site #30 is also level and may be convenient since it is also near an accessible RESTROOM. Campsite #109 is on the same level as an accessible RESTROOM with an asphalt approach to the doorway. You'll probably want to drive through and look at the sites before deciding where to set up camp. Parking is provided near the gently sloping dirt path that leads to the AMPHITHEATER and near the accessible TELEPHONE at the entry kiosk.

RESTROOMS near sites #23, #30, and #109 all have accessible features. All three have shallow stalls with high toilets, grab bars, and

---

Monterey Bay Area

WILDER RANCH STATE HISTORIC PARK

From the 1850's, D.D. Wilder supplied the Santa Cruz Mission with produce from his 4,000-acre ranch. Later, his son and family built the business into a most innovative and successful dairy ranch. Many original ranch buildings and family homes remain today. They are preserved and restored as a testament to the hard work and ingenuity of the Wilder family. If your interest lies in photography, this is the place for you. The decorative, historic architecture and lovely gardens are the perfect setting for some creative photos.

A gated road leads to the cultural preserve. With a handicap-indentification placard, you may request special access to the ranch exhibits. The attendant at the entry kiosk will direct you through the gate. Be sure to ask for a self-guided walking tour folder. It is a very descriptive guide to the buildings and history of the ranch, and since you may not be able to get into some structures, the guide will add interest to your visit. Before you enter the ranch, an accessible _RESTROOM_ and _DRINKING FOUNTAIN_ are provided in the main parking area not far from two designated _PARKING_ places.

Much of the grounds around the main ranch buildings have been left in their original state. Some buildings have asphalt access at the entrances, but rough dirt surrounds most of them or there are steps at the doorway. The 1897 Victorian home of Melvin Wilder

and a water-driven _MACHINE SHOP_ out back have recently been renovated, and are accessible by wheelchair users with some help. Mr. Wilder was very proud of his innovative ranch and took full advantage of "modern technology." Among other devices, you'll get to see the belt-driven Pelton Water Wheel that supplied electricity to the ranch four years before electrical service was available in nearby Santa Cruz.

Wilder Ranch SHP   *(Photo courtesy CDPR)*

On weekends, docents dressed in period attire enhance the atmosphere of this picturesque ranch. When available, a docent will be happy to take you on a personal tour of the Victorian Wilder home. A _WHEELCHAIR LIFT_ will carry you to the main floor where much of the turn-of-the-century decor is preserved and showcases Melvin Wilder's modern electrical touches. Demonstrations and special tours inside the Wilder home can be arranged by calling ahead to the Monterey Bay Natural-Historical Association (408) 426-0505.

Wilder Ranch State Historic Park
1401 Coast Road
Santa Cruz, CA 95060
(408) 423-9703
Pajaro District Office
(408) 688-3241

*Self-Guided Walking Tour Folder
   Available
Location—Two miles north of Santa
   Cruz, west of Hwy 1
Elevation—25 feet*

NATURAL BRIDGES STATE BEACH

Natural Bridges State Park is named for unusual wave-torn rock formations in the water just off the bluffs. Not only does it have a lovely beach, but is also a wintering area for migratory Monarch butterflies. Beginning in September, thousands of them flutter into the eucalyptus grove at the park. They reside there until February, when they return to their homes in Canada and the northern states. The sight is beyond description.

Wheelchair users will appreciate the accessible facilities at the park During butterfly season, you can visit the Monarchs on a _BOARDWALK_ through the trees. The newly refurbished _VISITOR CENTER_ is readily accessible as is a beach _RESTROOM_.

Boardwalk

Every park visitor has an opportunity to experience this phenomenon of nature. A _BOARDWALK_ leads ¼ mile into the midst of the trees where there is a viewing platform with benches. Chances are, you'll want to linger awhile here as the fluttering silence envelopes you. The park is particularly crowded on Monarch Day, celebrated the second weekend of October. With a reservation, the park docents offer an accessible _GUIDED_ _TOUR_ of the monarch area in the fall. The trail is open year-round, but during times of drought, the rangers close it to protect unsuspecting visitors from dangerous falling limbs.

Visitor Center

Now that the visitor center has its new access ramp, everyone may now enjoy learning a bit more about the butterfly migration and the coastal geology of the Santa Cruz area. _PARKING_ for the boardwalk and visitor center is at the upper end of the park road. There are two designated _PARKING_ places near the visitor center, across the road from the trailhead. Picnic tables on the nearby lawn are scattered among eucalyptus and pine trees. There are curb cuts at regular intervals around the parking lot. At the opposite end of the upper parking lot, an asphalt walk-

way leads 200 feet to the beach below. The path has a very steep (20%) segment at its end.

Beach Access

For the best beach access, park near the accessible _RESTROOM_ on the beach level half way in on the park road. From the paved designated _PARKING_ there is access to the restroom (shallow stall, low toilet with grab bars) and direct access to the sand just beyond. But, you'll have to cross another 500 feet of deep sand to get to the shoreline.

Natural Bridges State Beach

2531 West Cliff Drive
Santa Cruz, CA 95060
(408) 423-4609

Location — North side of Santa Cruz
Take Swift Avenue west from Hwy 1
or follow West Cliff Drive until it ends
at the park.
Elevation — Sea level

SANTA CRUZ MISSION STATE HISTORIC PARK

The Neary-Rodriguez Adobe, built in 1791, has been restored to showcase the fine craftsmanship of the California mission era. It also commemorates the days when religion was the crux of Western society and the lives that revolved around the Santa Cruz Mission. The roof has been newly thatched, lashed with leather strips, and tiled. Aged walls have been restored; public access ways are being developed. At the east end of the adobe, a portion of the original walls is not restored, but maintained in a state of arrested decay, showing just how intricate yet sturdy they are.

Through the Mission years, the adobe has housed the original native Americans who helped build the Santa Cruz Mission, the Mexican workers who later maintained

The notable landmark of Natural Bridges SB.   _(Photo courtesy CDPR)_

the grounds, and early American settlers who lived in the area during the Americanization of California. The rooms along the adobe's central hallway are decorated in a style exemplary of each time, offering you a historical perspective on the varied populations of Santa Cruz. In addition, one room contains a few of the archaeological finds of the region that date long before the advent of the mission.

A concrete VERANDA runs the length of the building inside the park gate and the doorways are at least 27 inches wide. Paved PARKING is is planned for the east end of the adobe with paved entries to an accessible RESTROOM building and the adobe. The interior hallway is wide enough for a wheelchair, but there are sharp turns required from the entrance that may preclude some visitors with larger wheelchairs. The parks department plans to have this historic building open to the public in late 1991. It is advisable to call the park for current access information.

Santa Cruz Mission State Historic Park

Contact Pajaro District Office
(408) 688-3241

Location — In downtown Santa Cruz. Take Mission Road to Emmet Road at the Mission Plaza, then take School Road to the end.
Elevation — 100 feet

LIGHTHOUSE FIELD STATE BEACH

A picnic and a stroll along the beach cliffs are activities often enjoyed at Lighthouse Field State

Beach. Local residents favor this rugged shoreline for surfing as well. They share a piece of the water known, as "Steamer Lane," with an active sea lion population. From a paved WALKWAY along the cliffs, you'll have a bird's eye view of the action in the surf below. You probably will spot sea lions on the rocks nearby as surfers ride the waves. A surfing museum occupies the original lighthouse at Santa Cruz Point, but is not accessible.

There is designated PARKING near the lighthouse or in a lot across the street near the picnic area and accessible RESTROOM. The RESTROOM offers a small approachable sink and a large stall with grab bars and a high toilet. An accessible TELEPHONE and DRINKING FOUNTAIN are available nearby. Picnic tables on a dirt surface dot the field near the parking lot, or you may want to take your snack out to a bench at the point overlooking the water.

Lighthouse Field State Beach

Contact City of Santa Cruz
(408) 429-3777

Location — On Westcliff Drive at Santa Cruz Point
Elevation — Sea level

TWIN LAKES STATE BEACH

Twin Lakes State Beach is a popular sandy beach for swimming and picnicking but there are no accessible accommodations. Multiple barriers impede a wheelchair user from reaching the shoreline. Only highly coveted street parking is provided on either side of the Santa Cruz small craft harbor.

Twin Lakes State Beach

Contact Pajaro District Office
(408) 688-3241

Location — On either side of the small craft harbor in Santa Cruz along East Cliff Drive
Elevation — Sea level

NEW BRIGHTON STATE BEACH

Perched on the wooded bluff overlooking northern Monterey Bay, New Brighton State Beach is a consistently popular park for day use and camping. Visitors enjoy the lovely setting, mild weather and camping accommodations. In the summer, the park is very heavily used. It is a good idea to make reservations early if you are planning a stay.

New Brighton State Beach has no camping or day use facilities specifically designed for wheelchair users, except two retrofitted RESTROOMS. Wheelchair users visiting this park will need help navigating the slippery beach access and difficult camping surfaces. Unless you plan on staying around your campsite, this park is best for the more adventuresome wheelchair user.

Beach

An asphalt service road leads 1,500 feet from the day use parking down to the sandy beach. The first 900 feet of the road are steep (10%), and the last 600 feet are level but usually covered with sand, making the surface very slippery. From the end of the road near the restroom, the shoreline is another 75 feet through deep sand. The *RESTROOM* at the beach has a 28-inch doorway, shallow stall with grab bars and a low toilet.

Camping

Both camping loops at New Brighton wind through a stand of tall pine trees. Sparse vegetation between campsites offers minimum privacy. Most sites are flat and have a table, fire ring, and food storage, all on the pine needle-covered dirt. If you're lucky, you may get a site with an ocean view.

Though there are no designated campsites, the first camping loop has an accessible *RESTROOM* with a shower. An asphalt path leads to the restroom building where the shallow stall has grab bars and a low toilet. The small *SHOWER* has a 30-inch doorway, grab bars, and a small seat in the corner. The control knob is 45 inches from the floor, and the shower head is high.

The main *PICNIC AREA* and *CAMPFIRE CENTER* are located in the camping section. Tables and stone BBQ's on the forest floor can be reached from nearby parking. At the campfire center, rangers give regularly scheduled talks on the natural history of the park. Most of the area is level, but the dirt surfaces are uneven. Loose dirt can create traction difficulties in some spots.

New Brighton State Beach

1500 Park Avenue and Hwy 1
Capitola, CA 95010
(408) 475-4850

Location—Four miles south of Santa Cruz in the town of Capitola, Park Avenue exit from Hwy 1
Elevation—Sea level

SEACLIFF STATE BEACH

The small town of Aptos is home to a unique fishing pier on the stretch of sand known as Seacliff State Beach. As with all the sandy beaches in the Monterey Bay area, Seacliff is a very busy place. During the summer months, temperatures are mild and the water inviting. In addition, the promise of a good catch and fair weather draws fishermen to a unique *PIER* at the park.

Wheelchair users can access most park features. A shaded *PICNIC AREA* with a great beach view is reserved near a beach access ramp and day use *PARKING* and *RESTROOMS* are accessible. There is also accessible facilities at the *RV CAMPGROUND*. Plan ahead and arrive early or make camping reservations well in advance to avoid disappointment at this popular destination.

Pier

Not only is pier fishing fun at Seacliff, this pier is quite unusual. It is actually a concrete-hulled supply ship built during World War I. As fate would have it, she never served, but instead was towed to this location and became an amusement center in 1929. It now rests on the sandy bay bottom. Over the years heavy storms have taken their toll, but her top deck can still support a throng of fishermen. Fishing along the Monterey Bay yields perch, kingfish, sole, flounder, halibut, lingcod, cabazon, salmon, steelhead, and an occasional rockfish. A wooden plank ramp leads to the 650-foot pier where the maximum slope is 6% in places. Even if you don't wish to fish, a stroll on the pier can be fun.

Day Use

Four *PARKING* places are designated along the road at the foot of the pier. For fishermen, a *BAIT AND TACKLE SHOP* is just across the street. Its outdoor service window is a high 46 inches. Next to the bait shop, a *SNACK BAR* offers outdoor service or an indoor eating area accessed by a ramp with a 1-inch lip at the doorway. A paved walkway leads to a nearby accessible *DRINKING FOUNTAIN* and *RESTROOM*. Its shallow stall has a 27-inch doorway and grab bars. A large-size changing stall has no privacy door and is directly in line with the open entry door.

Visitor Center

At the **Seacliff Visitor Center**, words and pictures interpret the story of the concrete ship, *Palo Alto,* and the natural history of the area. Designated *PARKING* places are provided near a ramp that leads to the doorway of the building. There are no restrooms here.

Beach Access

Along the beach road, two ramps allow access to the sandy beach from paved designated *PARKING*. You'll find a paved ramp at the northernmost day use parking lot. A second ramp at the southernmost end of the picnic area, is near the designated *PICNIC SITE*. From there, a paved path parallels the beach along a short bluff from one end of the park to the other. At other beach access points along the path, there are stairs at regular intervals. There are no accessible restrooms in the northern day use area.

Picnic

You'll have a great beach and shoreline view from the picnic area south of the pier. As you drive south on the park road, shade ramadas with picnic tables and BBQ's on packed dirt line the beach. Parking is on the dirt alongside the road. On the opposite side of the tables, a paved path runs the distance of the picnic area. There is direct access to the beach by way of a dirt and sand ramp at the southernmost end of the picnic area. Nearby is a designated *PARKING* place and table. All restrooms south of the pier have at least a 4-inch step at the entrance. The only accessible restrooms in the park are opposite the pier and at the northernmost end of the camping area.

Camping

RVer's enjoy the ocean views from their campsites set just above the beach at Seacliff. Curbing surrounds each of 100 developed sites that has a picnic table, electric and water hook-ups. An accessible *UNISEX RESTROOM* and *SHOWER* are available at the northernmost restroom building. There is designated *PARKING* and a curb cut out front. The 35" by 43" shower room has a bench seat and the lever control is 44 inches from the floor. Camping is limited to RV's only.

Seacliff State Beach

Hwy 1 and State Park Drive
Aptos, CA 95003
(408) 688-3222
Location — Off Highway 1 on State Park Drive in the town of Aptos, 5½ miles south of Santa Cruz
Elevation — Sea level

MANRESA STATE BEACH

Another of the lovely sand beaches on Monterey Bay is Manresa State Beach. From a parking lot at the bluff, you have a splendid view of the rolling waves on the bay as they curl toward Monterey to the south and Santa Cruz to the north. Four designated *PARKING* places are provided near the fully accessible *RESTROOM*. Another is located near a packed dirt ramp that leads to picnic tables on the bluff. A concrete ramp (15%) with handrails at 43" leads down to the deep sand beach. From the bottom of the 200-foot ramp, the shoreline is another 200 feet away.

Manresa State Beach

c/o Sunset State Beach
201 Sunset Beach Road
Watsonville, CA 95076
(408) 724-1266
Location — Thirteen miles south of Santa Cruz off Hwy 1 on San Andreas Road
Elevation — Sea level

SUNSET STATE BEACH

Tall sand dunes provide a wind barrier for the pine-covered campgrounds at this windswept beach on Monterey Bay. As with the other sandy beaches of the area, mild climate and scenic beauty make Sunset State Beach a year-round destination for picnickers and campers alike.

Except at the group camping facility, the park is not wheelchair-friendly. Access to the beach is difficult and not recommended for those without assistance.

Day Use

Parking for beach access is provided in one of two places. At the entry kiosk, day users may park on a bluff and follow a paved maintenance road down (15%) to the beach level 450 feet away. At the southern beach access *PARKING* area, one designated place is near a restroom that has no access modifications. Another is next to a steep boardwalk that climbs over the top of a large sand dune. Drifting sand is not frequently removed from the walkway. From either location, the shoreline is at least 300 feet away. A *TELEPHONE* at the entry kiosk is accessible, but the restroom nearby has a 27-inch doorway and no converted stalls.

Camping

Three family campgrounds share 90 campsites at Sunset Beach. Most pine-studded sites have a table, food storage, and a fire ring on a forest floor surface. An abundance of pine needle debris makes the going rather slippery for a wheelchair user. The *GROUP CAMP*, on the other hand, is accessible for wheelchair users. There is pavement from designated *PARKING* to many tables and to an accessible *CHEMICAL TOILET*. Group campsites are reserved for larger parties. You must arrange to use this and other group sites by calling MISTIX (800) 444-7275.

South Camp — There is plenty of shade at South Camp. An asphalt road and paved parking pull-ins make wandering easy through this level campground, but the restroom has no access modifications. Each site has a table and a fire ring.

Pine Hollow—Campsites at Pine Hollow have dirt pull-ins that are level and firmly packed. An asphalt road runs through this campground and slightly inclines to a restroom near sites #38 through #41. There are no grab bars in the stall, but the toilet is high. The adjacent shower is very small, has no seat and the controls are 46 inches from the floor. Parking is provided nearby. You'll find the park _AMPHITHEATER_ up a 12% asphalt walkway, 75 feet from the road.

Dunes—An asphalt road undulates through Dunes campground. Campsites here are more private than at Pine Hollow. Unfortunately, curbing surrounds the restroom and the stalls are not retrofitted for access.

Sunset State Beach

201 Sunset Beach Road
Watsonville, CA 95076
(408) 724-1266

Location—Sixteen miles south of Santa Cruz via Hwy 1. Take Hwy 129 west, left on Beach Road, then right on San Andreas Road to Sunset Beach Road and follow the signs.
Elevation—Sea level

MOSS LANDING STATE BEACH

Protected from onshore winds by the dunes of Moss Landing State Beach, the calm waters of Elkhorn Slough open into the picturesque harbor at Moss Landing. Picnickers and bird-watchers enjoy the peaceful environment here. Meanwhile, the windward side of the dunes is Monterey Bay's most popular surfing beach. The tireless wave action on the west-facing shoreline also attracts surf fishermen. In October of 1989, the Santa Cruz earthquake destroyed the road to the park. As of this publication date, a new access road has yet to be constructed.

Moss Landing State Beach

Contact Monterey District Office
(408) 649-2836

Location—Off Hwy 1 on Jetty Road West between Santa Cruz and Monterey
Elevation—Sea level

ZMUDOWSKI STATE BEACH and SALINAS RIVER STATE BEACH

Both Zmudowski and Salinas River State Beaches are quiet, out-of-the-way spots favored by surf fishermen and beach-goers who seek an escape from the madding crowd. Just north of Moss Landing, Zmudowski occupies a spot of land surrounded by farms. The northern beach perimeter of the park is a preserve offering refuge for nesting snowy plovers.

Salinas River State Beach is just south of Moss Landing at the end of either Portero Road or Madera Road. Both parks have dirt parking lots with chemical toilets. Access to the beach is by way of a steep ladder-like boardwalk over a bank of dunes.

Zmudowski State Beach
Salinas River State Beach

Contact Monterey District Office
(408) 649-2836

Location—Just north of Moss Landing
Elevation—Sea level

MARINA STATE BEACH

Gentle shoreline bluffs and just the right onshore winds from Monterey Bay provide hang gliders with a perfect "jumping off place" at Marina State Beach. Perhaps the most scenic place to watch the colorful wings leave the beach is from an accessible _BOARDWALK_ that meanders through the sand dunes on the edge of the bay.

A hang gliding concessionaire offers lessons or rentals and sells snacks and gifts in his accessible trailer _HEADQUARTERS_. An accessible _RESTROOM_ and _TELEPHONE_ aren't far from a designated _PARKING_ space in a small paved lot near the beach.

A portion of the dunes vegetation is protected from human footsteps by a _BOARDWALK_. It takes you on a stroll through the preserve beginning near the hang gliding office. With its steepest slope at 10%, the first 1/3 mile of the boardwalk is level, and there are benches along the way. After this, the remaining 1/4 mile of the boardwalk becomes more steep and undulating. At the 1/3 mile point, you'll be able to pull off the main walkway at a lookout. This is a great place to relax and enjoy the excellent view south to Monterey and north to the beaches forming a crescent to Santa Cruz.

Across from the hang gliding office, a ramp approach leads to a fully accessible _RESTROOM_. Thick sand that drifts across the ramp may create an obstacle at times. Access to the beach can only be accomplished through a break in the fence where there is a steep drop-off into the sand. From there the shoreline with its sometimes treacherous waves is about 150 feet away.

Marina State Beach

Contact Monterey District Office
(408) 384-7695

Location — Ten miles north of Monterey, off Hwy 1 on Marina exit
Elevation — Sea level

MONTEREY STATE BEACH

The calm flat beach north of Fisherman's Wharf in Monterey is a favorite place for evening beach walks and kayak launches. Unfortunately, there is no designated approach to Monterey State Beach from the road. Access points at the end of Del Monte Avenue, Aquajito, or Sand Dunes Road are merely curbed roadside parking with steep drop-offs to the beach. There is no other parking provided specifically for beach access.

Monterey State Beach

Contact Monterey District Office
(408) 649-2836

Location — On the waterfront in Monterey from Seaside to Fisherman's Wharf
Elevation — Sea level

MONTEREY STATE HISTORIC PARK

The town of Monterey served as capitol of California from 1775 to 1850, while under Spanish, Mexican, and early U.S. rule. Many historic homes and businesses of that era are open for public visitation. A self-guided town tour begins at the **Custom House** in the Plaza at the foot of Fisherman's Wharf. The buildings in this complex were the hub of government and a thriving trade business of the time. The Custom House, California State Historic Landmark No. 1, is the oldest governmental building on the west coast.

Custom House Plaza

The best parking near the Plaza is in the lot at Fisherman's Wharf in one of several designated *PARKING* places. Directly across the street, you'll find an accessible *RESTROOM* with a low toilet and standard sink with push fixtures. An accessible *TELEPHONE* and *DRINKING FOUNTAIN* are located outside the building. Several hundred feet beyond is the main historic section of the Plaza. The Monterey State Park district office is located here. You can get information about the park and a self-guided tour map at the office. A few doors away is the entrance to the main level of Custom House. You will need help over the 6-inch step at the doorway. After that, the main floor is explorable.

Because of their historic nature, most of the buildings included in the tour are not accessible for wheelchair users. They have narrow doorways and multiple steps between rooms. In addition, the roads in town are quite narrow and always busy. Crossing the street unassisted is challenging, and all parking is curbside.

Cooper Molera Adobe

John Rogers Cooper was a noted sea captain, dealer in hides and tallow, and a respected member of the Monterey community. In about 1823, he built a Victorian house, Spanish-style adobe, a store, barns, and a warehouse for his growing family and trade business. The Cooper-Molera Adobe stands on the corner where Polk and Munras meet to become Alvarado, three blocks from Custom House Plaza. It is the only historic structure with accessible features and a

Monterey State Beach   *(Photo courtesy CDPR)*

148

The Plaza at San Juan Bautista SHP

(Photo courtesy CDPR)

fully accessible *RESTROOM*. There is no designated street parking and the only curb cuts are at the corners, so getting out of the car on these narrow roads can be hazardous. You enter the adobe through the warehouse, which is now a *GIFT SHOP* and docent center. From there you will enter the gardens and then the lower floors of the Cooper Home. The Victorian house is cluttered with period furnishings, while the Diaz house contains a simple Spanish motif. Some passageways are a bit narrow for larger wheelchairs. The barn out back houses a carriage display.

Monterey State Historic Park

525 Polk Street
Monterey, CA 93940
(408) 649-7118

Location—Within a 20-square-block area at the foot of Fisherman's Wharf in Monterey
Elevation—Sea level

San Juan Bautista Area

SAN JUAN BAUTISTA STATE HISTORIC PARK

Besides serving as a military and commercial center during California's territorial days, San Juan Bautista was also an important religious center. Among the other thoughtfully preserved and restored historic buildings at the original town plaza is Mission San Juan Bautista. Founded in 1797, it is now a parish church where mass is still celebrated. A mixture of Mexican adobe and American Period structures, most of the homes and businesses that face into the plaza are accessible with assistance. While asphalt paving encircles the Plaza, access to the exhibits on its perimeter is mostly by way of level hard-packed decomposed granite. There are

ramps at several doorways and two *RESTROOMS* are accessible.

Museum

The Plaza Hotel houses the park museum. A 1-inch door sill at the entrance and worn door sills between rooms are the only barriers in the interior of the hotel. You'll feel as though you've stepped back in time to the days of stage coaches and bustles as each carefully decorated room recreates the flavor of the past. All of the exhibits are visible from a seated position. A ramp leads to a movie room where volunteers show a short film about the town's history.

Breen Adobe

The Breen family, survivors of the infamous Donner Party tragedy, purchased the Mexican adobe from Jose Castro just after the United States claimed California as its territory. Displayed in each

149

room is evidence of the day-to-day lifestyle and living arrangements of this 1870's family. A two-inch lip leads to the lower level of the Breen Adobe.

Livery Stable

Wood plank ramps at both front and rear entrances take you through big barn doors into the livery stable. Inside is an excellent display of horse and buggy equipment. In a shed to the rear of the livery, a complete blacksmith shop is also on display. As with most of the unpaved areas of the park, the hard-packed dirt surface around the stable is level and even.

Plaza Hall

For a look at the lifestyles of a later period, stroll by the Plaza Hall near the livery stable. You can peek through the boarding house windows for a view of a late-1800's parlor. Ramp access at the rear of the building (east side) leads to a 2-inch step up to the viewing area on the veranda.

Mission

Since 1797, **Mission San Juan Bautista** has endured as the religious heart of civilization in the region. You may visit the gardens and ante rooms of this holy place anytime; the chapel is open when services are not being held. The mission's heavy adobe construction required large door sills and room transitions. Some sills are ramped, but the visitor entrance is through the gift shop. It has its very narrow aisles and a 2-inch lip at the door. Displays in the ante rooms are protected behind glass. Since the windows are a minimum of 37 inches from the floor, visibility is

difficult for some. Most wheelchair users will need help to navigate the rough dirt transitions to the central gardens and small cemetery on the side of the mission.

Picnic

Across the road from the Plaza Hotel is a small groomed picnic garden. A curb cut leads from street parking to this quiant shady corner, where there are a few tables and firm dirt paths.

Restrooms

Restrooms are located in three places: behind the livery stable, southeast of the Plaza Hotel near the jail, and in the courtyard of the mission. The livery stable *RESTROOM* approach has a rough transition to a concrete slab. The roomy lateral-transfer stall has grab bars and a high toilet. A brick path leads to the *RESTROOM*, jail, and accessible *DRINKING FOUNTAIN* surrounded by packed decomposed granite. The stall here is a wide, pivot-transfer type with grab bars and a low toilet. The men's restroom at the mission is not modified for accessibility. The women's side has a lateral-transfer stall with grab bars and no other accessible features. Both restrooms are small, requiring tight turns for access.

**San Juan Bautista
State Historic Park**
PO Box 1110
San Juan Bautista, CA 95045
(408) 623-4881
Location—In the city of San Juan Bautista on State Route 156, seven miles west of Hollister
Elevation—210 feet

FREMONT PEAK STATE PARK

When John C. Fremont raised the American flag atop the tallest peak in the area, he did so knowing that United States territorial rule would soon replace the Mexican government. Almost 150 years later, the land around the 3,169-foot mountain top is now a state park that bears his name. A pine and oak woodland provide a home for birds and other wildlife in this 244-acre primitive refuge. In the spring and summer, park staff give tours of an astronomical *OBSERVATORY* located near the summit.

After traveling up the very winding park road you'll soon realize that most of the terrain in the main park activity area is very hilly and unpaved. Only two pit toilets are provided; approaches to both are on a hillside. Tables in the campground and the picnic area are situated in an oak forest on the rolling landscape. The trail to Fremont Peak, though wide and hard-packed, is understandably steep. There are no other accessible trails on the mountain.

Observatory

Between April and October, Fremont Peak State Park offers informative programs at its *OBSERVATORY* during the 1/3 and first quarter moon phases. The wheelchair accessible building houses a 30-inch reflector telescope and a number of photographic displays of the stellar studies. After a slide presentation, you'll have an opportunity to look through the eyepiece of the telescope and spot a se-

Families enjoy riding at Hollister Hills SVRA.   *(Photo courtesy CDPR)*

lected constellation. For those who cannot climb a short ladder to the eyepiece, high-powered binoculars can be trained on an image to be viewed from a seated position. You can make arrangements to visit the observatory by calling the park office.

To reach the observatory, take the cut-off 0.3 mile in from the park entrance. With a handicap-identification placard, you may park next to the building. Two hundred feet uphill, along gravel-covered dirt, a wooden ramp leads through the observatory threshold; there are no barriers inside. An accessible *RESTROOM* is down the hill from the observatory.

Fremont Peak State Park
    Contact Gavilan District Office
    (408) 623-4255
Location — Eleven miles south of San Juan Bautista on San Juan Canyon Road
Elevation — 2,750 feet

HOLLISTER HILLS STATE VEHICULAR RECREATION AREA

In the days of the Wells Fargo wagon delivery, Hollister Hills was a family ranch producing hay for the express teams. Later it became a world renowned walnut ranch. In the 1940's, the Bird Creek Hunting Club began using off-road vehicles to patrol for trespass violators. Subsequently, there began a series of hill-climbs and off-road races. By 1970 the ranch was open to public off-road vehicle riding. Today its 3,322 acres offer an assortment of off-road experiences for riders and drivers of all skill levels and vehicle types.

Eighty miles of trails and hill climbs wind and weave among the brush and oak-studded fields at the lower ranch. This 2,400-acre area is limited tor motorcycle and ATV use only. Besides the trails, there are special tracks for motocross, ATV's, TT bikes, and mini-bikes. If you wish to go four-

wheeling in the 800-acre Upper Ranch area, there are 60 miles of trails to explore. It is best to make arrangements for this day trip in advance at the park office. In the interest of safety, there must be two vehicles in your party to use the Upper Ranch.

Of the four campgrounds and two picnic areas in the Lower Ranch, Walnut Camp provides accessible *RESTROOMS* with hot and cold *SHOWERS*. The *RESTROOMS* at the picnic area near the park office are also accessible. The *CAMP STORE*, midway on the park's main dirt road, can be accessed on surrounding hard-packed dirt, and there are no doorway barriers. The telephone outside the camp store is too high to reach from a seated position.

Lodge, Bee, Madrone, and **Walnut Camps** all have similar campsite facilities. Mostly hidden in the oak-shaded hollows and valleys between hills, each packed dirt site has a table and fire ring. A new, fully accessible *RESTROOM/ SHOWER* complex was recently installed at Walnut Camp. Presently, it can only be reached across a heavily gravel-coated surface. The restroom has a lateral-transfer stall with grab bars; the hot shower has low controls and an interior seat. In addition, an outdoor cold shower is available with a low push-button control. All campsites are first-come-first-served and there are no designated sites.

Not far from the entry gate, ramadas shade the picnic area near the motorcylce wash. Tables and the approach to an accessible *RESTROOM* nearby are on hard-packed dir. The restroom stalls have grab bars and a pivot transfer to a low toilet.

Hollister Hills
   State Vehicular Recreation Area
   7800 Cienega Road
   Hollister, CA 95023
   (408) 637-3874

Park Folder Available
Location — Six miles south of Hollister
*   on Cienega Road*
Elevation — 800-2,900 feet

PINNACLES
NATIONAL MONUMENT

Twenty-three million years ago, in south central California, volcanic activity seeping through the rift between the Pacific and North American plates created a steep mountain of lava. No sooner had it formed than the plates began to shift, splitting and tearing at the mountain's sheer formations along the infamous San Andreas Fault. Today, millions of years later, a large portion of the lava mountains rest 195 miles north of their original location at Pinnacles National Monument. As the Pacific Plate continues on its inch-by-inch journey northward, it is one of the most famous active geological wonders in North America.

Rugged crags and spires jut skyward in the middle of smooth rolling hills. Appropriately named, Pinnacles, the land around this modern day phenomenon was dedicated as a National Monument in 1908. There are two locations from which to see the pinnacle formations and visit the park. You can reach the main facilities and the park's day use area from the east entrance. In the southern shadow of the pinnacles, you'll be able to watch a sysmometer in action at the VISITOR CENTER and enjoy an accessible shady PICNIC at Chalone Picnic Area. The western en-

trance to the park offers a unique prospective of the park landscape. Here you'll find a picturesque CAMPGROUND and various trailheads leading up into the mountains. In the summer, daytime temperatures climb into the 90's. Many visitors prefer to visit when the wildflowers bloom in the milder spring weather.

Visitor Center

A curb cut and an asphalt approach from a designated PARKING place lead to the small visitor center. Inside, you'll find a large three-dimensional layout of the park mounted on the wall, book sales, and a sysmometer that measures the current activity of the San Andreas Fault in this area. A ranger is on duty to answer your questions.

Across from the visitor center, a gentle asphalt ramp leads from a designated PARKING place to an accessible DRINKING FOUNTAIN and RESTROOM. The diagonal-transfer stall has a low toilet and grab bars. Though there are a few modified picnic tables at the visitor center area, they may not be placed in appropriate locations for wheelchair users.

Picnic

At **Chalone Picnic Area,** all the oak-shaded tables have extended ends. BBQ's are also provided. During a busy day of exploring, this cool spot could be just the place youneed for a bit of relief from the sun. A PARKING lot surrounds the flat picnic area and there is one designated place near an accessible RESTROOM with a ½-inch door sill, an accessible sink, and a stall with pivot transfer, grab bars, and a high toilet.

Camping

Chaparral and small conifers dot the hillsides while rugged Pinnacles dominate the southern landscape at **Chaparral Campground**. From this exceptional setting you can watch the shadows and colors change and move throughout the day. Shaded only by the early shadows of the pinnacles, each simple campsite has a modified table and a BBQ, and sits on the perimeter of an asphalt parking lot. Near campsite #6, there is a designated PARKING place and a rough asphalt walkway that leads to an accessible RESTROOM. A small ranger station at the campground entrance has an accessible TELEPHONE, a few exhibits, and book sales. (FCFS)

Trails

Though wheelchair riders have attempted to hike many of the park trails, at one time or another, none are accessible. They are wide and well-traveled, but can be rocky, sandy or off-camber and are sometimes very steep (more than 20%). There are no flat trails; many cross stream beds or narrow bridges. If it's a challenge you're looking for, your best bet is to check with a ranger, who may be able to direct you to a suitable hike.

Pinnacles National Monument
   Paicines, CA 95043
   (408) 389-4485
Park Folder Available
Location — East Entrance: 32 miles
*   south of Hollister on Hwy 25 then 5*
*   miles west on Hwy 46. West*
*   Entrance: From Soledad off U.S.*
*   Hwy 101, 11 miles east on Hwy 146.*
*   Much of the road is narrow and*
*   winding, so trailers and wide RV's*
*   are not recommended.*
Elevation — 1,000-1,400 feet

The contorted rocks and crags of Pinnacles National Monument   *(Photo courtesy NPS)*

Carmel and Big Sur Coast

ASILOMAR STATE BEACH & CONFERENCE GROUNDS

Beach

At the tip of the Monterey Peninsula, Asilomar State Beach lies just north of the famous Pebble Beach golf course. One half-mile of *BOARDWALK* wanders amid rolling dunes that separate the beach from Asilomar Conference Grounds. Established in 1913 as a YWCA summer retreat, the conference grounds are now operated by the Pacific Grove-Asilomar Operating Corporation. Nestled among pine trees on a gentle hillside,

groups or individuals can reserve the retreat facilities for meetings, recreation, dining and sleeping accommodations.

From street parking at the beach, a *BOARDWALK* leads 150 feet out to an *OBSERVATION DECK* 50 feet from the waterline. From there, steps descend onto the sand. Across the street, a *BOARDWALK* with a handrail at 39 inches leads 450 feet up to the conference center and takes a side trip through the dune environment. There are benches at regular intervals along the ½-mile loop; inclines are no more than 7%. Access to the boardwalk on either side of the street is often coated with a thick layer of drifted sand. There is a 1-1/2-inch transition onto it.

Conference Grounds

The conference grounds are modified to include accessible *RESTROOMS* in designated *GUEST ROOMS* with high toilets, and grab bars in the tub and toilet areas. Doorways at *MEETING ROOMS* and the *RECREATION HALL* are ramped; there are accessible *RESTROOMS* at each. Some paved walkways through the grounds are steep and may require help.

Asilomar State Beach

Contact Monterey District Office
(408) 372-4076

Conference Grounds

800 Asilomar Boulevard
Pacific Grove, CA 93950
(408) 372-8016

Location—One mile south of Monterey off Hwy 1 on Hwy 68
Elevation—Sea level

153

CARMEL RIVER STATE BEACH

Before the Carmel River empties into the ocean it forms a lagoon where ocean birds congregate. Though a pleasant place for a beach walk and bird watching, the only access to the shoreline is by a narrow dirt path. Restrooms with flush toilets at the beach are not accessible.

Carmel River State Beach

Contact Monterey District Office
(408) 649-2836

Location — Two miles south of Carmel on Hwy 1
Elevation — Sea level

POINT LOBOS STATE RESERVE

Wildlife on land and sea abounds at the 550-acre Point Lobos State Reserve. One hundred years ago, this was a busy whaling and fishing port. The point housed hundreds of fishing and cannery personnel who made their living from the sea at Whaler's Cove. Now, with civilization gone, sea otters, seals and sea lions have returned to reclaim the rugged, rocky coastline. A full compliment of furry and feathered critters again inhabiting the inland forests and meadows. California Gray whales are a common sight from the shore especially in winter as they migrate south to give birth. Many trails crisscross the reserve, but none are accessible.

To maintain the unspoiled beauty of the reserve, rangers closely monitor the number of park guests that pass through the gates. In the busy summer months this may cause a delay at the entry gate, but has the advantage of assuring enough space for everyone to enjoy their visit. The reserve is open from 9 a.m. to 5 p.m. daily, with extended hours in the summer.

Information Station

Park volunteers staff a portable information station near the parking lot at **Sea Lion Point.** They are well versed on the natural and human history of Point Lobos Reserve. Sometimes the docents will set up a telescope for viewing offshore marine life. If you are unable to reach the edges of the bluffs overlooking the water the telescopes are a great way to enjoy the activities there. Pamphlets, books, and postcards are available for sale at the information station. Two designated *PARKING* places are provided, but the chemical toilet nearby is not accessible.

Picnic

The park map lists three restrooms as accessible — Whaler's Cove, the information station, and Piney Woods. **Whaler's Cove** is the preferred *RESTROOM* as it has a paved approach from parking. In addition, there are shady picnic tables for a pleasant picnic near the underwater reserve.

Situated among a stand of Monterey pines, **Piney Woods** is the most shady place on the reserve for a picnic. Most of the tables stand on a sloping knoll. A dirt path leads to a 2-inch lip at the door of the restroom that has a shallow stall, grab bars, and pivot transfer to a low toilet.

Trails

Sea Lion Point Trail — Popular for its proximity to parking and the great views of wildlife on the rocky coastline, Sea Lion Point Trail is probably the most traveled of the reserve's many paths. Departing from the information station, the trail starts out wide and sandy. It becomes increasingly soft and steep (up to 13%) 650 feet from the start. From its highest point, you can watch sea lions and seals play or sun bathe on the rocks near the shoreline below. Beyond here, steps descend to the remaining portion of the trail.

Stairs or narrow passageways create barriers for wheelchair users and soft sandy spots are common on most of the trails in the reserve. For an ocean view, you will need assistance to manage the beginning of some trails.

Point Lobos State Reserve

Contact Monterey District Office
(408) 624-4909

Park Folder Available
Location — Three miles south of Carmel on Hwy 1
Elevation — Sea level

GARRAPATA STATE PARK

A four-mile stretch of beach and many miles of rigorous trails in the Big Sur area are the main features of Garrapata State Park's largely undeveloped 2,879 acres. From turn-outs on Hwy 1 you'll have a great view of the sea otter refuge offshore, so bring your binoculars. Access to the beach is steep and difficult.

Garrapata State Park

Contact Big Sur District Office
(408) 667-2315

Location — Ten miles south of Carmel on Hwy 1
Elevation — 50 feet

POINT SUR STATE HISTORIC PARK

Established in 1889 by the U.S. Coast Guard, the Point Sur Lighthouse and fog station is in operation today. For over 100 years it has steadfastly signaled passing ships, preventing mishaps on the rocky shores of the Big Sur coast. Four lighthouse keepers and their families lived a secluded life out on the point until automation eliminated their jobs in 1975.

On Sundays, docents give tours of the grounds around the lighthouse, workshops, and turn-of-the-century homes where the families lived and worked. Group size is limited and based on reservation. Since access roads to the lighthouse are treacherously narrow and steep, you must be transported there by a park van that has no wheelchair lift. If you have a means to get into the van, you'll find that the paved lighthouse grounds are accessible. If you call ahead and discuss your needs, the docents will arrange special access to the lighthouse. To arrange a visit to the lighthouse, call the information number and ask to speak with the tour director. She will be happy to accommodate you in any way possible.

Point Sur State Historic Park
   Contact Big Sur District Office
   (408) 667-2315

Location — Fifteen miles south of Carmel on Hwy 1
Elevation — 300 feet

ANDREW MOLERA STATE PARK

The 4,800 acres of Andrew Molera State Park were donated to the Nature Conservancy with the condition that they not be developed. As such, only trails, fire roads, and a primitive campground disturb the natural landscape that spans from the ocean, across Big Sur River, to the inland forested mountains.

Two trails are not strenuous and offer wonderful views of the ocean and experiences with the abundant wildlife at the park. **Bobcat Trail** follows the river along its course dividing the park, and **Bluffs Trail** gives you plenty of time to enjoy the ocean breezes as you overlook the beach. Sorry, neither trail is recommended for wheelchair users.

The campground, a large primitive trail camp, is very popular and well-known among cyclists of the coastal highways. It is located along a path about 1/3 mile from the dirt access road. There is an accessible *PIT TOILET*. A firm, smooth path to the campground for wheelchair users, is planned for completion some time in 1993. Call the park office for information on its progress.

Andrew Molera State Park
   Contact Big Sur District Office
   (408) 667-2315

Park Folder Available
Location — Twenty-two miles south of Carmel on Hwy 1
Elevation — 60 feet

PFEIFFER BIG SUR STATE PARK

Ask Californians to name a park in the redwoods they love to visit and you'll likely hear "Big Sur." Just about midway between the Mexico and Oregon borders, Pfeiffer Big Sur draws visitors year round from north and south to its scenic coastline location.

The park has something to make everyone's outdoor experience memorable. Many hiking trails thread through lush redwoods, mixed conifers, and oak forests where streams and a waterfall add to the enjoyment. For day use, there is a large group picnic area and playing field as well as an accessible family *PICNIC AREA* with a *RESTROOM* nearby. An extensive campground offers accessible *CAMPSITES* and restrooms and even has its own laundromat and *CAMP STORE*. For those that don't care to "rough it," the Big Sur Lodge offers cabins for rent. An accessible *RESTAURANT* and *GIFT SHOP* will help keep you fed and occupied for a while.

Visitor Center

South of the main park entrance on Hwy 1, the California State Parks and Recreation Department, the U.S. Forest Service, and Cal-Trans are combining in a joint effort to establish a Big Sur visitor center and information station. According to plans, the building will be totally accessible and also will house the district offices of each department. Look for completion by 1992.

Kids enjoy a dip in the Big Sur River at Pfeiffer Big Sur SP.

(Photo courtesy CDPR)

---

the doorway. The staff is very helpful and willing to help in making your stay comfortable. For further information contact Big Sur Lodge, PO Box 190, Big Sur, CA 93920, (408) 667-2171.

Camping

Two hundred eighteen campsites are spread between two camping areas along the Big Sur River. Shaded by huge redwoods and other evergreens, the campground is well-used, and as such, there is little under-growth for privacy between sites. Asphalt roads service each paved pull-in and run through the entire campground. The flat, shady sites have a table and a fire ring on a packed dirt surface. Three campsites are designated, totally paved, and available for reservation through MISTIX (#6, #120 and #188). Each is conveniently located near an accessible *UNISEX RESTROOM, SHOWER,* and *DRINKING FOUNTAIN* reached by continuous pavement. There are no barriers to the *LAUNDROMAT, CAMP STORE,* and *TELEPHONE.*

Pfeiffer Big Sur State Park
Big Sur, CA 93920
(408) 667-2315
Park Folder Available
Location—Twenty-six miles south of Big Sur on Highway 1
Elevation—215 feet

Picnic and Campfire Center

There are plans to make the bridge between the accessible *CAMPSITE* #6 and the *CAMPFIRE CENTER* usable for wheelchairs. Until then, you can get to the campfire center from the day use side of the Big Sur River. A lighted concrete path leads from two designated *PARKING* places 200 feet to the *CAMPFIRE CENTER,* where there is a platform at the top for your chair. The same path leads another 80 feet to an oak-shaded picnic site with a modified *PICNIC TABLE* where you'll have a view of the river. If you and your family are picnickers or you'd like to try to catch a glimpse of an autumn steelhead trout swimming upstream, this is the place for you. An accessible *RESTROOM* at the parking area is retrofitted to include a lateral-transfer stall with grab bars and a high toilet.

Gift Shop and Restaurant

If the great outdoors makes you hungry and you aren't planning a magnificent cookout at your camp-site, a *RESTAURANT* awaits just inside the park gates. A designated *PARKING* place is provided near an asphalt ramp where there is an accessible *TELEPHONE.* Both the restaurant and an accompanying *GIFT SHOP* are accessible and have a fully accessible *RESTROOM.*

Trails

Presently, none of the trails in the park are accessible to wheelchair users, but there are plans to widen and smooth the self-guided nature trail across from the picnic area. The threat of poison oak along the narrow trail is enough to keep bare legs or arms away from the area for now.

Lodging

Lodge cabins complete with swimming pool line a meadow north of the main park entrance where you may reserve a self-contained unit for any number of days. There are no cabins with access modifications; each has one step through

JULIA PFEIFFER BURNS STATE PARK

The rocky coastline of Julia Pfeiffer Burns State Park is most recognized for its 50-foot waterfall that drops straight down into the ocean at McWay Canyon. The only way to see the falls is by taking the Waterfall Trail under Hwy 1 to the falls overlook. There are plans to eliminate the stairway to the gently sloping trail, but for now, wheelchair users cannot access the falls trail. Located in the canyon etched by McWay Creek, most of the terrain in the day use area other than the parking lot is steep. Access to the restroom, telephone and picnic areas is at least a 15% slope. Though this park is exceptionally picturesque, it doesn't offer much access for a visitor with limited mobility.

Julia Pfeiffer Burns State Park

Contact Big Sur District Office
(408) 667-2315

Park Folder Available
Location — Twelve miles south of Pfeiffer
  Big Sur State Park on Hwy 1
Elevation — 400 feet

San Luis Obispo County

HEARST SAN SIMEON STATE HISTORICAL MONUMENT

William Randolph Hearst named it "La Cuesta Encantada." The "Enchanted Hill" is set like a huge diamond against the Santa Lucia Mountains on a coastal knoll overlooking a broad expanse of rolling grassland and ocean. One hundred twenty-seven acres of intricate gardens, dramatic pools, and three magnificent guest houses surround the 125-foot-high Hispano-Moresque mansion, La Casa Grande.

This overwhelming structure with its accompanying service buildings took 30 years to design and build and still remains incomplete. The mansion housed Mr. Hearst's collection of prized European antiques and art pieces, many of which are still in place. His library is filled with hundreds of volumes of assorted titles and subjects. As a leading publisher and newspaper tycoon, William Randolph Hearst had the opportunity to entertain a multitude of influential guests from all walks of life. He often invited them to stay at his place. Given his opulent life style and his authoritative presence as a media mogul, it is no wonder that this home on his 250,000-acre ranch became known as Hearst Castle.

The park offers four different guided tours of the mansion at least once an hour from 8:20 a.m. to 3 p.m. daily. There are expanded hours in the summer and on weekends and holidays. The park closes on Thanksgiving, Christmas, and New Year's Day. You may make regular reservations through MISTIX no sooner than eight weeks in advance. Reservations are especially important to have in the summer months when park visitation is at its peak. You may call the National Toll-Free number (800) 444-7275 to make reservations for the regular tours. *TOURS FOR WHEELCHAIR USERS CANNOT BE MADE THROUGH MISTIX. CALL (805) 927-2020. FOR SPECIAL TOUR INFORMATION AND RESERVATIONS.*

Wheelchair Accessible Tour

For those who use wheelchairs or simply cannot climb the multiple stairs encountered on a regular tour, the park staff gives a special tour at least three times a day throughout the year.

Aerial view of Hearst Castle

(Photo courtesy Hearst Monument/
John Blades ©)

If walking any distance is a problem for you, a wheelchair is available on request. In either case, you must provide an assistant that can maneuver the chair up and down long inclines and narrow ramps. You should make reservations directly with the Castle at least ten days before your visit. This way, you'll be sure to be included at the time of your choice.

The special access tour is most like Tour 1 in the park brochure. It is modified to avoid stairs, but you'll be able to enjoy most of Tour 1 along with the regular tour group. The special group gets a personal tour of Casa Del Mar, Mr. Hearst's ocean view guest house, and the lovely gardens nearby. After an exclusive entry through massive castle doors, the groups then merge and stay together for the remainder of the tour inside the Hearst home. All tours cycle simultaneously, so it is also possible for other members of your party to take a different tour while you and your assistant are on Tour 1.

The park staff strongly encourages disabled visitors to explore and enjoy the grounds. They go to great lengths to provide each individual with a fulfilling visit. Every special tour guide is sensitized to the needs of wheelchair users and arranges the tour setting so that you can see as much as possible. When you are with the main group, they see to it that the wheelchair users are in the front nearer the speaker. On the personal portion of the tour, you'll be directed to locations along the way with the best views from a low perspective.

Arrive at least twenty minutes before your appointed tour time, stop

at the ranger kiosk at the north end of the visitor center. If you have not already purchased your tickets, the attendant at the booth will take your money inside to the ticket window and purchase them for you. You will receive further instructions from the attendent. You will be given a magnetized passcard to insert in a slot that opens the gates on the roadways. You will be asked to follow the regular tour bus,. As you wind up

A special access tour includes a grand entry through the castle's main doors.
(Photo courtesy Hearst Monument/ John Blades ©)

the five-mile road to the "Castle," you will experience a 1,600-foot elevation gain. Your your interpretive guide will be waiting for you near designated parking where a wheelchair lift will take you to the main castle grounds level. Due to the slow speed of the wheelchair lift, only one wheelchair user in a party of up to six can be accommodated on each special tour. Of course, exceptions can be made in special cases. Discuss your individual needs when you make your reservation. The regular fee is charged for this tour. The total time for the tour is approximately one hour and forty-

five minutes, including the drive to and from the Monument.

Visitor Center

One million visitors a year come to see Hearst Castle. All of them must pass through the modern visitor center complex before riding the bus up the hill. Besides the *INFORMATION DESK* and *TICKET COUNTER, A SNACK BAR, GIFT SHOP, MUSEUM* and excellent *EXHIBIT ROOM* are designed to entertain and inform you while you wait for the next tour. If you will be following the bus on the special wheelchair-accessible tour, it is not necessary to make arrangements for your tickets inside. But, since the only accessible restroom at the park is near the entrance to the visitor center, most folks make a stop here anyway.

In the exhibit building you'll be able to watch while antiques and artifacts from the castle are restored in a climate-controlled conservation room. A broad wall of windows beginning 41 inches from the floor allows unobstructed viewing of most of the displays. Across the hall, the visitor's museum offers a pictorial history of the castle and the legacy of William Randolph Hearst.

Directly in front of the main entrance, there are several prominently marked designated *PARKING* places. A gradual sloping, pebble-embedded walkway leads to the main lobby door or to the *RESTROOMS. RESTROOM* stalls offer lateral transfer, high toilets, and grab bars. All of the doors in the complex are heavy and difficult to open. In the lobby, the counters at the *TICKET BOOTH* and *SNACK BAR* are low, and there is an accessible

TELEPHONE available. Even the _GIFT SHOP_ displays and counters are no higher than 48 inches.

The uniqueness and unequaled grandeur of the Hearst estate coupled with efforts of the staff to provide each visitor with a complete experience, make Hearst San Simeon State Historic Monument an excellent park to visit.

Hearst San Simeon State Historical Monument

750 Hearst Castle Road
San Simeon, CA 93452-9741
(805) 927-2020

Information—**(805) 927-2000**
Reservations for the Physically
Challenged—**(805) 927-2020**

Park Information Available: Park Folder, Hearing Impaired Visitor Packet, Park Guide in Braille
Elevation—0-1,600 feet

WILLIAM RANDOLPH HEARST MEMORIAL STATE BEACH

Protected from rough currents and winds, the secluded little cove at William Randolph Hearst Memorial State Beach is a quaint place to cool off in the afternoon sun. Anglers also enjoy a bit of pier fishing, while picnickers can seek out shade in the small park on shore. Accessibility here is limited, however. On the park's upper level, picnic tables have elevated fire rings, but the whole area is surrounded by curbing, and the nearby restroom is not modified for access. A 6% ramp access leads to a snack bar and tackle shop. If you'd like to fish from the 200-foot pier, they'll sell you a state fishing license. For beach access, drive to the lower level where an uneven hard-packed dirt surface covers the parking and picnic area. Thick beach sand begins here and extends to the shoreline.

Knowledgeable park staff provide wheelchair accessible tours of the Castle.
(Photo courtesy Hearst Monument/ John Blades ©)

William Randolph Hearst Memorial State Beach

Contact San Simeon District Office
(805) 927-2020

Location—Directly across the street from Hearst San Simeon State Historical Monument entrance road on Hwy 1
Elevation—Sea level

SAN SIMEON STATE BEACH

A two-mile stretch of interesting and varied coastline is the focal point of San Simeon State Beach. Most travelers pass right by the road to the beach unaware that the rocky shores are teaming with salt water birds and other wildlife. A stream, a marsh and acres of open meadow beckon those who like to wander, but none of the trails are accessible for wheelchair users. Both campgrounds are accessible, but a beach visit for wheelchair users probably is limited to a view from the day use area parking lots.

Day Use

Near the main park entrance there is a large day use picnic area with an accessible *RESTROOM*. Picnic tables are on a dirt surface, and there is no designated parking. A sandy dirt path with steep inclines runs beneath the highway to the beach which lies on the opposite side. While this may serve as an adequate rest stop, access to the beach from here is not favorable.

Further south on Hwy 1, three other day use areas bring you close to the ocean spray and varied coastline. To reach them, take Moonstone Drive, which fronts the highway. Both **Santa Rosa Creek** and **Vista Point** offer great blufftop views of the beach but have no other facilities. **Leffingwell Landing** also offers spectacular views, a designated *PARKING* spot, and a fully accessible *RESTROOM* (low toilet) and *DRINKING FOUNTAIN*. You can park at the foot of a dirt trail that leads to the restroom. Loose gravel and pine needles make this cross-sloping trail slippery and hard to manage as it climbs at 8% for about 200 feet to the restroom.

Camping

North of San Simeon Creek, five miles south of Hearst Castle, the main park entrance is the gateway to two year-round campgrounds. They serve as the nearest state campgrounds to Hearst San Simeon State Historic Monument. Near the kiosk, you'll also find an accessible *TELEPHONE* and an RV dump station. There is parking and an accessible *TELEPHONE* at the ramp access to the campground *AMPHITHEATER*.

San Simeon Creek — Three designated *CAMPSITES* are available at the broad grassy campground at San Simeon Creek. Smooth paved roads serve the flat lower section. Every site has an asphalt pull-in and very little shade. All three designated sites are near an accessible *RESTROOM*. Site #73 is completely paved under a modified table and fire ring, and there is an accessible *WATER SPIGOT* nearby. The pull-in at site #45 is quite long but the modified table and elevated fire ring are on a grass surface. Site #41 has a wide pull-in and similar features to #45.

The accessible *UNISEX RESTROOM* near site #73 has a concrete approach and an accessible *DRINKING FOUNTAIN*. There are no barriers to the *SHOWER*, which has a seat both inside and outside the stall and a twist control knob 49 inches from the floor.

Washburn — From your vantage point on the bare flattened hilltop at Washburn Campground, you'll have a 360-degree view of the countryside. Waves of grass cover the hillsides and flow through the open meadows to the rocky coastal bluffs. The simple campground is suitable only for RV camping. Most of the surfaces including the road are rough decomposed granite, but two designated *CAMPING SPOTS* have asphalt paving in the parking space, under a modified table and around an elevated fire ring. An asphalt paved path leads to an accessible *CHEMICAL TOILET* at each site. There is an additional overflow *ENROUTE CAMPGROUND* by Washburn. Keep in mind that campers at Washburn may not use the facilities at San Simeon Creek Campground.

San Simeon State Beach

Contact San Simeon District Office
(805) 927-2020
Location — Five miles south of San Simeon on Hwy 1
Elevation — Sea level

CAYUCOS STATE BEACH

A sandy beach and lighted fishing pier are central to the downtown district in the city of Cayucos. A paved sidewalk runs the length of the beach to the pier. Designated *PARKING* is 300 feet away. Typical of most small beach towns, bait shops, snack bars, and rental services line the street across from the pier. While there is no wheelchair access to the beach from the street, the 600-foot *PIER* is accessible.

Night fishing is popular at the pier where anglers pull in mackerel and smelt by the buckets full. Though most of the pier is level, some segments have slopes as steep as 7%, and the railing is 43 inches high. The accessible _RESTROOM_ at the foot of the pier has a shallow stall with grab bars and a low toilet.

Cayucos State Beach

Contact San Luis Obispo County
(805) 549-5200

Park Folder Available for the area
Location—Five miles north of Morro Bay at the foot of Cayucos Drive in the city of Cayucos
Elevation—Sea level

MORRO STRAND STATE BEACH

During the roaring 20's, a developer named E.G. Lewis was attracted to Morro Bay, picturing it as a major tourist spot. He began to build a hotel and sell ocean front lots, but the crash of 1929 brought an end to his development. All that is left of his oceanside dream is a vacant lot at the west end of San Jacinto Street and three miles of sandy beach and windswept dunes that today draws surf fishermen, windsurfers, and beach campers to what is now Morro Strand State Beach.

The beach can be reached at two different locations. A parking lot at the northern section is next to the sand and has no accessible facilities. The southern section, formerly known as Atascadero State Beach, provides an RV campground snuggled beside low-lying dunes. The dunes block the access and view to the beach and shoreline. Curbing surrounds the parking lot-style campsites, leaving no way to access the tables and fire rings. The only ramps over the curbing are at the restrooms, which have no modifications for wheelchair access.

Morro Rock, a notable landmark at Morro Bay SP   *(Photo courtesy CDPR)*

Morro Strand State Beach

c/o Morro Bay State Park
(805) 772-2560

Park Folder Available; Park newspaper, Tidelines *covers the San Luis Obispo District*

Location — North section is two miles south of Cayucos at 24th Street off Hwy 1, south section is off Hwy 1 at Yerba Buena

Elevation — Sea level

MORRO BAY STATE PARK

On the central California coastline located half way between Los Angeles and San Francisco, Morro Bay State Park offers a variety of outdoor recreation opportunities for locals and tourists alike. Hikers will enjoy exploring trails that skirt one of the largest undisturbed saltwater marshlands on the California coast. While playing 18 holes at the Morro Bay State Park Golf Course, golfers have sweeping views of the ocean and the famous Morro Rock that lies at the entrance of Morro Bay. Boating enthusiasts can rent a boat from the small harbor concessionaire at the park marina. Campers relax in the 135-site campground nestled in a pine and eucalyptus forest just across the street. An exercise trail and frisbee golf course are next to the campground, and picnic facilities are available for day users. In addition, the park is quite proud of its Museum of Natural History, which represents the wildlife and Native American history of the region.

Morro Bay State Park is a lovely place to visit. Unfortunately, for a wheelchair user, there is little that is easily accessible at this scenic spot. The campground offers a meager retrofit on one restroom and wheeling surfaces are either very rough roadways or are soft dirt campsites. The *MUSEUM* and an asphalt *VIEWING AREA* are accessible, but the approach to it is steep and needs a few minor modifications for wheelchair users.

Museum

The **Museum of Natural History** is a special attraction at the park. Located on White Point, its observation area overlooks much of the saltwater marsh, marina, and bay. From here there are views of Morro Rock to the northwest and the blue heron rookery natural preserve to the northeast. Many displays of the local wildlife and early heritage are high on the walls of the museum, but there are no barriers and plenty of room to maneuver. Two designated *PARKING* places are marked in a lot 250 feet from the entrance down a 17% access road. Another 150 feet of rough asphalt leads around a rocky outcropping for a fantastic view of the bay and marina. Bring your binoculars; you may be able to catch a glimpse of the pair of rare peregrine falcons that nest near the top of Morro Rock.

Marina

A long narrow sand spit juts across a cove to create a calm bay for an inviting small boat harbor. The concessionaire at Morro Bay State Park Marina will rent you a boat or a slip and runs a small accessible cafe. A small gravel boat launch is available for kayakers and canoeists who wish get a closer look at the bay or the saltwater marsh. Most of the surfaces at the marina are roughly paved, and the restroom is not accessible. For more information, contact the concessionaire by calling the park number.

Campground

You should make reservations early for this popular year-round campground at Morro Bay, especially in the busy summer months. Shaded by pines and eucalyptus, the level dirt campsites offer rock-based concrete tables, stone BBQ's or fire rings, food storage, and dirt pull-ins. You should consider asking for a *TABLE EXTENSION* at the kiosk. The table ends do not extend far enough out to allow wheelchair access. Of the 135 sites, twenty offer paved pull-thrus with electricity and water hook-ups.

The only *RESTROOM* that is modified for access is next to site #129, located directly across from the day use picnic area and campfire center. A rough asphalt approach leads to the building where a wide door and pipe grab bars have been added to an otherwise standard shallow stall.

Other Features

Other features of the park have varying degrees of accessibility. One designated *PARKING* place is provided near an asphalt path to the amphitheater where rangers give campfire programs regularly in the summer season. Picnic tables for families or groups occupy the shade nearby. In a level eucalyptus grove next to the campground is a frisbee golf course (played like progressive horseshoes) and exercise track. Soft dirt and fallen leaves could present an obstacle for this unique pastime. For your convenience, an accessible _TELEPHONE_ is available at the entry kiosk and an RV dump station is provided near the day use area; the approaches to both are dirt.

Morro Bay State Park

State Park Road
Morro Bay, CA 93442
(805) 772-2560

Park Folder Available; also District Newspaper, Tidelines
Location—Morro Bay Boulevard exit from Hwy 1
Elevation—Sea level

The view from Montaña de Oro bluffs is magnificent!   _(Photo courtesy CDPR)_

MONTAÑA DE ORO STATE PARK

The seven-mile shoreline of Montaña de Oro State Park is comprised of rugged cliffs, headlands, and a dune-covered sand spit at Morro Bay to the north. Chaparral dusts the hillsides of this largely undeveloped 8,000-acre park. The landscape, dotted with live oak, is host to variety of animals that compliment the neighboring ocean species. Monterey pines shade a few picnic tables at the park office, and primitive camping is available for the stout-hearted. Of the many trails that meander through the park, you may find the Bluff Trail accessible. Other visitors like to take their four-wheel drive vehicles down to the sand spit for a closer look at the crashing waves and mountainous sand dunes. Beachcombing is excellent in the soft sand but would be difficult for a wheelchair user.

Trails

The **Bluff Trail** is the most level of the park trails as it makes a loop out onto a coastal bluff. You can begin either at the southernmost end of the park road, or about 50 feet beyond a dirt parking area south of the ranger station. This is not a trail for everyone. The first 75 feet are rough and cross-sloped. You'll probably need a strong assistant, a wide brimmed hat, and some water for this 1½-mile trip. There is no shade on the bluff, and some brief segments of the hard-packed dirt trail can be as steep as 15%. On the bluff's edge, your efforts will be rewarded with a special perspective of a tangle of coves and sea caves carved by the violent wave action below. In addition, you'll have a panoramic view as far south as Point Sal and north to Piedras Blancas.

For access to the sand spit separating Morro Bay from the ocean, a four-wheel drive road known as Army or Dune Buggy Road inter-

sects Pecho Valley Road about ½ mile north of the park entrance. There are no facilities at the dunes and access is limited by thick sand on most surfaces.

Camping

Monterey pines offer shade at some primitive campsites at Montaña de Oro. The uneven dirt sites have picnic tables and food storage. The asphalt pavement on the roads and the pull-ins is also rough and uneven. The campground is level, but the only restrooms are large pit toilets with a 2- to 4-inch step at the doorway. Inside, the stall has lateral transfer to a low toilet with grab bars. A 70-foot asphalt footpath takes you from a designated _PARKING_ place to the unpaved sloping campfire center. If you need a place to rest for the night, _ENROUTE CAMPING_ is also available on a dirt lot with no restroom facilities.

The only accessible _RESTROOM_ at the park can be found near the ranger station. A 20-foot paved ramp leads to a pit toilet with grab bars and lateral transfer to a low toilet.

Montaña de Oro State Park

Pecho Valley Road
Los Osos, CA 93402
(805) 528-0513

Park Folder Available; District Newspaper, Tidelines
Location—Seven miles south of Los Osos on Los Osos Valley Road to Pecho Road
Elevation—0-50 feet

LOS OSOS OAKS STATE RESERVE

An impressive grove of 700-year-old coast live oaks is preserved in Los Osos Oaks State Reserve. Based on their age, you would expect to find tall, stately trees. Instead, among the thicket of branches and undergrowth, dwarfed oaks of no more than eight feet evidence the mineral-depleted soil of ancient sand dunes. While development encroaches on the 8½-acre park, it remains in its natural state, serviced by only a small dirt parking lot and a narrow trail wandering through. You will not find wheelchair access here.

Los Osos Oaks State Reserve

c/o Montaña de Oro State Park
(805) 528-0513

Park Folder and District Newspaper Available
Location—Seven miles south of the junction of Los Osos Valley Road and South Bay Boulevard in the town of Los Osos
Elevation—Sea level

PISMO STATE BEACH

Clamming was once the most popular pastime at Pismo Beach State Park, but these days you'll rarely dig up a legal-sized Pismo Clam. Meanwhile, the broad white-sand beach is still a lovely place to spend a day in the sun. With its accessible *PICNIC AREA* and *CAMPGROUND*, the park invites everyone to be a part of the year-round activities at Pismo Beach. In the winter months, thousands of Monarch butterflies migrate to a grove on the perimeter of the park, attracting hundreds of curious tourists and passersby on Hwy 1.

Day Use

At the southern end of the park, the day use lot provides designated *PARKING* near a fully accessible *RESTROOM* and a concrete picnic area with a modified *PICNIC TABLE*. While there are no accommodations for wheelchair users in the nearby restaurant, you'll find an accessible *TELEPHONE* on the south side of the building.

Beyond the restroom, an accessible *BOARDWALK* reaches 150 feet out onto the sandy beach. From there you have a great view of the activities nearby and of Pismo Dunes State Vehicular Recreation Area to the south. Stairs are the only access to the beach from this point. To get to the beach in a chair, you'll need to take the sidewalk behind the restaurant that leads down to the beach. For better beach access, you may prefer to enter through Pismo Dunes State Vehicular Recreation Area right next door.

Monarch Butterfly Tree Trail

As the winter sun begins setting low in the sky, so arrive hundreds of thousands of migrating Monarch butterflies from Canada and the northern states to take up residence in a small eucalyptus grove at North Beach Campground. A seasonal dirt parking lot within the park and a dirt pull-out area on Hwy 1 are situated on either end of a very soft dirt footpath leading through trees that are heavily laden with black and yellow wings.

A shady observation area with benches and hand rails 350 feet from either parking area is a pleasing spot to experience the silent flight of these delicate creatures. Log railing lines the main trail, which can be soft in places and has no more than a 7% slope. From designated *PARKING* on the campground side, a short, steep (15%) section must be crossed before you arrive at the main trail. Access from Hwy 1 is straight and level, but the parking is on the dirt shoulder of the highway.

Camping

North Beach—Most of the campsites at North Beach are level, and all have asphalt parking areas. A set of dunes separates the grassy open campground from the beach and blocks the winds and blowing sand. Each site has a table, food storage, and a fire ring, but none of the restrooms is modified for wheelchair users. The *CAMPFIRE CENTER* can be found on the west end of the campground. From designated *PARKING*, a rough asphalt path with a maximum slope of 12% leads 125 feet to a concrete wheelchair platform. The walkway continues over the dunes to the beach and ends at the sand 250 feet from the shoreline.

Oceano — Two miles south of North Beach Campground, a row of sand dunes protects Oceano Campground from offshore winds. Campsites border a quaint creek-fed lagoon that attracts waterfowl and other wildlife to its banks. A small footpath outlines the water's edge but is too narrow for wheelchair travel. Instead, an accessible *VIEWING PLATFORM* has been built near a designated *PARKING* spot.

The campground offers either RV camping with electric and water hook-ups or multiple use sites. Designated *SITE* #18 in the hook-up area is paved around the table and fire ring, and is near a fully accessible unisex combination *RESTROOM/SHOWER*. This is the only accessible restroom in the campground. You will need a key; ask for it at the kiosk, or check with the campground host. All roadways, pull-ins and pull-thru's are paved for easy access; each site has a table and a fire ring. The multiple use campsites have rock

BBQ's, and there is more shade, but there are no accessible restrooms in this area.

Pismo State Beach

555 Pier Avenue
Oceano, CA 93445
(805) 489-2684

Location — Two miles south of the town of Pismo Beach on Hwy 1
Elevation — Sea level

PISMO DUNES STATE VEHICULAR RECREATION AREA

The Pismo Beach sand dune area has long been recognized to be the finest, most extensive coastal dunes remaining in California. As such, vehicles are prohitted from a portion of the fragile dune environment to the south. For the most part, 3½ miles of beach at Pismo Beach State Vehicular Recreation Area are open for beach and sand dune play to all types of off-road vehicles. In addition, vis-

itors can bring their personal water craft with them and play in the waves.

You can camp on the beach, but there is no campground. Make camping reservations through MISTIX (800) 444-7275. You'll have to bring your own drinking water, and the only accessible restroom is at the entrance gate. Otherwise, chemical toilets are placed at regular intervals along the shore.

Not far from the park entrance, a designated *PARKING* place overlooks the beach. Near the parking place, two ramped curbs will take you to a picnic table on a paved beach overlook. If you bring along a pair of binoculars, you can watch the vehicles whiz around on the dunes to the south.

Not far away, a long, smooth concrete walkway (30 feet of which has a 14% incline) leads from the dirt parking area to the accessible *RESTROOM*. The shallow pivot-transfer stall has a high toilet and a grab bar.

Pismo Dunes State Vehicular Recreation Area

576 Camino Mercado
Arroyo Grande, CA 93420
(805) 473-7220

Park Folder Available
Location — Just south of Pismo State Beach
Elevation — Sea level

There are miles of sand dunes to ride on at Pismo Dunes SVRA.

(Photo courtesy CDPR)

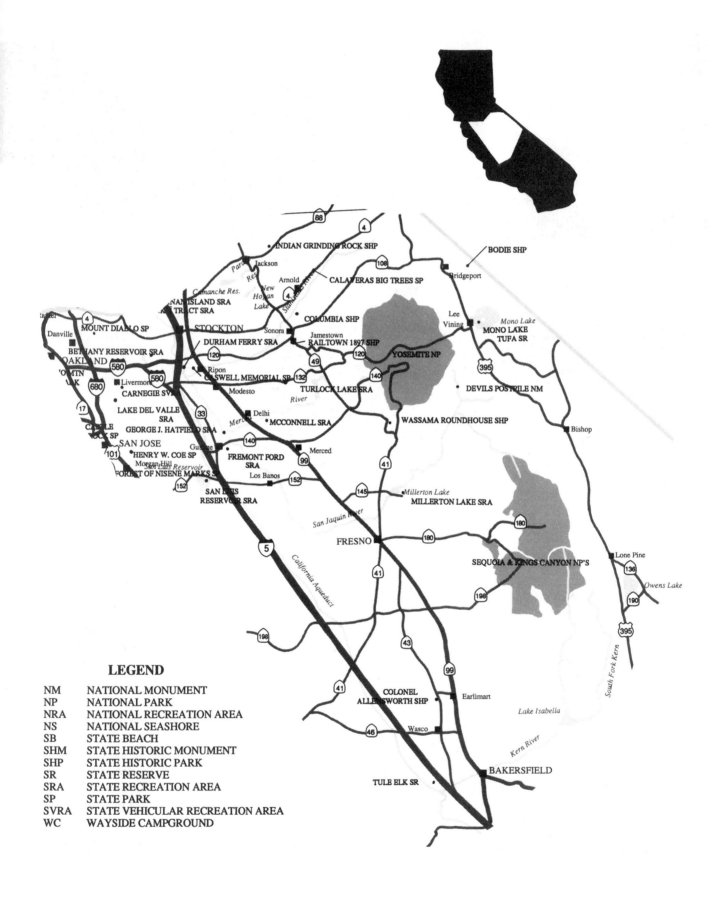

LEGEND

NM   NATIONAL MONUMENT
NP   NATIONAL PARK
NRA   NATIONAL RECREATION AREA
NS   NATIONAL SEASHORE
SB   STATE BEACH
SHM   STATE HISTORIC MONUMENT
SHP   STATE HISTORIC PARK
SR   STATE RESERVE
SRA   STATE RECREATION AREA
SP   STATE PARK
SVRA   STATE VEHICULAR RECREATION AREA
WC   WAYSIDE CAMPGROUND

There was gold in them thar hills at Bodie SHP.

CENTRAL CALIFORNIA INLAND

Eastern Sierra Nevada

DEVIL'S POSTPILE NATIONAL MONUMENT

Hidden in the spectacular mountain scenery of the Sierra Nevadas is one of the world's finest examples of columnar basalt. Standing like a sentry over the Middle Fork of the San Joaquin River, the Devil's Postpile is a geologic phenomenon explainable in the early years by folklore alone. Only the devil himself could have bundled these huge rock posts and stand them on end in such a beautiful valley. Towering sixty feet tall, the effects of time, weather, and earthquake activity have taken their toll, causing many columns to fall and fragment onto the slope below. Visitors to Devil's Postpile National Monument come not only to view the rock, but also to enjoy the marvelous hiking trails that lead through meadows, along streams, and into the mountains.

To ease the impact on this limited area in the summer, most visitors must use the shuttle bus service when it operates during the peak summer season. The bus leaves from the Mammoth Mountain Inn, taking its passengers to various trailheads and features in the valley. If you display a handicap-identification placard, you may drive directly to any part of the valley any time.

It is unfortunate that there are few accessible facilities at the Monument for wheelchair users. Once you arrive at the day use area in the valley, parking and most of the surfaces are dirt. The restrooms in both the day use area and the

167

Devil's Postpile National Monument   *(Photo courtesy CDPR)*

campground offer no accessible stalls. The ranger station has a ramp access that leads to a 1-inch door sill. The telephone nearby is low, but there is a 2-inch transition onto the pavement surrounding it.

Trails

Although the trail from the parking area to Devil's Postpile is short, it is very steep and sandy in places. Just before you arrive at the exhibit, there is a series of high steps to climb. All other trails leading into the backcountry from the Monument are steep and narrow in places, and not accessible.

Camping

Camping on the mountainside is pleasant, but far from accessible. High foliage provides little shade at the campsites. Each site, including a table, fire ring, and pull-in dirt parking, is sloping. There are no accessible restrooms.

Devil's Postpile National Monument

Contact Inyo National Forest
Mammoth Ranger District
PO Box 148
Mammoth Lakes, CA 93546
(619) 934-2505

Park Flyers Available
Location—From U.S. Highway 395,
take Highway 203 through Mammoth
Lakes to Minaret Summit, then 7
miles down a winding road to the
Monument.
Elevation—7,600 feet

BODIE
STATE HISTORIC PARK

Take a step back in time to 1877 and imagine yourself in the midst of the California Goldrush. You are surrounded by thousands of prospectors frenzied by the recent discovery of gold in the eastern Sierras. The hotels and saloons are filled with lucky miners, and hopeful newcomers as well as a slew of no-goods who have come

to prey on them all. The town of Bodie was just such a place. Named for Waterman S. Body, the first man to discover gold in "them thar hills." In 1859, the residents changed the name to insure its proper pronunciation. As quickly as the fervor began, the gold was completely mined out, and folks left town in pursuit of other dreams. By the time the town was designated a historic park in 1962, only 1/10th of the original town structures remained. The rest have been lost to weather, fire, and vandalism.

Bodie State Historic Park is now being maintained in a state of "arrested decay." Due to the historic designation of the town, few of the buildings will be modified for access. Most of them are not open to the public anyway. Much of the tour involves peering through windows at displays ranging from coffins in the slumber room at the undertaker's office to merchandise stacked on shelves at the general store. Many commercial buildings still stand complete with goods and furniture, which are visible through the high windows. Some have stairs or a high step up to a veranda or a boardwalk. The roads in town are packed decomposed granite and are rough in some areas. Use your imagination when you visit Bodie. Picture in your mind wagons and horses clattering through town to pick up supplies, or maybe even an explosive gunfight in the street over a mining claim dispute.

Be sure to pick up a state park folder at the entry kiosk. It is a helpful guide to the existing historic buildings and important town sites. It also will aid in recreating the aura of the Bodie Goldrush days. There is no designated parking in the main lot, but there are fully accessible *RESTROOMS* here. Down the road from the parking lot is a dirt and grass area set aside for picnics. It has standard tables, but no other amenities.

If you want to avoid both the loose gravel in the parking lot and the trail downhill to the town, display your handicap-identification placard and drop passengers off at the head of Green Street. The walking tour of the town begins here at Sheriff Dolan's House. Don't miss seeing the Miner's Union Hall (#58 on the tour), which now serves as the park *MUSEUM*. A ramp access takes you to this large

building. It is crammed full of memorabilia and interesting stories of the women and men who lived in or passed through Bodie.

Though views into some historic buildings are limited and the buildings are widely scattered, this trip to a page out of the Old West at Bodie State Historic Park will be worth your effort.

Bodie State Historic Park

PO Box 515
Bridgeport, CA 93517
(619) 647-6445
Park Folder Available
Location—Seven miles south of Bridgeport off Hwy 395, ten miles east on Hwy 270 (8 miles of dirt road)
Elevation—8,400 feet

MONO LAKE TUFA STATE RESERVE

As far as scientists know, the Mono Lake ecosystem has existed for more than 700,000 years and could be the oldest lake in North America. Though the surroundings appear barren and inhospitable, salty Mono Lake supports an abundant population of brine shrimp and brine flies. This is why, in late summer and fall, hundreds of thousands of nesting and migrating birds flock to the protection and plentiful food source that the lake provides. Snowy plovers make their nests on the windswept flats along the eastern shore. Migrant birds, including the Eared Grebe, arrive in numbers of up to 800,000. In fact, 90% of all California gulls are born at Mono Lake!

Step into the past at Bodie SHP

(Photo courtesy CDPR)

Mono lake tufa formations

(Photo courtesy CDPR)

For thousands of years, natural underground springs that are rich in calcium have mixed with the alkaline Mono Lake water to form underwater calcium carbonate towers. These formations are called tufa. Since 1941, when Los Angeles began diverting water draining into Mono Lake, the water level of the lake has continued to lower. The receding waterline exposed many tufa formations along the lake's western shoreline. Lake salinity has risen to over twice that of the ocean and it continues to increase as water levels drop. Consequently, Mono Lake Tufa State Reserve has been set aside to preserve the remnants of this unique ancient sea ecosystem.

Tufa

The South Tufa area is the most accessible route for a close-up visit to the tufa formations. Take Highway 395 south from Lee Vining. Drive five miles to the South Tufa turn-off at Hwy 120. Exit there and follow the signs to a dirt parking lot. This is where a one-mile self-guided nature trail loop begins. At the trailhead you'll find a guide brochure. The lake shore and tufa formations are approximately ¼-mile from the parking lot. The path is wide and has a gentle downward slope. On the way to the lake, you'll pass some small, weather-beaten tufa standing on the trail. Regular handling by visitors has worn some of the

crusty edges off these formations, but you can get a feel of these calcium carbonate towers. There are intermittent sandy patches along the trail and the packed dirt surface becomes softer as you near the shoreline.

Gulls and other birds feed on masses of swirling brine flies above the shallow waters at the lake's edge. Pinnacles of larger tufas stand defiantly both in the lake and on the shore east as far as Navy Beach. From your vantage point on the shore, you'll be able to see Paoha Island in the middle of the lake. Bring a pair of binoculars with you. Incredible numbers of birds come to nest on the island in the fall and winter. As the trail

170

continues eastward, it becomes more hilly and rough. It may be best to backtrack from here. There are no trees, accessible toilets, or drinking water at South Tufa. Keep that in mind when you plan your visit.

For a personal visit to Paoha Island and the tufa formations, paddlers use the gentle shores of Navy Beach to launch their kayaks and canoes. Be careful when boating on Mono Lake. Strong winds can come up quickly and make your boating trip hazardous.

Boardwalk

One-and-a-half miles north of Lee Vining, at the old marina site, there is an accessible boardwalk that takes you near the lake. Surrounded by tufa-coated pumice boulders, this walkway takes you to a spot with a panoramic view of the water and a great view of birds on Paoha Island. Due to the continual recession of the lake, the end of the boardwalk is now approximately 30 feet from the water's edge. To find the boardwalk, turn in at the Mono Lake Access. Continue past an exhibit shelter and follow the blue signs to paved designated *PARKING* place near the foot of the boardwalk.

Visitor Center

The Mono Basin National Forest Scenic Area and Mono Lake Tufa State Reserve have combined their efforts to protect more than 117,000 acres of diverse natural features on the shore of Mono Lake. North of Lee Vining, on a bluff overlooking the Mono Lake Basin, the National Forest Service recently completed a fully accessible *VISITOR CENTER*. The road from

Hwy 395 to the visitor center is well-marked with paved designated parking near the entry. Interpretive displays and a short movie in the exhibit hall describe the dramatic natural and human history that have shaped the lake. You can pick up folders, books, and other printed material at the information station. A ranger is there to help you and a fully accessible *RESTROOM* is also available.

Mono Lake Tufa State Reserve
PO Box 99
Lee Vining, CA 93541
(619) 647-6331
Park Folder Available
Location — On Highway 395 at Lee Vining
Elevation — 6,417 feet

YOSEMITE NATIONAL PARK

"Yosemite is one of the great gestures of the Earth. It isn't that it is merely big, it is also beautiful, with a beauty that is solid and apparent as the granite rock in which it is carved." Ansel Adams, famous photographer and Sierra Club activist found solace at Yosemite National Park, and called it his home for many years. This vast tract of land is about the size of the state of Rhode Island, with elevations ranging from 2,000 to 13,000 feet. It contains some of the most wondrous scenery in the Sierra Nevada mountain range, inspiring many an artist and poet.

World renowned for its captivating waterfalls, sheer granite mountain walls, and endless streams of tourists and hikers, Yosemite National Park draws more visitors than any

other State or National Park in California. While most of the 3½ million annual visitors drive directly to Yosemite Valley, there is much more to explore and appreciate in the park.

Tioga Road crosses the park's northern high country, winding through fragile alpine meadows, sparkling lakes and granite domes polished by glacial ice. At the park's northeast entrance, Tioga Pass is California's highest automobile pass. You can sometimes spot big-horn sheep from the highway at this 9,945-foot elevation.

In Yosemite's southern section, Wawona Road takes you for a look at the pioneer history of the Sierra Nevadas and to the historic Wawona Hotel. Standing guard near the southern park entrance is the Mariposa Grove, largest of the three giant Sequoia groves preserved in the park.

Yosemite Valley is the most famous of all park attractions and undoubtedly the most frequently photographed. The Valley is a familiar landmark to people throughout the world. With its majestic waterfalls and overwhelming geological formations it is understandable that most people who come to view Yosemite's awesome beauty will visit the Yosemite Valley.

General Information

The National Parks Service has directed their efforts to provide everyone with an opportunity to share in the natural wonders of Yosemite. The disabled and those with mobility limitations are given special consideration. As a service to the mobility impaired, the park will provide you with a *DISABLED*

PLACARD at any entrance station or visitor center. When it is displayed in the front window or on the dashboard of your vehicle, you will be allowed to drive onto some restricted roads and park in spaces designated by the International Access Symbol. With your placard, you may drive your vehicle on the Happy Isles Loop road to Mirror Lake, on the service roads in the village, to the visitor center in Tuolumne Meadows, and you may follow the tram as it tours the Mariposa Grove. To help the rangers identify those in need of special access, you should use the park's placard even if you have a handicap-identification placard from your state.

The Park Service provides each visiting vehicle with a park map and a copy of _Yosemite Park Guide_. This newspaper-style edition of seasonal park activities and events is a very helpful tour planning tool and can be mailed to you in advance of your visit upon written request.

A free _SHUTTLE BUS_ service runs on a regularly scheduled route in the eastern end of the Yosemite Valley. It makes stops at all of the main places of interest, lodging and campgrounds. (You can refer to _The Yosemite Guide_ for bus stop locations.) Three of these busses are equipped with front door wheelchair lifts and tie-downs for two wheelchairs. All of the other busses have a 12-inch step with handrails for boarding. In winter, only two modified busses are running. To get the bus schedule, call Yosemite Transportation System (209) 372-1241 or ask a driver to let you know when the next wheelchair-equipped bus will be at the stop.

For those who enjoy sightseeing by car, numbered roadside markers stand at many scenic views and points of interest in the park. _The Yosemite Road Guide_ is an 80-page booklet keyed to these markers and includes informative descriptions of each stop, other maps and illustrations. The guide is available for purchase at any of the Visitor's Centers and most gift shops in the park, or by writing to The Yosemite Association, PO Box 545, Yosemite National Park, CA, 95389, (209) 379-2646.

The Northern Section — Mather District

In the high mountain country of the Mather District, you will be delighted with the changing scenery waiting for you around every corner. About 1½ hours from the Valley, Tioga Road (Hwy 120) takes you to Tuolumne Meadows, the focal point of the park's northern section. As the Sierra's largest sub-alpine meadow, Tuolumne holds a special place in the hearts of many outdoor-lovers who return regularly to visit its forest, lakes, springs, and the ominous granite formations on its perimeter.

Features

Lembert Dome—Along Hwy 120, at the east edge of the meadows, is the striking presence of Lembert Dome. This is a favorite place for rock climbers to practice their skills, so bring your binoculars. You'll have a great view of climbers from a picnic area set at the base of this monolith. To get to the picnic area you'll have to cross an uneven, decomposed granite surface for a short distance. The tables here are not mo-

dified for wheelchair use. There is a designated dirt _PARKING_ place with an accessible _RESTROOM_ nearby. A ramp with grab-railing leads to the ample _UNISEX SHASTA TOILET_. Its large stall provides lateral transfer to a low toilet with grab bars.

Soda Springs Trail—A quarter mile down the road that leads to Tuolumne Meadows Stable is the trailhead for Soda Springs Trail. A mile down the trail is **Parson's Lodge**, where Robert Underwood Johnson and John Muir conceived the idea of Yosemite National Park. The broad, firm trail is embedded with rock; you also will encounter some sandy patches. During your one-mile hike to the lodge, you'll pass some of Yosemite's natural soda springs. Unlike other water sources in the park, this salty water comes from deep underground and has not yet been contaminated by animals or humans. In the spring the trail can be muddy, so before setting out, it's best to check with a ranger for trail conditions.

Tenaya Lake—Seven miles west of Tuolumne Meadows, Tenaya Lake is a quiet place along the road for a scenic picnic lunch. From the asphalt parking lot, a firm dirt path leads 600 feet to the lake. It has a lake sand coating, so you may need some help to get to the lake shore. At the edge of the lake's sparkling waters, you'll find picnic tables in a shady pine grove. If you like to canoe, the gentle shoreline here is a perfect place to launch your boat. There is another picnic area on the north shore of Tenaya Lake near **Murray Creek Trailhead**. The picnic tables there have a great lake view and are shaded by an abundance of pine trees, but there is no paved parking lot, and the forest floor surfaces are uneven and soft in places. Neither the restrooms at the lake parking lot nor those at Murray Creek Trailhead are accessible.

Tuolumne Grove of Giant Sequoias—Six miles east of the Big Oak Flat entrance is the Tuolumne Grove of Giant Sequoias. You will come upon the grove one mile down the Tuolumne Grove Road off Tioga Road. These towering trees, largest of all living things, have stood watch over the history of the western world for more than one thousand years. Parking is at a premium here, and the trails are rough and steep as they climb into the grove. A much larger, more accessible grove of these lofty giants is located at the Mariposa Grove in the Wawona section of the park.

Visitor Services

There are two main points of entry in the northern portion of the park; Tioga Pass and Big Oak Flat. The **Big Oak Flat Entrance Station** includes a _RANGER STA-TION/INFORMATION CENTER_ with ramp access, accessible _VENDING MACHINES_ and _TELEPHONE_. The accessible _RESTROOMS_ have an extra large stall and changing area with a low toilet and grab bars. There are no visitor services at the **Tioga Pass Entrance Station**.

At **Tuolumne Meadows** you'll find the camp store, Tuolumne Grill, post office and an accessible _UNISEX RESTROOM_. There is one designated _PARKING_ place with an asphalt ramp to the curb near the _RESTROOM_ and accessible _DRINKING FOUNTAIN_. The Tuolumne Grill and the camp store each have 1- to

2-inch lips at the doorways, and the outdoor post office window is at 45 inches. There is no walkway or ramp from the designated _PARKING_ area to the entrances of these facilities. They are fronted by a concrete walk that is a few inches higher than the parking area. _GASOLINE_ is available just up the road, west of Tuolumne Campground and an RV dump station is provided near the visitor center.

Mark Wellman: "Tenaya Lake is a great place for a paddle."   *(Photo courtesy NPS)*

The **Tuolumne Visitor Center** is ¼-mile west of the store and is a warm inviting place to linger on a chilly Tuolumne morning. Visitors with a handicap-identification placard may follow the authorized vehicle road up to a lot where designated _PARKING_ is on the same level as the building. The well-marked wheelchair entrance is on the opposite side of the building. Rangers are available at the _VISITOR CENTER_ to help you with questions about the park. On cool days, they keep the wood stove stoked, creating a cozy atmosphere. Displays of native flora

and fauna are readily visible from a seated position. A plentiful supply of books and pamphlets is also available for sale. _RESTROOMS_ for the visitor center are located in a modular unit at the lower parking lot. With railed ramp access and a heavy door, the restroom offers a long, pivot-transfer stall with a low toilet and grab bars.

Lodging and Camping

Tuolumne Meadows Lodge is nestled in the trees just off Tioga Road. Designated _PARKING_ is 400 feet from the registration office and restaurant. There is a 6-inch door sill at the entrance and an accessible _TELEPHONE_ on a concrete slab just around the corner. In the camping area, rustic style tent cabins are situated in and along sloping, uneven dirt walkways. The management considers three of their cabins to be accessible, but they are not designated and must be specially requested. Unlike the other cabins, #7, #21, and #66 have little or no lip or steps at the doorway. You may drive up the service road to load and unload supplies at the door step. The restrooms have a set of stairs at each entrance and limited turning space in the building. Reservations for Tuolumne Meadows Lodge are available by calling Yosemite Curry Company at (209) 252-4848.

Tuolumne Meadows Campground—The park has plans to build a designated accessible site at Tuolumne Meadows Campground, but at this time, camping here is a challenge. The sandy, dirt roads that wind through the grounds are rutted and very dusty. Each site has a table, fire ring, and food storage, and most lie on a shady sloping forest floor surface. Approach to the restrooms is either through thick gravel and pumice or up a sloping hillside. There is a 2- to 4-inch transition from the dirt to the concrete restroom slab and no added access modifications. A steep dirt path with a jagged 8-inch step transition up to asphalt leads to the campfire center and would not be considered accessible.

West of Tenaya Lake off Tioga Road, you'll find several campgrounds that are similar to one another. **Porcupine Flat, Yosemite Creek** and **Tamarack Flat** (FCFS) each has shady sites with dusty pull-ins, picnic tables, food storage, and fire rings. Camping surfaces are uneven and sometimes hilly. The only restroom at each campground is a standard chemical toilet.

The campground at **White Wolf** (FCFS) is similar to the three campgrounds previously mentioned. In addition to regular campsites, this area rents tent cabins. However, all of them have stairs to the entry, and there are no accessible restroom accommodations. A set of stairs also leads to the General Store at White Wolf.

At **Crane Flat** and **Hodgdon Meadow** there are many shady, level campsites. The approach to the restrooms is through a patch of gravel. To add to the difficulty, there is a 1-inch transition to a concrete slab and the fixtures are not retrofitted for access. The park lists the campfire center at Crane Flat in its literature as an accessible location. However, there is an excessively steep (35%) grade on the 75-foot asphalt path that leads to the seating area. A _GAS STATION_ and an accessible _TELEPHONE_ are located just outside the campground.

Camping reservations at Tuolumne Meadows, Crane Flat, and Hodgdon Meadow may be made with MISTIX by calling (800) 365-2267.

The Southern Section—
Wawona District
and Glacier Point

The forested mountainsides in the southern portion of the park are rich in the history of Native American homelands and pioneer settlers. As you drive through the area, you can almost imagine what it would have been like in the late 19th century, when gentlemen and their ladies sought out the gracious Wawona Hotel for a holiday in the high country. You'll also want to spend some time among the towering trees in a Giant Sequoia Grove.

The **Pioneer Yosemite History Center** is just north of the Wawona Hotel. A collection of historic buildings and equipment recalls the contributions and pioneering individuals of Yosemite National Park's history. Each building is well marked for a self-guided tour. The walkways in the exhibit area are flat. Unfortunately, wood chips or shavings cover segments of the paths, making the walking surface unstable and access nearly impossible for a wheelchair. Ranger-led tours are available Spring through October, but all of the buildings have obstacles like steps, or boards at the entrances, making close-up viewing difficult for wheelchair users.

For a scenic ride through old Wawona, why not try a stage coach ride? At the Grey Barn on Chilnualna Falls Road, the staff will be happy to help you aboard for a ten-minute tour of the historic town. A fee is charged for the ride.

Picnic—If a shady picnic is more your style, there is a designated _PARKING_ place and _PICNIC TABLE_ at the east end of the parking lot, across from the History Center entrance. Presently, the _TABLE_ has extended ends and rests on a flat surface covered in gravel, but there may be plans to return the surface to packed dirt. Up a short paved walkway from the picnic table is an accessible _UNISEX RESTROOM_ including a high toilet and grab bars.

Mariposa Grove—Two miles from the park's south entrance or about 1¼ hours from Yosemite Valley, Wawona Road turns toward the Mariposa Grove. Mariposa is the largest of three Giant

Sequoia groves in Yosemite. Every 15 minutes, from mid-May to mid-October, a tram takes visitors from the parking lot on a _GUIDED_ _TOUR_ of these stately giants. With your handicap-identification placard you can follow behind the tram in your vehicle. The tour takes you to such trees as the 2,700-year-old Grizzly Giant or one of two tunnel trees cut in the 1800's.

When you get to the gate at the grove entrance, notify the tram dispatcher that you would like to follow the tram. The dispatcher will open the gate for you and provide you with a recorded tour message to guide you along the way. Please stay with the tram at all times and park only in specified locations. There is an accessible unisex _RESTROOM_ in the parking lot; the key is available at the kiosk. An accessible _TELEPHONE_ is next to the gift shop.

Visitor Services

Gift shops, a post office, and a small market are in the north parking area near the Wawona Hotel. There is no designated parking, and log parking stops block access to the walkway in front of the shops. Each shop has a 1-inch lip at the door. _GASOLINE_ is available in front of the Wawona Hotel and an RV dump station is just east of the history center. The ranger station, located past the stables on Chilnualna Falls Road, is not accessible.

Lodging and Camping

Wawona Hotel—First constructed in 1876 and updated in 1879, the Wawona Hotel offers its guests a step back in time when

the hotel was central to a Yosemite visit. Ramp access to the _LOBBY_ and _DINING_ _ROOM_ of the Wawona is behind the main building by way of the walkway on the south side of the hotel. Everyone who comes to the Wawona enjoys a stroll along the paved walkways that wander through the rolling lawns and gardens of the hotel.

The hotel provides _FOUR_ _ROOMS_ in the Annex building that the management considers to be accessible. Two rooms share a central bathroom or may be rented individually with or without the bathroom. A ramp takes you to your room, where the doorway is wide enough for a wheelchair, and grab bars are installed in the bathrooms. Another accessible _REST-ROOM/SHOWER_ is available behind the pro shop at the end of the Annex building. This is the only accessible public _RESTROOM_ at the hotel. It is important to make prior reservations for the accessible rooms up to a year and a day in advance by calling (209) 252-4848.

The Redwoods—Northeast of the Wawona Hotel is a portion of privately-owned land that lies within the park. The Redwoods, a property management company, rents cabins year round to park visitors. Currently they rent _FOUR_ _UNITS_ that are accessible by ramp and have wide doorways and other special accommodations for the disabled. Contact them for further information and reservations: The Redwoods, PO Box 2085, Wawona Station, CA, 95389, (209) 375-6666.

Wawona Campground (FCFS) has one designated _CAMPSITE_. This flat, gravel-covered site has a picnic table with an extended end.

Unfortunately, the restroom near the designated site is not modified for access, and the gravel makes wheeling very difficult.

Glacier Point

Most visitors have a spectacular view of the Yosemite Valley with its domes, pinnacles, and waterfalls from Glacier Point. Wheelchair users will find that the railing and safety wall at the observation area restrict the view downward to the valley floor, leaving only a 10-inch gap at a height of 30-40 inches for viewing from a wheelchair. There are plans to build an open grating at three locations along the wall for those unable to see over the existing wall.

In the large paved parking lot, several designated _PARKING_ places are close to the concrete walkway. The walkway leads to a path that takes you to Glacier Point and to an accessible _RESTROOM_ about 150 feet away. There is a small lip at the doorway of the restroom, and the stalls provide lateral transfer to a low toilet with grab bars. The handle on the entry door is high, so you may require assistance to open the door as you leave.

Beyond the restroom, the walkway splits in two directions. The right fork leads to the snack bar area. The _SNACK_ _BAR_ and _GIFT_ _SHOP_ have a boardwalk access with a 2-inch lip. An accessible _TELEPHONE_ is located just outside the gift shop. The view of Half Dome and Little Yosemite Valley is wonderful from here, but the trail to the Point on this fork is impassable for wheelchair users. Blue signs along the left fork of the walkway denote *SPE-CIAL ACCESS* to the point. Smooth pavement stretches in gradual inclines and declines for a distance of approximately 1/3-mile from the parking lot.

Glacier Point is located 32 miles from Yosemite Valley by way of Wawona Road to Chinquapin; then take Glacier Point Road to the end. Glacier Point is 25 miles north of Wawona. Glacier Point Road east of Badger Pass is closed in winter.

Badger Pass

In the winter, when snow blankets the Yosemite Valley, the **Badger Pass Sit Ski Program** goes into full swing. If you have lower body paralysis but would love to experience the thrill of speed and motion on skis, the Yosemite Ski School's sit ski lessons are designed for you. Introduced in the 1980 Winter Park Ski Area, the program has spread nationwide and has become highly popular among paraplegics, quadriplegics, and others with involvement of the lower extremities.

The sit ski is a kayak-like device that is controlled by the skier's upper body and short, hand-held poles. Safety of the sit skier and others is provided by "tethering" to an able-bodied, trained skier holding an attached rope behind the sit ski. The sit ski consists of a reinforced Fiberglass shell, push bar seat and leg cushion, leg straps, harness, tethering straps, security line, lift evacuation straps, and hand-held picks.

To rent a sit ski, you must take a lesson. The Yosemite Ski School teachers have received special training as Sit Ski Instructors. The

ski instructor will familiarize you with Badger Pass and teach you how to get on and off the chairlift, control your speed, roll, turn, and stop. Because the number of sit skis and trained instructors is limited, advance registration is required for sit ski lessons. To reserve your lesson, call (209) 372-1330 or write to Yosemite Ski School, Badger Pass Ski Area, Yosemite National Park, CA 95389.

The Badger Pass day lodge was one of the first ski lodges constructed in California. As such, it was not designed with handicapped skiers in mind. To enter the day lodge, drive to the far left of the building, passing around the Yosemite Cross-Country Ski Center. At the rear of the building is a level entrance to the day lodge and sun deck. You'll find designated *PARKING* there. For your comfort, a fully accessible *UNISEX RESTROOM* has been added to the lodge. To get to the ski area from the lodge, you'll need to cross some snow. The ski instructor will be happy to help you to your lesson or you can have an able-bodied friend lend a hand. The park staff is anxious to make this a wonderful experience for you and will help in any way they can. If you have any questions or special concerns, call the ski school at (209) 372-1330.

Yosemite Valley District

Think of Yosemite National Park and what comes to mind is a mental picture of the Yosemite Valley with its cascading waterfalls and magnificent granite cliffs towering over a tree-filled river basin. At first glimpse from the highway, the Yosemite fulfills the promise of unsurpassed scenic beauty. Once you're deep within the glacier-

carved valley surrounded by 3,000-foot walls of granite, the awesome power of nature seems to dwarf the importance of Man.

A tribe of the Ahwahneechee Indians called the Yosemite Valley their home, sharing it with the animals and plants native to the region. As word of the Valley and its splendor got out, it was not long before settlers came to claim it for themselves. In the mid-1800's they established a small community. Now, after over 100 years as a National Park, Yosemite Valley is host to most of the 3½ million visitors who come annually to find beauty and recreation among its open meadows and mixed-conifer forests.

Features

Bridal Veil Fall is at its picturesque best in the spring when streams are high and the wind-blown waters descending the mountainside are more dramatic. There are no designated parking spaces or accessible restrooms in the asphalt parking area near the falls. If you have a willing assistant and want an up-close experience with Bridal Veil Fall, take the trail that starts at the east corner of the parking lot. It begins with 150 feet of rough asphalt road (max 9%). Then the trail narrows and becomes quite steep (some short 19% grades) to the observation area for a total distance of 450 feet. From there you'll be able to watch the water twist and turn as it drops to a bed of rocks nearby. If you're not up to the hike, a stop here for the view of the fall from the parking area is still worthwhile. There is an accessible *TELEPHONE* in the parking lot.

Yosemite Falls, a focal point in the valley, are especially spectacular in the spring and early summer when torrents of mountain run-off tumble over sheer cliffs. By late summer and fall, the flow slows to a mere trickle. The trailhead to the falls, marked by a yellow and black pole, is three spaces down from the designated _PARKING_. For the first 100 yards, this asphalt trail is level and shady. Just before the trail begins to climb, there is a viewing area with benches and shade. The second half of the trail is very steep in places (up to 22% grade) and its surface is rougher. At the end of the trail is a level rest area with benches. In the spring, when you sit here, you can feel the power of the falls as they tumble to the valley floor. The _PARKING_ lot has two designated spaces near an accessible _UNISEX RESTROOM_ that has a high toilet with grab bars, an accessible sink and mirror.

The Happy Isles Nature Center is at the southeasternmost end of the valley. Not far away, the park staff is developing the **Happy Isles Loop Trail** for use by visitors of all abilities. The trail leaves from the Nature Center on a self-guided tour of the interesting flora and fauna of a mountain stream.

With a handicap-identification placard, you may drive up the maintenance road and park anywhere in the dirt behind the _ICE CREAM STAND_ or near the Nature Center. From there, take the uneven dirt trail leading past the ice cream stand and along the stream bed for 150 feet to the ramp entrance at the Nature Center. Inside you'll find a great artificial stream simulating the natural ecology of a wetlands environment. The only accessible _RESTROOM_ in this area is near the Happy Isles shuttle bus stop.

Vernal Fall—The trailhead to Vernal Fall is just across the stream from the ice cream stand. While it is one of the most well-traveled trails in the Valley, the

Yosemite Falls, Yosemite NP

(Photo courtesy CDPR)

Vernal Fall trail is very steep in places and would be a challenge for the heartiest of wheelchair users. Restroom facilities at the falls are not accessible.

Mirror Lake was once a crystal blue body of water at the base of Half Dome. A rock slide dammed melting water from a retreating glacier, thus forming the lake. Gradually, sediment has filled the lake causing it to recede almost entirely from view. Geologists call this process, succession. The filled lake becomes a lovely meadow much like the one that has replaced the ancient Lake Yosemite in Yosemite Valley. With your handicap-identification placard, you can drive to Mirror Lake on the service road for a look at modern geological history in the making. When driving on the service roads, be aware that the hikers and bicyclists who use this road are not expecting to share it with vehicles.

Yosemite Village

As the hub and main activity center of the park, the village has many services of a small town. Wheelchair access is a consideration in nearly every building, meaning that most visitors will have access to the many features in the Village. A privately-operated _DENTAL_ and _MEDICAL CLINIC_ are available for emergencies and accessible at the rear entrance. There is a _SERVICE STATION_ and a Versateller machine in the village.

You'll find designated _PARKING_ in the following locations: next to the administration building, behind the post office, and in the market parking lot. For the easiest access to the village and visitor center,

follow the service road and park near the administration building. See your park map to locate these buildings.

Visitor Center

A good place to begin your Yosemite Valley experience is the **Valley Visitor Center**. It is a main gathering place for people exploring the Park. The information desk, manned daily by park rangers, is usually bustling with activity. A portion of the counter is lowered for wheelchair users. The rangers are very helpful and will direct you to accessible park features. Besides the information desk, there is a large section of book and map sales, and a very well-designed exhibit area with accessible displays and films about the natural, historical, geological, and archaeological stories of Yosemite. Once inside the heavy door, the concrete surface is smooth and gently slopes through the exhibits. Handrails are provided at elevation changes.

An accessible _RESTROOM_ is near the entrance to the visitor center. Beyond the heavy door is a wide, lateral-transfer stall with a low toilet, tilted mirrors, low hand driers, and a _DRINKING FOUNTAIN_; _the sinks are difficult to access._

Tours—Many _RANGER-LED WALKS_ originate from the visitor center, and most of the _CAMERA OUTINGS_ begin at the hotel lobbies. These tours generally follow asphalt walkways and bike paths, making them ideal for wheelchair users. The ranger or workshop leader will be happy to modify the tour according to the needs or requests of the visitors in each group. Talk

to the ranger ahead of time, and be sure to include yourself in all of the park activities you can. Look for the schedule of walks and camera outings in your _Yosemite Park Guide._

Auditorium—In the evening, you may enjoy a live theater production or a film in the _AUDITORIUM_ located behind the visitor center. Plays about the life and times of John Muir are presented in the summer season. In addition, there are colorful slide shows and films featuring the natural history of the park, its many varieties of wildlife, and its splendid scenery. Consult the _Yosemite Guide_ for current topics and fees. The steep (11%) ramp access to the entrance may require some assistance, but there is plenty of room for wheelchairs inside. Not only will you appreciate the quality entertainment, a stroll to the theater is a perfect way to appreciate the Valley's lovely summer evenings.

Indian Village Walk—Located behind the visitor center, a level _PATH_ leads to a Miwok Indian village, re-created as it may have appeared in 1872. Descriptive markers line the paved path to and from the packed dirt surfaces at the dwelling area. There is a small transition getting on and off the pathway. An informative pamphlet is available at the beginning of the path to make your visit more meaningful.

Indian Museum—Next to the Indian Village, the Indian Museum houses displays and exhibits about the Native Americans that preceded us in the Yosemite Valley. Once inside the heavy door, there are no barriers, and exhibits are visible from a seated position. The

Pioneer Cemetery, across the street from the designated _PARKING_ by the administration building, is preserved without access improvements. Tombstones arranged on an uneven dirt surface, are a reminder of the Valley's pioneer history.

Gallery—Both the **Ansel Adams Gallery** and the **Art Activity Center** have ramp access. The lower floor of the Ansel Adams Gallery is accessible from the front entrance. For access to the film processing area and other exhibits, ask the clerk at the desk for assistance to the upper level entrance.

Visitor Services

The best access to the _POST OFFICE_ is at the west side door. You can reach _DEGNAN'S FAST FOOD DELI_ and a _GIFT SHOP_ from the main village patio. An accessible _TELEPHONE_ and _RESTROOM_ are located below the stairs for Degnan's Restaurant; the restroom has a medium-heavy door. The stall has lateral transfer to a high toilet with grab bars, and the sinks, towels, and mirror are accessible. There is designated _PARKING_ behind this building, but from there, the asphalt road downhill is very steep 17%.

A 30-foot ramp entrance (3%) leads from designated _PARKING_ in the adjacent lot to the _VILLAGE STORE_, a grocery and gift shop. Behind the market is a _HAMBURGER STAND_ and a _SPORT SHOP_ with a

ramp access (6%). The _RESTROOM_ in the sport shop has lateral transfer to a high toilet, grab bars, and an accessible sink. Behind the sport shop, a concrete walkway leads to an accessible _AUTOMATED TELLER MACHINE_ and check cashing window. Camera and photo supplies may be purchased on the _PHOTO PROCESSING SHOP_ at the edge of the market parking lot.

Picnic

One of the activities most everyone looks forward to in the outdoors is having a picnic. In Yosemite Valley, there are four picnic areas. Each with a little different setting. set up with tables, and chemical toilets. Of these four, one is modified for access. It offers a great view of an open meadow sprinkled with wildflowers, flowering shrubs and an occasional grazing deer. From here, you can pick up the asphalt bike path and take a hike across the meadow. This picnic area has a designated _PICNIC SITE_ with a modified table and accessible _CHEMICAL TOILET_. As you drive

on the incoming park road, it is the third picnic area on the left. A designated _PARKING_ space is provided.

The other three picnic areas are more primitive. Picnic sites are scattered among the valley trees and the natural surfaces, though level, are quite uneven. Only standard chemical toilets are provided.

Trails

Miles of smooth asphalt hike/bike trail lace Yosemite Valley. Well-marked, two-way lanes take visitors through varying landscapes of inspiring scenery and past campgrounds and other park features. There are photo opportunities around every corner. A favorite is the meadow just east of the village where deer regularly visit to graze in the shadows of sheer mountain cliffs towering overhead. If you follow the bike trail to the middle of the meadow, you'll have an unobstructed 360° view of the surrounding valley walls.

Yosemite Valley, Yosemite NP

(Photo courtesy CDPR)

Lodging

To get maximum enjoyment out of your trip, it is imperative that you plan your visit well in advance. If you'd like to camp, you can make your reservations through MISTIX (800) 365-2267, no more than eight weeks ahead of the first day you wish to stay. If you call exactly eight weeks ahead, you will have the best chance of getting the dates and campgrounds of your choice. Lodging accommodations are available for reservation one year and a day ahead of your visit. For lodging accommodations contact Yosemite Park and Curry Co. at (209) 252-4848. Because of the limited number of accessible rooms, it is advisable to call as soon as you know your plans.

Yosemite Lodge offers two accessible _HOTEL ROOMS_ and 16 _CABINS_ that have accessible features. A convenient access ramp and designated _PARKING_ are provided near the lobby. Within the Lodge complex is a _CAFETERIA_, _RESTAURANT_, _GIFT SHOPS_, _MARKET_, and an _AMPHITHEATER_. You can reach them either through the Lodge lobby or by the patio near the _SWIMMING POOL_. Surfaces in the patio area vary from smooth asphalt to pebble-embedded concrete and have rough transitions in places. Three accessible _RESTROOMS_ in the complex are all similar (pivot-transfer stall with grab bars and a low toilet). You will find one in the lobby, one at the restaurant entrance, and another in the cafeteria.

Of the two _LODGE ROOMS_ considered accessible, one is very accommodating for a wheelchair. It has wide doors and plenty of room in the bathroom for access. The oth-er room has more limited space with wide doorways. Each of 16 accessible _CABINS_ has an access ramp and accessible showers. Some have dirt parking directly in front of the door. When reserving a cabin, ask for the code "B4WA" (wheelchair accessible). Both the cabins and the lodge provide linens and housekeeping service.

The illustrious **Awahnee** hotel is a great place to spend some time. You'll want to explore its various sitting rooms that are filled with old tapestries, memorabilia, and photographs of the early days in the Valley. The _DINING ROOM_ is accessible and is an elegant place for a special evening (shorts and tee shirts are not allowed at dinner). A fully accessible _UNISEX RESTROOM_ is near the elevator on the mezzanine. _SPECIALTY SHOPS_ along the entry foyer are accessible but store aisles are narrow. The hotel _SWIMMING POOL_ can be reached along a paved path with an accessible _TELEPHONE_ and _DRINKING FOUNTAIN_ enroute. The Awahnee offers two _COTTAGE ROOMS_ and two _HOTEL ROOMS_ each with an accessible _BATHROOM_ and _SHOWER_. _TWO DESIGNATED PARKING_ places are opposite the covered hotel _ENTRANCE_.

Curry Village

In the shadow of Glacier Point, a community of white-sided tents reminiscent of an old miner's camp is tucked into the valley location known as Curry Village. Set apart just enough from Yosemite Village to avoid the heavy tourist traffic, wooden boardwalks and service buildings give the village a rustic flavor and Western town atmosphere.

All of the _SHOPS_ and _RESTAURANTS_ are accessible in the village, as are the _PUBLIC POOL_ and _SHOWER_. This is also one boarding areas for the valley tour bus. Unfortunately, the Valley floor tour busses are not modified for wheelchair access, and the staff is not prepared to help you on board

Visitor Services

A boardwalk connects each of the Curry Village shops, restaurants, and lounge. The remaining area has a packed dirt surface with a sandy coating. You'll find accessible restrooms in three locations: west of the lounge, in the cafeteria, and at the shower building east of the dining pavilion. The _CAMPFIRE CENTER_ for Curry Village is beyond the boardwalk on hard-packed dirt between the dining pavilion and the lounge. There are no obstacles to the campfire center, but the ground is soft sand in places.

The lounge, post office, and telephones are located behind the reservation office and up two steps. The _DINING PAVILION_ is opposite the lounge along the boardwalk and offers an indoor cafeteria and an outdoor _BAR_, _PIZZA_, and _ICE CREAM_. A ramp near the cafeteria entrance leads to this patio area. A heavy door opens to the fully accessible _CAFETERIA_ that serves breakfast, lunch, and dinner in the summer only. The _RESTROOM_ inside has a wide stall door (low toilet with grab bars). A _HAMBURGER STAND_, _BIKE SHOP_, _MARKET_, and _MOUNTAIN SHOP_ can be reached by way of a ramp on the parking lot side of the building. There are three designated _PARKING_ places and an accessible _DRINKING FOUNTAIN_ nearby.

Curry Village Pool and Showers are located behind the cafeteria up a paved service road which leads from the parking lot. The showers are free to the guests of Curry Village. Others are charged a small fee. These are the only public showers in the Valley. Disabled visitors can be dropped off in front of the shower building or park in the designated spaces at the foot of the road, 200 feet downhill from the entrance. The accessible SHOWER with grab bars is very roomy, but has no bench or shower seat. You'll need to ask for a chair when you arrive. The shower head is at 65 inches, and the control knob is low at 38 inches. In the RESTROOM, the roomy stall offers lateral transfer to a low toilet with grab bars. A mirror, hand dryer, and sink are accessible.

Lodging

Curry Village offers two hard-sided cabins with ramp access. Each has two double beds and limited room to maneuver. Bathroom doorways are 27 inches wide, and grab bars have been added near the toilet. Units 2A and 2B are close to designated PARKING near the reservation office. Besides a few hard-sided cabins, Curry Village accommodations are mostly tent cabins. Each cabin has steps to the doorway. None has an access ramp. Reservations for Curry Village may be made up to a year and a day in advance with Yosemite Curry Co. by calling (209) 252-4848.

Yosemite Valley Camping

All camping reservations in the valley (except Sunnyside walk-in campground (FCFS)) are handled by MISTIX, (800) 365-2267. The summer season is highly popular. For the best selection, you should make reservations exactly eight weeks ahead of the first day of your visit. You must have your MISTIX ticket to enter your assigned campground.

Most of the campgrounds have similar features. Asphalt roads connect the mostly grass and packed dirt campsites.

Each site provides a table, fire ring, food storage box, and a paved parking place. Restrooms are generally located central to each camping loop on a concrete slab surrounded by dirt or grass. Unless otherwise mentioned, all restrooms should be considered to have standard fixtures with no access modifications. Most camping in the valley is level, so many sites near an accessible restroom might be adequate. If you check ahead of time, the attendant at the kiosk may be able to run an extension cord to your site to charge the battery for a motorized wheelchair.

Upper River—Located in tall trees with very sparse low growth, the sandy banks of the Merced River trace the outskirts of Upper River Campground. This campground is exclusively for tent campers. One designated CAMPING SITE (#16) has a concrete walkway to an accessible DRINKING FOUNTAIN and RESTROOM with lateral transfer to a low toilet with grab bars. There are no other accessible features at this site.

Lower River—Much like the Upper River Campground, this area offers very little privacy. There are sites for RV's up to 35 feet in length, but no designated sites. At the AMPHITHEATER, a gently sloping, smooth concrete ramp leads from a designated PARKING place to the seating area where there is space for a wheelchair. An RV dump station is located near the amphitheater.

Upper Pines—As the name implies, a thick forest of pine trees shades the Pines Campgrounds offering cooler sites than those at the River Campgrounds. Although no campsites are designated, the "A" loop has an accessible RESTROOM. **It** offers lateral transfer to a low toilet with grab bars in a large stall that has a bench seat. An RV dump station is located near the kiosk.

Lower Pines—The three unpaved designated CAMPSITES (#5, #12 and #14) provide an accessible TABLE, and a raised BBQ close to the restroom and amphitheater. The RESTROOM in this loop has an asphalt approach and a concrete walkway to the door. The stall is roomy, with lateral transfer to a low toilet with grab bars and has a bench seat. The other restrooms in the campground have retrofitted stalls with grab bars, but each building has a 2- to 4-inch step at the doorway. The AMPHITHEATER can be access by a forest floor trail or by a smooth asphalt walkway leading from a nearby parking place.

Housekeeping Camp—Housekeeping Camp is a cluster of hard-sided tent cabins with concrete slab floors and soft-sided privacy screens. Each cabin comes with mattress and frame beds, fire ring or BBQ, and a food storage box. Sheets and blankets may be rented, or you can bring your own. Hard-packed dirt surrounds the tents and the nearby parking. There is a designated DIRT PARKING place near the accessible RESTROOM and accessible _SHOWER ROOM_. The _RESTROOM_ provides an accessible sink, and the stall has lateral transfer to a low toilet with grab bars. In the _SHOWER_, the control is at 32 inches from the floor, and the hand-held shower head bracket is at 48 inches. There is a seat in changing area only. When you check in, be sure to get the key to the shower room at the office. If requested, the staff will get you an extra mattress to raise the level of the bed for easier transfer. Coin laundry facilities are near the office where the approach from the parking area is rough asphalt.

Sunnyside Walk-in (FCFS) — Though it is unusual to include a walk-in campground in this access summary, Sunnyside is unique in its camping features and accessibility. Used as a base of operations for climbing the many granite faces and domes in the park, this campground is always abuzz with activity. Climbers are organizing their gear, planning their next climb, or sharing stories of their latest conquest. You can pitch your tent anywhere within the boundary lines of the camp.

There are some level sites on the packed dirt surface, but tables and other niceties are at a minimum. An accessible _UNISEX RESTROOM_ is centrally located. You may need to get the key at the entry station.

Yosemite National Park

PO Box 577
Yosemite, CA 95389
General Park Information
(209) 372-0624

Weather & Road Information
(209) 372-4605

Lodging reservations:
Yosemite Park and Curry Co.
Central Reservations
5410 East Home
Fresno, CA 93727
(209) 252-4848

Camping Reservations:
MISTIX - **(800) 365-2267**

Location — 72 miles northeast of Merced via SR 140, 63 miles north of Fresno via SR 41, 13 miles wet of Lee Vining via SR 120, 102 miles east of Stockton via SR 120.

Elevations — Tioga Pass 9,945 feet; Tuolumne 8,600 feet; Wawona 4,012 feet; Glacier Point 7,214 feet; Yosemite Valley 3,966 feet.

INDIAN GRINDING ROCK STATE HISTORIC PARK

Long before the "White Man" came to California seeking gold, the Northern Miwok Indians inhabited much of the western Sierra Nevada region. For thousands of years, large numbers of Miwoks would come together at this location in the winter to continue their hunting and gathering activities. Several types of structures similar to those used by the tribe for shelter and community assemblies are recreated from bark and logs. Most notable of Indian artifacts is the huge low-lying marbleized limestone outcropping pitted with hundreds of mortar cups. Centuries of acorn and seed grinding formed these small depressions, called chaw'se. You can almost picture the Miwok women as they exchange the news of the day while tirelessly grinding out their staple diet of acorn meal. Indian Grinding Rock State Historic Park is dedicated to these and other Native American tribes that made their home in California.

A concrete _WALKWAY_ leads through the entire outdoor display of Miwok buildings. There is even a _BOARDWALK_ to take you out over the middle of the 173' by 82' grinding rock. An impressive roundhouse

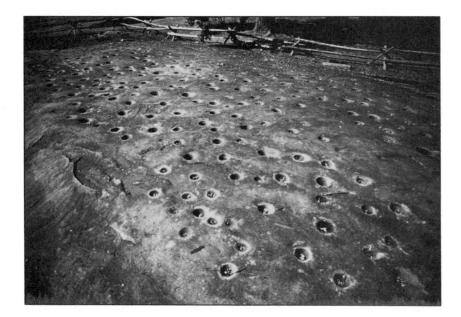

A boardwalk leads over the morteros at Indian Grinding Rock SHP.

(Photo courtesy CPDR)

stands near the grinding rock. Many California Indian communities considered this their social and ceremonial heart. Several different tribes still use the roundhouse for joint gatherings. From the trail you'll be able to peek into a teepee-shaped structure made of bark and logs (Bark House) used as sleeping quarters. You'll also get a look at an Indian football field. A *SELF-GUIDED TOUR* begins at the parking lot near the Chaw'se Regional Indian Museum. From there, a 9½% slope takes you to the mostly flat display area. The paved portion of the walkway ends 600 feet from the parking lot at the roundhouse. Benches are provided at regular intervals along the path.

Visitor Center

The **Chaw'se Regional Indian Museum** contains original works and interesting displays of Indian art and handcrafts. In the spring and summer, weekend visitors will be delighted with special demonstrations of various Miwok craftmaking at the museum. Most other days, an artifact reproduction display allows everyone to touch many tools and personal items that local tribes used daily. In addition, a colorful visitor orientation video tape is shown downstairs. Two designated *PARKING* places are very close to a gentle ramp at the main upstairs entrance. The video viewing room, accessible *RESTROOMS*, and a *DRINKING FOUNTAIN* can be accessed on the lower level from the outside walkway. A wall-mounted telephone there is too high to reach from a seated position.

Camping

Indian Grinding Rock Campground sites, smothered in pines and oaks, stand on a hillside near the Indian football field. Most of the asphalt pull-ins are on a different level than the tables. Each site has a table, food storage, BBQ, and a fire ring. The centrally-located restroom is not accessible. Though the campsites are private, they are not at all practical for wheelchair users.

Indian Grinding Rock (Chaw'se) State Historic Park
14881 Pine Grove-Volcano Road
Pine Grove, CA 95665
(209) 296-7488
Park Folder Available
Location — Off Hwy 88 from Jackson to Pine Grove on Pine Grove-Volcano Road
Elevation — 2,418 feet

CALAVERAS BIG TREES STATE PARK

Giant Sequoias predate humans by millions of years. Combined with other redwood species, they dominated the forests of North America. In the days of early humanity, the trees were the subject of awe and admiration by Native Americans of the West. Today, climate changes and society's intervention have diminished the redwood growing regions, leaving only a few isolated patches of sequoias that dot the western Sierra Nevadas.

When A.T. Dowd stumbled onto these beauties while chasing a wounded bear in the 1850's, his reports of 300-foot trees initiated a flood of curiosity and exploitation.

He and others cut down trees or stripped them of their bark for exhibits in the big cities and traveling shows in the East. The "Big Trees" soon became a tourist destination. There was even a dance floor built on the stump of the first tree felled in the forest. The colorful history of the grove, coupled with the fascinating redwoods, still draws thousands of visitors each year to Calaveras Big Trees State Park. Now, irreverent disbelief has been replaced by respect and understanding of the need to preserve and protect the few remaining redwood groves on the West Coast.

Just as the pioneers discovered the wonders of the Giant Sequoia, park visitors with mobility limitations are discovering that the park is very hospitable for those with special access concerns. The *VISITOR CENTER* and *RESTROOMS* are accessible, as is the one-mile *BIG TREES TRAIL*. In addition, the docents will loan you a *WHEELCHAIR* if you feel your day at the park will be more than you can manage on foot. To assure your comfort when you arrive, you may arrange for a chair by calling the park office.

Visitor Center and Day Use

For day users, *PARKING* is designated near the visitor center and at the north end of the main parking lot near the amphitheater trail. A short ramp leads to an accessible *RESTROOM* at the edge of the main day use parking lot. The *VISITOR CENTER*, housed in a cozy log cabin, displays the wildlife and colorful human history of the Calaveras Big Trees. There is also variety of books and pamphlets available for purchase. Children and adults alike are drawn to the "touchy-

183

The path at North Grove - Big Trees Trail is smooth and inviting.

(Photo courtesy CDPR)

feely" exhibit where they can handle some of natures artifacts. A twenty-foot ramp (6%) takes you from designated *PARKING* to the entrance.

Trails

North Grove — Big Trees Trail — Accessible ranger-led *NATURE WALKS* leave the visitor center once a day during the peak season or you may take the self-guided North Grove — Big Trees Trail on your own. Plan at least an hour for this very interesting walk through time. The broad, well-packed trail is smooth and flat. Ramps, wooden walkways, and platforms avoid the heavy surface roots, allowing disabled visitors, wheelchair users, and those who would like a closer look at the trees to get right next to the bark of broad tree bases. There are plenty of benches at strategic locations along the way so you can just sit a while and enjoy the view. The guide to the trail is also available in audio tapes or braille, so everyone may share the experience.

Three Senses Trail — The North Grove also features a *SPECIAL TRAIL* that begins beyond the campfire center. The Three Senses Trail is designed to help everyone see the wonders of the forest by using their senses of touch, smell, and hearing. Guide ropes placed along the 600-foot trail lead blind visitors between display markers written in large print and braille. At most of the markers, you are encouraged to feel, listen to, or get a whiff of a part of the forest, thus identifying the world around you through all your sensory perceptions. The trail is similar in surface to the Big Trees Trail, and is open for all people to enjoy.

Picnic

In addition to the picnic area at the west end of the North Grove camping loop, other shady spots along the Walter W. Smith Memorial Parkway provide picnic tables on forest floor settings. In the **North Grove Picnic Area,** several tables with BBQ's skirt Big Tree Creek. The restroom central to this picnic area has a 2-inch lip at the doorway and narrow stalls with no modified fixtures.

Further down the park road beyond Oak Hollow Campground, tables and BBQ's are scattered along the loop drive at **River Picnic Area**. Nearby, a small _PARKING_ stop with designated spaces offers a view of the Stanislaus River where a steep set of stairs descends to the water's edge. Just beyond the river, a steep gravel ramp leads up to two tables in a flat shady alcove above the roadway at **Oak Leaf Spring Picnic Area**. To use this spot, you must park across the street in a pull-out. As you drive to the end of the parkway, **Beaver Creek Picnic Area** offers sightseers a look at the swimmers and sunbathers on the rocky creek banks at Beaver Creek. The densely-shaded walk-in picnic area here has tables and BBQ's. None of the picnic areas are modified for access.

Camping

North Grove — Giant sequoias and a mixed canopy of pine and cedar trees shade the North Grove campground. Its paved camping loop completely encircles a lovely open meadow at Big Tree Creek where forest creatures often come to feed in the late afternoon. Each level site has a forest floor or asphalt pull-out in the trees next to a table and fire ring. Designated _CAMPSITE_ #19 is designed for maximum accessibility. Asphalt covers the parking, the surface surrounding the table, and a path that leads 50 feet beyond the site to a fully accessible _UNISEX RESTOOM/SHOWER_ combination. Water is also available at the campsite. You'll need to get a key to the restroom from

the kiosk attendant at the time you register.

A 300-foot asphalt path from the visitor center leads to the park's _AMPHITHEATER_. An asphalt platform is next to the seating so wheelchair users don't have to be separated from their party. A dirt trail from the main day use parking lot also leads to the amphitheater. Campers of all ages enjoy the campfire programs that the rangers give nightly during peak summer season.

Oak Hollow — Four miles from the park entrance, paved campground roads loop among oaks and pines in a small valley called Oak Hollow. The hilly roads and steep campsites at Oak Hollow Campground are not desirable for wheelchair users. There are no modified restrooms or showers at this campground.

Calaveras Big Trees State Park
PO Box 120
Arnold, CA 95223
(209) 795-2334

Park Folder Available; also, A Guide to Calaveras North Grove Trail
Location—Four miles northeast of the town of Arnold on Hwy 4
Elevation—4,000 to 4,800 feet

Columbia SHP

COLUMBIA STATE HISTORIC PARK

When the Golden State was in its Goldrush heyday, towns and cities sprang up overnight in the hills and back country of California. In 1850, Dr. Thaddeus Hildreth found his fortune waiting for him in the hills of the western Sierra above American Camp, a tent and shanty town he named. Dr. Hildreth's strike was so rich, in fact, that American Camp developed into the town of Columbia, and his gold discovery became known as the "Queen of the Southern Mines." Thousands of fortune-hunters filled the town, making it the second largest in California at the time. Unlike many other Goldrush towns of the 1870's, Columbia was never completely deserted when the mines were depleted; a small community stayed on. A California State Historic Park since 1945, Columbia is now being preserved and restored for its 19th-century appeal. Miners have been replaced by vendors and tourists, and the town thrives once again.

The narrow streets of the main business district are closed to mo-

(Photo courtesy CDPR)

torized vehicles, making them safe for children and available for easier access. Shops in town, open every day except Thanksgiving and Christmas, offer variety of diversions and delectables; interesting stores include a bakery, souvenir shop, candy store, blacksmith, and several restaurants, saloons, and snack shops. In addition, there are all sorts of special events held in town. Consult your park flyer for schedules of square dancing, the melodrama theater, and stage coach rides.

The **Columbia Museum** will be of special interest to history buffs. Personal artifacts and Goldrush memorabilia fill the walls and display counters at the _MUSEUM_ to overflowing. Every two hours, park docents show a movie recounting the fascinating story of Columbia's Goldrush days. To get into the museum, there is a special ramp entrance around the corner off the main road. Near the museum entrance, a brick ramp leads to a small accessible _RESTROOM_ that has a shallow stall, low toilet and grab bars.

STAGE COACH RIDES and horseback riders leave all day from the livery area at the south end of town. If you're game, the stage drivers are willing to help you on board for an authentic stage coach trip through town. For information about the stage coach ride call (209) 523-0663. You also can take a tour through a working hardrock gold mine, the only one of its kind open to the public. Gold mine tours leave by bus from the Matelot Gold Mine Supply Store. At the mine, most of the trails are hard-packed dirt, but there are a few mine car tracks to maneuver over. The bus does not have a wheel-

chair lift. You will need help buying tickets at the ticket counter, assistance on and off the bus, and someone to get you around small obstacles in the mine. This trip is a lot of work, but certainly a different experience. For further information about the mine trip call (209) 532-9693.

Because of the historic nature of the town and the park's intention to preserve the buildings in their original state, many doorways and walkways are not accessible for wheelchair users. At times you'll find yourself having to take a detour into the street to avoid a stretch of boardwalk or a set of steps. Besides the one near the museum, there is another accessible _RESTROOM_ at the north end of town near the Street Charles Saloon.

If you park in the lot on the south end of town, you'll have access to Main Street near the livery stable or to the large picnic and BBQ area. A paved path leads from the parking and passes an accessible _RESTROOM_ (shallow stall, grab bars, and low toilet). Beside the path, two modified _PICNIC TABLES_ occupy a paved slab on the lawn. From this spot, you can watch the town goings-on or get in on the picnic activities.

PARK HEADQUARTERS is on Broadway and Washington. There is ramp access from designated _PARKING_ and an accessible _TELEPHONE_ at the entrance. You may pick up park brochures at the headquarters or the museum. Be sure to get a Columbia State Historic Park folder. It will make your visit to this lively town much more enjoyable.

Columbia State Historic Park

PO Box 151
Columbia, CA 95310
(209) 532-4301
Park Folder Available
Location— Four miles north of Sonora via Hwy 49 and county road
Elevation— 2,100 feet

RAILTOWN 1897 STATE HISTORIC PARK

In the late 19th century, the railroad was a vital link connecting the lumber mills and mines of Tuolumne County with the rest of the world. Today, the Sierra Railway Company continues to operate the original vintage steam locomotives taking delighted visitors for short rides or long excursions through the Mother Lode Country. The charm of railroading endures at the depot, where a gift shop, ticket counter, and museum carry through the old-fashioned theme. On the _ROUNDHOUSE TOUR_, you'll experience one hundred years of railroading history through the sights, smells, and sounds of the roundhouse. This turn-of-the-century building is still in use today as a maintenance and display shed for antique passenger cars, a variety of steam engines, and maintenance equipment. If you're a train buff or would like to experience a ride on an old steam train, this is definitely the right place for you to visit.

Wheelchair access is considered in much of the park's 26 acres. In the lot to the left as you enter the park, you'll find paved designated _PARKING_ near the depot _BOARDWALK_ access. Otherwise, the rest of the

Railroad history comes alive at Railtown 1897 SHP.

(Photo courtesy CDPR)

lot is gravel-coated. The accessible *BOARDWALK* encircles the depot building, and each *SHOP* in the building is also accessible. On the track side of the building, a heavy *RESTROOM* door opens to an ample lateral-transfer stall with fully accessible fixtures.

Train Rides

The train runs April through November on a regular schedule, and special trips are planned throughout the year. You may obtain a train schedule at the ticket counter or by contacting the park. The staff is happy to help passengers on board, but keep in mind that the access doorway on the train is only 27 inches wide. You may wish to call the depot with specific questions regarding your access needs.

Tour

Except for access to the turntable, the *TOUR* of the six-track roundhouse and blacksmith shop is accessible for most visitors with limited mobility. From the *MUSEUM* at the depot, where you'll see a short film, the tour leads down a paved path through a sloping grassy picnic area to the historic roundhouse building. Many displays are at eye level from a seated position. The tour guide will see to it that your visit is enjoyable

and provide you with the best vantage points along the tour. You can take a tour daily, May through September and year round on weekends.

Railtown 1897 State Historic Park

c/o Columbia State Historic Park
(209) 984-3113
Park Flyer and Train Schedule Available
Location—Hwy 49 to Fifth Avenue just
north of Main Street
Elevation—2,000 feet

WASSAMA ROUNDHOUSE STATE HISTORIC PARK

Similar to the roundhouse at Indian Grinding Rock State Historic Park, Wassama Roundhouse is a tribal gathering place for Native Americans from the Sierra foothill region. An organization of Native Americans called the Wassama Association operates the park. In July, the association holds its annual special Native American

events. Other gatherings take place throughout the year. For more event information call the Wassama Association at (209) 683-8869.

Reservations can be made for a guided tour, or a self-guided tour brochure may be obtained at the park. There is a small fee charged, and the hours of operation vary seasonally. The above-ground roundhouse and bark houses stand on a dirt surface at the base of a small knoll. From the dirt parking lot, the terrain follows a gradual downhill slope to the exhibit area. There are no paved access paths and the only restrooms are standard chemical toilets.

Wassama Roundhouse State Historic Park

Contact San Joaquin Valley
District Office
(209) 822-2332
Location—Seven miles north of
Oakhurst on Hwy 49
Elevation—2,300 feet

TURLOCK LAKE STATE RECREATION AREA

Before American and European settlers came along, the San Joaquin Valley was wild and magnificent, abounding in a profusion of plant life. In the last 200 years, civilization has changed the face of this Western Sierra valley. The rolling hills have become prime grazing lands for cattle ranchers and dairy farmers and are now grasslands for as far as the eye can see. Dredger tailing piles that line the highway are lasting evidence of gold mining endeavors here in the mid-1800's. In 1913, the Tuolumne River was impounded and used for irrigation purposes, creating Turlock Lake.

As a result, we now can enjoy camping and water sport activities at Turlock Lake State Recreation Area. At the _PICNIC AREAS_, a mixture of mature trees offers a shady canopy from the hot summer sun. The swimming beaches are pleasant and sandy. The _BOAT LAUNCH_ has plenty of car and trailer parking. Anglers try their luck for trout, black bass, crappie, blue gill, and catfish in the waters of the Recreation Area. At the wooded campground, you'll have the opportunity to see the indigenous plant life that once thrived along all the rivers of the San Joaquin Valley.

Boat Launch

Boaters, water skiers, and fishermen launch at the ramp between the east and west picnic areas. Two designated _BOAT_ and _TRAILER PARKING_ places are provided are near the launching ramp. The _LOADING DOCK_ is accessible. You'll

have to bring along your own gas, however. The concessionaire-operated snack bar and marina were destroyed in a fire and, as of 1991, are not rebuilt.

Picnic

Two _PICNIC TABLES_ at the eastern picnic area are covered with concrete and accessible for wheelchair users. A 50-foot paved pathway leads from designated _PARKING_ to this oak-covered knoll. These tables are popular because they have a great view of the swimming beach below. A fully accessible _UNISEX RESTROOM_ and _DRINKING FOUNTAIN_ are conveniently located near the parking places.

Cottonwoods, sycamores, and willows shade the picnic area west of the boat launch. An _ASPHALT PATH_ with guard railing skirts the perimeter of the grassy knoll for views overlooking the lake. If you wish, you can follow this path all the way to the boat launch. The restroom here is not accessible.

Camping

Down the highway from the day use area, a grove of cottonwood trees between the Tuolumne River and Turlock Lake lies in what was once the river's natural flood plane. A heavy growth of wild blackberries on the river bank is an added enticement to berry-pickers in mid-July through October. If you plan to pick berries from one of the narrow dirt trails among the bushes, be sure to watch out for poison oak!

Most of the sites at the campground are level and located on the perimeter of asphalt or gravel parking. Each has a table, fire

ring or BBQ, and food storage. The restrooms have narrow access doors that are less than 25 inches wide. There are no designated campsites or accessible restrooms in this campground.

Turlock Lake
State Recreation Area
22600 Lake Road
La Grange, CA 95329
(209) 874-2008
Park Folder Available (includes Caswell Memorial SP and MCConnell SRA)
Location — Twenty-three miles east of Modesto off Hwy 132
Elevation — 248 feet

MILLERTON LAKE STATE RECREATION AREA

Millerton Lake is located almost exactly in the center of California, where the San Joaquin River flows down from the Sierra Nevada range and is collected by the Friant Dam. The land at the base of the dam at Millerton Lake State Recreation Area was the Fresno County seat from 1856 to 1874.

Now that Millerton Lake has been created, the area offers a wide range of outdoor pleasures. There are several developed _CAMPGROUNDS_ with accessible _RESTROOMS_ and _SHOWERS_, many picnic grounds with varying accessibility, and boat launching ramps at the marina and campground. You also may visit the original Millerton County Courthouse, circa 1867. The Parks Service saved the building from rising waters when the dam was built in 1941 and carefully reconstructed it near the dam at Mariner's Point as it appeared over 100 years ago.

Directions

Before arriving at Millerton Lake, Hwy 145 splits to the north and south. Road 145 runs to the north then cuts off eastward, leading directly to the campground area at the lake's north shore. Road 206 to the south, veers east and becomes Millerton Road where it passes the park headquarters, day use areas, and boat marina on the south shore.

Courthouse

The Millerton County Courthouse served as the main offices for the county of Fresno after Millerton grew from a military encampment at Camp Barbour into a thriving city, now 200 feet below the lake. The courthouse is open to the public during the day. *PARKING* is designated near the *COURTHOUSE* entrance where a concrete walkway leads to the entry doors. The courtroom and adjoining offices have been decorated in the post-Goldrush style. Period furnishings and interpretive exhibits enhance your appreciation of the era.

Picnic Areas

The hills surrounding the lake tend to be steeper and higher on the eastern side. Each picnic area beginning at La Playa near the dam and ending with South Finegold, have difficult access to the picnic tables and other features.

An accessible *CHEMICAL TOILET* is placed somewhere near each day use area but can sometimes be difficult to reach due to the slope of the ground or its surface texture. None of the picnic sites are paved, nor are any of the tables modified.

La Playa—Most of La Playa picnic area is poised on the side of a sloping grassy knoll with plenty of digger pines and oak trees for shade. Along the lake access road, there is a level overlook area where the tables are more accessible than those on the hillside. However, unless the lake level is high, this spot isn't very appealing. Nearby, three designated *PARKING* places are next to a restroom with

Millerton Lake scene   *(Photo courtesy CDPR)*

a wide doorway, but there are no other access modifications.

Grange Grove—Pine and eucalyptus shade the sloping grassy lake bank at Grange Grove Picnic Area. Here, you will find some tables on a level grass and dirt surface. Two designated *PARKING* places are marked in the asphalt lot near an accessible *DRINKING FOUNTAIN* and *UNISEX RESTROOM* that can be reached by way of a 7% sloping path.

Blue Oak—Blue Oak Picnic Area is a series of rough dirt turn-outs.

Each has parking next to a few tables under clusters of blue oak trees.

South Bay—At South Bay Picnic Area, a dirt and gravel access road leads to parking near an accessible *CHEMICAL TOILET*. Tables and BBQ's are very difficult to access on the adjacent hillsides.

McKenzie Point—There is very little shade at the swimming beach and small McKenzie Point Picnic Area. There are no ramps or walkways down the steep incline to the beach that lies about 150 feet (at low water level) from the parking area. There is an accessible *CHEMICAL TOILET* in the dirt and gravel parking lot.

South Finegold Picnic Area is at the end of Sky Harbor Road, 6 miles from Millerton Road. The sloping picnic sites are similar to the other picnic areas. Near the parking area, a dirt approach leads to a restroom that has a wide door but no other accessible features.

Camping

On the north shore of Lake Millerton, a series of five campgrounds line Dumna Cove. In each section, you'll find that many campsites are level and have a view of the lake. Sites have paved parking with a table, fire ring, and food storage on a dirt surface. An occasional tree provides sparse shade at some sites. Facilities at **Mono**, **Rocky Point** and **Fort Miller** campgrounds offer fully accessible UNISEX RESTROOMS and barrier-free SHOWERS with low controls and a retractable bench. A paved approach from the road is not yet developed, so each restroom has a 1- to 4-inch transition onto a concrete slab from the surrounding dirt. It is best to take a drive through the campground to choose a suitable site before paying your camping fee.

A designated CAMPSITE is located at the end of Road 145 at **Meadow Campground**. The entire surface of site #121 is paved except for a flat dirt section for a tent. Like most of the other campsites, there is little shade, so you'll want to bring some protection from the mid-summer sun. A concrete walkway leads from the site to an accessible RESTROOM that has a large converted stall with grab bars, a high toilet and an accessible DRINKING FOUNTAIN. The shower room stall has a bench, and the controls are 47 inches from the floor. This restroom is scheduled for an upgrade in 1992.

The boat launch ramp at Meadow Campground has an inaccessible dock. When the water level is low, you can drive onto the gently sloping beach from the boat ramp for access to the water. During the summer, park rangers give campfire programs at the AMPHITHEATER. It is up a dirt path from a parking area along Road 145. The restroom in the parking lot is not accessible. An RV dump station is provided near the group camping area across from Fort Miller Campground.

Millerton Lake State Recreation Area

PO Box 205
5290 Millerton Road
Friant, CA 93626
(209) 822-2332
Park Folder Available
Location—Twenty miles north of Fresno on Hwy 145 (Millerton Road)
Elevation—600 feet

SEQUOIA and KINGS CANYON NATIONAL PARKS

Thousands of years ago, the giant sequoia's early redwood ancestors ranged over the entire northern hemisphere. As the climate changed over millennia, the huge trees retreated to the western slope of the Sierra Nevada mountains and are now found only in scattered groves. In the mid-1800's, when white settlers discovered groves of these massive beauties, John Muir and others feared that what remained of nature's largest living things would go the way of the saw blade. It was not until 1890 that legislators were successful in naming the Sequoia and General Grant areas as America's second National Park. Since then, more acreage in Kings Canyon and Mineral King has been added to preserve the land that surrounds one of the few survivors of the last Ice Age, the giant sequoia.

As home to the largest living things on earth, Sequoia and Kings Canyon National Parks include variety of spectacular scenery ranging from high mountain peaks (six are over 14,000-foot elevation) to canyons deeper than the Grand Canyon. Just out of sight, Mt. Whitney towers over the Owens Valley on the eastern park boundary as the highest mountain in the contiguous United States, reaching 14,494 feet. In contrast to the dense forests of giant trees, low-growing chaparral covers the dry foothills to the west. Wildlife of all sorts abounds. Mountain lions prowl the hills, and an occasional black bear is still attracted to campsites by the prospect of finding some improperly stored food.

The General's Highway, open year round, is the main road that connects Sequoia and King's Canyon National Park. It winds through the sequoia belt for a pleasant two-hour drive of 46 miles. Most of the park roads are narrow and curvy as they thread through the mountainous terrain. So give yourself ample time to get to your destination.

At either the Big Stump Entrance of Grant Grove or at the Ash Mountain Entry Station, you will be given a copy of *Sequoia Bark*, a semi-monthly newspaper with a detailed description of current activities and features in both the Sequoia and Kings Canyon areas. In addition, you'll receive a *Sequoia/Kings Canyon Map and Guide* to help you find your way around these large parks. It would be helpful to write or call ahead for this information to help you plan your visit.

If you plan to stay at either of the parks, you can make lodging reservations through Sequoia and Kings Canyon Guest Services, Sequoia National Park, CA, 93262, (209) 561-3314. Reservations for Lodgepole campground must be made with MISTIX, either by mail or telephone. For camping information at Lodgepole Campground, contact MISTIX Customer Service, PO Box 85705, San Diego, CA 92138, (800) 365-2267. All other campgrounds are available only on a first-come-first-served basis and cannot be reserved. There are some designated sites available. Most polite campers understand that these sites are reserved for campers with a handicap-identification placard unless there are no other sites available. In the busy summer season, you should arrive early in the day to choose your campsite.

KINGS CANYON NATIONAL PARK

Grant Grove

The Grant Grove area of Kings Canyon National Park was dedicated just after Yosemite National Park. Originally named General Grant National Park, it was established to preserve the last natural environment of the giant sequoias. When the Kings Canyon area was added to the National Park system, it absorbed Grant Grove. This section of Kings Canyon National Park begins at the Big Stump Entrance on Hwy 180 and ends one mile north of the Grant Tree Trail turn-off.

Village and Visitor Services

Grant Grove Village is the center of activity in the Grant Grove section of Kings Canyon National Park. Besides the _PARK OFFICE_ and _VISITOR CENTER_, you'll find a market, _FOOD SERVICES_, a _GIFT SHOP_, _POST OFFICE_, _LENDING LIBRARY_, and _GAS STATION_. All of the surfaces at the village are paved and smooth. Though there is a large parking lot near the gift shop, the only designated _PARKING_ is across the street near the visitor center.

A ramp with handrailing leads to the entrances of the accessible _GIFT SHOP_ and _COFFEE SHOP_. An accessible _TELEPHONE_ is just outside. The lodging reservation desk is located in the lobby of the coffee shop. The coffee shop has a restroom, but it is too small for wheelchair access. A 24-hour _POST OFFICE_ is just down the walk from the gift shop; there is a small sill at the doorway. Perched on a knoll near the rustic cabins, the market is located down the village road past the post office. From a parking area below it, there is an uphill push all the way to the steep (20%) 15-foot access ramp.

At the _VISITOR CENTER_, you can check with a ranger for the current programs and services available in Grant Grove. Exhibits and book sales are within view of a seated person and films shown regularly in the _THEATER_ are accessible as well. You'll find the _LENDING LIBRARY_ at the end of a concrete path around the side of the visitor center. The _RESTROOM_ at the visitor center has a wide but shallow stall and a high toilet with grab bars. There is one designated _PARKING_ place just outside the visitor center.

Picnic

Columbine — A dirt road takes you to a secluded picnic area enveloped by sequoias and pines where you may park next to your chosen table. Most of the tables and fire rings are not on level surfaces, and there are no modified tables or paving. The restrooms here are not accessible.

Trails

General Grant Tree Trail — Considered by some to be "the nation's Christmas tree," naturalists estimate the General Grant Tree to be between 2,000 and 2,500 years old; it has a circumference of over 107 feet — wider than many city streets! You can view this massive sequoia at a distance from the large parking lot or up close and personal, as it towers beside a very popular paved trail. From the parking lot, the trail leads uphill to a 1/3-mile self-guided nature loop that takes you through the forest leading to General Grant Tree. If you seek a more informative tour, take a _RANGER-LED WALK_ on the trail, offered most days in the summer season. Or, rent a cassette tape at the visitor center to take along with you. The first bit of the trail is steep and will require assistance, but the path is broad and well traveled. Like many other park trails, this one requires effort., but a walk through this giant forest is worth it. Though there are no designated parking places, there is an accessible _RESTROOM_ in the parking lot with a roomy, lateral-transfer stall with a high toilet and grab bars.

Big Stump Trail — This interesting trail traverses an area that was clear cut for timber in the late

1880's. Evidence of the logging endeavor is still visible along this one-mile self-guided walking trail that winds on a hilly course through sequoia stumps and sawdust piles. Unfortunately, the trail tread is rough and sometimes too steep and narrow in places to allow passage by wheelchair. Picnic tables are distributed on raised grassy areas on the outskirts of the paved parking lot. There are no curb cuts onto the grass except at the accessible RESTROOM. A wide doorless stall in the restroom has a high toilet and grab bars.

Camping

Sunset (FCFS) — Giant sequoias and other mixed conifers shade 200 campsites at Sunset Campground, most of which are on rolling terrain and not very level. Each site includes a table and forest floor parking, which are not always on the same level. There are no designated campsites here. The campfire center at the entrance to the campground serves all of Grant Grove. A large paved parking lot is nearby. Although there are no designated parking places, a gentle (5%) paved path leads 200 feet to the totally paved CAMPFIRE CENTER. Rangers offer nightly programs during the summer season, here. Sunset Campground is open from early May to mid-October.

Azalea (FCFS) — Open year round, Azalea Campground is a series of five small loops with campsites on hilly terrain. A paved road serves the campground, and each site's pull-in is paved. All campsites have a table and fire ring on a forest floor surface. Trees in this area are sparse, but there are several flat sites with some protection

from the sun. The designated CAMPSITE #51 offers little shade but is near an accessible RESTROOM and has a modified PICNIC TABLE. The RESTROOM directly across the road has an extra large doorway and lateral transfer to a low toilet; the sink is not accessible. An RV dump station here is closed in winter.

Crystal Spring (FCFS) — Sunlight filters through the trees at the rolling terrain of Crystal Spring Campground. Designated SITE #6, like most of the other sites, is not very level. Besides the asphalt pull-in, site #6 has a fire ring and modified TABLE on the forest floor camping surface and is close to a fully accessible UNISEX RESTROOM. Crystal Spring Campground is open from early May to mid-October.

Lodging

Those who like a roof over their head at night, can arrange a stay at the **Grant Grove Cabins** that are spread over a hilly area near the visitor center at Grant Grove Village. Paved walkways that wind through the cabin area are be steep in places, requiring assistance to reach the entry ramps to each designated cabin. The management lists three cabins with bath (#7, #8, and #9) and one rustic cabin (#511) as accessible. The only accessible feature of the cabins is a ramp at the doorway. Otherwise, the bathrooms are standard and have no modifications for access. One cabin (#9) has a step at the doorway. The rustic cabin has no running water or electricity with only a wood-burning stove for heat and kero-

sene lamps for light. You can reach the restrooms for the rustic cabins on a paved path. There is a small step at the entry, and there are no widened stalls nor grab bars. While the cabins with bathrooms are available year round, the rustic cabins are closed in winter.

Lodging is also available in the private community of Wilsonia at the Wilsonia Motel, but there are no special accommodations for wheelchair users.

Cedar Grove

Cedar Grove nestles in a thickly-forested area on the banks of the South Fork of the Kings River. Campgrounds and the Cedar Grove Village are surrounded by an impressive steep-walled valley whose solid granite peaks rise one mile above the river. By driving to the end of the park road, you'll have many opportunities for mountain, canyon, and meadow views. For a complete self-guided tour of the canyon from your vehicle, return on the Cedar Grove Motor Nature Trail.

Village

Most visitors to the Cedar Grove area stop at the Village for supplies or a quick bite to eat at the **Cedar Grove Lodge**. The lower floor of the lodge contains the lodge's reservation desk, and a SNACK BAR and MARKET where you can purchase food, gifts, and camping supplies. Some aisles in the market are narrow, and there are small sills at each doorway. Two designated PARKING places are provided near a 40-foot wooden ramp with a handrail leading to the lower floor entrance. A *RESTROOM* on this floor has a stall wide enough for wheelchair access, but there are no other modifications. You'll also find a *SERVICE STATION, PUBLIC SHOWERS,* and the visitor center in the vicinity of the market.

Visitor Center — There are designated *PARKING* places in front of the small one-room ranger station that also serves as a visitor center. A small step and door sill at the entry prevent unassisted access. The *RESTROOMS* here have an accessible sink and a wide stall with a high toilet and grab bars. An accessible *DRINKING FOUNTAIN* is just outside.

Shower Building — The shower building near the gas station contains the *PUBLIC SHOWERS, A RESTROOM,* and a laundromat. The showers are small, with a 26-inch doorway, and there is no seat in the stall, but a shower chair is available on request. The shallow *RESTROOM* stall has a wide door, grab bars, and a low toilet.

Trails

Roaring River Falls — In years of heavy runoff, the river lives up to its name as it roars over the falls from the gorge above. Even in dry years the falls are impressive. You'll have an uphill climb all the way on the asphalt paved path that takes you to the base of Roaring River Falls. There are no other established trails beyond the top of this tree-lined path from which only the lower portion of the falls is visible. At its steepest,

this 800-foot trail is a strenuous 20% grade. The parking area contains no designated spots, but a crude asphalt ramp leads over the curbing to the trailhead.

Zumwalt Meadow — The Zumwalt Meadow Trail traces a path near the Kings River, crosses a suspension bridge, and gradually climbs above Zumwalt Meadow. The first portion of the trail has few elevation changes but much of it is quite rocky. This trail is not accessible for wheelchair users though there is a designated *PARKING* place near the trailhead.

Motor Nature Trail — To complete your driving tour of King's Canyon, take the Cedar Grove Motor Nature Trail on your way back from the end of Kings Canyon Highway. There is a self-guided trail map at the beginning of the dirt road, but you would have to get out of your vehicle to get one. It would be better to pick one up at the visitor center before you go. As you slowly make your way back to Cedar Grove Village along this scenic dirt road detour, follow along in the pamphlet as it describes the canyon's history and natural features.

Camping

Sentinel (FCFS) — Of all the campgrounds at King's Canyon, Sentinel Campground offers the most shade and is the most convenient to Cedar Grove Village. Designated campsite #9 has a paved parking place and a picnic table with an extended end. An asphalt trail leads from the site to an accessible *RESTROOM* that the visitor center shares. The *CAMPFIRE CENTER*

for all the campgrounds is located here. Parking is nearby; you must cross a bed of slippery pine needles to get to the campfire center.

Sheep Creek (FCFS) — At Sheep Creek Campground many sites near the river are level and shady, and you can park your vehicle on an asphalt pull-in. Like the other campsites in the park, these have a table, a fire ring, and food storage on a dirt surface. Unfortunately, there are no accessible restrooms or modified campsites at this campground.

Canyon View and **Moraine** (FCFS) — Campsites at both Canyon View and Moraine Campgrounds are not level and have little shade. A rough asphalt road circles these small camping loops where each site has a dirt pull-in, a table, and food storage. There are no designated sites at either campground.

Lodging

In the summer season, **Cedar Grove Lodge** offers motel rooms, each with two queen beds and a full bathroom. The management of the lodge has partially modified one room on the second floor for improved accessibility. The doorways are widened and there is a hand-held shower in the tub. At this time, there have been no grab bars placed, and the sink and toilet are not modified for access. A series of ramps (12%) provides access to this room on the second floor. For reservations or information, call (209) 561-3314.

193

The Trail for All People is a highlight in Sequoia National Park.

(Photo courtesy "The Fresno Bee")

SEQUOIA NATIONAL PARK

Lodgepole Area

The Lodgepole area is located between Grant Grove and Giant Forest on the General's Highway. With its 260 campsites and modern village stores and services, Lodgepole is a very popular family campground. It is often used as a home base for exploring the rest of Sequoia and Grant Grove. Campers who use wheelchairs will be happy to discover that Dorst Campground, north of the village on General's Highway, now offers accessible *CAMPSITES* and *RESTROOMS*.

Visitor services available at the Village include a *MARKET*, laundromat, *GAS STATION*, *DELI*, *GIFT SHOP*, *ICE CREAM SHOP*, *POST OFFICE*, and *PUBLIC SHOWER*. The *VISITOR CENTER* and campground reservation office are also in the vicinity. A paved marketplace and central plaza houses the Village shops. Several designated *PARKING* places are provided around its perimeter. Concrete walkways with an occasional gentle slope connect all of the buildings and doorways. However, many doors are heavy and have a 1-inch door sill.

In the *VISITOR CENTER*, books and pamphlets are available for purchase, and there is an accessible *AUDITORIUM* where rangers give talks. Consult your Sequoia Bark for the program schedules. A 4-inch step leads to the nearby campground reservation office. Until it is modified, you should do your business with them by telephone, (800) 365-2267. A short ramp leads to the doorway of an accessible *RESTROOM* located near the visitor center. The extra long stall has a high toilet and grab bars.

Public Shower—After a long day of exploring, an accessible *SHOWER* may be just what you're looking for. The designated stall in the public shower has a wide door and roomy interior with grab bars. A low shower chair is provided, and the twist control knob is 36 inches from the floor. A nearby *RESTROOM* stall offers lateral transfer to a low toilet with grab bars. There is a nominal charge to use the shower.

Nature Center—The Nature Center is just inside the campground entrance at the edge of the amphitheater parking lot. A small cabin serves as a children's activity center and is lined with nature displays and youngsters' projects on low tables and counter tops. There are steps at the front door, but an access ramp (12%) is available at the rear entrance.

Camping

Dorst—If you drive north from Lodgepole on General's Highway, just before you reach Kings Canyon NP, you'll see Dorst Campground on your left. In 1991, park staff and volunteers began a project to provide accessible family and group camping. In camping Loop G, eight accessible family *CAMPSITES* with an accessible *RESTSROOM* nearby are projected for completion in the Spring of 1992

Each level site has a hardened dirt surface, modified *PICNIC TABLE* and a raised *COOKING GRILL*. The fully accessible *RESTROOM* has a paved approach and designated *PARKING*. A wide doorway opens to a lateral-transfer stall with a high toilet, grab bars and an accessible sink.

Lodgepole—Steep granite cliffs and dense pine forests protect Lodgepole Campground on three sides. Campsites are distributed along in the midst of a large stand of lodgepole pines the banks of the Marble Fork of the Kaweah River. Rocky dirt roads wind through many camping loops along the river where high foliage topping the lodgepoles offers only sparse shade. In this busy community of hundreds of tents and RV's, each site has a table, a fire ring, and food storage. An old asphalt path takes you 550 feet to the *AMPHITHEATER*. Coated in places with decomposed granite or pine needles, the trail can be slippery. You may park in the lot near the Nature Center, but there are no designated spaces. An RV dump station is provided in this parking lot.

Designated *CAMPSITES* #69 and #70 are very close to the only accessible *RESTROOM* in the campground. However, these two sites are not convenient for wheelchair users. Bordered with large rocks, the sites are very uneven and have narrow parking places. If you don't need to be right next to the restroom, do not request a designated campsite. Many of the other 266 sites are more level, have wider parking, and are more desirable.

Surrounded by a dirt surface, the accessible *RESTROOM* is next to the Nature Center. The accessible stall is wide and extra long with grab bars and a high toilet. It also has a sink with knee room.

Giant Forest Area

At Giant Forest, you won't have to hike into the back country to see some fine groups of giant sequoias. The largest living thing on earth, the General Sherman Tree is sure to be of interest. It towers ominously over a paved trail at the northern edge of the Giant Forest along General's Highway. Other paved trails will take you on a pleasant loop around a grassy meadow or up into the tall trees beyond the General Sherman Tree. If you plan to stay in the Park, you'll be happy to find comfortable, accessible accommodations at the Giant Forest Lodge.

Visitor Services

Before taking off to see more of the park, **Giant Forest Village** is the place to stop for a meal or groceries. There is cafeteria near two designated *PARKING* places. A walkway leads to the entrance where there is a steep ramp at the doorway. Along the walk, you'll find an accessible *TELEPHONE* and *DRINKING FOUNTAIN*. The nearby market has very narrow aisles and a short, steep ramp access at the doorway. Steps create a barrier to both the gift shop and the information booth in the village. Neither the restrooms behind the information booth nor those in the cafeteria are accessible.

Trails

Trail for All People—The Trail for All People was conceived and designed for visitors with limited mobility. Not far from Giant Forest Lodge, this paved 0.6-mile walk skirts the edge of the open creek-fed area of Round Meadow, one of many meadows that add special beauty to the Giant Forest. You can stroll in the shadows of towering sequoias that surround this open space. From descriptive exhibit markers along the self-guided trail, you'll learn about meadow ecology and other wonders of the redwood forest. Designated *PARKING* and an accessible

CHEMICAL TOILET are provided in the northern parking area near the trailhead. The trail begins across the road with a short steep downhill access, but the rest of the trail is smooth and almost flat.

General Sherman Tree—In 1879, when James Wolverton discovered this tree, he decided to name it in honor of the General under whom he served in the Ninth Indiana Cavalry. Based on total volume, the General Sherman Tree is "The Largest Living Thing in the World." It is difficult to appreciate the size of this magnificent specimen. Although, when you consider that it would take at least 30 rail cars to transport the trunk alone, you get some idea of its gigantic proportions.

Since the General Sherman Tree is quite an attention-getter, there is always a lot of activity in the parking lot. One hard-to-find designated *PARKING* place is provided near the restroom at the parking lot entrance. From here you take the asphalt trail that makes a steady but gradual uphill climb to the base of the tree about 300 feet away. The restroom in the parking lot is not modified for wheelchair access.

Congress Trail—For an exciting introduction to the giant sequoia, a paved portion of the Congress Trail branches off the Sherman Tree Trail and leaves from the opposite end of the parking lot. At both locations, the beginning of the trail is very steep but levels out more as it ascends to the Alta Plateau section of the Giant Forest where many big tree groupings stand watch over the trail. Most wheelchair users will need help for the steep sections of this two-mile loop trail. An excellent pamphlet,

available for a small fee at the beginning of the trail, offers fascinating insights into the nature of this unique forest.

Crystal Cave—For thousands of years, underground springs at Grant Grove have slowly and steadily worn at a vein of marble lying just under the surface of the Sierra granite mountains. The softer marble substance is gradually being washed away, leaving behind the fantastic marble caverns called Crystal Cave. The Sequoia Natural History Association gives seasonal tours of the cave, but the very hilly terrain and several sets of stairs prohibit wheelchair access.

Lodging

Giant Forest Lodge offers year-round accommodations ranging from deluxe motel units to rustic cabins. Paved walkways and service roads meander through the grounds and lead to the dining room and to the accessible *AMPHITHEATER*. Walkways are steep in places and may require assistance. The main office is up a steep incline from the closest parking place. It is advisable to call ahead and make check-in arrangements. Behind the office, a ramp leads to a fully accessible *RESTROOM*.

Five *DELUXE MOTEL UNITS* at Giant Forest Lodge are modified and reserved for disabled visitors. Room #240, and #243 through #246 are enlarged and offer two queen-sized beds and an accessible bathroom with a removable seat in the tub/shower combination. There are grab bars in the shower and around the elevated toilet and raised sink.

When you make reservations, be sure to ask for the handicap-accessible rooms so that your reservation will take priority for these modified accommodations. You can park at the bottom of a gated service road that has a slight grade about 150 feet from the rooms. If you call ahead or speak with the clerk in the lobby, the staff will unlock the gate so you may unload your things next to the wooden ramp that leads to the doorway of your room. For further information, you may call the Lodge office at (209) 565-3381.

Located behind the Lodge, the dining room has a series of four steps that precludes wheelchair access, but, if you wish, the staff will be happy to lift you onto the decking and help you over the step into the dining area. Otherwise, meals are available at the village cafeteria.

Foothills

Covered with grasses and oaks common to the eastern Sierra, the foothills present a stark contrast to the mountainous woodlands at the upper elevations. Depending on your direction of travel, you'll want to be prepared for a 10° to 20° variation in temperature. While the weather is mild in Giant Forest, summers in the foothills can be downright hot.

To enter the park from the south, take Hwy 198 as it gradually climbs from Visalia in the San Joaquin Valley into the foothill region of Sequoia National Park. You'll find the Park Headquarters and **Ash Mountain Visitor Center** one mile north of the entry station.

All of the visitor center features are accessible, including a *TELEPHONE,* *DRINKING* *FOUNTAIN*, and a fully accessible *RESTROOM*. Rangers are on duty daily and can offer information on the road conditions, weather or park activities. Maps, brochures, books and postcards are for sale and you can watch a film in the visitor center.

Across the street, a grassy area with tables and plenty of shade invites you to relax a while before continuing your journey on the steep twisting road to Giant Forest. If you didn't stop at Ash Mountain, you'll have another chance to stretch and refresh at the **Hospital Rock** picnic and rest area. The Hospital Rock area offers one designated *PARKING* place near a curb cut to an accessible *RESTROOM* (high toilet with grab bars), *TELEPHONE* and *DRINKING* *FOUNTAIN*. Oak trees shade the picnic tables just off the asphalt pavement.

Camping

Potwisha (FCFS) — Shaded by an abundance of oaks that offer relief from the hot summer sun, the Potwisha Campground is the first campground you encounter as you enter the park from the south. An asphalt road connects the level campsites; pavement extends to each pull-in or pull-thru. Designated *SITE* #39 has pull-thru parking near a concrete walkway that leads to an accessible *RESTROOM*. As with the others, the table, food storage, and fire ring are on a dirt surface. The *RESTROOM* has a wide stall, a high toilet with grab bars, and no other access modifications. Campsite #40, though not designated, is similar to site #39 and is also near the restroom.

Buckeye Flat (FCFS) — Across from Hospital Rock picnic area, a narrow road winds down to the oak-covered hillside at Buckeye Flat. Anything but flat, the campsites are arranged so that the parking and the table area are not on the same level. The restrooms are not accessible, and there are no designated campsites.

Mineral King

The promise of mountains rich with silver ore prompted miners to call this area Mineral King. Unfortunately, wealth was not to be derived from the rock, and the little town of Silver City is only a remnant of its former self. But the grandeur of the forested peaks and sub-alpine meadows remains for stout-hearted hikers and campers to explore. In keeping with its primitive nature, facilities at Mineral King are rustic and limited. There are very few accommodations made for wheelchair users. For more information, contact the Mineral King ranger station (209) 565-3341 extension 812.

Sequoia and Kings Canyon National Parks
Three Rivers, CA 93271
(209) 335-2315 — Kings Canyon
(209) 565-3341 — Sequoia
24-Hour Information
(209) 565-3351

Lodging reservations:
Sequoia and Kings Canyon Guest Services
Sequoia National Park, CA 93262
(209) 565-3373 or
In California — **(800) 824-9364**

Camping reservations for Lodgepole Campground only — **(800) 365-2267**

Pamphlets and Maps Available:
Sequoia and Kings Canyon Official Map and Guide; Sequoia Bark, *semi-monthly newspaper;* *Flyers — general information, access information, campground information, General Sherman and*

General Grant Sequoia information, assorted hiking information
Elevation—Grant Grove 6,589 feet; Cedar Grove 4,635 feet; Lodgepole Area 6,700 feet; Giant Forest 6,412 feet; Foothills 2,820 feet; Mineral King 6,935 feet

---

Diablo Range

MOUNT DIABLO STATE PARK

Views of the Livermore and Diablo Valleys become more breathtaking around every turn as you follow the narrow winding road up the grassy mountainside at Mount Diablo State Park. As you near the summit (elevation, 3849 feet), oak studded fields give way to sage-covered hillsides. From the top, on a clear day you'll be able to see over 40,000 square miles of central California, from the Golden Gate to the Sierra Nevada range and from Lassen Peak to the Mount Whitney area!

Picnic

Picnic areas snuggle into nooks and crannies along the road leading to the summit. All of them except Horseshoe Picnic Area have very difficult access around rocks or up narrow paths. You'll find **Horseshoe Picnic Area** just past the Live Oak Campground near Curry Point lookout. Here you can park near a gently sloping paved site that has a table, BBQ, and *DRINKING FOUNTAIN* shaded by oaks overlooking Curry Canyon. There is a *PIT TOILET* nearby with ramp access, a wide door and grab bars.

Trail

The most spectacular vantage point from which to view Mount Lassen is on the **Fire Interpretive Trail** that begins near two designated *PARKING* places just below the summit. The trail was built to demonstrate Mount Diablo's recovery from a devastating 6,000-acre fire in 1977. The first paved portion of the trail is level and leads around the summit to the north for approximately 1/3 mile. At the trailhead is a modified *PICNIC TABLE*; the restroom nearby has a wide stall door and no other access modifications.

Camping

All three campgrounds at Mount Diablo State Park cling to the hillsides. Roads through each are steep and campsites are understandably sloping. Restrooms are not accessible, and there are no designated sites.

Mount Diablo State Park
   PO Box 250
   Diablo, CA 94528
   (510) 837-2525
Park Folder Available
Location—Five miles east of I-680 in Danville on Diablo Road or off Ygnacio Valley Road from the city of Walnut
Elevation—3,849 feet

BETHANY RESERVOIR STATE RECREATION AREA

Bethany Reservoir is set in the rolling grassy hillsides of northwestern San Joaquin Valley. Surrounded by a farm of wind generators whirring in the breeze and cattle grazing on the hillside, this small secluded reservoir is well-known to local fishermen and windsurfers. The wide variety of lake fish includes large mouth and striped bass, blue gill, catfish, and crappie. The park also serves as the northern terminus of the California Aqueduct Bike Trail, a graded dirt and gravel roadway that follows the aqueduct to San Luis Reservoir, 70 miles to the south.

Day Use

There is no overnight camping at the reservoir, but day users have their choice of two developed areas. Both areas have accessible *PARKING* places, *PICNIC TABLES*, a *BOAT LAUNCH*, and *FISHING PLATFORMS*. Since there are no trees around the reservoir, cabanas protect both picnic areas from the hot summer sun. In addition, the wind often sails through this end of the valley, so be prepared to "batten down the hatches."

The first day use area you encounter on the park road has many accessible features. Most of the parking area is paved, and a concrete walk leads to accessible *PICNIC TABLES*. The *BOAT LAUNCH* here has a gently sloping concrete walkway with handrails at 32 inches that takes you to the *BOAT DOCK* and *FISHING PLATFORM*. Designated *PARKING* is provided near an accessible *CHEMICAL TOILET*. Designated *PARKING* at the other day use area is on rough asphalt near the picnic cabanas and an accessible *CHEMICAL TOILET*. From the tables, there is a gently sloping asphalt ramp down to the *FISHING PLATFORM*. There are no railings on either fishing platform.

**Bethany Reservoir
State Recreation Area**

Contact Diablo District Office
(510) 687-1800

*Location—Ten miles east of Livermore,
seven miles north of I-580 via
Altamont Pass then north on
Mountain House Road to Kelso
Road west, then south on Bruns
Avenue to the end of Christensen
Road*
Elevation—247 feet

CARNEGIE STATE VEHICULAR RECREATION AREA

Motorcyclists of all abilities come to Carnegie State Vehicular Recreation Area to play in its rolling hills, canyons, and gulches. You'd never know that the hills once supported a booming clay brick and pottery factory. Long since razed, the factory went bankrupt in the early 1900's, and until the 1960's, cattle grazed on the hillsides.

Overnight camping is available at the primitive campground Friday and Saturday nights as well as the nights preceding a holiday. Day Users can explore the park year round on their motorcycle, three-wheeler, or quad. Park rangers are trained in emergency medical treatment and patrol the park regularly for your safety.

Camping facilities at the SVRA are limited and simple. Besides an accessible *TELEPHONE* and *CHEMICAL TOILET* near the entrance, there are no special access features. Camping is allowed only in your vehicle; you may not use a tent. Scattered oak trees or an occasional ramada

provide shade for picnic tables and fire rings.

The picnic and camping areas in the valley parallel the park road. Riding trails lead from every parking location, taking you to a network of trails on the hills and steep slopes nearby. To make your off-road visit more fun and to acquaint yourself with the park regulations, you should call and have a park folder sent to you ahead of time. Don't forget your helmet!

**Carnegie State
Vehicular Recreation Area**

PO Box 1105
Tracy, CA 95378
(510) 447-9027 or 447-9361
Park Folder Available
Location—Ten miles west of Tracy (6 miles west of I-580) on Telsa/Corral Road
Elevation—600 to 3,000 feet

LAKE DEL VALLE STATE RECREATION AREA

Nestled in the hills south of Livermore, the crystal blue waters of Lake Del Valle lie in sharp contrast to the golden grasses and chaparral of the surrounding oak-studded hills. There is a variety of outdoor activities to enjoy at Lake Del Valle State Recreation Area. On the eastern lake shore, you'll find a *BOAT LAUNCH* and a *BOAT RENTAL* concessionaire who will help boaters and fishermen with special access needs. Acres of wide open rolling grassy space can accommodate hundreds of picnickers and a sandy swimming beach gently slopes to the water. From the patio of the seasonal *SNACK BAR*, you'll have a great view of the windsurfing action on the lake. Across the

bridge on the western side of the lake, another grassy day use area overlooks the water. From this side of the lake, horseback riders saddle up for a journey into the hills, and a campground is just down the road.

East Lake

Day Use Area

The day use area on the east side of Lake Del Valle, is a modern, well-planned, and accessible place to spend a relaxing day. An asphalt *WALKWAY* with gradual inclines follows the shoreline for the entire distance of the day use area. You'll find picnic tables in flat grass or dirt areas and on pavement beside the walkways. Accessible *DRINKING FOUNTAINS* are provided at regular intervals along the path. There are designated *PARKING* places and curb cuts at every point of access to the lake shore. Accessible *RESTROOMS* and *TELEPHONES* are located throughout the day use area.

Snack Bar

Open during peak summer season and weekends, the snack bar is only 100 feet away from the nearest designated *PARKING* place. The patio around it is paved, and there is an accessible *TELEPHONE* nearby. If you're having a snack at the modified *PICNIC TABLES* in the patio, you'll have a clear view of windsurfers and first-timers near the swimming beach where windsurfing gear is rented by the hour.

Restrooms

Eagle's View—A 50-foot walkway leads from designated *PARKING* up a ramp with a maximum 10%

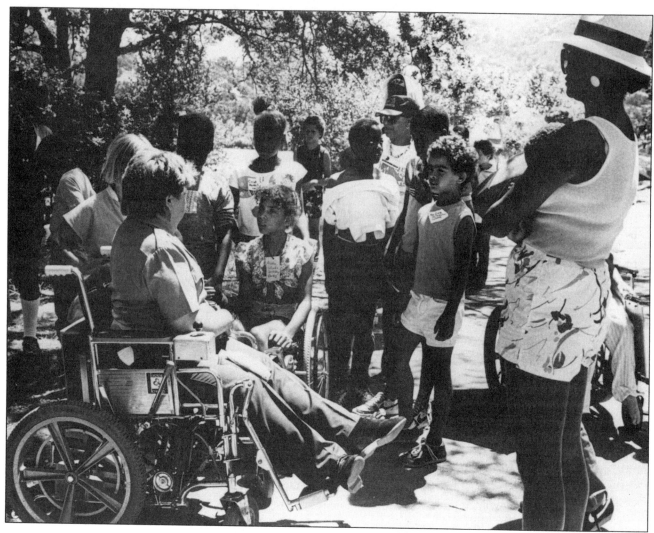

(Photo courtesy East Bay Regional Parks and Recreation)

grade to the <u>RESTROOM</u>. The accessible stall has a lateral transfer, high toilet, and grab bars. The sink is also high.

Oak Point and Snack Bar — The <u>RESTROOM</u> in this section has only a wide door and grab bars. No other access adaptations are made. There is an open changing area with benches in each of these buildings.

Boat Launch — This restroom is not accessible.

Boat Launch and Rental

Rainbow trout, large and small-mouth bass, white catfish, yellow bullhead, sunfish, and blue gill are the catch of the day at Lake Del Valle. There are regular trout plants from October to May; large-mouth and smallmouth bass bite well in the spring and summer. To launch your boat, take the east lake road north to its end. Park in one of two designated <u>PARKING</u> places for vehicle and trailer. A 4% decomposed granite approach leads from the parking to the boat dock gangway. The 25-foot gangway can be as steep as 15%, has a non-slip surface and handrails at 42 inches. For those without a boat, a concession employee will rent you a fishing or patio boat at the dock and help you on board For more boating information call (510) 449-5201.

West Lake

Day Use Area

On the west side of the lake, the swimming beach and most of the picnic locations are about 600 feet downhill from a large parking. A designated _PARKING_ place is illogically marked far from the lot's only curb cut. Asphalt walkways crisscross the grassy area and lead to the _VISITOR CENTER_ and a seasonal _SNACK BAR_. The large _RESTROOM_ and dressing room building has a stall with a wide door and grab bars, but there are no other modifications. From the visitor center, you'll have a splendid perspective of the lake below and access to the south swimming beach. Be sure to look for the display on the visitor center marking the lake's high water level — it's amazing.

Camping

One hundred fifty oak-shaded campsites lie along two creeks that feed into Lake Del Valle. On a quiet day, you may see wild turkeys come down from the hills to scavenge acorns and crumbs from last night's dinner. It's also not uncommon to spot deer foraging in the fringes of the campground. Watch them from a distance, and don't encourage them by offering them food. Asphalt roads take you to each campsite; the paved parking is either pull-in, pull-off, or pull-thru type. Twenty level sites are available with sewer and water hook-ups (no electricity), and an RV dump station is near the entrance.

The campground is arranged in a series of four camping loops. The fourth loop is the newest and has a fully accessible _RESTROOM_ and _SHOWER_. Though none of the campsites here are modified for access, many are level and within close range of the restroom. _RESTROOMS_ in this camping loop have lateral transfer to a high toilet, an accessible _DRINKING FOUNTAIN_ and _TELEPHONE_, and an electrical outlet. The _SHOWER_ has a retractable seat, low fixtures in the stall, and a changing bench in the drying area. All of the other restrooms in the campground have shallow accessible stalls with grab bars and standard fixtures. The other _SHOWERS_ have a 1-inch step, grab bar, 40-inch high control knob, but no seat.

There are two designated _PARKING_ places near the centrally located _AMPHITHEATER_. From there, a lighted asphalt path leads 150 feet to the seating area. For a short distance the path has a slope of 13%. Near the campground entrance is a modular unit housing the _CAMP STORE_ and office. A ramp access leads to the doorway there. The park and campgrounds are operated by the East Bay Regional Park District, headquartered out of Oakland. You can make reservations for the family campground by calling (510) 562-2267.

Lake Del Valle
State Recreation Area

Contact East Bay Regional Park District Office
(510) 531-9300

Park Folder Available — Ask for the Del Valle Campground map also. It gives detailed park information as well as campground information.
Location — Nine miles south of Livermore from I-580, take the N. Livermore exit (it becomes Tesla) to Mines and follow the directional signs to the park
Elevation — 800 feet

Henry W. Coe SP has marvelous scenery, but is not wheelchair-friendly.

(Photo courtesy CDPR)

HENRY W. COE STATE PARK

Once part of a sprawling 12,500-acre ranch belonging to the Coe Family, Henry W. Coe State Park is now a favorite getaway for horsemen and backpackers. Two hundred miles of riding and hiking trails lace the park ranging in elevations from 900 feet to 3,600 feet. As you wind your way up the narrow 13-mile road to the park headquarters at the site of the old Coe Ranch, the panoramas and habitat seem to change around every corner. The park is largely undeveloped, open grasslands and chaparral, dotted with oaks and sycamores — ideal for a horseback ride.

Part of the ranch house now serves as the visitor center and the equipment barn now houses a wagon and carriage display. Docents are sometimes on hand at the small museum that depicts life on the ranch in the late 1800's. Books and maps are also for sale. Parking is downhill from the park headquarters and visitor center on a sloping asphalt road. Covered in pea gravel, the approach to the visitor center is challenging, and there is a 4-inch step at the door. There are more steps inside the museum that limit access. The telephone at the visitor center is placed too high for access from a seated position.

The primitive campground (FCFS) near the visitor center is suggested only for the more adventurous camper. Twenty sloping sites with dirt pull-ins, picnic tables, shade ramadas and concrete BBQ's are connected by a steep asphalt road. A table extension is available on request at the visitor center. The approach to the nearby pit toilets is steep and not accessible. While Henry W. Coe State Park is a beautiful place to visit, but the hilly terrain severely limits wheelchair use.

Henry W. Coe State Park

PO Box 846
Morgan Hill, CA 95038
(408) 779-2728

Park Folder Available
Location — Fourteen miles from Morgan Hill on East Dunne Avenue, a steep and winding road
Elevation — Visitor Center 2,200 feet

San Joaquin Valley

DURHAM FERRY STATE RECREATION AREA

By the San Joaquin River in an open grassy setting, Durham Ferry State Recreation Area is popular with river fishermen and equestrians. A special section of the park, devoted to horsemen, has pipe corrals and trailer parking. In addition, marksmen will enjoy a full size archery range. Since there is no boating or swimming allowed in this section of the river, fishermen cast their lines for catfish, black bass, and perch from the ½-mile riverbank frontage, none of which is accessible for wheelchair users.

Because the park development is relatively new, the trees sprinkled on the rolling landscape are still immature, so ramadas shade the picnic tables. Pavement leads from ample packed dirt parking to the picnic areas and to accessible *UNISEX RESTROOMS* at both the day use and camping areas. There is an uphill slope of 8% to the restroom in the picnic area.

Campsites at the park are generally level. Two designated *SITES* are close to the accessible *UNISEX RESTROOM* and *SHOWER*. Each site has a table with ramada, BBQ, and parking on packed dirt. At the end of a rough asphalt path, the first door you come to at the *RESTROOM* building opens into a large accessible unisex unit that includes an accessible *SHOWER*. The 40" by 48" stall has no seat and the control knob is 41 inches from the floor. An RV dump station is provided at the campground. You can make reservations for the campground by calling the park at (209) 953-8800.

Durham Ferry State Recreation Area

Contact San Joaquin County Parks and Recreation Department
(209) 953-8800

Location — Ten miles west of Ripon off Airport Way near the junction of Durham Ferry Road and Kasson Road (J4)
Elevation — 60 feet

CASWELL MEMORIAL STATE PARK

The valley oak, native only to California, once blanketed the river banks and flood plains of the San Joaquin Valley. With the continued demand for agricultural land and firewood, only a few isolated stands remain. At Caswell Memorial Park, a dense forest of virgin valley oaks covers the banks of the Stanislaus River. The thick foiage provides shelter and a lush habitat for an abundance of wildlife and plants. In the heat of the summer, visitors come to play in the cool river, take a walk on the Oak Forest Nature Trail, or just relax in the shade. A tangle of undergrowth offers extra privacy for these secluded campsites. There is an accessible TELEPHONE at the entry kiosk and an accessible RESTROOM in the picnic area.

Day Use

Picnics are a pleasure in the shady oak grove near the river. A paved portion of the picnic section is near two designated PARKING places in the second day use parking lot. An accessible RESTROOM with a lateral-transfer stall, grab bars, and an accessible sink is conveniently located near the tables.

Kids and grown-ups alike enjoy splashing in the refreshing waters of the Stanislaus River. To get there from the picnic area, take the broad, hard-packed dirt trail that find its way eastward through the trees to the river bank. The surface here becomes sandier and gradually slopes toward the water's edge. Because the path is uneven in places and soft near the river, most wheelchair users will require help to get to the river.

Fishing from the banks of the Stanislaus is particularly good in the summer when there are striped, largemouth, and smallmouth bass, sturgeon, blue gill, catfish, shad, and buffalo carp. In the fall you can try your luck for salmon and steelhead.

Trail

At the south end of the picnic area is the trailhead for the **Oak Forest Nature Trail**. This broad, packed, undulating trail wanders for a mile through sturdy valley oaks. Markers along the trail point out many features of animal and plant environment that you'll encounter along the Stanislaus River. The trail takes some steep dips in places that will require help to cross.

Camping

Shrubs and a profusion of vines and undergrowth make each campsite a private haven at Caswell Memorial State Park. The paved roadways and pull-ins connect level dirt sites, each offering a table, BBQ, and food storage. Though there are no designated campsites, many would be acceptable, but the restroom at the campground is not accessible. There is a 3-inch lip at the doorway, and there have been no modifications made in the stalls. A smooth dirt trail leads to the AMPHITHEATER.

Caswell Memorial State Park

28000 South Austin Road
Ripon, CA 95366
(209) 599-3810

Park Folder Available — (includes McConnell SRA and Turlock Lake SRA)
Location — Six miles from Hwy 99 south of Ripon on Ripon Road west to South Austin Road
Elevation — 40 feet

MC CONNELL STATE RECREATION AREA

McConnell State Recreation Area is a spacious park with lawns and tall trees that provide a relaxing atmosphere near the Merced River. Picnic tables and BBQ's are scattered on the grass, and several narrow footpaths lead to the river. In the hot summer, local residents often find this a refreshing place to cool off. Except for the RESTROOM at the campground, the facilities at the park are not modified for wheelchair access.

Seventeen campsites border either side of an asphalt road in a tree-shaded grassy area. Camping is best at the north end of the camping loop near the accessible RESTROOM, SHOWER, and DRINKING FOUNTAIN. The RESTROOM has a high toilet with grab bars, and the adjacent SHOWER has a seat, grab bars, and low controls. Designated PARKING is provided in front of the restroom. Rangers lead campfire talks on Saturdays at the amphitheater near the group campground, but you'll have to cross a grassy knoll down hill to access the seating area.

McConnell State Recreation Area

McConnell Road
Ballico, CA 95303
(209) 394-7755

Park Folder Available — (includes Caswell MSP and Turlock Lake SRA)
Location — From the town of Delhi on Hwy 99, take Santa Fe Avenue (J7) to El Capitan. Go west to Pepper, then south to McConnell Avenue.
Elevation — 104 feet

GEORGE J. HATFIELD STATE RECREATION AREA

Bounded on three sides by the Merced River, George J. Hatfield State Recreation Area is a favorite among fishermen. Close to the confluence of the San Joaquin and Merced Rivers, the area abounds with birds and other wildlife that find refuge in the surrounding valley oaks and river bank vegetation. Because of the lushness of the area, it is not surprising that California Indians often sought food and shelter here.

Wheelchair users will find the park difficult to access. Picnic tables are centered on a broad grassy knoll rimmed by rugged oaks about 300 feet uphill from the parking area. The twenty-one campsites that skirt the paved parking lot are at least 50 feet away from the nearest parking place. Each has a brick BBQ and a table. The only restroom at the park has a very narrow doorway and is not accessible. The narrow, rocky, nature trail that leads through the animal habitat near the river is not accessible.

George J. Hatfield
State Recreation Area

4394 North Kelley Road
Hilmar, CA 95324
(209) 632-1852

Location — From I-5 take the Newman exit into Newman, continue east on county road J-18 for five miles to the San Joaquin River bridge.
Elevation — 62 feet

FREMONT FORD
STATE RECREATION AREA

There are no developed facilities at Fremont Ford, only access by river bank trail to the San Joaquin River, where fishermen cast their lines from the shore hoping for bass, catfish, or a fall strike of salmon or steelhead.

Fremont Ford
State Recreation Area

Contact Four Rivers District Office
(209) 826-1196 or 429-2251

Location — Five miles east of Gustine on Hwy 140
Elevation — 66 feet

SAN LUIS RESERVOIR
STATE RECREATION AREA

San Luis Reservoir State Recreation Area nestles in the hills that once were the home of the Northern Valley Yokuts. But, by the 1850's, settlers had driven out the Indians. As early as 1871, local farmers began building a network of canals to service the growing needs of the agricultural community in the San Joaquin Valley. Construction of the existing reservoir on the west side of the valley began in 1962. San Luis Reservoir stores extra run-off water from the Sacramento Delta region that would otherwise flow into the ocean. Water stored here feeds much of the fertile San Joaquin valley through the canal system.

Fishing is the main attraction at all three bodies of water in the Recreation Area — San Luis Reservoir, O'Neill Forebay, and Los Banos Creek Reservoir. Striped and black bass, white and channel catfish, crappie, and blue gill arrive through the canal system from the Sacramento area. They grow and thrive in the forebay and in San Luis Reservoir. On the other hand, Los Banos Creek Reservoir is stocked with trout, crappie, blue gill, and catfish. Since the winds can be tremendous on the lake, a system of lights warns boaters of possible dangerous wind condi-

tions. If you are planning any type of recreation on the reservoirs or forebay, be sure to request a copy of the state park regulations about to your sport. The park service will provide you with safety information pertaining to fishing, hunting, windsurfing, camping, and swimming at the park.

San Luis Reservoir

Park Headquarters

Though it is not a visitor center, you may stop at the park headquarters for information and literature; park rangers and staff are available to help you. The office is located off Hwy 152 in the Basalt Area. There is designated *PARKING* near the entrance and a 2-inch step at the doorway.

Visitor Center

The Department of Water Resources operates the Romero Overlook Visitor Center just north of the San Luis Dam. From a vantage point high over the water, you'll have a bird's-eye view of the entire reservoir through huge glass windows. Pictorial displays and a film describe the history of the California Water Project and the rationale of water storage. There are two designated *PARKING* places at the entrance; a gentle ramp leads to a heavy door that will require help to open. The telephones are not accessible, but the *RESTROOM* is fully accessible. The turn-in for the overlook is easy to miss, so keep an eye out for the directional sign north of the dam.

Boat Launch

The new boat launch in the Basalt area has an an accessible *RESTROOM* in the parking lot, and a *LOADING DOCK* that is accessible from the boat ramp. At Dinosaur Point, the launching area is primitive and has no accessible features.

Camping

Typically, the Basalt area is characterized by rolling grass-covered hills, parched by hot summer sun. The park has planted eucalyptus, pine trees and shrubbery at the Basalt Campground providing campers with shade and privacy. Asphalt roads and parking offer smooth surfaces for access within the campground. A table, food storage box, and concrete BBQ are provided in each flat, firm, decomposed granite campsite. Paving surrounds the table and BBQ at designated *CAMPSITE* #32, which is near the accessible *RESTROOM*.

Designated *PARKING* is provided near each centrally located accessible *RESTROOM*. All offer a wide, but shallow pivot-transfer stall with grab bars and a high toilet. The sinks are standard, but hand driers are within reach and there is an electrical outlet available. The *SHOWER* has a 27-inch doorway and no seat in its 46" by 52" interior. Though there are no access barriers, the shower nozzle is high, and the controls are 51 inches from the floor.

As you enter the Basalt area, you'll find parking and an accessible *TELEPHONE* at the entry kiosk. A little further up the road is an rv dump station. On weekend evenings, rangers give programs at the *AMPHITHEATER*. Designated *PARKING* is on the upper campground road. A weathered asphalt walk will take you 50 feet to a paved area provided at the rear of the campfire seating.

O'Neill Forebay

While anglers try their luck in the reservoirs, most of the water sports and recreation are centered at O'Neill Forebay, nationally known for its excellent sailboarding. Windsurfers relish the strong spring and summer west winds that whistle through the valley. While the south shore of the forebay is a common place to launch, the most challenging rides are at Catfish Flats near Hwy 152. You can watch the action from an observation area off the day use road or from the forebay's south shore.

At a large day use area on the western shore of the lake, picnickers and swimmers have plenty of room to enjoy a day in the sun. In addition, there are two small-craft boat launches and a primitive campground suitable for RV's.

Day Use

At San Luis Creek Day Use Area, grassy knolls with picnic tables on concrete slabs overlook the swimming beach and dock. From the parking above, smooth asphalt paths cross the lawns and parallel the shoreline for convenient access to the entire day use area. You'll find accessible *RESTROOMS* and *DRINKING FOUNTAINS* at regular intervals along the path and in the parking areas.

The access road for the San Luis Creek day use facilities begins at Hwy 152 across from the dam and takes you directly to the main day use parking area. A chain of parking lots border the picnic area to the north and south. For ease of access, the lower north beach parking lot is preferable. With two designated *PARKING* places, the

lot is closest to the boat launch and swimming beach. There are picnic tables and a *RESTROOM* on the same level as the parking, or you may wish to choose a table along the path closer to the water. The other parking lots have designated *PARKING* places about 450 feet from the beach. The pathways to the picnic areas from these lots are steep in places, with grades up to 13%. All of the *RESTROOMS* in the parking areas are similar. Each has a paved approach, accessible *DRINKING FOUNTAIN*, high sink, and pivot-transfer stall with a high toilet and grab bars.

In the summer months, lifeguards are posted at the *SWIMMING BEACH* north of the boat launch. The coarse forebay sand begins at the shoreline path and gently slopes to the water's edge. The loading dock at the paved boat launch is accessible and has no railing. South of the boat launch on the shoreline path is a seasonal *SNACK BAR* and *FISHING SUPPLY SHOP*. At the *SNACK BAR*, an asphalt path leads to a covered *BOAT DOCK* from which you can fish. From the path, a metal gangway with handrails leads to a 2-inch drop onto the wooden surface. Depending on the water level, the gangway may be steep, and you will need help.

Camping

Medeiros Campground (FCFS) —Primitive campsites at Medeiros line the gravelly south shore of the forebay. Each has a table with a ramada for a welcome respite from the hot summer sun. One site with a modified table is designated but is gravel-coated like the rest of the campground. The only restroom here is a standard chemical toilet. At the Madeiros Campground, self-contained RV camping is allowed in the large dirt parking lo next to the boat launch. The boat launch is similar to the one at San Luis Creek Day Use Area.

Los Banos Creek Reservoir

Los Banos Creek Reservoir was created to prevent storm runoff from flooding the canal system. Off the beaten track, Los Banos is a quieter place to fish or camp. You can reach the reservoir from Hwy 152 east of I-5, by taking Volta Road south. Then follow the signs east on Pioneer Road and south on Canyon Road for a total of about six miles.

You'll find the boat launch, picnic, and camping areas on the north shore of the reservoir. The loading dock at the boat launch is not accessible, but there is one designated _PARKING_ place for a vehicle and trailer nearby. A picnic area skirts the perimeter of the paved parking lot and has a view of the lake, but there are no curb cuts. Across from the boat launch is another picnic area with ramadas on a dirt surface. There is a curb cut for access to this area and an accessible _CHEMICAL TOILET_ nearby.

To find the primitive campground (FCFS), follow the narrow dirt road to the hard-packed dirt of the lake shore. Each sloping shoreline site has a table and BBQ in the

shade of a ramada. You can park your vehicle next to your site. Drinking water and standard chemical toilets are provided.

San Luis Reservoir
State Recreation Area
31426 West Highway 152
Santa Nella, CA 95322
(209) 826-1196 or 429-2251
Park Folder Available
Location — Twelve miles west of Los
_ Banos on Hwy 152_
Elevation — 400 feet

COLONEL ALLENSWORTH
STATE HISTORIC PARK

In 1908, an enterprising group of black Americans decided to establish a town where black people could take pride in their personal accomplishments and improve their economic and social stature. The goup was led by Colonel Allen Allensworth, a former slave and the highest ranking negro army officer of his time. They settled in the San Joaquin Valley, involving themselves in the agriculture and

commerce. The town of Allensworth prospered for almost a decade, but transportation changes and the death of Col. Allensworth in 1914 were a blow to the town. However, the biggest obsticle, ans one that the people of Allenstown could not overcome was a severe lack of water. This eventually led to the demise of Allensworth.

The town streets, named for prominent black Americans, are lined with many original structures that are now in the restoration and preservation process. All the buildings of this period had porches, so wheelchair access ramps are being built. Eventually, they all will have a ramp access. Meanwhile, ramps lead to the rear of only a few homes and businesses. Others that are still being developed, have partial boardwalks requiring travel over the surrounding dirt onto 3-inch transitions. For directions to accessible exhibits, pick up a map at the visitor center or the park entrance.

Visitor Center

A modular unit near the schoolhouse is the current home for the

Some of Allensworth's early settlers

(Historic photo courtesy CDPR)

park visitor center where you can watch a visitor-initiated ½-hour orientation video (control button at 40 inches). An 8% ramp with handrails ascends from a gravel-covered designated *PARKING* place to a shady picnic veranda in front of the visitor center entrance. There is a small door sill. Picnic tables are also scattered on the schoolhouse lawn. If the ranger is not at the visitor center, you'll usually be able to spot him somewhere in town, busily at work.

Camping

Immature trees offer little shade to the fifteen campsites with asphalt pull-ins near the visitor center. Two designated *CAMPSITES* have a wider-than-standard parking area; each site is flat and has a table and BBQ on a hard-packed surface. The accessible *RESTROOM* is housed in a modular unit with a 5% ramp access and board hand-rails at 30 inches. There is designated *PARKING* at the foot of the ramp. The unisex stall has a low toilet, grab bars, and a high sink. The rv dump station for the park is located on the road near the schoolhouse.

Colonel Allensworth
State Historic Park

Star Route 1, Box 148
Earlimart, CA 93219
(805) 849-3433

Park Folder Available
Location—Fifteen miles west of
* Earlimart on County Road J22*
Elevation—205 feet

Tule Elk   *(Photo courtesy CDPR)*

TULE ELK STATE RESERVE

In the Goldrush days, the huge population shift to California brought with it a need for more food and the inevitable exploitation of natural resources. Tule Elk that roamed freely in the San Joaquin Valley soon became the target of the hunter's gun when land was cleared for farming. By 1874, the elk herd had been decimated to near nonexistence. Henry Miller, a cattleman with foresight, arranged for a portion of his land to be used to restore the Tule Elk. Since then, their numbers have grown to the point that some of the herd has been relocated to other areas of their natural habitat in California.

At the 953-acre Tule Elk State Reserve, a fenced observation area with shady picnic site is provided for visitors who wish to get a glimpse of these majestic creatures. Sometimes you'll spot them in the fields grazing; however, the best time to visit is during the dry

season when rangers supplement their diet. Park rangers feed them daily at 2 p.m. near the observation area, giving you a chance to see them up close. Be sure to bring your camera!

On the central lawn of the observation area, you'll find picnic tables situated under the trees. A narrow walkway leads to the *RESTROOMS* that have a shallow stall with pivot transfer, grab bars, and a low toilet. The visitor center is open Sunday afternoons and is around the corner from the park office.

Tule Elk State Reserve

Route 1, Box 42
28577 Station Road
Buttonwillow, CA 93206
(805) 765-5004

Park Folder Available
Location—Twenty-seven miles west of
* Bakersfield, the Stockdale Hwy exit*
* from 4 miles from I-5*
Elevation—300 feet

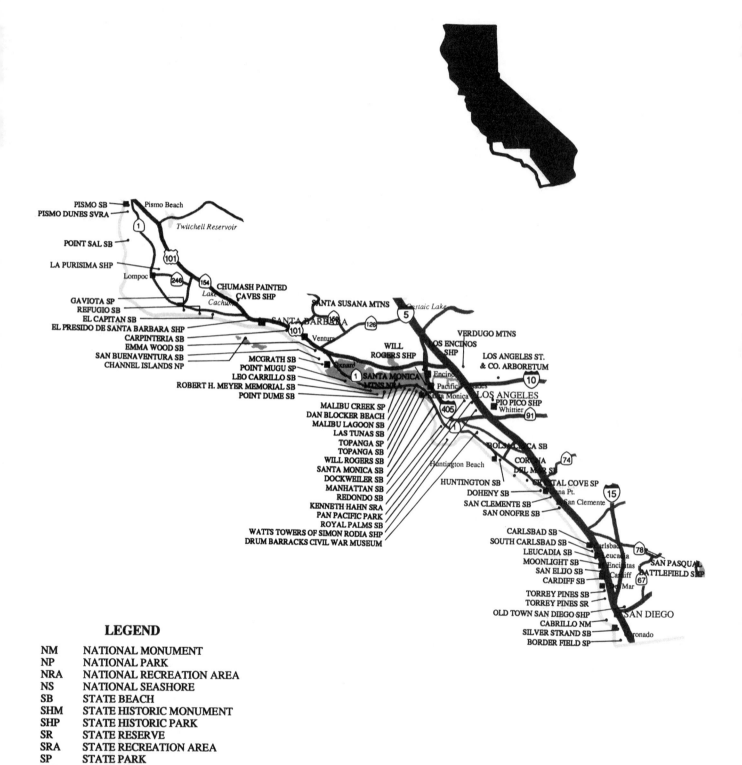

LEGEND

NM	NATIONAL MONUMENT
NP	NATIONAL PARK
NRA	NATIONAL RECREATION AREA
NS	NATIONAL SEASHORE
SB	STATE BEACH
SHM	STATE HISTORIC MONUMENT
SHP	STATE HISTORIC PARK
SR	STATE RESERVE
SRA	STATE RECREATION AREA
SP	STATE PARK
SVRA	STATE VEHICULAR RECREATION AREA
WC	WAYSIDE CAMPGROUND

Leo Carrillo State Beach (Photo courtesy CDPR)

SOUTHERN CALIFORNIA COAST

| Santa Barbara Area |

POINT SAL STATE BEACH

Isolated on the coast at the end of a hilly dirt road, Point Sal State Beach is, according to some park rangers, one of California's most beautiful state beaches. Rarely are there enough people on the sand to disturb the multitudes of sea birds and seals that congregate near the shore. Access to the beach is a challenge even for the able-bodied. Parking is provided on a small unimproved strip of private property. From there, a steep bluff trail picks its way through the rocks and sand to the water below. Sometimes in the winter, the four-mile dirt section of Brown Road is impassable.

Point Sal State Beach

c/o La Purisima Mission
State Historic Park
(805) 733-3713

Location—Nine miles southwest of Guadalupe via Hwy 1 and Brown Road
Elevation—Sea level

LA PURÍSIMA MISSION STATE HISTORIC PARK

Misión La Purísima Concepción de María Santísima is the most completely restored of California's twenty-one Spanish missions. However, the grassy knoll where you see it today is not its original location. As a result of a great earthquake in 1812, the original mission across the Santa Ynez Valley was destroyed and subsequently rebuilt where it currently stands. The structures again fell to ruin after the mission system closed down and it was not until the 1930's that seven years of re-construction and restoration began anew. While ongoing restoration projects continue, the mission stands now much like it stood over 180 years ago. To give you the flavor of a true-to-life visit, displays include livestock and vegetation similar to that used by the original settlers.

The park folder offers an informative self-guided tour of the mission grounds. Much of the tour follows a rough, but level dirt path; if followed in total it will take at least two hours to complete. Tools and artifacts of the mission era are artfully displayed in a series of rooms in the shops and residence buildings. You'll find more furniture and equipment displayed in other parts of the mission. Most of the mission doorways have a traditional adobe entry sill of more than 4 inches, making unassisted wheelchair access difficult. Trail tread around the buildings varies from Spanish tile to grass. Central to the mission buildings, the garden area is a pleasant respite from the sometimes piercing summer sun. The smooth paths and shady trees of the garden make this a good place to take a breather. Due to the distances, some difficult wheeling surfaces, and obstacles,

you should bring along a friend to help.

Near the entrance to the mission grounds there is paved designated _PARKING_. A reproduction of old mission out-buildings houses the visitor center, bookstore, and a restroom. Seventy-five feet of loose, soft sand leads from the parking to the mission history museum at the visitor center. In keeping with the historic nature of the mission, the doorways are narrow and have high door sills or steps. A cramped bookstore sells small gift items, trinkets, and curios; an equally confining restroom is not accessible. The only accessible _RESTROOM_ at the park is at the opposite end of the mission grounds on the north side of the cook building, about 1,500 feet from the parking lot. It has a pivot-transfer stall with grab bars and a high toilet.

**La Purísima Mission
State Historic Park**

2295 Purisima Road
Lompoc, CA 93436
(805) 733-3713

Park Folder Available
_Location — Three miles from Lompoc off
  Hwy 246 at Purisima Road_
Elevation — 75 feet

GAVIOTA STATE PARK

Just a little off the beaten path, Gaviota State Park is the place to go for a camping or beachcombing experience. Soldiers of the Portola Expedition of 1769 gave the white sands of this south-facing beach the Spanish name of "seagull". This protected cove at the mouth of Gaviota Creek is a popular surf fishing spot and a quiet place for beach campers. The landmark Southern Pacific Railroad trestle frames the beach as it runs overhead. At times, a stiff breeze from around Point Conception can cool even the warmest day on the beach, so be prepared for gusty weather. From the accessible _FISHING PIER_, you'll have an added scenic view of the western Santa Barbara coast. Also, you can buy groceries and fishing tackle at the small seasonal _PARK STORE_.

After entering the park, the road separates in two directions. The right fork parallels the beach north of the pier with clifftop views of the water. The left fork leads to the beach, pier, picnic area and campground. You'll find the _CAMP STORE_ and restrooms at the edge of the large day use parking lot. Two designated _PARKING_ places are marked near a restroom that has a

The chapel at La Purisima Mission SHP

(Photo courtesy CDPR)

210

wide door and high toilet, but no other access modifications. Fine beach sand begins at the parking lot edge and runs for about 300 feet to the water. Picnic tables are 50 feet from the pavement on a bed of sand and pebbles. You'll find the only accessible TELEPHONE located just inside the park entrance.

The park also includes a bit of "high country" across the highway from the beach. About 2½ miles north of the main park entrance there is a frontage road where Hwy 1 separates from U.S. 101. From a parking area, hikers take a narrow steep trail past a warm sulphur spring and ultimately to Gaviota Peak (2,458 elevation). The trail is not appropriate for visitors with limited mobility.

Pier

On the west end of the beach, a lighted 575-foot pier with self-operated 3-ton boat launch is open from 6 a.m. to 9 p.m. To use this unique hoist, you lift your boat off the trailer, swing it over the railing, and lower it to the ocean. There is no charge for this service. Anglers try their luck off the pier, from a boat, or in the surf for halibut, barred surf perch, and Pacific mackerel common to this region. At the end of the pier, you'll have a fine view of the Santa Barbara coast as it unfolds to the east.

Camping

The day use parking lot separates the beach from the campground. The campground is divided into two sections, one for RV's and the other for tents. Rows of tamarisk trees line the paved RV section; there are no hook-ups. Some grassy tent sites border Gaviota Creek as the paved road continues into the main tent camping loop. Each tent site has a table, BBQ, food storage, and fire ring. The tent loop restroom is in the middle of a very uneven grass and dirt surface. There is a 1-inch transition onto the concrete slab that surrounds the building. The stall inside is 30 inches wide but has no grab bars or other access modifications. The shower stall is small, the access door is 28 inches wide; the shower head is high, and the control for it is 41 inches from the floor. You cannot make reservations for this campground (FCFS).

Gaviota State Park

Contact Gaviota District Office
(805) 968-1711

Location — Thirty-three miles west of Santa Barbara on U.S. 101
Elevation — sea level

———————

REFUGIO STATE BEACH

Palm trees line portions of the 1½-mile sandy beach lending a tropical air to this popular 40-acre state park. Swimmers, surfers, campers, and picnickers enjoy the park's mild climate and proximity to Santa Barbara. A variety of trees shade flat campsites and pleasant grassy picnic areas. Roadways and parking lots are paved, RESTROOMS are accessible, and there is a small seasonal STORE near the beach. For bikers and hikers with plenty of energy, a blufftop BIKEWAY connects Refugio with El Capitan State Beach 2½ miles to the east.

Day Use

From the shady picnic area on the west side of the park you have a beautiful view of the cove that surrounds the mouth of Refugio Creek. Tables and BBQ's share a lawn with swings and a horseshoe pit near the beach. A small MARKET is open in the summer from 9 a.m. to 5 p.m. and there is an accessible TELEPHONE nearby. To get to the sand you'll need to climb over a small bank that is not accessible to wheelchair users. The RESTROOM in the parking lot has a wide concrete approach and a pivot-transfer stall with grab bars and a low toilet.

Camping

As you drive through the campground on the paved road, you'll notice that many sites have a paved double-wide parking place. A table, food storage, and fire ring are provided on the dirt and grass surface near the pavement. UNISEX RESTROOMS and SHOWERS on the east and west ends of the campground are fully accessible, and there is designated PARKING nearby.

Refugio State Beach

Contact Gaviota District Office
(805) 968-1711

Location — Twenty-three miles northwest of Santa Barbara off U.S. 101 on Refugio Road
Elevation — Sea level

———————

EL CAPITAN STATE BEACH

Wooded blufftops rim the sandy beaches and rocky point at El Capitan State Beach. Protected from northerly ocean swells by Point Conception and from southerly swells by the Channel Islands, the surf on this sunny south-facing beach is usually gentle. The park is popular for its shady campground and bicycling opportunities. A paved _BIKE PATH_ follows the bluff contours 2½ miles westward to Refugio State Beach. A small _VISITOR CENTER_ at the park entrance will orient you to the natural ecology and geological history of the coast east of Point Conception. You'll find an accessible _TELEPHONE_ just inside the campground road nearby.

Day Use

The day use parking lot at the foot of the park road provides access to the beach. There are designated _PARKING_ places at the west end of the lot near an accessible _PHONE_ and _DRINKING FOUNTAIN_ at the _CAMP STORE_ and _SNACK BAR_. A concrete ramp will take you to the level of the seasonal store. Unfortunately, curbing surrounds this parking area; the only curb cut allowing access to the paved walkway is illogically place midway in the lot.

Beach Walk—From either corner of the parking lot, a steep (16%) rough concrete walkway with handrails at 37 inches, winds 110 feet down a bluff to another paved path. The path parallels the beach for 400 feet then brings you back up to the other end of the parking lot. The beach along the walkway

Though scenic, picnic spots at El Capitan State Beach are not easy to access.

(Photo courtesy CDPR)

is reached either by a set of stairs at the west end or down a 4-foot embankment. A restroom at the west end of the path has a pivot-transfer shallow stall with grab bars and a low toilet, but a 4-inch lip at the entry does not allow for easy wheelchair access.

Picnic

At the east end of the beach walk overlooking the beach, there are several picnic tables in the sand. Also, a gently sloping, paved path leads from the east end of the parking lot to additional tables near the water's edge, but, to get there, you must cross about 100 sloping feet of coarse sand. Standard chemical toilets are provided. Other picnic tables also are at the east end of the parking lot on a rough, grassy surface. The beach parking and day use areas are open from 8 a.m. to sunset year round. Lifeguards are on duty from Easter week through October.

Camping

Oaks and sycamores shade the bluff top campground at El Capitan State Beach, providing campers with the feeling of a getaway in the woods. Every site has a table and fire ring on a dirt surface. Though there are no designated sites, many are flat. The _RESTROOMS_ in Loops C and D are accessible. All of the campsite parking is paved and most spaces are double wide.

In **Loop C** there is a mixture of trees and bushes scattered about for shade and privacy. _RESTROOM_ #5 near site #103 has a short 10% paved approach, a high toilet with grab bars and an accessible hand dryer. The _SHOWER_ stall has a seat inside with grab bars, and controls at 39 inches.

Bushes and undergrowth are more dense but there are fewer trees in **Loop D**, so there is privacy but less shade here. The _RESTROOM_ in this loop is similar to restroom #5.

Loop A, shrouded in oaks, is in a hollow near the campfire center.

Rangers give weekly programs at the campfire center but the only access is by way of narrow dirt paths. Sites in both Loops A and B are sloping and the restrooms are not accessible. An RV dump station is available off the road between Loops C and D.

El Capitan State Beach

Contact Gaviota District Office
(805) 968-1711

Park Folder Available
Location—Twenty miles northwest of Santa Barbara off U.S. 101
Elevation—Sea level

CHUMASH PAINTED CAVES STATE HISTORIC PARK

For thousands of years the Chumash Indians lived in the Santa Barbara region, harvesting plants and animals from the land and sea. Their lives were directed by a very elite sect of medicine men, called shamans. The shamans performed secret ceremonies in caves such as the one at Chumash Painted Cave State Historic Park. They documented the history and supernatural events of their people in the form of pictographs on the cave walls.

To reach the cave, park in the wide spot in the road near the State Park sign. (This road is not recommended for long vehicles or trailers because there is little turn-around room at the cave.) From there, a very steep path threads its way uphill among loose rocks and roots to the small sandstone rock cave. The paintings are readily visible by peering through the metal grate that protects the cave from vandals. There are no facilities of any kind at this location. The hike to the cave, though short, requires a degree of agility.

Chumash Painted Cave State Historic Park

Contact Gaviota District Office
(805) 968-1711

Park Folder Available—Ask for El Capitan State Beach folder
Location—From U.S. 101, take Hwy 154 west for 8 miles to Painted Cave Road A small street sign on the right marks the narrow bumpy road that winds two miles to the cave.
Elevation—1,750 feet

EL PRESIDIO DE SANTA BARBARA STATE HISTORIC PARK

In the days when the Spanish ruled California, they built four presidios to serve as military fortresses and governing centers, the last of which was the Santa Barbara Royal Presidio. Established in 1782, the presidio predated Junipero Serra's Mission Santa Barbara by four years. As the centuries have passed, many of the presidio walls have vanished. Now rejuvenated through painstaking excavation, research, and guidance of the Santa Barbara Trust for Historic Preservation, they are being restored on their original stone foundations. Because of the park's historical nature and the demands for accurate restoration of door-ways and walking surfaces, wheelchair access is difficult.

El Presidio Chapel is reconstructed and decorated with Spanish and Mexican artifacts representative of 18th century

Cave paintings at Chumash Painted Caves SHP are now protected from vandals by a fence.

(Photo courtesy CDPR)

213

Christianity. From the sidewalk on East Canon Perdido, a sloping dirt surface leads to the chapel doors. There is a 1- to 2-inch transition onto a tile entry. The tile extends down the front of the padres' quarters to the visitor center; there is a small step at the doorway. A large scale model of the complete fort, built by the Santa Barbara Trust, is on display there. The park docents will be happy to answer your questions and also will show a short film about the Presidio history.

The padres' quarters and park office open onto a courtyard where the surfaces are mostly uneven packed dirt. A side door from the chapel steps down to the courtyard, or you can reach it at the southwest side of the building near a service driveway. There is a Spanish tile walkway to the park office, then the surface becomes dirt. Most of the doorways to exhibits in the padres' quarters have at least a 1-inch sill with stones embedded on either side.

The only designated *PARKING* near the Presidio is across East Canon Perdido Street near the post office. Parking here would require that you travel to the end of the block and cross at the light where there is a curb cut. Otherwise, street parking and corner curb cuts are on both sides of Canon Perdido.

Also across the street, the restored **El Cuartel**, Santa Barbara's oldest adobe, houses a gift shop/book store. There are two steps up to a brick-paved courtyard, but the access door is too narrow for wheelchair access. The closest accessible public *TELEPHONE* near the park is located next door at the post office.

El Presidio de Santa Barbara State Historic Park

PO Box 388
123 East Canon Perdido Street
Santa Barbara, CA 93102
(805) 966-9719

Park Folder Available from the Santa Barbara Trust for Historic Preservation
Location—In downtown Santa Barbara on East Canon Perdido Street between Anacapa and Santa Barbara Streets
Elevation—75 feet

———————

CARPINTERIA STATE BEACH

For thousands of years, Chumash Indians inhabited the Santa Barbara region and adapted well to their seaside environment. They were so adept at building seaworthy canoes from driftwood, tar, and fiber ropes, the Spanish named this area Carpinteria, meaning "carpenter shop." The white sand beaches and dunes of Carpinteria State Beach flank the mouth of Carpinteria Creek, where the Chumash launched their boats to fish and hunt in the waters off the Channel Islands.

Today the 48-acre park is a popular destination for beach campers, surfers, and sunbathers. Over 425,000 visitors come to Carpinteria each year for its mild weather, campgrounds, and day use beaches. Because it is so close to Santa Barbara, the beaches at the park get a great deal of summer use. There are some access modifications in the day use *RESTROOM* and *PICNIC AREA*. One campground also has an accessible *RESTROOM*.

Day Use

From a grassy lawn below a large day use parking lot, you'll have direct access to the beach sand. A sloping (8%) ramp takes you to the *RESTROOMS* on the east end of the lot. The shallow accessible stall has a high toilet and grab bars. Behind the restroom, there is a grouping of tables on a concrete surface, none of which are modified for wheelchair use. The ramp to get there is a steep 10%.

Accessible *TELEPHONES* are at the entry kiosk and at both restrooms in the Santa Rosa camping area. A convenient RV dump station is on the outgoing road of the RV camping area.

As you enter the park on Palm Avenue, a small crossroad to the right will take you to the *VISITOR CENTER* and ranger station. The visitor center has a variety of displays and sells books about the natural and human history of the region. On weekends during the summer season, park rangers offer programs at the *CAMPFIRE CENTER*. You'll find it along an uneven asphalt path connecting the entry kiosk and visitor center.

Camping

Four separate camping areas with a total of 252 campsites cover the length of the park. Each site has a table and fire ring on dirt or grass, and asphalt parking. Every campground has restrooms and hot showers.

Anacapa—Anacapa Campground, located north of the day use parking area, has one designated *CAMPSITE*. Designated *SITE* #7 has a double-wide paved parking place but no other accessible provisions. A table stands on the campsite grass, and there is very little foliage for shade or privacy. Site #7 is the farthest north on the camping loop, thus it is quite a distance from the centrally located accessible RESTROOM and SHOWER. Designated PARKING is provided near a fully accessible UNISEX REST-ROOM/SHOWER combination at the restroom building. The restroom offers lateral transfer to a high toilet with grab bars; the shower has a retractable bench and both high and low controls and shower heads. Most of the campground is level, so if double wide parking is not a necessity, you'll want to choose another campsite that has more shade and is closer to the restroom. You may not bring your trailer on this loop.

Santa Cruz—Eucalyptus trees and bushes surround the generally flat campsites at Santa Cruz Campground. Located just east of the day use entry kiosk, a row of sand dunes protects the sites from onshore breezes, but limits your beach views. Tables at each site are near a paved pull-out in the soft dirt or grass. Both RESTROOMS located in Santa Cruz camping loop have a modified stall with grab bars and a low toilet. You may not use a trailer in this loop.

Santa Rosa and **San Miguel**—These parking lot-style campgrounds with great ocean views are for RV's only. Curbing and sand surround the paved parking area and there are no curb cuts for access to the picnic tables. Restrooms at either end of each camping area have accessible stalls but there are short steep (30%) ramp approaches to the doorways. Shower stalls have small step-

downs into a limited space (36" by 42"); they have no seats or special fixtures. To get to Santa Rosa and San Miguel Campgrounds, go east on the park road over the Carpinteria Creek bridge.

Carpinteria State Beach

5361 6th Street
Carpinteria, CA 93013
(805) 684-2811
Park Folder Available
Location—Twelve miles south of Santa Barbara, in Carpinteria at the foot of Hwy 224 off U.S. Hwy 101
Elevation—Sea level

Ventura Area

EMMA WOOD STATE BEACH

At Emma Wood State Beach, visitors experience the seashore at a cobble beach, grassy camping area, and freshwater marsh just off U.S. Hwy 101. Located near the mouth of the Ventura River, this park is actually two different parks with separate entrances and operators. You'll find Ventura River Group Camp at the intersection of Main Street and U.S. Hwy 101 in Ventura. The state operates this grassy group camping facility that includes bicycle and ENROUTE CAMP-ING.

At the north end of the park, 61 family campsites with beach and ocean views are spread over a mile-long section of old Pacific Coast Highway paralleling the Southern Pacific Railway tracks. At these sites you'll park along the old asphalt road and camp on the adjacent beach. In some places, the asphalt ends in a drop-off to

the sand below. At the sites to the north, the beach is more rocky, but the picnic tables there are on firmer ground and may be easier for you to access. Accessible CHEMICAL TOILETS are provided in the parking area at regular intervals. An RV dump station and an accessible TELEPHONE can be found near the entrance. The County of Ventura operates this portion of the park.

Emma Wood State Beach

Contact Channel Coast District Office
(805) 643-7532
(805) 654-3951—County of Ventura
Location—Off U.S. Hwy 101 about one mile from the northern boundary of Ventura
Elevation—Sea level

SAN BUENAVENTURA STATE BEACH

Two miles of sandy beach, a pleasant concrete BOARDWALK, and a 1700-foot pier beckons sunbathers, surfers, beach-walkers, and fishermen to the mild weather and friendly surroundings at San Buenaventura State Beach. Summer brings a crowd of tourists to the sunny beach conveniently located near the fairgrounds in the city of Ventura. Also, there is a spacious grass picnic area for family gatherings or an outdoor lunch. For the active visitor, an asphalt BIKE PATH extends the length of the park connecting Ventura to the south with Emma Wood State Beach to the north. Accessible RESTROOMS are available near the pier and in the picnic areas.

In the summertime, there is always something happening at San Buenaventura State Beach. *(Photo courtesy CDPR)*

Pier

At the landmark Ventura Pier, anglers try their luck for bonita, surf perch, shark, bass, and corbina. In addition, the pier features an accessible *SNACK BAR*, *FISH HOUSE RESTAURANT* and *BAIT AND TACKLE SHOP*. (To enter the bait and tackle shop, you'll need to use a short, steep ramp at the doorway.) If you wish, you can be dropped off at the foot of the pier. Otherwise, there is a long grade up a paved sidewalk from the designated *PARKING* at beach level in the lot north of the pier. The *RESTROOM* in this parking lot has an accessible stall with pivot transfer to a high toilet and grab bars. You'll also find an accessible *TELEPHONE* at the foot of the pier.

Boardwalk

Hundreds of beach lovers enjoy strolling on the broad ½-mile concrete *BOARDWALK* that runs from the pier to the County Fairground at the northern park boundary. If you're a people-watcher, you can keep an eye on the beach activities from viewing areas that are cut in the sea wall (30 inches high), or relax on one of the many benches that are provided along the walk. Just north of the pier, a pair of steep (13%) ramps will take you directly onto the sand about 200 feet from the water's edge. Other locations along the boardwalk have stair access to the beach level. At the pier, the boardwalk becomes a smooth asphalt bike path that continues southward for the length of the park to a large picnic area near San Pedro Road.

South Sector

Park headquarters and the grassy picnic section of the park can be reached by following Harbor Boulevard south to San Pedro Road. Smooth asphalt paving laces the green lawns behind the beach, connecting restrooms and the park office to the bike path and parking areas. All of the picnic tables are arranged in the grass on individual concrete slabs among a smattering of Monterey cypress and pines. Several small *RESTROOMS* in the area have stalls with wide doors and varying access modifications. As it continues south from the pier, the bike path passes a *SNACK BAR* and *EQUIPMENT RENTAL SHACK* surrounded in pavement, that are open during peak season.

San Buenaventura State Beach

Contact Channel Coast District Office (805) 654-4611

Location—Off Harbor Boulevard just north of the Seaward Avenue exit from U.S. 101

Elevation—Sea level

CHANNEL ISLANDS NATIONAL PARK

The Channel Islands, known even in ancient times for their bounty of life and natural sustenance, continue to harbor a multitude of animals and plants in a unique ecosystem. Harbor seals and dolphins play in the warm and cold water currents of the Santa Barbara Channel. In the winter, California Gray whales pass on their way to give birth in the lagoons of Mexico. Pelicans and other waterfowl nest in the bluffs overlooking the water and feed from the abundance of sea life near the shore.

Channel Islands National Park consists of five islands fourteen miles off the coast of Ventura. Designated in 1980 as our 40th National Park, the islands of Anacapa, Santa Cruz, Santa Rosa, San Miguel, and Santa Barbara, and the waters one nautical mile surrounding them, can only be reached by boat. So as to protect the character of the park environment, park rangers carefully supervise and limit visitation. While there is no wheelchair access onto the islands, tour operators offer special services for those who cannot go ashore, and you can visit the fully accessible _VISITOR CENTER_.

Visitor Center

All visitors will enjoy a stop at the Channel Islands National Park Visitor Center. In the theater, you can watch a colorful film presentation about the islands. In the main hall, wildlife and plant life displays cover the walls and ceilings, and a miniature tidal pool ecology has been recreated for visitors to learn from and enjoy. Park naturalists and docents are on hand to help you with any questions you may have.

From Harbor Boulevard, Spinnaker Drive leads to the park headquarters, and ends in a cul-de-sac in front of the visitor center. From designated _PARKING_ at the opposite side of the cul-de-sac, curb cuts and gentle sloping pavement take you to the entrance. On your way, you'll pass the **California Native Plant Trail** where a rough paved concrete path winds through a garden with marked specimens of native vegetation. Through the heavy front door, all of the displays and facilities are accessible in the spacious guest area.

Opposite the _THEATER_, an _ELEVATOR_ will take you to the observation tower on the third floor. If you cannot stand, views of the marina, the jetty, and the coast are blocked by a wall 35 inches high and a railing at 43 inches. Panels describing local geology line the wall.

A _RESTROOM_, accessible _TELEPHONE_, and _DRINKING FOUNTAIN_ also are near the theater. A heavy door opens into the _RESTROOM_ where the stall is fully accessible with lateral transfer, grab bars, and a high toilet. The sinks are high and a hand dryer is accessible.

The visitor center occupies a choice location on the Ventura Harbor Marina. On the veranda, you can eat your lunch at a modified _PICNIC TABLE_ and have a lovely view of the boat docks and harborside goings-on. If you're hungry or want to inquire about an island excursion, take the paved path next to the visitor center that leads down to the private docking area. There you will find a _SNACK BAR_ and island tour concessionaire.

Excursions

Depending on your needs and abilities, you can arrange a visit to the Channel Islands by boat through Island Packers, the park concessionaire for boat excursions. To land on the islands, you must be able to climb stairs or a rung ladder, and hike a short distance. If you cannot do that, Island Packers is happy to schedule a half-day _NON-LANDING TOUR_ for you. If the rest of your group is able to make the shore landing, and you would like to see more, the crew will help you aboard their skiff for a personalized tour of other parts of the island.

Island Packers goes the extra mile to provide a personal adventure to those with special access needs and will help you in any way possible to make your Channel Island visit memorable. Their office is next to to the visitor center; their information number is (805) 642-1393. With a call ahead, you can personalize your visit and discover for yourself the richness and beauty of these island shores.

Channel Islands National Park

1901 Spinnaker Drive
Ventura, CA 93001
(805) 644-8262
Park Folder Available
Location — At the end of Spinnaker Drive off Harbor Boulevard
Elevation — Sea level

MC GRATH STATE BEACH

The windswept beaches of McGrath State Beach are refuge to hundreds of species of water fowl and other birds. Sand dunes overlook the beach to the west where strong currents tug at the shore. The Santa Clara Estuary Natural Reserve on the park's northern boundary is home to two endangered species: the California Least Tern and the Belding's Savannah Sparrow. Meanwhile, McGrath Lake, in the south sector of the park, is alive with the warbles and twitters of birds and other small animals.

McGrath has a small parking lot for able-bodied explorers, and some visitors use the campground for a home base. Roads near the entrance and through the campground are paved, but all other routes are narrow paths of uneven dirt and sand. There is no wheelchair access to the **Preserve Nature Trail**. Presently, rocks and roots cover the narrow footpath leading to the preserve. An access ramp will take you to the small modular visitor center near the park entrance, but there is a 3-inch step at the doorway. An accessible _TELEPHONE_ and an RV dump station are provided near the parking.

Camping

Three sections of the campground offer level sites with some bushes and small trees for privacy. A row of dunes protects the sites from onshore breezes and blowing sand. Uneven, loose sandy dirt surrounds the paved pull-ins at each site, which includes a picnic table

and fire ring. The _RESTROOMS_ central to each section have a shallow accessible stall with a high toilet and grab bars. The entry doors may require help to open; they are very heavy. The showers are not accessible. You will probably need help to cross a section of rough dirt and exposed roots on the way the campfire center in the middle camping loop.

McGrath State Beach

Contact Channel Coast District Office
(805) 654-4611
Park Folder Available
Location—South of the Santa Clara
River off Harbor Boulevard in Oxnard
Elevation—Sea level

Santa Monica Mountains

POINT MUGU STATE PARK

The Chumash Indians native to the Santa Barbara Coast called this area "muwu," meaning beach. Later renamed Mugu, today's Point Mugu is far more than just a beach. It encompasses almost 15,000 acres of hills, canyons, and savannah prairies stretching from the ocean to Newbury Park. Rich in cultural history of Native American Indians, Spanish, Mexicans and American ranchers, the land is now preserved in a mostly primitive state so others may enjoy the natural beauty of the disappearing wilderness on California's coastline.

The park has something to offer every visitor year round. In the fall, monarch butterflies return to

the safety of the huge sycamore trees that line Sycamore Canyon, their genetically assigned wintering grounds. In late winter and early spring, you can spot California Gray whales on their annual migration. In December and January, the shallow waters off the cove are often a resting place for the whales as they make their way to the warm Mexican lagoons for the winter. In early spring you'll sometimes see them as they swing close to shore on their return journey to their northern Pacific home. And of course, the summer brings beach-goers. All this can be enjoyed from the accessible developed areas around Sycamore Canyon and Sycamore Cove.

Access Mats

A few years ago, the Santa Monica Mountains Conservancy sponsored the development of a new way for wheelchair users to access soft sandy areas without the restrictions of a permanent walkway. The result is a portable 4' by 10' plastic mat that can be laid over a soft surface. With two of these devices and the help of a friend, the mats can be laid progressively in front of one another so a wheelchair user can travel in any direction as far onto the beach as desired. The mat is called a "Ritter Ring" and weighs about 15 pounds.

The park staff will be happy to provide Ritter Rings for you. With 24 hours notice, they will place two mats on the sand near the parqueted path described below. Call the dispatch office at (805) 488-1827 and let them know when you'll be arriving so your mats can be ready for you.

Day Use

For a day of sunning or whale-watching, the day use area at Sycamore Cove is a pleasant spot. In the warmer months the beach comes alive with sunbathers and swimmers. An ample picnic area with tables and BBQ's overlooks the sandy beach where everyone enjoys the waves.

A shady picnic area at the beach has an accessible _CHEMICAL TOILET_ and designated _PARKING_ spaces. Parqueted railroad ties have been laid around the restroom and lead down a sloping path (max 14%) over the beach sand. From here, you'll have a view of the activities at the shore. Because it is so rough and steep in places, the path is difficult to use in a wheelchair without assistance.

Trails

Sycamore Canyon Trail — Hiking, biking, and horseback riding trails lace the canyons, and prairies in the park's backcountry. Rangers at the park recommend the Sycamore Canyon Trail for wheelchair hikers. The trail begins at the wooden gate at the end of the Sycamore Canyon Campground road. It is actually a service and fire road for the over 18,000 acres of open space at the park. Graded annually, the road follows the base of the canyon for five miles with only a 75-foot elevation gain. A canopy of sycamore trees shades most of the trail as it crosses dry stream beds and guides you into the quiet of the backcountry.

At the five-mile point, the road is paved and serves as a service road from the north for the group

A happy hiker enjoys his "Wilderness Experience" on the Sycamore Canyon Trail.
(Photo courtesy Wilderness Institute, Inc.)

campgrounds at the Danielson and Sycamore Multi-Use areas. Some groups, such as Wilderness Institute's "Wilderness Experience" hikers, begin their downhill hike from here and travel to Sycamore Cove. The road becomes steeper about one mile beyond the Danielson Area. (Note: Wheelchair users will need some help across the stream beds. You may wish to bring along a Ritter Ring to help you cross the soft spots. You will only encounter water in the stream beds immediately after a heavy storm.)

La Jolla Canyon Trail — There is designated _PARKING_ and an accessible _UNISEX RESTROOM_ at the trailhead of the La Jolla Canyon

Trail, but don't let that mislead you. The start of the La Jolla Canyon Trail appears broad and even. Eventually, it becomes steep and weathered as it winds through the canyon to the walk-in campground 1.9 miles away. Though not a strenuous walk for the able-bodied, it is a difficult trip by wheelchair due to the rough service-road trail tread.

Camping

Thornhill-Broome Beach (Formerly called La Jolla Beach) — For those who enjoy camping by the beach, Thornhill Broome Beach Campground offers campsites on the sand, 400 feet from the water where surf fishing and clam dig-

219

ging are shoreline pastimes. A deep underwater rift just offshore can cause rip currents and treacherous wave action in this area, so use caution if you're going near the water.

All the campsites and tables are on the beach sand. In the north section, curbing surrounds the asphalt parking area. A ridge of rocks blocks the wind as well as the ocean view from these campsites. In the south portion, there is no curbing but there is a drop-off to the sand, making access to the campsites difficult. Accessible *CHEMICAL* *TOILETS* are provided and there is an RV dump station and accessible *TELEPHONE* at the entrance to this RV campground.

Big Sycamore Canyon—You will find the campground across from the main day use area at Sycamore Cove much more accessible. Big Sycamore Canyon Campground offers 55 wooded campsites, each with a table and fire ring. A stand of sturdy sycamore trees shelters much of the canyon, but a fire that blazed through the canyon in 1989 burned through a section of the campground and eliminated some shady sites. Nevertheless, it is still an inviting place for small animals, birds, and deer who share the floor of the canyon with friendly campers.

Two designated *SITES* are available for disabled visitors. Site #58, close to the camp entrance, is about 150 feet from an accessible *RESTROOM* and *SHOWER*. The site has a double-wide paved pull-in. Site #36 is a shady pull-thru space suitable for a trailer or RV. Both sites are paved under the table and around the fire ring and water spigot. A paved path also leads to the adjacent *RESTROOM* and *SHOWER*.

Both *UNISEX* *RESTROOMS* have lateral transfer, grab bars, and accessible sinks outside the building. Controls for the roomy walk-in showers are at 48 inches and there is no seat in the stall. An RV dump station is at the campground entrance.

Ritter Rings offer beach access to wheelchair users.  *(Photo courtesy Wilderness Institute, Inc.)*

Point Mugu State Park

9000 West Pacific Coast Highway
Malibu, CA 90265
(818) 987-0383 or
(805) 499-2112

Park Folder Available
Location—Fifteen miles south of
Oxnard on U.S. 101
Elevation—0-500 feet

_____

LEO CARRILLO STATE BEACH

The famous radio and television actor of the 1950's who served on the Park and Recreation Commission shares his name with this popular scuba diving and fishing location. Leo Carrillo State Beach also encompasses a part of the Santa Monica Mountains where hikers and mountain bikers climb Arroyo Sequit Ridge for superior panoramic views of the coastline. Access is limited for wheelchair users in the park, however.

Day Use

Day use *PARKING* for the beach at Leo Carrillo is located on the east side of Pacific Coast Highway beyond the entrance station. An accessible *CHEMICAL TOILET* is provided near designated *PARKING* at the north end of the lot. To reach the beach, you'll take the concrete walkway with railing that starts here. It will lead you under the highway to a restroom and changing area on the beach side. The pavement ends at the restroom area and meets sand that slopes steeply away to the shoreline about 250 feet away. With 24-hour notice, the park staff will bring two Ritter Rings to this location so

Ritter Rings can be placed at either Point Mugu or Leo Carrillo.
(Photo courtesy Wilderness Institute, Inc.)

wheelchair users or those requiring special assistance can more easily access the shore. (See the Access Mats section of Point Mugu State Park for the details.)

Picnic

A picnic area is arranged on the pavement at the south end of the North Beach Campground. Among the picnic tables and BBQ's that overlook the sandy beach and ocean horizon, two modified *TABLES* have lowered *BBQ GRILLS*. Accessible *UNISEX RESTROOMS* are available at the campground 200 feet away.

Camping

Canyon—Complete with a *CAMP STORE* and accessible *CAMPFIRE CENTER*, the Canyon Campground is similar to Sycamore Campground at Point Mugu State Park except that there are no designated sites. While most of the campsites are

level, the camping surfaces are grassy dirt and most are uneven. Each of four combination *RESTROOM/SHOWER* buildings in the campground offers an accessible *UNISEX RESTROOM* and two accessible *UNISEX SHOWER ROOMS*. The *RESTROOMS* have a high toilet with grab bars, accessible sink, towels and mirror. There is a retractable bench in each *SHOWER* and a high and low shower head; the controls are low enough to reach from the bench.

You can get provisions and snacks at the *CAMP STORE* near the middle of the campground. Rough asphalt inclines to the doorway; the aisles are narrow but passable. An accessible *TELEPHONE* is just outside. Parking and a paved access route are provided at the amphitheater. You'll also find an *RV DUMP STATION* located near site #103.

North Beach—There are 32 RV pull-thru sites lined up in parking lot style at North Beach Campground. (RV's must have a maximum clearance of 8 feet to clear the low highway underpass.) Designated _CAMPSITE_ #16 has extra room on one side for access to a BBQ and table. It is directly across from an accessible _UNISEX RESTROOM_ with an accessible _TELEPHONE_ and cold outdoor shower. From an opening in the chain link fence that surrounds the campground, access to the beach drops down one foot onto the sand.

Leo Carrillo State Beach

35000 Pacific Coast Highway
Malibu, CA 90265
(818) 706-1310 or
(805) 499-2112

Park Folder Available
Location — Twenty-eight miles west of Santa Monica on Hwy 1
Elevation — Sea level

SANTA MONICA MOUNTAINS NATIONAL RECREATION AREA

Whether you're looking for a secluded spot in the mountains for an intimate picnic, or a concert on the green, the Santa Monica Mountains National Recreation Area has something to offer you. Federal, state, county, and city parks departments work in cooperation to offer park-goers a diverse and interesting melange of places to go and activities in which to participate. Several organizations offer all types of programs and entertainment throughout the year at the various park locations.

One reason the Santa Monica Mountains were chosen as a national recreation area is because of the exceptional plant communities found here. This area is part of a unique coastal Mediterranean ecosystem found in few places of the world. Types of chaparral have been found here that normally grow only in the region between Palm Springs and Baja California. In addition, there are many endemic species that grow only in the Santa Monica Mountains. Preservation of these unique communities and rare plants is one main goal of the recreation area.

Twenty-nine separate sites comprise the National Recreation Area; seven of these are State Parks. Of the remaining 22, the National Parks Department considers nine to have accessible features and has marked them with a wheelchair symbol in park literature. For a detailed schedule of seasonal activities and a park map and brochure, you may call the National Recreation Area office at (818) 597-1036. You may also look for a site map that is usually somewhere close to the entrance of each unit.

Since the park consists of steep hillsides and backcountry trails, improved areas are most often at trailheads where horsemen, mountain bikers and hikers can park their car and take off into the wilderness. Though marked with a wheelchair symbol on official literature, essentially, the only accessible feature at **Arroyo Sequit National Area**, **Diamond X Ranch**, and **Tapia County Park** is a _RESTROOM_ with an uneven dirt approach.

Cheeseboro Canyon

For over 150 years, the rolling grasslands of Cheeseboro Canyon were prime grazing land for ranch cattle. The plants and animals native to the area were all but decimated by the indiscriminate tastes of the cattle. Now that this area is public parkland, the park service is trying to restore the native plants to the land and reestablish its ecosystem to its pre-modern-Man status.

Trail — Though there is no drinking water or restroom facilities here, wheelchair users often take short hikes on the Cheeseboro Canyon Trail. Once a ranch access road, the broad dirt trail has gentle grades. It runs through grasslands for about a mile along a stream bed to a live oak riparian zone. A stream bed crossing here will be a barrier for some, but most wheelchair users can cross with the help of a friend. Further on, you'll come upon a sulphur spring. You'll probably smell the "rotten egg" odor before you get there. Be sure to bring a hat and something to drink as there is little shade along the way.

Directions — To find Cheeseboro Canyon, take Cheeseboro Road exit off the Ventura Freeway. Turn right on Palo Comado Canyon Road and right again on Cheeseboro Road.

Circle X Ranch

Circle X Ranch is used mainly as a home base by hikers as they explore the many fascinating hills and valleys of the Santa Monica Mountains. From the entrance at Yerba Buena Road, the ranch

A hike into Cheeseboro Canyon   (Photo courtesy NPS)

lodge, used for group functions, and the picnic area are downhill in sloping a forested glen. A primitive camping area is along a dirt road 1¾ mile from the entrance. To reach the ranch, take Yerba Buena Road from Hwy 1 for about five miles. A ranger station and accessible _RESTROOM_ is on the road level. The _UNISEX_ _RESTROOM_ has diagonal transfer to a low toilet with no grab bars.

Franklin Canyon Ranch

If you hadn't just driven through it, you won't believe that the busy city of Los Angeles sprawls just on the other side of the canyon walls at Franklin Canyon Ranch. At the park's remarkably quiet day use area, jacarandas in purple bloom and tall leafy sycamores shade a peaceful green lawn.

The Spanish style stucco house that overlooks the sloping lawn was built by the Doheny family in

1935. It now contains park offices and an accessible information office about 350 feet from the parking area. An accessible _TELEPHONE_ is nearby.

Restroom—In the paved parking area, the accessible _UNISEX RESTROOM_ has a high toilet with grab bars, high sink, low hand dryer and an accessible _DRINKING FOUNTAIN_. From the parking lot, an asphalt walk leads uphill for 75 feet to the lawn.

Trails—Three hiking trails begin in the general vicinity of the parking lot. Though two of them are easy hikes for the able-bodied, they are all too narrow for wheelchair access.

Directions—To find Franklin Canyon Ranch from the Ventura Freeway, take Coldwater Canyon Drive south to Beverly Drive. Turn right at the Beverly Hills Fire Station #2 and go one mile to Franklin Canyon Drive. Turn right and

drive 1½ miles through a residential area to Lake Drive. To find the ranch from Sunset, go north on Beverly Drive and follow the sign to Coldwater Canyon Drive. Turn left at the Beverly Hills fire station #2 and proceed as above.

Paramount Ranch

In the 1920's and 30's, moviemaking was a booming industry and the talkie developed into America's main source of entertainment. Paramount Pictures purchased 2,700 acres in the Rancho Las Virgenes area to use for natural sets in their burgeoning movie business. With the advent of television in the 1940's, the movie industry waned and Paramount Ranch was sold in parcels to various parties. William Hertz purchased 326 acres where he and his family developed an independent movie and television set. For several years before he sold it, the set was home to television westerns such as "Bat Masterson" and "The Cisco Kid."

The western town was revitalized in 1984 and is one of few remaining western sets in California used by independent movie companies. When they're filming, you can come and watch the actors and crew in action, or just drop by any day and take a surreal walk down the dirt roads of Main Street. Every so often, the ranger will lead a one-hour tour of the old western town.

As you take your _SELF-GUIDED_ _TOUR_ of the movie sets and entertainment facilities, most of the surfaces are uneven dirt and can be rutted in places. The facades include the standard western boardwalks making an up-close view difficult for wheelchair users. But the visit is still fun and there is plenty of room in the road for an old-fashioned cowboy shoot-out.

Also at this site, the Parks Service is making an effort to reestablish the valley oak. After years of cattle grazing on the hillsides, the lands where the oak once thrived has been trampled, discouraging new plant growth. A 5K jogging trail passes through the oak restoration area as it winds its way through the site. Though level, the trail is quite rough in places and not wheelchair accessible.

Paramount Ranch is open daily for jogging, hiking and riding on the many trails that meander through the surrounding hills and valleys. A wide-open grassy picnic area, suitable for group events, borders the western town. At various times throughout the year, an open air pavilion is the stage for music festivals, auctions or dancing. The pavilion has a short steep ramp up to the floor and is accessible.

Restrooms — Two _RESTROOMS_ at the site are accessible. At the main entry gate to the movie lot, there is a modular _RESTROOM_ building with ramp access. The accessible stall has a low toilet with grab bars. You'll find an accessible _UNISEX RESTROOM_ at the end of a concrete walk that leads between the hotel and the jail.

Directions — The site is open between sunrise and sunset unless special events or entertainment is scheduled. To find Paramount Ranch from the Ventura Freeway, take Kanan Road south for ¾ mile.

Take a left at the sign reading "to Cornell Road" and veer to the right. Go south for about 2½ miles and the entrance is on the right.

Peter Strauss Ranch

Until the early 1900's, the land around Peter Strauss Ranch was wild and undeveloped. It is likely that homesteaders grazed their cattle on the same hillsides that the Chumash Indians roamed for thousands of years. Then in 1923, Harry Miller, the developer of the automobile carburetor, built a stone house on the property along with a caretaker's house, aviary, look-out tower and small zoo enclosure. But he lost his ranch in the depression years. It was later purchase by two entrepreneurs who had dreams of transforming the quaint setting into a "fairyland of charm and paradise for children and adults." They constructed a dam on the creek to form a small lake that they named Lake Enchanto. By the 1950's, the amusement park they envisioned was in full swing with rides, parties, children's summer camps, fishing, dancing and overnight cabanas.

Little of the amusement park was still there when Peter Strauss purchased Lake Enchanto in 1977. Not long after that, the ranch was purchased for the National Recreation Area. The charming ranch setting is now host to a regular schedule of concerts and other outdoor events. Art shows are often held in the garden or on the large terrazo dance floor near the house. A _WHEELCHAIR LIFT_ onto the ranch house veranda provides access to functions inside the house.

Amphitheater — Some concerts and gatherings held at the ranch are held at the amphitheater. To get to the seating area from the designated _PARKING_, you'll need some assistance up a dirt path for about 200 feet, part of which is as steep as 16%. Park officials have expressed that any number of people would be available to help you get there.

Picnic — If you follow a paved path beyond the amphitheater, you'll find a children's playground and picnic area shaded by eucalyptus and oaks. The paved path ends at an overlook where you can see the remains of the original Lake Enchanto dam, most of which was destroyed by flooding in 1969. With much imagination, you may be able to picture the lake with families frolicking along the shore or casually fishing from rowboats.

Parking — The dirt parking lot for the ranch is on the opposite side of the creek bed from the house. Normally, you would have to cross the bridge at the street and return to the house down a long dirt drive. With a handicap-identification placard, you may drive up the entrance roadway directly to designated _PARKING_ near the house. Though flat, the parking surface has a layer of pea gravel embedded in the dirt. You may wish to call ahead to be certain that the gate will be open when you arrive. If there isn't someone there to open it for you, you may park at the gate instead of in the lot across the creek.

Restroom — Accessible *RESTROOMS* are located on the opposite side of the house from *DESIGNATED* parking and can be reached along a concrete walk. The restroom has a lateral-transfer stall to a high toilet with grab bars. The sinks are high, the hand dryer and mirror are accessible and there is an accessible *DRINKING FOUNTAIN* nearby.

Directions — To find Peter Strauss Ranch from the Ventura Freeway, take the Kanan Road exit south for 2.8 miles to Troutdale Road. At the end of Troutdale you'll see the arched entrance to the ranch. On the other side of the creek to the left, is the arched entrance to the main parking lot.

Rancho Sierra Vista/ Satwiwa Site

In keeping with the rancho traditions and cowboy heritage of Southern California, Rancho Sierra Vista maintains a collection of highly trained horses and a selective breeding program. Moorpark College equine training and management program, in cooperation with the National Park Service operates the ranch. Every Saturday and Sunday the students offer tours of the ranch and riding demonstrations that begin at the ranger station.

The dirt grounds are just what one would expect of a horse ranch. Horse corrals and an assortment of out buildings provide breeding facilities and classrooms for this learning center. One small barn serves as a visitor area where displays line the walls and a film is shown. Wheelchair ramps are provided at the doorways. Near

the ranger station is a small picnic area among mature fruit trees with tables on uneven grass and dirt. But, a 4-inch transition from the sidewalk to the lawn makes access a challenge.

The paved public parking lot for the ranch is downhill from the barns and corrals. To get to the ranch from there, you have to walk along a dirt path to the main barn area. With a handicap-identification placard, you will be allowed to drive up the service road entrance and park near the ranger station on an uneven packed dirt surface. If you need ranger assistance, a series of concrete ramps will take you to the front door of the ranger office. Near the ranger station is an accessible *UNISEX RESTROOM* with a low toilet, grab bars, high sink and accessible *DRINKING FOUNTAIN*.

Satwiwa, meaning "the bluffs," was the name of a Chumash Indian village located near the ranch. Historians believe that the canyons in this area were part of a Chumash Indian trade and travel route. A portion of the canyon is reserved for regional Native Americans to perpetuate the Indian culture and share traditions and accomplishments. Not far from the ranch buildings further up the service road, you'll find the **Satwiwa Native American Indian Cultural Center**. Housed in an older ranch dwelling, the cultural center with its displays and gift items is open only on Sundays and is not accessible. Sometimes special gatherings or events are held under the shade trees on the lawn. At those times, you will be allowed to take the service road directly to

the Cultural Center and park on the uneven dirt nearby. Otherwise, you'll have a ¼-mile walk on a firm dirt path from the public parking lot near the ranch.

Directions — To find Rancho Sierra Vista, take the Ventura Freeway to Wendy Drive exit in Newbury Park. South on Wendy to Portero Road west (right). Just before Pinehill Road, the service road entrance is on your left.

Rocky Oaks

Pleasant oak-covered rolling hills and washes characterize the 198 acres of Rocky Oaks. A favorite of local horsemen, a web of trails winds through the changing terrain at this section. About 150 feet from the parking area is a group of picnic tables and a small amphitheater where ranger schedule summer talks. During seasons of normal rainfall, you can enjoy a nature walk along a dirt trail that leads a short distance to a natural pond.

Though several acres of Rocky Oaks are level and shady, there are no special accessible features. The trail to the amphitheater is level but has a thick layer of soft dirt that is difficult to manage. Near the entrance of Rocky Oaks is a large *PIT TOILET* with grab bars and a heavy door. Parking is provided nearby on dirt and gravel.

Directions — Rocky Oaks is located south of the Ventura Freeway, off on Kanan Road then right on Mulholland Highway. From Pacific Coast Highway, take Kanan Dume Road north to Mulholland Highway and turn left.

**Santa Monica Mountains
National Recreation Area**

30401 Agoura Road, Suite 100
Agoura Hills, CA 91301
(818) 597-1036
Park Folders Available
Elevation — 0-3,000 feet

MALIBU CREEK STATE PARK

Once used by Twentieth Century Fox as a location for television and movies, the Malibu Creek area has always been an important watershed for the Santa Monica Mountains. The 6,600 acres preserved by Malibu Creek State Park protects the major water gap that drains 100 square miles of surrounding canyons and rugged terrain. Oaks and sycamores are painted onto the rims and valleys, and the remaining vertical landscape is awash with chaparral. Because it is so close to the metropolitan Los Angeles area, hikers and horsemen from the city enjoy exploring the urban wilderness on trails and fire roads.

A portion of the park at the entrance on Las Virgenes Road, developed for camping and picnicking, serves as a trailhead assembly area. The park road bisects a wide-open meadow and ends in a seclusion of oak trees at the campground. Picnic tables are scattered in the meadow grasses, and three paved day use *PARKING* locations along the road have accessible *UNISEX RESTROOMS*.

Visitor Center

The accessible *VISITOR CENTER*, with ramped entrance, offers pictorial and physical exhibits of the flora, fauna, and geology of the Santa Monica Mountains region. You'll enjoy the hands-on table-top display of plants and animal pelts that you can personally examine. In addition, the ranger shows films and slide presentations in the accessible *MEDIA ROOM*. There you'll learn about the history of man in the park and about other parks in the area. The visitor center also has an accessible *UNISEX RESTROOM* with grab bars and a high toilet. The visitor center is open Saturdays, Sundays, and holidays only, from noon to 4 p.m. To get there, you must hike along a dirt service road (Crags Road) that will take you for about ¾ mile from the main park road. (See Crags Road-High Road description below.)

Trails

Crags Road-High Road — As mentioned above, Crags Road can be used for access to the visitor center. The hard-packed dirt road is level and follows along the south side of a creek, then crosses a concreted stream bed. Most wheelchair users probably will need some help to manage the grade changes at the stream bed. As you make your way along the trail, you'll pass an occasional oak tree and have a wide view of the surrounding canyon walls. For a change of scenery, you can take the high road north of the creek on your return trip. It leads back to within ¼-mile of your original starting point on the main park road. You can reach the high road just across the creek near the visitor center. The total hike is approximately 1½ miles.

All-Persons Trail — Across from the last day use parking area a 60-inch-wide hard-packed trail is specially designed for wheelchair users. The trail leads 800 feet through a meadow to a picnic table at the base of a huge oak tree inviting you for a shady stay. (There is no paving or table modifications.) The trail has a very gradual slope until you get to the fork near the tree, then the trail narrows to 30 inches. The right fork is narrow and steep (10%), so take the left fork.

Campground

Meadow campsites at Malibu Creek are ringed by valley oaks. An asphalt road serves the campground and the pull-in sites. Each uneven dirt and grass site has a table, concrete BBQ and very little shade. An abandoned entrance road that is level but now quite weathered, leads through the trees to the day use parking area across from the trailhead mentioned above.

Both *UNISEX RESTROOM* buildings in the campground have asphalt walkways to the doorway and accessible sinks outside. Of the two accessible restrooms, the east building is preferable because it also contains an accessible *SHOWER* with a seat. Though an RV dump station is provided near the park entrance, the campground is not suitable for large RV's or trailers. (FCFS)

Malibu Creek State Park

Contact Santa Monica Mountains District Office
(818) 706-8809 or **(805) 499-2112**
Location — Four miles south of U.S. 101 on Las Virgenes Road (Route N1)
Elevation — 700 feet

TOPANGA STATE PARK

Laced with hiking trails and fire roads, Topanga State Park, encompasses over 9,000 acres and is the world's largest undeveloped parkland within the boundaries of a major city. Hikers and rugged nature-lovers enjoy getting into the back country that is strewn over the ridges and peaks of the Santa Monica Mountains.

At the park entrance, a fully accessible *UNISEX* *RESTROOM* is near two designated places in a large paved *PARKING* lot. At the opposite end of the parking lot, the *RANGER* *STATION* and *TELEPHONE* are also accessible. Picnic tables on the sloping grounds around the parking lot are difficult to access. From this point, many trails lead into the hills and rugged park terrain. Though there are some fire roads, trails are too difficult for wheelchair users.

Topanga State Park
20825 Entrada Road
Topanga, CA 90290
(213) 455-2465 or (818) 706-1310
Park Folder Available
Location—Eight miles south of U.S. 101 off Topanga Canyon Boulevard (Hwy 27), east on Entrada Road
Elevation—1,500 feet

Malibu Area

ROBERT H. MEYER MEMORIAL STATE BEACH

Robert H. Meyer Memorial State Beach consists of three small sandy coves hidden at the bottom of steep coastal cliffs midway between Point Dume and Leo Carrillo State Beaches. Signs along the highway mark the small paved parking lots that serve each location. Each lot has an accessible *CHEMICAL* *TOILET* and limited views of the water below.

Robert H. Meyer Memorial State Beaches
Contact Santa Monica Mountains District
(818) 706-1310 or (805) 499-2112
Location—Along Hwy 1 about ten miles west of Malibu
Elevation—Sea level

POINT DUME STATE BEACH

By the popular Zuma Beach, the headlands, cliffs, and secluded coves of Point Dume State Beach offer a variety of recreation opportunities, but access to these areas is limited. Starting at the end of Westward Beach Road a string of parking lots follows the foot of the bluff bordering the beach. This portion of the park is administered by the County of Los Angeles and has no accessible facilities.

Point Dume State Beach
Contact Santa Monica Mountains District Office
(818) 706-1310 or (805) 499-2112
Location—Eighteen miles west of Santa Monica off Westward Beach Road from Hwy 1
Elevation—Sea level

DAN BLOCKER BEACH

Highway 1 traverses the shoreline bluffs until it drops to the level of the beach between Corral and Solstice Canyons at Dan Blocker State Beach. To access the mile-long sandy shore from the highway, you must climb down a short cliff, and there are no facilities here other than standard chemical toilets.

Dan Blocker Beach
Contact Santa Monica Mountains District Office
(213) 620-3342 or (818) 706-1310
Location—Thirteen miles west of Santa Monica on Hwy 1 at the foot of Corral Canyon Road
Elevation—Sea level

MALIBU LAGOON STATE BEACH

Whether you call it Surfrider or just Malibu Beach, many remember Malibu Lagoon State Beach as the home of Beach Blanket Bingo and the Beach Boys. With beachgoing as popular as ever, the park service has set aside the lagoon at the mouth of Malibu Creek as a protected wildlife sanctuary. Throughout the year, birdwatchers have sighted up to 200 species of waterfowl and migrating species from the primitive trails at the preserve. South of the lagoon, a piece of Malibu's rich historic past stands at the Adamson House and Malibu Lagoon Museum. The famous Malibu tile was manufactured by the family that built this ornate mansion. Parts of the wildlife sanctuary, mansion, and museum are accessible and open for your pleasure.

Lagoon

For bird watching at the lagoon, enter the park at Cross Creek and Pacific Coast Highway. A ¼-mile nature trail leads through this rare coastal wetland. The firm but sometimes uneven trail crosses a foot bridge over a narrow place in the lagoon and continues to the beach where it becomes very soft. If you are planing a day trip to the refuge, it would be a good idea to check with the ranger for current wildlife sightings and parking lot hours. The parking area has an accessible _CHEMICAL TOILET_ and _DRINKING FOUNTAIN_.

Beach

In the summer, the popular beach north of the Malibu Pier is crowded with sun-worshippers. Street parking lines Pacific Coast Highway, and there is a parking lot near the Adamson House, but both are quite a distance from the water. A paved sidewalk runs the full length of the beach along the highway, but there are no special access arrangements to the sand. Restroom facilities, surrounded by sand, have no modifications for access.

Museum

As a Californ ia Landmark and National Historical Site, the **Adamson House** preserves some lavish ceramic tile artistry produced by Malibu Potteries as well as other skilled handiwork of the

early 1900's. As the last family to own the Malibu Spanish Land Grant, the Adamson's took full advantage of their beautiful beach location. Their home is a showplace for wood carvings, hand-painted murals, filigreed ironwork, and lead-framed bottle glass windows.

Docent-led _TOURS_ of the house and grounds are available hourly every Wednesday through Saturday from 10 a.m. to 2 p.m. Wheelchair users will be able to view the lower floor of the house by way of a ramp access into the kitchen at the rear of the building. As the tour continues to the pool and garden area, you'll pass some beautiful ornate fountains in a central lawn. Some assistance may be required across the lawn to the pool decking. For special access arrangements or other questions, call the Malibu Lagoon Museum Association at (213) 456-8436.

The **Malibu Lagoon Museum** adjoining the Adamson House contains a collection of artifacts, rare photographs, other publications, and a film relating to the colorful history of "The Malibu." It occupies the original garage inside the Adamson House gates and is the meeting place for the Adamson House tour. With a handicap-identification placard, you may drive through the main gate and park near the front of the Adamson House. The interior of the museum has ramps between exhibit rooms, sloping at no more than 8%.

Footpaths wander through the gardens outside the museum and lead also to a quaint gift shop on a

knoll above the parking area. Most of the paths are firm soil with slopes of no more than 8%. Access is difficult to the tiny gift shop due to a large door sill. Across the garden from the parking area, a fully accessible _RESTROOM_ has been added in the corner of an old garage building. However, there is a steep dip down to a very steep 2-foot ramp access to the building. This restroom cannot be accessed without help.

Malibu Lagoon State Beach

23200 Pacific Coast Highway
Malibu, CA 90265
(213) 456-8432
Beach Information—(213) 456-9497
Park Folder Available for Adamson House
Location—On Hwy 1 just east of Malibu Canyon Road
Elevation—Sea level

LAS TUNAS STATE BEACH

Once covered with prickly pear cactus ("las tunas" in Spanish), Las Tunas State Beach is most popular with scuba divers who enjoy exploring the sea life at an offshore reef. Parking for the beach is along the highway, and the only shore access is down a bluff trail.

Las Tunas State Beach

Contact County of Los Angeles
(213) 305-9503
Location—One mile west of Topanga Canyon Boulevard on Pacific Coast Highway (Hwy 1)
Elevation—Sea level

TOPANGA STATE BEACH

This one-mile sandy beach in Malibu is a haven for surfers and swimmers. Though there is no special access to the water, the restroom facilities are accessible, and there is designated *PARKING* on the beach level. If you have a handicap-identification placard, don't park in the upper lot. The road leading down to the beach is just past the southern end of the parking lot. A hard right turn will take you down to the designated spaces where a paved walk leads to an accessible *RESTROOM* and *DRINKING FOUNTAIN*. The restroom offers lateral transfer to a low toilet, an accessible sink and hand dryer. The concrete ends with a drop-off directly to the thick sand of Topanga State Beach.

Topanga State Beach

Contact Los Angeles County Office
(213) 455-2465
Location — Pacific Coast Hwy (Hwy 1) at Topanga Canyon Boulevard in Malibu
Elevation — Sea level

> **Greater Los Angeles Valley Areas**

LOS ENCINOS STATE HISTORIC PARK

For thousands of years in the arid Southern California region, native Californians relied on the life-giving waters from natural springs and other sources. When "modern" Spanish explorers arrived in 1769, they soon discovered the warm fresh water spring at the foot of the Santa Monica Mountains. The small body of water became a welcome rest stop for scouts and pioneers between the Topanga Pass and Sepulveda Pass. By the mid-1800's, the Mexican Governor Pio Pico had the land divided, distributing a 4,000-acre parcel including the spring to the de la Osa family. The family subsequently built a fine adobe home and raised 15 children here. As years went on, the ranch changed ownership several times and became a regular stage coach stop.

In 1872, two Basque sheepherders living on the ranch, built a limestone house similar to one in their French homeland. Today, a tiny portion of the original ranch including the adobe, limestone house, and natural spring remain at Los Encinos State Historic Park.

Each room in the adobe is restored in period furnishings reflecting the tastes of the various owners and eras of the ranch. Most of the rooms and exhibits are accessible. The best access to the long patio that runs the length of the building is at the west end near the spring; there is a 1-inch transition from grass to pavement. At the south end, the thick concrete slab is two steps up from the ground.

The spring still flows near the adobe, but is contained in a fenced concrete pond providing safety for a collection of waterfowl. On a warm day, you'll want to spread your blanket out on a sloping lawn near the spring and watch the birds play in the water.

Restoration of the French-style home built by Eugene and Phillipe Garnier is planned for sometime in 1992. The limestone structure will contain a fully accessible visitor center and information station.

A little piece of history is preserved right in the middle of the city at Los Encinos SHP.

(Photo courtesy CDPR)

229

The 5-acre park, located in a residential section of Encino, is surrounded by a chain link fence and curbside parking. The grounds around the historic buildings, including the gently sloping entrance on Moorpark Street, are a hard-packed dirt or grass surface. Accessible UNISEX RESTROOMS are located below the adobe in another lawn area where you'll also find several picnic tables on level grass shaded by olive trees. Since there is no paving to the restroom, you'll have to cross about 50 feet of grass and dirt to get there from the park entrance. The ranger offers TOURS of the park most days in the afternoon. A call ahead to verify the tour schedule would be helpful. The park is closed on Mondays and Tuesdays.

Los Encinos State Historic Park
16756 Moorpark Street
Encino, CA 91436
(818) 784-4849 or (805) 499-2112
Elevation—757 feet

SANTA SUSANA MOUNTAINS

The Santa Susana Mountains area will preserve parts of an old stagecoach road that dates to 1860 as well as some remnants of the Native California Indian history. It is still in the acquisition stages and there are no developed visitor facilities. Contact the park at (213) 620-3342 or call the Southern Region Headquarters at (619) 237-7411.

VERDUGO MOUNTAINS

Once part of a huge land grant to the Verdugo family, 200 acres of the Verdugo Mountains area preserves mountainous open spaces that overlook the San Fernando and San Gabriel Valleys. There are no improvements for visitors other than hiking trails that connect adjacent parks. The trailheads can be reached west of the 210 Freeway on La Tuna Canyon Road. Contact the park at (213) 620-3342 or call the Southern Region Headquarters at (619) 237-7411.

LOS ANGELES STATE AND COUNTY ARBORETUM

Amid the hustle-bustle of the busy city, there is a refuge for nature-lovers seeking tranquility and natural beauty. Within its 127 acres, the Los Angeles State and County Arboretum contains a world of plant life. It is a haven for horticulturists and those who appreciate a peaceful stroll through fragrant gardens. The collection of plants at the Arboretum is so vast that whether your interest is in flowering plants, exotics, or herbs, there is an exhibit you'll enjoy. In addition, flower shows and informative demonstrations scheduled throughout the year will highlight your visit.

The gardens are arranged in sections circumscribed by rolling paved walkways with short grades of up to 15%. Each section represents a geographical or historical habitat where markers describe plant species along the walkway. In some sections, firm, smooth, dirt pathways meander into the foliage for a look at special plant or historical exhibits.

Besides the gardens, the Arboretum includes a herbarium with a collection of dried plants, a 26,000-volume plant science reference library, two greenhouses for tropical and shade plants, and an accessible COFFEE SHOP, GIFT SHOP, and RESTROOM. To add to your interest, you may wish to participate in an accessible docent-led tour of the gardens offered on Wednesdays. Four designated PARKING places are provided near the garden entrance. An accessible TELEPHONE is on the parking level. From the there, a wheelchair access walkway with a 10% grade, bypasses the stairway to the entry level, where you can access the visitor center, gift shop, or garden entrance.

Visitor Center

For a brief orientation to the Arboretum, visit the visitor center located near the entrance to the garden. There you'll find a pictorial history of the park and a continuous video tape about the wide variety of plants you will encounter on your tour of the gardens. You may need some help to open the heavy entry door. There are no barriers in the room, but some displays are a bit high for comfortable viewing from a seated position.

The Lucky Baldwin coach barn at the Arboretum is quite interesting.

(Photo courtesy CDPR)

Historical Section

The historical section of the Arboretum is a popular area. Here, buildings with period furnishings and manicured gardens depict transitions of San Gabriel Valley civilization. With some help you can tour recreations of wickiups dating from the time of the Gabrielino Indians, an old adobe, and a coach barn for a late 1800's Queen Anne Cottage. Also in the historical area is a completely furnished Queen Anne Cottage and a railroad depot, symbol of the transportation that spawned California's rapid growth. Neither of these buildings is modified for access.

The restored interior of the coach barn is beautifully hand-crafted and houses an extensive collection of 19th century livery items. In addition, some original documents and correspondence of the former owners of the ranch is on display along the walls. If you like historical artifacts and memorabilia, a trip along the dirt path to the

steep (20%) plank ramp of the coach barn is definitely worth the effort.

Tours

Every Wednesday at 11:00 a.m., a park docent will take you on an informative guided *WALKING TOUR* of the grounds. Since there is such a variety of plant exhibits to learn about, tour routes are very flexible; the docent will modify your tour to meet the your needs. There is no need to call ahead for special arrangements. The staff also offers daily narrated tram tours; two steep steps onto the tram and very narrow doorways limit access.

Shops

Coffee Shop – The cafeteria-style **Peacock Pavilion Coffee Shop** is a very pleasant stop for a casual bite to eat. You have a choice of staying indoors or enjoying the sunny terrace, both have accessible *TABLES*. On the level below

you, a flock of peacocks spends the day sifting through the undergrowth for insects and strutting their stuff for the ladies, (peahens, that is). If you're coming from the direction of the entrance restrooms, a ramp of 10% leads to the coffee shop. The slope is more gradual from the walkway on the north side of the building.

Gift Shop – Before you leave the gardens, you'll probably want to make a stop at the docent-operated *GIFT SHOP*. Gift items have been tastefully selected. Along with the usual trinkets are a variety of decorator items, stationery and toys. You may find the perfect birthday gift here for your favorite aunt. You can get to the shop from the garden or the parking area through a heavy glass doorway that may require help to open.

Restrooms

There are three restrooms at the park, but only accessible one is near the tram station. From the garden entrance, a steep (15%) concrete ramp with grab railing will take you directly to the *RESTROOM* building. For gentle but longer route, paved garden walkways will eventually lead you there. The restroom stall is fully accessible (lateral transfer, high toilet and grab bars) including its accessible sink. In addition, there is an accessible TELEPHONE nearby.

Picnic

You may not take recreational equipment, radios, blankets or picnic baskets into the garden. A picnic area in the parking area is south of the entrance on shady median strips. There is a concrete ramp at the end of one median and a 2-inch transition onto the dirt surface.

Los Angeles State and County Arboretum

301 North Baldwin Avenue
Arcadia, CA 91006-2697
(818) 821-3222
Park Flyer and Calendar of Events Available

Santa Monica Bay

WILL ROGERS STATE BEACH

Because of their proximity to the Los Angeles basin, the broad sandy beaches at Santa Monica Bay are very heavily used by tourists and locals residents. Will Rogers State Beach is the northernmost of these beaches. The famous entertainer, Will Rogers, originally purchased the property as a substitute for the swimming pool that he did not have on his nearby ranch (see Will Rogers State Historic Park).

The beach is also the northern terminus of the **South Bay Bicycle Trail**, a 19-mile paved pathway that follows the shoreline from here all the way south to Redondo State Beach. Much of the path is

level, but there are some sections that climb up and over small knolls that would require an extra push or two.

Two parking lots are provided along this 1¾-mile beach. The main parking lot is at the foot of Temescal Canyon Boulevard, where there are several designated PARKING places, lifeguard station, and an accessible TELEPHONE near the entrance. A paved walkway that skirts the parking lot and overlooks the beach can only be accessed at a curb cut near the parking lot entrance. Asphalt ramps lead from the walkway directly to the sand. The only accessible RESTROOM you'll find in this area is at the lifeguard station. The stall is narrow (27 inches) and shallow with a high toilet and grab bars.

The parking lot at the foot of Entrada has a short ramp (10-12%) at either end with access to the bike path and an accessible UNISEX RESTROOM with designated PARKING nearby.

Will Rogers State Beach

Contact the County of Los Angeles
(213) 305-9545
*Location — Pacific Coast Highway (Hwy 1) and Temescal Canyon Road on the Santa Monica Bay
Elevation — Sea level*

SANTA MONICA STATE BEACH

The South Bay Bicycle Trail continues along over three miles of broad sandy shoreline at Santa Monica State Beach. As it winds

its way south, it passes the popular Santa Monica Municipal pier with its famous carrousel and other amusements. Gymnastics equipment draws the athletic crowd at "Muscle Beach," while further south concessionaires will sell you a snack or a beverage. Plenty of benches are provided along the bike path for resting and people-watching at this very popular beach.

Beach Access

To get a closer feel of the beach activities, a smooth BOARDWALK extends onto the sand just south of the SNACK BAR near RESTROOM #2. It ends just before a crest of sand about 150 feet from the bikeway. Your view of the shoreline from the end of the boardwalk is limited, but you can to share the sand with other beach enthusiasts like yourself.

Parking — A series of parking lots along Pacific Coast Highway serves the beach. The main parking entrances are south of the pier at the foot of either Bicknell or Ocean Park. You'll find designated PARKING places near cuts in the concrete curbing that parallels the bikeway. There are several small parking lots north of the pier along Hwy 1. For wheelchair users, access to the beach is minimal from these lots.

Restrooms — All of the restrooms lie along the bikeway and are numbered in ascending order beginning at the south end of the beach. Restrooms #1 through #5 are accessible and located about 500 feet from designated parking places. Each has a stall with lateral transfer, grab bars, and a changing bench. The sinks are accessible as are the telephones outside each building. Further north, restrooms #6 through #11 do not have accessible stalls.

Santa Monica State Beach

Contact the City of Santa Monica
(213) 305-9545 or 394-3266

Location — On Pacific Coast Highway near the Santa Monica Municipal Pier
Elevation — Sea level

DOCKWEILER STATE BEACH

The 3½ miles of Dockweiler State Beach shoreline are flat, broad, and perfect for a scenic stroll on the *BIKE PATH*. You can access the path from the foot of Culver, at the snack bar parking lot, or near the RV *CAMPGROUND*. For those who are enamored with jet planes, you can watch from the beach as airliners take off from Los Angeles International Airport.

North of the park entrance you'll find a seasonal *SNACK BAR* and *RESTROOM*/shower area near a large lot with designated *PARKING* places. The *UNISEX-STYLE LADIES ROOM* is on the street side of the building. The *MEN'S ROOM* is similar and faces the ocean. Each has a large room with grab bars, high toilet, accessible sink, and changing bench. The snack bar is generally open on weekends, holidays, and in the summer. It has an expansive concrete patio with an ocean view, but there are no accessible tables.

Culver Street marks the northern boundary of the beach. You can get to an accessible *RESTROOM* and *TELEPHONE* on the bike path from street parking. The stall has a high toilet with grab bars; an accessible *DRINKING FOUNTAIN* is outside.

Camping

The RV campground at Dockweiler is the only beach campground in Los Angeles. It is open year round for self-contained RV's; hook-ups are available. From the paved parking-lot-style sites, you'll have direct access to the South Bay Bicycle Trail and a nice view of the sun setting over the ocean.

Four *CAMPING SPACES* are reserved for visitors with special access needs; two in the hook-up area and two in the self-contained spaces. Hook-up sites #47 and #49 are both near a central restroom that has sharp turns to narrow stalls. Unlike any of the other sites, sand surrounds the table at site #47; site #49 has no table at all. Any other hook-up site is better, especially those near the restrooms at the front office. Designated non-hook-up sites #84 and #118 are on either end of the parking lot near accessible restrooms.

An 8% downhill grade leads to the south restroom from site #84. Both the north and south campground *RESTROOMS* have a large, lateral-transfer stall with a high toilet, grab bars, and a raised sink.

Dockweiler State Beach

Contact the County of Los Angeles
(213) 305-9503 or 305-9545

Location — At the western terminus of Imperial Hwy at Vista Del Mar
Elevation — Sea level

MANHATTAN STATE BEACH

The broad sandy beaches of the Santa Monica Bay area are well represented at Manhattan State Beach. Two miles of shoreline are punctuated with over one hundred volleyball nets and accentuated by the Manhattan Beach Pier. The South Bay Bicycle Trail continues its course south to Redondo State Beach (see Will Rogers State Beach)as if to underline the sandy shore.

Parking is limited near the beach, but there are two unmetered, designated *PARKING* places near the bike path as it passes the pier and nearby restroom. Though the *600-FOOT PIER* is accessible, it has no special accommodations for wheelchair users. In 1992, there are plans to update and remodel the pier, its neighboring restroom, and the lifeguard station. The current *RESTROOM* has a large changing area, high sink, and an accessible stall with lateral transfer, high toilet, and grab bars. A *TELEPHONE* booth is accessible at the foot of the pier.

Manhattan State Beach

Contact the County of Los Angeles
(213) 372-2166

Location — At the western terminus of Manhattan Beach Boulevard
Elevation — Sea level

REDONDO STATE BEACH

With the bluffs of Palos Verdes Peninsula extending from the south, and the sweeping coastline of the Santa Monica Bay to the

The ranch home of the tall tale-teller, Will Rogers.

(Photo courtesy CDPR)

north, Redondo State Beach is the prettiest Los Angeles beach. For many people, a ride or stroll along the **South Bay Bicycle Trail** is the best way to enjoy the beach. The smooth, paved bikeway begins near a parking area at the foot of La Playa and will take you on a 19-mile journey to Will Rogers State Beach in northern Santa Monica.

The only designated *PARKING* places at Redondo can be found near the Redondo Beach Pier at the northern boundary of the park. From that location, or at the foot of Avenues "C" or "I," a 200-foot ramp (15%) with handrails at 34 inches leads down to the bike path at the beach level. Additional parking lines the roadside along a low bluff overlooking the beach. Parking is metered, and there are no designated parking places, but curb cuts are provided at the foot of each intersecting road. Two *RESTROOMS* along the bike path are accessible by a 60-foot ramp system (10%) with handrails at 34 inches. Each has an accessible sink, and the stall provides lateral transfer to a high toilet with grab bars.

Redondo State Beach

Contact the County of Los Angeles
(213) 305-9545

Location — On Esplanade Boulevard between Avenue "A" and La Playa in Redondo Beach
Elevation — Sea level

Los Angeles Metropolitan Area

WILL ROGERS STATE HISTORIC PARK

Through a legacy of radio recordings, newspaper clips, and motion pictures, Will Rogers will be remembered as the "Cowboy Philosopher." By 1922, he had become a successful stage show entertainer. He purchased a large parcel of land in the hills above Sunset Boulevard with a view of Los Angeles, Santa Monica, and the ocean. As time passed, he built a ranch house, polo fields, and stables to share with his family and friends. A visit to his unusually decorated home will give you a feel for the kind of simple whimsy that characterized Will Rogers.

The grounds and buildings of Will Rogers State Historic Park are maintained as they were when the family lived on the ranch. The old ranch house garage contains a visitor center and small gift shop. There, among the assorted memorabilia, you may view a short film about Mr. Rogers' colorful life. An audio self-guided tour of the home and ranch begins at the visitor center. Unfortunately, the ranch house is not retrofitted for wheelchair access. By taking a route on the lawn, you can avoid two sets of stairs that lead from the visitor center to the veranda of the house. From there you'll be able to peer through the windows into the main sitting room; there are two steps to the entrance of the lower floor. (The park staff is developing a film of the upstairs and other non-accessible features of the ranch. It will be ready for viewing in 1992.)

When you enter the park, you'll pass an accessible *RESTROOM* with a shallow stall and grab bars. Designated *PARKING* nearby overlooks a polo field that is still used regularly. The *VISITOR CENTER* and ranch home are up a driveway from the main parking lot. There are no accessible telephones at either the restroom or the visitor center.

Further uphill, beyond a broad expanse of lawn, horse lovers board and train their mounts at the main stables and riding ring. With a handicap - identification placard, you may park in a designated dirt *PARKING* place near the barn and look around. The grounds in the barn area are all uneven dirt surfaces, so you may need some help. From here, the popular two-mile loop trail to **Inspiration Point** begins. The trail is actually a fire road of varying surface consistencies with as much as a 13% incline. You wouldn't need to take the entire trail; views of the ocean are wonderful from part way up. Visitors using wheelchairs would require assistance both uphill and downhill.

Will Rogers State Historic Park

14235 Sunset Boulevard
Pacific Palisades, CA 90272
(213) 454-8212

Location — Take Sunset Boulevard to Will Rogers State Park Road 4½ miles northeast of Hwy 1
Elevation — 400 feet

PAN PACIFIC PARK

The famous Pan Pacific Auditorium of classic Depression- era architecture was the star of Pan Pacific Park until a fire destroyed it in 1989. The auditorium, with its "Streamline Moderne" facade and eye-catching towers hosted all sorts of sporting events and shows. Only the charred and deformed facade of the auditorium remains today; a chain link fence prohibits visitors from a close-up look.

While at the park, you also may wish to pay a visit to the **Holocaust Memorial**. Marked by six tall triangular columns at the north end of the park, the memorial's background panels tell the stories of the internment and extermination camps of World War II. You can access the open air panels on either side of the memorial; a dramatic stairway leads to the front entrance.

To the south, the balance of the narrow 27-acre downtown strip of land is a beautifully designed urban recreation park. Bounded by homes and a busy city street, the park was developed for multiple uses. Miles of broad, smooth concrete walkways of no more than 8% grade crisscross sloping grass and connect all of the facilities at the park. Several sport fields, paved *PICNIC AREAS*, an outdoor *AMPHITHEATER*, and accessible *RESTROOMS* make this urban park particularly suitable for most everyone. Designated *PARKING* is provided near the Holocaust Memorial on Stanley. From there, a concrete path will take you directly to the memorial and natural grass *AMPHITHEATER*, then on to rest of the park. The *RESTROOM* on the west side of the park has a lateral-transfer stall with a low toilet and grab bars, but the sink is not accessible. An accessible *TELEPHONE* is near the restroom.

Pan Pacific Park

7600 Beverly Boulevard
Los Angeles, CA
(818) 798-1173
County of Los Angeles

Location — Park access is best off the 7600-block of Third Street at Stanley
Elevation — 75 feet

WATTS TOWERS OF SIMON RODIA STATE HISTORIC PARK

Made without the aid of power tools, welding torches or scaffolding, steel pipes and rods were wrapped in wire and mesh then covered with mortar. Thousands of porcelain pieces were added to create one of the most talked-about landmarks in the history of Los Angeles. It took Italian immigrant, Simon Rodia 33 years to complete the nine structures in downtown Los Angeles known as Watts Towers of Simon Rodia. As a State Historic Park, the unusual towers ranging from 13 feet to over 100 feet are undergoing a long-term restoration project. You'll need to call for a schedule of tours of the grounds and for current access information.

Watts Towers of Simon Rodia State Historic Park

1765 East 107th Street
Los Angeles, CA
(213) 933-1094 or **(818) 798-1173**
County of Los Angeles

Elevation — 75 feet

KENNETH HAHN STATE RECREATION AREA

Kenneth Hahn State Recreation Area (formerly Baldwin Hills SRA) is a popular suburban park offering many recreation opportunities. Set in gently rolling grassy hills, the park includes the site of the Olympic Village for the athletes of the Tenth Olympiad. You can picnic at one of many *PICNIC* and play areas, *FISH* in one of two fishing lakes, linger near a man-made stream, or take a hilly trail that winds through the **Olympic Forest** where a tree was planted for each country represented in the 1984 games in Los Angeles.

A series of _PATHWAYS_ reinforced with soil cement or paved with concrete improves access to most of the park. You can take a stroll around most of the lake area and up into the picnic grounds with no barriers, but some inclines may require an extra push. From several designated _PARKING_ areas along the park road, concrete walkways lead to fully accessible _RESTROOMS_ with lateral-transfer stalls and an accessible _TELEPHONE_.

Picnic tables on concrete slabs are scattered on the grassy hillsides; some are quite level. If a view is your priority, the upper park section is the place to go for prime ocean views and a panorama of the Los Angeles basin. It is more level than the lower section and has the same amenities.

For fishermen, a concrete walkway leads from designated _PARKING_ to the edge of the lake where an accessible _FISHING PLATFORM_ is rimmed with curbing. If hiking "off-road" is your interest, the Olympic Forest may be the place for you. Be aware that the trail, though hard-packed, is very uneven and can be steep in places.

Kenneth Hahn
State Recreation Area
4100 South La Cienega Boulevard
Baldwin Hills, CA
Contact the County of Los Angeles
(213) 291-0199
Elevation — 100 feet

_____

PIO PICO
STATE HISTORIC PARK

As the last Governor of Mexican California, Pio Pico's political and personal career was fraught with struggle and disappointment. He began his political career at the age of 25 and spent years opposing the Mexican military government. In 1845 he was sworn in as governor. He quickly moved to bring the capital of California to Los Angeles and increased his efforts to secularize mission lands. Only a year later, Americans invaded California. With no support from Mexico, Pio Pico relinquished his post as governor and became an entrepreneur. He used the wealth he had amassed in his 19-year career to develop education, banking, and town sites.

In 1850 he purchased 9,000 acres in the Whittier area and built his mansion in 1852. Subsequently, a flood destroyed his home, forcing him to borrow large sums of money to rebuild. Eventually his fortune dwindled to nothing and he died at the age of 93 — destitute. In later years, many old buildings in the area were salvaged, their stones used to repave Whittier Boulevard. Fortunately, the mansion was spared. But in 1987, an earthquake severely damaged the mansion. It is closed to the public until repairs are completed.

Pio Pico State Historic Park
6003 Pioneer Boulevard
Whittier, CA 90606
(213) 695-1217
Park Folder Available
Location — West of the 605 Freeway at Pioneer and Whittier Boulevards
Elevation — 50 feet

_____

DRUM BARRACKS
CIVIL WAR MUSEUM

In 1859, the U.S. Army, determined to expand into the far West, established a base in Wilmington. Materials were sent from around the Horn to build the twelve original structures at Drum Barracks. They originally housed 400 soldiers and served as a supply station for Southern California, Arizona, and New Mexico. The only building that remains today is the junior officers' quarters. It now houses an _ARMORY_ and _MUSEUM_ with artifacts and military memorabilia of the period between 1859 and 1866. In the _LIBRARY_, Civil War buffs pour over hard-to-find documents and information about California's contributions to the war.

There is wheelchair access to the rear of the _MUSEUM_ on the 1000 block of Banning Street where a fenced parking lot is open during museum hours. A _TOUR_ of the accessible lower floor includes a visit to the parlor, the armory, which includes an operable Gatling gun, and the library, containing historical documents and other interesting papers. There are also plans to move a huge diorama display downstairs from the upper floor. You can visit the museum by tour only; docents or park staff offer regularly scheduled tours. For times and days contact the park office.

Drum Barracks Civil War Museum
1053 Cary Avenue
Wilmington, CA
Contact the City of Los Angeles
(213) 548-7509
Elevation — 50 feet

_____

ROYAL PALMS STATE BEACH

Royal Palms State Beach is marked by a stand of palms on the bluffs overlooking waves crashing on the rocky shoreline. Once the site of the luxurious Royal Palms Hotel, built in 1915, you only see the overgrown building foundations on your way to a small sandy cove north of the White's Point on the Palos Verdes Peninsula.

Though access to beach and tide-pools is limited, there is an accessible *RESTROOM* near a designated *PARKING* place at the north end of the beach. A concrete walkway leads from the dirt parking to an accessible *DRINKING FOUNTAIN* and *RESTROOM* with an accessible sink. The lateral-transfer stall has a low toilet with grab bars.

Royal Palm State Beach
  Contact the County of Los Angeles
  (213) 305-9503
Location—Beach access on Paseo Del Mar, two miles north of Pacific Avenue
Elevation—0 feet

Orange County

BOLSA CHICA STATE BEACH
and
HUNTINGTON STATE BEACH

From the southern boundary of Seal Beach south to Newport Beach, broad, sandy shores at Bolsa Chica and the world famous surfing beach at Huntington extend a total of five miles. Large crowds of local residents and tourists flock to these beaches in the summer. Five thousand *PARKING* spaces, including many designated spaces, are provided in lots that line the highway. Similar in features and design, a lighted, paved *BOARDWALK* runs the entire distance of both beaches providing access to restrooms and concessions. Besides the usual beach fare, people-watchers get a kick out of the interesting variety of bike riders, skaters and sunbathers that parade up and down the promenade.

Access

For easier access to the sand, each beach has a smooth, broad asphalt *RUNWAY* that takes you out to within 75 feet of the water's edge. Elevated *FIRE RINGS* on the pavement nearby are just right for an evening bonfire. *RESTROOM* buildings with accessible *DRINKING FOUNTAINS* are placed at regular intervals along the bike path. Each building has one accessible unisex room with lateral transfer to a low toilet and grab bars. Food concession patios each have at least one *PICNIC TABLE* with wheelchair access and an accessible *TELEPHONE*.

ENROUTE CAMPING for self-contained RV's is available at Bolsa Chica. The entrance to the parking area at Bolsa Chica State Beach is about 1½ miles south of Warner Avenue. The entrance to Huntington State Beach is at the terminus of Magnolia Avenue.

Bolsa Chica State Beach
  (714) 846-3460
Huntington State Beach
  (714) 536-1454
Location—Along Pacific Coast Highway extending from Seal Beach to Newport Beach
Elevation—Sea level

CORONA DEL MAR
STATE BEACH

This small ½-mile sandy cove, enveloped by steep rocky cliffs and the Newport Harbor jetty, is a scenic spot for a day in the sun. Unfortunately, there are no accessible restrooms, drinking fountains or

The boardwalk at Bolsa Chica State Beach   (Photo courtesy CDPR)

tables here. Several designated *PARKING* spots are provided near the restrooms and dressing rooms, but doorways there are not wide enough for wheelchair access. In the northeast corner of the parking area an asphalt walk leads to a shady lawn with a group of standard picnic tables. The grass is very uneven and difficult to negotiate in a wheelchair.

Corona Del Mar State Beach

Contact the City of Newport Beach
(714) 644-3151 or 644-3044
Location — From Hwy 1 take Marguerite west, then north on Ocean Boulevard to beach access road
Elevation — Sea level

CRYSTAL COVE STATE PARK

Crystal Cove State Park preserves 2,791 acres of the last major open space on the Orange County coast, including parts of the San Joaquin Hills, over three miles of shoreline, and an off-shore underwater park. While the cove is a favorite among scuba and skin divers, mountain bike riders and hikers explore the inland canyons, enjoying the ocean views from a network of trails and fire roads in the back country.

Visitor Center

Rangers are on hand to answer questions at the *VISITOR CENTER* and park office in El Moro Canyon, on the east side of Hwy 1. From designated *PARKING*, an asphalt ramp takes you over the curb to the entrance. An accessible *TELEPHONE*

and *RESTROOM* (lateral transfer with grab bars and a low toilet) are near the front door. One hundred feet from the entrance is another restroom (unisex-type with a high toilet and grab bars).

Beach

At the base of the cliffs, prime diving territory to a depth of 120 feet is protected as an underwater park. When the water is clear, you'll see lots of activity at the **Reef Point** parking lot. Access to the beach from this parking area, is a very steep (23%) 600-foot road of rough concrete that ends abruptly in the sand quite a distance from the shore. At the end of a ½-mile all-purpose road that parallels Hwy 1 to the north, another steep concrete road does the same. At the south end of the parking lot, you can park in a designated spot near an accessible *UNISEX RESTROOM* with a low toilet, grab bars, and accessible sink. There is an accessible *TELEPHONE* near another accessible *UNISEX RESTROOM* in the center of the lot, but you'll have to approach it from the south end of the lot because there are no curb cuts nearby.

Trails

The trails in Crystal Cove State Park are hilly, very uneven, and are not accessible for wheelchair users.

Crystal Cove State Park

Contact Orange Coast District Office
(714) 494-3539 or 848-1566
Location — Between Corona Del Mar and Laguna Beach on Hwy 1
Elevation — Sea level

DOHENY STATE BEACH

From the shore of Doheny State Beach at Dana Point, you'll have a beautiful sweeping view of the coastline south to San Clemente. A mile-long white sand beach at the mouth of San Juan Creek invites visitors for a day in the sun. Palms and eucalyptus shade acres of lawn in the day use area, while across the creek to the east, overnighters relax in a comfortable campground with accessible *RESTROOMS* and *HOT SHOWERS*.

Day Use

Whether you're a traditional family picnicker with a checkered table cloth and wicker basket, or you prefer a BBQ by the shore, Doheny State Beach can accommodate you. Five acres of wide-open flat grassy park are laced with asphalt walkways and dotted with shaded tables on pavement. Closer to the water, a paved *PROMENADE* parallels the shoreline. Tables with BBQ's are situated just off the pavement on a packed dirt surface with a sandy coating. If cooking isn't your idea of fun, a seasonal *SNACK BAR* is also close by.

Designated *PARKING* is provided close to the day use area in the main parking lot where you'll also find an accessible *TELEPHONE*. Accessible *RESTROOMS* Visitor Center

The *INTERPRETIVE CENTER* at Doheny is chock full of wildlife displays and aquariums with living exhibits of underwater off-shore life at the park. The volunteer association also sells books and pamphlets at the visitor center. Paved walkways lead to the *VISITOR CENTER* from a designated *PARKING* area. There is an accessible *TELEPHONE* at the rear of the building.

Camping

The new beachfront campground at Doheny is designed for comfort and convenience. Smooth asphalt connects each site with a paved pull-in and firm-packed dirt around the table and fire ring. Two designated *SITES* are close to an accessible *RESTROOM*, but most campsites are comparable. In fact, many sites facing the beach have tables with extended ends. Families with bikes love this campground for its paved roads and access to smooth paths in the day use area. The small campsites have little foliage for privacy.

The campground has two restroom buildings and two shower buildings. Both *RESTROOM* buildings provide barrier-free access to a pivot-transfer stall with grab bars and a high toilet. Each *SHOWER* building has an extra large stall with a bench in the changing area and a retractable seat in the shower area, with water controls at 43 inches. A mirror and sink are also accessible. There is a designated *PARKING* place at all but one restroom and shower building, and there is an accessible *TELEPHONE* available at each. In addition, an RV dump station is provided near the campground entrance.

For an evening stroll, a concrete walkway from the campground takes you to a hard-packed service road that parallels the beach east of the creek. From there you'll have an unrestricted view of the sunset over Dana Point.

Doheny State Beach
25300 Harbor Drive
Dana Point, CA 92629
(714) 496-6172
Location—Off Hwy 1 on Del Obispo Street (Pt. Harbor Drive) in Dana Point
Elevation—Sea level

SAN CLEMENTE STATE BEACH

Perched on a seaside blufftop in southern Orange County, San Clemente State Beach draws all types of beach-goers. Sun worshippers come to the shore for the day, while surfers, swimmers and skin divers enjoy the water. With easy access off Interstate 5, San Clemente State Beach is also a favorite among RVers and campers.

Day Use

Day Users park in a lot at the head of a steep asphalt trail (25% max slope) to the beach. At the top of the trail, you'll also find the campfire center and cabana-covered picnic area (15% access grade). An accessible *RESTROOM* in the parking lot has a 41-inch-wide stall and a high toilet with grab bars.

Camping

Of the 157 campsites on the high bluffs at the shore, 72 have pull-thru's with full hook-ups. Unfortunately, the restrooms and showers in the hook-up area are not modified for access.

The campground road continues to a section of family camping loops beyond the hook-up sites, where

both of the *RESTROOM/SHOWER* buildings are accessible. The unisex restroom has a high toilet with grab bars. The controls for the high and low shower heads are 29 inches from the floor. There is a retractable bench in the shower and a stationery bench in the changing area. An accessible *TELEPHONE* is available outside the restroom near site #106.

Campsites in this area have paved pull-ins and uneven grass and dirt camping surfaces. On either side of each restroom, designated *CAMPSITES* (#104, #106, #134, and #156) are paved around the table, BBQ, and fire ring, and a paved path leads directly to the restroom building. These sites will be designated, but may not be listed as such on the MISTIX reservation sheet. There is an RV dump station between the hook-up and non-hook-up camping areas.

San Clemente State Beach
3030 Avenida del Presidente
San Clemente, CA 92672
(714) 492-0802
Location—Avenida Calafia exit from I-5 in South San Clemente
Elevation—Sea level

San Diego County

SAN ONOFRE STATE BEACH

Seemingly dwarfed by the San Onofre nuclear power plant and surrounded by Camp Pendleton Marine Base, San Onofre State Beach retains its reputation as one of the best surfing beaches in Southern California. Known to surfers as Trestles and Surf Beach,

Though no sites are designated, wheelchair users often camp at San Onofre SB.

(Photo courtesy CDPR)

its consistent waves bring surfers from San Diego, Orange, and Los Angeles Counties.

Camping lines a section of abandoned highway on the sandstone cliffs overlooking three miles of undeveloped beach. Over two hundred paved sites, some with an ocean view, are usually full in the summer. Many local families reserve a spot here for a family retreat. In addition, there is a newly developed campground near the marshy area at San Mateo Creek on a parcel of land leased from Camp Pendleton Marine Base.

For a good view of the surfing action, there is a separate entrance for Surf Beach bluff parking at the north end of the main beach (near the Southern California Edison facility). The accessible _RESTROOM_ in the dirt parking lot has a wide stall with grab bars and a high toilet, a foot flusher, a high sink and accessible _DRINKING FOUNTAIN_. Day Use hours are 6 a.m. to 10 p.m.

Camping

Main Beach—The abandoned highway along the bluffs serves as a camping area, but there is no wheelchair access to the beach below. With 221 developed sites on pavement, campsites are reserved either for RV or tent use. Make summer reservations for your site well in advance, since this is a very popular camping spot. Five _RESTROOMS_ are spaced over the ½-mile length of the campground; each has a stall wide enough for wheelchair access. A 12% ramp leads to the modular building that houses the camp store. Curbing surrounds the building, and it is open only in the summer.

San Mateo—At the northern boundary of Camp Pendleton Marine Base, San Mateo Campground is the newest addition to San Onofre State Beach. Each paved pull-in site is level and has a table and raised fire ring on a packed, uneven dirt surface. Young trees and bushes promise shade and pri-

vacy in years to come, but for now there is little of either.

For your convenience, a campsite is designated near each restroom (#1, #66, #81, #116, and #144), but has no special accessible features. Every _RESTROOM/SHOWER_ building in the campground has designated _PARKING_ and an accessible unisex restroom with a low toilet and grab bars. The shower stall is roomy and has a retractable seat and low controls at 28 inches. There is also a bench in the changing area.

From the hillside _AMPHITHEATER_, you'll overlook the campground and the San Mateo Creek Bed at Camp Pendleton. A lighted asphalt path leads uphill (6%) for 200 feet from designated _PARKING_ to the seating area. Check at the kiosk for the current schedule of summer programs.

To reach San Mateo Campground, take the Christianitos off-ramp at I-5 and follow it east 1 mile past the Camp Pendleton Marine Corps sign.

San Onofre State Beach

Contact Pendleton Coast District Office
(714) 492-4872 or 492-0802
Location—Near the Orange County/San Diego County boundary. Take Basilone exit from I-5 south of San Clemente and proceed about 3 miles south to the park entrance.
Elevation—Sea level

CARLSBAD STATE BEACH

Though the waves on Carlsbad State Beach are gentle as a rule, several severe southerly storms of the late 1980's took their toll on many beaches of North San Diego County. The storms caused erosion of the coastal bluffs and migration of beach sand. Currently, this mile-long beach is a combination of sand and smooth cobbles but still a very pleasant place for a day in the sun.

A newly-constructed *CONCRETE WALKWAY* bordered by a 45-inch seawall runs from Ocean Street south to Tamarak Avenue. From designated *PARKING* provided at the north end of the walkway, a 200-foot downhill asphalt sidewalk (12%) leads to the seawall and onto the beach below. The lot at the foot of Tamarak Avenue has designated *PARKING*. Access to the walkway from there is less steep. South of Tamarak Avenue the beach is at street level. A designated street *PARKING* place with a curb cut and direct beach access is provided near lifeguard stations #1, #2, #3, and #4. Standard chemical toilets are the only restrooms in this area.

On the blufftop above the beach, a concrete sidewalk with coastal views and an occasional bench follows its contours. You may want to stop for a while at one of several picnic tables along the walk just north of Tamarak Avenue. The sidewalk continues down a steep (12%) ramp to a restroom near the parking lot at the foot of Tamarak Avenue. The restrooms are not sufficiently modified for wheelchair access.

Carlsbad State Beach

Contact La Costa District Office
(619) 729-8947

Location — On Carlsbad Boulevard (S21) at the terminus of Tamarack Avenue in Carlsbad
Elevation — Sea level

SOUTH CARLSBAD STATE BEACH

Cool ocean breezes and an unobstructed blufftop view make for great camping at South Carlsbad State Beach. Over half the ample campsites have gorgeous ocean views, and there are no barriers to the camp store and laundromat. Ranger present slide talks and safety demonstrations at the amphitheater Monday and Wednesday evenings from mid-June through Labor Day. Lifeguards are on duty daily from mid-June to mid-September and on weekends for a month and a half before and after the summer season.

Open year round, the campground is very popular in the summer months. If you are planning a stay, make your reservation early. Two camping loops line the bluff. Of the two, the northern loop is more level, and campsite surfaces are firmer. Asphalt roads service the campground but parking at each site is on packed, decomposed granite. Campsites include a table fire ring and food storage. Thick bushes separate each site, offering some privacy and wind screen.

Each conveniently located *RESTROOM* is accessible, but the showers are not. The shallow restroom stalls have grab bars and high toilets. Accessible *TELEPHONES* are available near the ranger station, at the entrance, and at the laundromat. The *FIRST AID STATION* behind the ranger office is accessible. In addition, you'll find an RV dump station in the north loop.

Beach erosion has left the shoreline of South Carlsbad with a mixture of cobbles and sand. Long stairways descend to the beach from seven locations at the campground, except near campsite #184, in the south loop. Here, a steep (12%) asphalt service road rolls downhill for about 200 feet to a weathered dirt path. Reinforced with sand bags, the path continues another 200 feet to the cobble beach.

South Carlsbad State Beach

2680 Carlsbad Boulevard
Carlsbad, CA 92008
(619) 438-3143

Location — From I-5 take Palomar Airport Road west to Carlsbad Boulevard south to the park entrance
Elevation — Sea level

LEUCADIA STATE BEACH

Known to the local surfing set as "Beacon's" the rocky beach at Leucadia is only accessible by a long, steep stairway from clifftop parking overlooking the water. There is one designated *PARKING* place at the top of the stairs if you want to look around, but there are no other accessible features.

241

There is reserved parking an paved access to the beach at Moonlight SB.

(Photo courtesy CDPR)

Leucadia State Beach

Contact La Costa District Office
(619) 729-8947

Location — At the foot of Leucadia Boulevard at Neptune in the city of Encinitas
Elevation — Sea level

MOONLIGHT STATE BEACH

Like most beaches in the county, Moonlight State Beach is easy to get to and very popular in the summer months. A broad, paved mall has many benches arranged for a great view of the beach scene. Paving stretches from a special designated *PARKING LOT* to the opposite end of the park for easy access to the *RESTROOMS* and *SNACK BAR*. The beach is sometimes the victim of sand erosion and covered in pebbles.

If you have a handicap-identification placard, you may *PARK* in one of four designated spaces at beach level, at the foot of "B" Street next to the snack bar.

Parking here is free. Other parking is available in an upper lot on "C" Street. It is operated by the City of Encinitas; there is a seasonal toll booth. This lot contains no designated parking places, and you must take a steep (23%) paved path with a handrail at 35 inches for 250 feet to the beach level. There is another small lot at the foot of "C" Street with a smooth, steep (18%), off-camber paved path leading 120 feet to the beach.

An accessible *TELEPHONE* is near the reserved *PARKING* at the *SNACK BAR*. In the center of the paved mall area is a fully accessible *UNISEX RESTROOM* with a high toilet and grab bars. Lifeguards are on duty daily in the summer and on weekends in spring and fall.

Moonlight State Beach

Contact La Costa District Office
(619) 729-8947

Location — West of Interstate 5 on Encinitas Boulevard in Encinitas
Elevation — Sea level

SAN ELIJO STATE BEACH

Similar to South Carlsbad in appearance and services, San Elijo State Beach with its blufftop views draws large crowds of campers in the busy summer months. With 171 developed campsites for both tent and RV, reservations are essential if you want to stay and soak up the summer sun at this campground.

You'll be able to purchase food and general merchandise at the *CAMP STORE* or grab a quick bite to eat at the *SNACK BAR*, just inside the park entry. When it is time to do the laundry, you'll find a *LAUNDROMAT* around the corner from the *SNACK BAR*. At the nearby ranger station, first aid and an accessible *TELEPHONE* is available. If needed, an RV dump station is provided south of the entrance.

The campground road extends along the 1½ miles of coastal bluff forming one long, narrow camping loop to the north and three to the south. While the sites on the northern loop have better access to the store and are smoother, those to the south are closer to beach level. You can access the beach directly from some sites on the southernmost loop. The *AMPHIT HEATER* is also in the southern loop. To get to the *AMPHITHEATER*, you'll need to take a 100-foot dirt path that begins at near the restroom. For those who sleep lightly, you'll want to be aware that many campsites back up to U.s. Hwy 101. If it's an ocean view you want (and who doesn't?), look for sites #1 through #55 or #145 through #171.

Asphalt roads connect each campsite where parking is on packed decomposed granite near a table, fire ring, and food storage. Loose gravel covers most of the sites in the southern loop, making them unacceptable for wheelchair access. Sites are separated by thick bushes that offer some privacy and wind screen. An accessible *RESTROOM* in each loop has a shallow stall with grab bars and a high toilet. The showers are not accessible. For day users, a small parking lot doubles as an *ENROUTE CAMPING* spot at the northernmost end of the campground.

San Elijo State Beach

Contact La Costa District Office
(619) 753-5091

Location—Near the community of Cardiff-by-the-Sea on old U.S. Hwy 101
Elevation—Sea level

CARDIFF STATE BEACH

Cardiff State Beach is a ¾-mile level strip of clean white sand across from San Elijo Lagoon. There is a small parking lot north of the surfing beach known to the locals as "Swami's." The only beach access is down a very long set of stairs. Designated *PARKING* places are near an accessible *UNISEX RESTROOM* with a high toilet and an accessible *TELEPHONE* and *DRINKING FOUNTAIN*. The parking lot

and the beach are on the same level. Parking is also available on Pacific Coast Highway. Because automobile and bicycle traffic is usually heavy, it is better to park in the lot if you are planning to spend some time at this beach.

Cardiff State Beach

Contact La Costa District Office
(619) 729-8947

Location—On old Highway 101 between Cardiff-by-the-Sea and Solana Beach
Elevation—Sea level

TORREY PINES STATE BEACH

The broad white sands of Torrey Pines State Beach lie in the dusky backdrop of the pine-covered bluffs of Torrey Pines State Reserve. From the city of Del Mar, stretching south for 4½ miles to the famous Torrey Pines Golf Course, this expanse of sand is a peaceful northern San Diego

beach. Just inland, the lazy waters of Los Penasquitos Lagoon, also part of the Reserve, provide shelter and a perfect breeding ground for many varieties of waterfowl and fish.

Paved day use parking for the beach is located on the inland side of U.S. Hwy 101. A designated *PARKING* place is provided in the lot near an accessible *UNISEX RESTROOM* and accessible *TELEPHONE*. From there, an asphalt walkway with a maximum slope of 10% takes you under U.S. Hwy 101 and drops you off in the sand of Torrey Pines Beach at the mouth of Los Penasquitos Lagoon. It is a long way to the surf from there.

Torrey Pines State Beach

Contact La Costa District Office
(619) 729-8947

Location—One mile south of Del Mar off old U.S. Hwy 101 (Pacific Coast Highway) to Carmel Valley Road east ¼-mile to the parking lot entrance
Elevation—Sea level

The rare Torrey Pine tree is preserved at Torrey Pines State Reserve. *(Photo courtesy CDPR)*

TORREY PINES STATE RESERVE

The wind-sculpted Torrey pine tree inhabits only two regions in the world, Santa Rosa Island off the coast of Santa Barbara, and here at Torrey Pines State Reserve. In 1921, the land encompassing the Torrey pines was set aside to protect and preserve the primeval environment of this unique specie. A lattice-work of hiking trails wanders through the solitude of this urban wilderness for a personal experience with the trees. And in spring, mother nature puts on its annual wildflower show, making it a special season at the reserve.

To maintain the integrity of this rich plant community, automobile access to the park is limited. You'll find a designated *PARKING* place near the *VISITOR CENTER* and another near an accessible public *RESTROOM* across the road from the *VISITOR CENTER*. From the restroom parking, you must cross about 25 feet of decomposed granite surface to get to the entrance of the restroom. The reserve is open daily from 9 a.m. to sunset.

Visitor Center

When you visit the reserve, be sure to stop at the *PARK HEADQUARTERS* and *VISITOR CENTER*. Built originally as a restaurant in 1923, it is housed in a pueblo-style structure high on a hill. You'll enjoy excellent displays of wildlife and human artifacts as well as an interesting natural history exhibit and slide presentation. From the designated *PARKING* place, a paved walkway at the east side of the building will take you to a ramp access at the rear for a total of 250 feet. You'll need to arrange to have a set of double French doors opened for you. Due to the historic nature of the building, the doorway to the room used for the slide show is a narrow 27 inches.

Trails

If you are able, don't miss the awesome view from a rest area behind the visitor center. From the designated *PARKING* place, take a short, steep (10%) dirt path leading up to a group of picnic tables surrounded by a low concrete wall. From there you'll have an unforgettable 200-degree panorama of chaparral-covered hillsides of the inland valleys of San Diego County. Don't plan on a picnic at the reserve, though. To protect the health and welfare of local wildlife, there is no food allowed anywhere on the reserve except on the beach.

Another short trail that may be wheelable begins near the accessible restroom at the parking lot across from the visitor center. It leads to a bluff viewpoint on Red Butte overlooking the sandstone canyons and beach below. The hard-packed decomposed granite trail has some soft spots along the way that may require assistance, but the views from this trail are worth the effort of getting there. Check with the ranger for current trail conditions.

The park road continues from the restroom area on to the other side of the reserve for a mile more. Motor vehicles are prohibited in this section so it is a perfect place to continue your wilderness experience. From the road you'll have a limited view of **Fern Canyon** and easy access to the heart of the Reserve.

Park information on signs or handouts mentions the **Guy Fleming Trail** as being accessible. Though the trail is relatively flat, there are many root gnarls and other natural obstacles in the path, making it undesirable for visitors with mobility limitations.

Torrey Pines State Reserve

Contact La Costa District Office
(619) 755-2063
Park Map Available
Location — Two miles south of Del Mar off North Torrey Pines Road (Pacific Coast Highway)
Elevation — 330 feet

SAN PASQUAL BATTLEFIELD STATE HISTORIC PARK

The bloodiest conflict in California during the Mexican American War was fought in the San Pasqual Valley. On December 6, 1846, Californio lancers led by Captain Andres Pico met General Stephen Kearny and his American dragoons. The battle lasted less than half an hour but left 22 Americans dead or fatally wounded and the rest in retreat.

The San Pasqual Battlefield State Historic Park was built in remembrance not of the virtues of war, but as a reminder of the human passions that drive people to fight. Located in the peaceful San Pasqual Valley, eight miles east of Escondido, the 50-acre park is maintained in its natural state, marked only by an amphitheater and subterranean *VISITOR CENTER*.

Visitor Center

As with most Southern California regions, several cultures enfluences the course of San Pasqual Valley history. In the _VISITOR CENTER_ you can follow a pictorial history that included Native Americans, Mexican era settlers called the Californios, and American settlers. Park staff will play a 20-minute video for you about the Mexican American War and the events that led to the battle of San Pasqual. In addition, at an observation area, there is a view of the battlefield with corresponding diagrams of troop movements in the valley.

Except for the observation area, the visitor center is totally accessible. If you are seated, the battlefield display is at eye-level (43 inches) and hinders your view out the window to the battlefield site. But, there is a lower level nearer to the window (36 inches) where your view is better.

A lighted concrete _WALKWAY_ leads from the parking lot where there are two designated _PARKING_ places. This gently sloping path takes you through natural chaparral-covered landscape for 350 feet to the visitor center entrance. Along the way, take time to enjoy the peacefulness of the valley. It is hard to image this farmland as a scene of violent armed conflict. _RESTROOMS_ near the entrance have an accessible sink and a large lateral-transfer stall with a low toilet and grab bars. There is also an accessible _DRINKING FOUNTAIN_ nearby.

Amphitheater

Built into the hillside, the _AMPHITHEATER_ is located half way up the concrete walkway to the visitor center. Rangers and service organizations use it as a gathering place for park programs, guest speakers, and field trips. Picnic tables shaded by eucalyptus trees are near a historic bronze statue of Kit Carson and Edward Beal. Commissioned by Beal's granddaughter in 1910, the statue commemorates the battle of San Pasqual and was once displayed in the Smithsonian Museum.

Trail

Next to the amphitheater is a ½-mile loop trail leading onto the hillside. Parts of the self-guided dirt path are very steep. The path winds its way past numbered markers labeling the various plants used by the local Native Americans. The trail is not accessible without help.

**San Pasqual Battlefield
State Historic Park**

15808 San Pasqual Valley Road
Escondido, CA 92025
(619) 489-0076
Park Folder Available
Location—Eight miles east of
Escondido on San Pasqual Valley
Road (Hwy 78)
Elevation—400 feet

———————

OLD TOWN SAN DIEGO
STATE HISTORIC PARK

California life, as it was in the Mexican and early American periods from 1821 to 1872, is recreated and preserved at Old Town San Diego State Historic Park. Shops and restaurants occupy historic buildings illustrating the vast changes that have taken place in San Diego over the years.

During the Mexican period, the town of San Diego briefly became the state capital. Jedediah Smith, the first Yankee to cross overland into Mexican California, came here to pay his respects. Later, soldiers from the presidio on the hill began to settle here and eke out a living. Meanwhile, the presidio was abandoned, and the surrounding land divided into ranchos.

In 1846, the Americans landed their ship, the U.S. _Cyane_ to claim California for their own; gold was discovered, and the face of San Diego changed forever. Because of expanding gold rush excitement in the nearby Laguna mountains, Old San Diego became a thriving addition to the trade and transportation route east. In the 1860's, drought and the end of "gold fever" caused the town to decline. Interest shifted to ocean trade, and the activities at the old town slowed.

You should begin your visit to Old Town at the Robinson-Rose house on the west edge of the Plaza. Originally the commercial center of the town, the replicated two-story structure now houses the park _INFORMATION CENTER_. Here also, you can view a scale model of San Diego as it appeared in the 1800's. You can purchase a booklet entitled, _Old Town San Diego State Historic Park; Tour Guide and Brief History_. It is a very helpful and informative guide for your _SELF-GUIDED WALKING TOUR_ of Old Town. Look for docents in period costume throughout the grounds. They will be happy to talk with you and can direct you to the various park highlights.

245

For the most part, the Old Town WALKING TOUR is level and paved with concrete. The historic buildings have ramped entrances and no more than ¾-inch door sills. There are three exceptions: the Mason Street School, the Machado House, and the blacksmith shop at the livery stable. The Mason Street School and Machado House are away from the central plaza close to Congress Street. The approach to each is over sloping dirt surfaces, and access to the Machado House is poor. The school is not accessible due to two brick steps at the doorway. The best approach to the Black Hawk Smithy building is from Mason Street where there is a short boardwalk ramp (12%) that leads to the level dirt yard behind the building. Docents regularly demonstrate the art of blacksmithing in the shed here. (The access route to the blacksmith shed shown on the walking tour guide is a steep, narrow, decomposed granite walkway.) Across the dirt yard, a well-restored collection of carriages is housed behind glass in the barns. Each has a viewing platform, but there is a 3- to 4-inch step from ground level.

Other Tours

At 2 p.m. daily, docents give gided tours of Old Town (year round except Thanksgiving, Christmas, and New Year's Day). Accessible TOURS can be arranged by calling the park. The docents will personalize a tour specific to the needs of your party (619) 237-6766.

A commercial "trolley" bus service leaves from Twiggs and Calhoun Streets for a 90-minute tour of the highlights of San Diego. Busses run every 30 minutes from 9 a.m.

to dusk. You may disembark and reboard at any of twelve different attractions in the city, returning to Old Town when you like. Tour directors are sensitized to the needs of disabled passengers and will help lift you onto the bus. For more information call (619) 298-8687.

Parking

4005 Taylor Street—This large parking lot with three designated parking places near the Taylor Street entrance is a long walk on an asphalt sidewalk from the Old Town District. From here you also must cross a busy street.

Congress and Smith Streets—There are two designated parking places near an accessible restroom in this lot. The restroom has a 1-inch lip at the doorway, high sink, and lateral-transfer stall with a high toilet and grab bars. An uneven packed decomposed granite path leads from this lot to the park.

Juan and Wallace Streets—You'll find two designated PARKING places behind the Bazaar del Mundo. From there, you'll have direct access to the concrete walkway into the park. This is the most desirable parking location at Old Town.

Twiggs and Juan Streets—If you're going to the playhouse, the designated PARKING in the lot nearby has a ramp access to the theater veranda. For park access, two designated PARKING spaces are available in the lot across Twiggs Street.

Mason and Congress Streets—From the two designated park-

ing places in this lot, access to the park is by way of an uneven decomposed granite path.

Restrooms

Two accessible RESTROOMS are available at Old Town. Besides the accessible RESTROOM in the Congress and Smith Street parking area, there is another across from the Livery Stable. It has a shallow stall with a low toilet, grab bars, high sink, and accessible hand dryer. An accessible DRINKING FOUNTAIN is located at the east end of the Plaza.

**Old Town San Diego
State Historic Park**
4002 Wallace Street
San Diego, CA 92110
(619) 237-6770
Park Folder Available
*Location—An area bounded on four
sides by Twiggs, Congress, Wallace
and Juan Streets*
Elevation—60 feet

CABRILLO
NATIONAL MONUMENT

Named for the 16th century Mexican explorer, Cabrillo National Monument stands on the tip of Point Loma in tribute to the achievements of Juan Rodriguez Cabrillo and his valiant quest for discovery of the California coast. At 422 feet above sea level, the view of the San Diego Bay and city skyline is unsurpassed from this lofty headland. Because of this, in 1851 the U.S. Coastal Survey decided to place San Diego Bay's first lighthouse at the top of the point. Though 36 years later a new lighthouse was built at the bottom of the hill, the original still stands today.

From late December to the end of February visitors spend hours whale-watching from the overlook on the ocean side of the point where thousands of California Gray whales migrate past the park each season on their way to give birth in the warm waters of Baja California. Meanwhile, along the rocky coast below, low tide unveils over 100 species of ocean animals and plants thriving in the tide pools.

Stairs lead into the lighthouse at Cabrillo National Monument. *(Photo courtesy NPS)*

Visitor Center

The *VISITOR CENTER* stands high on the eastern bluff over the entrance to San Diego Bay. The view of San Diego harbor is magnificent from its tall glass windows or from a paved patio area outside. On a clear day, the city of San Diego sparkles across the water as hundreds of sailboats drift in and out of the harbor on afternoon breezes.

When you arrive at Cabrillo National Monument, you probably will want to stop by the *VISITOR CENTER* first. Here, you'll learn more about Cabrillo's voyage and the human history of Point Loma. You'll also be able to purchase books or gifts and pick up further park information.

The park administration building, auditorium, and accessible restrooms are also in this complex. Rangers present daily programs in the accessible *AUDITORIUM*. The only fully accessible *UNISEX RESTROOM* in the park is well-marked, and you'll find it behind the audi-

torium. An accessible *DRINKING FOUNTAIN* and *TELEPHONES* are also close by. A steep rampway (13%) immediately north of the visitor center, will lead you from the parking lot to a pleasant garden area where you may relax and enjoy the setting.

Access

On your way to the lighthouse and whale overlook, you may find the wayside exhibits of interest. All of the footpaths and exhibit areas are paved. While the grounds around the visitor center are fairly level, some smooth access routes to bay overlooks and the picnic area are as steep as 15% and will require assistance. In addition, you can arrange for a *GOLF CART RIDE* to and from the lighthouse on request. Plenty of designated *PARKING* is available near the visitor center. In addition, there are designated *PARKING* places at the West Point pull-out on Catalina Boulevard before you get to the main parking lot.

Lighthouse

Located directly in the middle of Cabrillo National Monument is the **Old Point Loma Lighthouse**. A paved sidewalk will take you all the way to the exhibit, or you may arrange to get a ride on an electric cart for the ¼-mile uphill trip. Once at the lighthouse, the terrain is level, and there are benches at regular intervals along the asphalt path that encircles it. Unfortunately, a set of steps renders the lighthouse inaccessible to wheelchair users. The restrooms nearby can only be reached by a steep set of stairs with a handrail.

Whale-Watching Lookout

From your vantage point at the whale overlook on a high bluff above the Pacific Ocean, you'll have a sweeping view of the San Diego coastline. In the winter, visitors come to the point looking to spot California Gray whales as they make their way from the frigid summer feeding grounds of the Bering Sea, headed for the sheltered waters of Scammons Lagoon and Magdelene Bay to have their young. A glassed wind screen will shelter you from cool ocean breezes as you scout the swells beyond the kelp beds for the water spouts of passing whales. Don't forget your binoculars! You'll find the whale-watching point beyond the lighthouse along an asphalt walkway.

Picnic

Secluded in bushes and trees on the north side of the lighthouse access road is a cozy picnic area. A paved path (13%) leads down to the area where hard-packed dirt surrounds a group of picnic tables. There is no view from this area. The only place to find food at the Monument is at vending machines near the auditorium.

Tide Pools

The shores of Point Loma are a favorite spot for tide pool enthusiasts in the spring, fall, and winter. At low tide, the pounding surf recedes to uncover a bounty of sea life protected by the nooks and crannies of the rocks. Dirt trails rim the tidepools from two parking areas, but the only access to the water is down a 10-step staircase.

Cabrillo National Monument
PO Box 6670
San Diego, CA 92106
(619) 557-5450
Park Folder Available
Location—At the southern tip of Point Loma in San Diego. From Rosecrans Street turn right on Canon Street then left onto Catalina Boulevard to the end.
Elevation—422 feet

SILVER STRAND STATE BEACH

Silver Strand State Beach stretches along a narrow isthmus of sand connecting the City of Coronado to the southern community of Imperial Beach. This peninsula helps to enclose the San Diego Bay and provides the park with frontage on both the bay and ocean sides.

On the ocean side of the park, you'll have a sweeping view of the Pacific. On a clear day, you'll be able to see the Coronado Islands that lie 18 nautical miles offshore. During the summer months, lifeguards are on duty and the *FIRST AID STATION* and *SNACK BAR* are open. The ranger station is located north of parking lot #2 and is wheelchair accessible. Each of four *PARKING* lots has designated spaces located near accessible *UNISEX RESTROOMS*. Accessible *DRINKING FOUNTAINS* can be found outside each building.

The bay side is accessible only by a paved tunnel leading under the highway with approaches of 11%. Asphalt walkways wind through several groupings of picnic ramadas in the sand and stretch along the full length of the beach. Ramadas shade several modified *PICNIC TABLES* on paved surfaces and offer excellent views of the bay from the shoreline. In the summer, the staff places a rubber mat on the sand so you can wheel your chair to water's edge. Each *RESTROOM* along the walkway has one double-wide stall (some do not have grab bars).

ENROUTE CAMPING for self-contained vehicles is available in parking lot

#4, where there are two designated *PARKING* spaces near the accessible *UNISEX RESTROOM.*

Silver Strand State Beach
5000 Highway 75
Coronado, CA 92118
(619) 435-5184
Location—Four and a half miles south of Coronado on Hwy 75
Elevation—Sea level

BORDER FIELD STATE PARK

With the Tijuana Bull Ring hovering to the south, Border Field State Park lies directly on the border of the United States and Mexico. A developed picnic area here is a favorite family gathering spot. Often on weekends, mariachi singers come out to entertain park visitors, adding a festive air to this seaside locale.

Estuary

Almost half the park's 680 acres lies within the boundary of the Tijuana River Estuary, one of the few remaining salt water marsh habitats in the state. Hikers and horseback riders explore the sand dunes and vegetation on a network of trails where many varieties of birds and waterfowl reside. Though most of the estuary is flat, trails are often muddy or soft and sandy, precluding wheelchair travel.

Picnic

Situated on a bluff overlooking the shore, a 33-inch block wall encircles the picnic area. At the south end of the lawn, a chain link fence and surveyors' monument denote the Mexican border. From here you can see the La Playa area of Tijuana. The fully developed picnic area has paved designated *PARKING* near the *RESTROOM*, and concrete pavement bordering the grassy table sites. The tables are made of formed concrete; none are modified for wheelchair access. The *RESTROOM* has a shallow stall with grab bars and a low toilet.

Another parking area is available at the water level. From the paved parking here, there is direct access onto the broad, white sand beach but no other facilities. The park is open Thursday through Sunday for day use only.

Border Field State Park
Monument Road
San Diego, CA
(619) 237-6766
Park Folder Available (estuary)
Location — From I-5 in Imperial Beach
 take Hollister Road south, then
 Monument Road west
Elevation — Sea level

———————

The beautiful Anza-Borrego Desert State Park

(Photo courtesy CDPR)

6

SOUTHERN CALIFORNIA INLAND

Mojave Desert

DEATH VALLEY NATIONAL MONUMENT

As the hottest and driest place in North America, Death Valley National Monument is a region of uncommon contrasts and fascinating history, both geological and human. In a region with less than two inches of rainfall in the average year, and where summer temperatures of 120° are not unusual, one would expect to see a desolate wasteland. Instead, evidence of humanity and the natural adaptive evolution of plants and animals is apparent from the sub-sea-level valley to the magnificent rugged peaks.

Millions of years ago, major geological tumult created the valley and its surrounding mountain ranges. Several Indian cultures have inhabited the area for over 9,000 years. But it was only recently that Death Valley received its name and reputation. In the winter of 1849, a group of pioneers looking for their fortunes in gold, crossed the valley thinking it was a shortcut. As they proceeded their water and provisions became low, so the group dispatched two men over the Panamint Mountains for supplies. Most of the party was saved, but as they left, they bid farewell to "Death Valley." Later, modern exploitation of Death Valley began with the discovery of the mineral borax.

Tolerating the climate and surviving in this wealth of geological formations, are over 200 species of plants and animals, ranging from the Salt Creek pup fish to the bobcat, mountain lion, and coyote. Beside the more common sort, twenty-one species of plants are unique to the valley, including the Panamint daisy and the Death Valley sage.

You can enjoy a great deal of Death Valley National Monument from your car. The morning and afternoon hours are especially satisfying when shadows drift with the sun's shifting light, and the color spectrum fades from golden bright to violet haze. You should check in at the VISITOR CENTER for road guides to the park and refer to the visitor guide newspaper for travel tips. Remember to keep your gas tank full; the only gas stations in the park are at Furnace Creek, Stovepipe Wells, and Scotty's Castle, so plan ahead.

Furnace Creek Area

Visitor Center

Most people who come to Death Valley National Monument stop in at the **Furnace Creek Visitor Center** at Furnace Creek. It is the main hub of activity in the park; docents and rangers are on hand to help you. You'll enjoy browsing in the MUSEUM over memorabilia, art, and other cultural resources significant to the history of the valley. In addition, every half hour a film is shown in the accessible AUDITORIUM. Park brochures and pamphlets are plentiful, and you can purchase books and gift items as well.

Four designated PARKING spaces, accessible TELEPHONES, and a DRINKING FOUNTAIN are near the visitor center entrance. RESTROOMS in the foyer have heavy entry doors

and accessible stalls with grab bars.

Features

Harmony Borax Works — Descriptive markers along the Harmony Borax Works Interpretive Trail, north of Furnace Creek, recount the history and human drama of borax mining in Death Valley. It was in this valley that two entrepreneurs determined to make their mining venture succeed, memorialized the famous Twenty-Mule Team method of hauling borax.

The interpretive trail is a roughly-paved 1/3-mile hillside loop. The upper loop (8%) takes you to the refinery and mining displays. The lower loop (13%) leads to the twenty-mule team wagons.

Death Valley Museum — The rapidly-expanding mining industry required all sorts of equipment to transport ore and minerals from one location to another. Many wagons and other representative mining gear are on display at the outdoor Death Valley Museum located in Furnace Creek Village. In this same area next to a quaint but cramped rock shop, gemologists, antique collectors, and others sometimes set up displays or small booths in the courtyard to show or sell their wares.

A weather-worn parquet boardwalk leads to uneven packed dirt on the museum grounds, making unassisted wheelchair access very difficult. There is some ramping, but you must cross very rough ground to get to most of the exhibits.

Badwater Self-Guided Auto Tour — For an informative and enjoyable excursion through some of

Death Valley's most fascinating landscape, take the self-guided auto tour. It begins at the Furnace Creek Visitor Center and directs you on a 40-mile journey (80 miles round trip) to such points of interest as Mushroom Rock and the **Devil's Golf Course**. On your return from **Badwater**, the lowest place you can drive to on the western hemisphere, the route cuts off onto **Artist's Drive** for a closer look at strange and beautiful alluvial fans of the desert hills. By following along in your tour guide and stopping at each marked pull-out, you will learn about the mysteries of the valley terrain and its changing landscape. You may purchase the pamphlet, entitled *Badwater Self-Guiding Auto Tour*, at the visitor center or any of the other park gift shops.

Zabriskie Point — If you and a friend are game for a steep (20%) hike up a smooth asphalt road, your efforts will be rewarded by a breathtaking view of the badlands from Zabriskie Point. The turnout, just south of Furnace Creek on Hwy 190, and access route are on smooth asphalt, and there are several benches along the ¼-mile climb. The view from the point gives you a new perspective of the colorful Death Valley terrain.

Visitor Services

Furnace Creek Village — You'll find most of the basic services you need at Furnace Creek Village. There is designated PARKING near the POST OFFICE or the GENERAL STORE. Several food establishments are close by, including a COFFEE SHOP, CAFETERIA, STEAK HOUSE, SALOON, MEXICAN RESTAURANT and

PIZZA SHOP. CAR REPAIR and GASOLINE are available as well.

Be aware that Furnace Creek Village offers many access challenges. The designated PARKING place at the general store is over 30 feet from the ramp that crosses the curbing to a flagstone patio. Then, to get to the store, you must climb a short concrete ramp of 15%. Restaurants, on the same level as the store, have makeshift ramps over the thresholds of each doorway. Access to any of the restaurants also involves tight turns. The RESTROOM in the cafeteria has an accessible stall with grab bars and a low toilet.

Tours — Several different Death Valley van tours leave from the parking lot at Furnace Creek Village. You will need someone to help you on and off the tour van; there are no wheelchair lifts and the drivers cannot help you on board. For tour information, call the Fred Harvey Transportation Company, (619) 786-2345, extension 222.

Camping and Lodging

Furnace Creek Campground (FCFS) — The flat desert terrain hosts 136 campsites at Furnace Creek Campground. A firm dirt road services several camping loops sprinkled with desert foliage. Each site has a dirt pull-in with a fire ring and table. The tent camping area has an accessible RESTROOM with designated PARKING. The restroom's lateral-transfer stall has a high toilet with grab bars, and there is an accessible sink, DRINKING FOUNTAIN, and laundry tub. From there, an asphalt walkway marked with the international access symbol leads to the RV sec-

tion of the campground. Sites #50, #72, and #73 are near the path and have a modified table on their dirt camping areas. The asphalt walkway then leads on to the Furnace Creek Visitor Center. Other restrooms in the campground have a wide stall, but no other accessible features. Near the entrance to the campground, you'll find an accessible TELEPHONE and an RV dump station.

A small commercial RV campground near the general store offers full hook-ups with some shade. The restrooms and showers there are not accessible. For reservations or information call (619) 786-2345.

Sunset Campground (FCFS) — Across the highway from the Village at Furnace Creek, a huge flat parking area hosts self-contained RV's on a packed desert floor surface. There are no tables or BBQ's, but an RV dump station is provided. Close to the highway in Loop A, a DESIGNATED SECTION of 16 paved sites lined in blue adjoins an accessible RESTROOM that has an electrical outlet. From there, a paved path leads across the highway for easy access to the Village. This campground is only open from November through April.

Texas Spring Campground (FCFS) — Back from the highway past Sunset Campground, Texas Spring Campground finds haven in a rocky outcropping where generator noise is forbidden. Of the two camping loops, the lower loop is flatter. There is an accessible CHEMICAL TOILET in the upper loop, but the sites there are rocky and not quite level. Weathered asphalt roads lead to each campsite, where

parking is on the desert floor near a table and fire ring. This campground is only open from November through April.

Furnace Creek Ranch — FOUR DELUXE ROOMS on the ground level at Furnace Creek Ranch are modified for access: room #603, #705, #803, and #903. From designated PARKING nearby, ramps lead through ample doorways to each room, equipped with two double beds and an accessible bathroom. There are grab bars near the toilet and on the end and side of the tub/shower combination (14-inch-high tub). In addition, ceiling hooks have been installed over the tub, toilet, and bed. Parking surrounds the ranch office at the Village Center. There is a steep ramp (8%) to the registration desk, but designated parking is not provided. For Ranch reservations you may dial toll free (800) 528-6367.

Furnace Creek Inn — The four-star Furnace Creek Inn has no special modifications for wheelchair users, but the management suggests that if you call and express your specific access needs, they will try to accommodate you. Furnace Creek Inn offers a dining room, an Italian restaurant open for dinner, and a lounge with evening entertainment. The Inn is closed in the summer season. Furnace Creek Resort, PO Box 1, Death Valley, CA 92328, (619) 786-2345.

Stovepipe Wells Area

Prospectors traveling old Indian trails between what are now the ghost towns of Rhyolite and Skidoo, dug for water near the sand dunes in this area. To mark the hole, someone stuck a length of stovepipe in the sand beside it. Thus, the name Stovepipe Wells came into being and today identifies the village near the sand dunes. Stovepipe Wells Village will be happy to share their trip planning flyer and map if you give them a call at (619) 786-2387.

Visitor Services

All of the services at Stovepipe Wells center around the Village area. The MOTEL, RESTAURANT, and GIFT SHOP are on the south side of Hwy 190. Designated PARKING IS near the ramp entrance to the gift shop and motel registration desk. There is an accessible TELEPHONE near the motel lobby and an accessible RESTROOM in the courtyard with a high toilet and grab bars. Since there is a set of stairs at the entrance to the restaurant, the management has arranged a rear access for wheelchair users. You should notify the host or call ahead to the dining room and they will be happy to direct you to the rear entrance and unlock the door for you. Call (619) 786-2387 and ask for the dining room.

A GENERAL STORE containing hot and cold foods, gift items and sundries, and GAS STATION are across the highway from the motel. There is ready access to the market on pavement from designated PARKING. But, the self-serve gas station next door has a difficult 12% access to the pay window. Also, the approach to the restroom on the gas station side of the general store is too rough and steep for wheelchair users to attempt without some help. It has a rough

transition from the desert floor approach to the concrete walk at the entry.

Trails and Picnic

Salt Creek Interpretive Trail IIn the hot, parched landscape of Death Valley, it is a pleasant surprise to find water flowing on the desert surface. Salt Creek threads its way along a path on a valley floor that, many thousands of years ago, was covered by a fresh-water lake. Now, the water has become salty, and all that remains is this two-mile stretch where only algae and a few plant and animal species can survive.

You can visit the creek and follow its path for ½ mile at the Salt Creek Interpretive Trail. The gradually sloping BOARDWALK trail begins at a dirt parking lot located on Hwy 190 between Mud Canyon and the Beatty Cutoff. There is a 1-inch transition from the dirt at the trailhead to the slightly off-camber boardwalk. Chemical toilets and picnic tables in the sandy dirt parking lot are not accessible. Trail guides for the creek walk are available in a box at the trailhead (48 inches high) or at any of the gift shops or visitor centers.

Sand Dunes Picnic Area — As you travel along the highway east of Stovepipe Wells Village, a vast area of dunes north of the road seems to beckon you with ethereal waves of sand. There is no wheelchair access out onto the ever-changing sands, but you can stop at Sand Dunes picnic area for a closer look. Surfaces in the parking lot are firm but sandy, and the only facilities here are picnic tables and chemical toilets. Five miles from town on the opposite side of the road, eerie clumps of

arroweed stand at **Devil's Cornfield** like corn stalks after a harvest.

Camping and Lodging

Emigrant Campground (FCFS) — Near the Emigrant Ranger Station eight miles west of Stovepipe Wells, ten dirt campsites sit out in the open near a parking lot. Water is available, but campfires are not allowed, and the telephone and restroom nearby are not accessible. The campground is open April through October only.

Stovepipe Wells Campground (FCFS) — At Stovepipe Wells Campground, a large, flat parking area entertains over 200 RV and tent-camping units. While the parking-lot style sites are mainly for self-contained RV's, there are a few hook-up sites near the store and an handful of tent-only sites on the fringes of the campground that have tables, fire rings, and some grass. A modular restroom building with a short set of stairs is central to the parking area. It serves as the campground restroom while upgrades are completed on the regular restroom. Until then, accessible CHEMICAL TOILETS have been placed near the modular unit. Stovepipe Wells Campground is open November through April only.

Stovepipe Wells Motel — The motel at Stovepipe Wells offers TWO UNITS with a king-size bed and adapted bathroom fixtures and lever-type door handles. The extra large tub in each unit has a seat and a hand-held shower. There are grab bars at the high toilet and in the tub area.

The accessible tour of Scoitty's Castle is a highlight of a trip to Death Valley NM.   (Photo courtesy NPS)

Grapevine Area

The Grapevine Ranger Station serves as the northern entrance to the park. To get there from outside the park drive southwest on Hwy 267. From inside the park, you get there by traveling north on the main park road. Designated PARKING is provided near an accessible TELEPHONE and a RESTROOM that has a long pivot-transfer stall with a low toilet, high sink, and an electrical outlet.

Ubehebe Crater

Long ago, a huge volcanic explosion formed this 800-foot crater, 5.2 miles west of the Grapevine Ranger Station. A paved overlook rims this gaping depression, but unfortunately, there are no curb cuts from the parking lot to the pavement. If you stay in your vehicle, you'll only be able to see the sides of this tremendous crater.

Scotty's Castle

As an official part of the National Monument for only twenty years, Scotty's Castle is a major attraction for most Death Valley visitors. Originally owned by a wealthy businessman, Albert Johnson, and his wife, Bessie, the castle was the result of a truly fantastic scheme devised by a devil-may-care adventurer and raconteur named Death Valley Scotty. The rangers retell the intriguing story of the Johnson's and Death Valley Scotty when you take the 50-minute TOUR through this magnificent desert mansion.

You'll be happy to know that most of the CASTLE TOUR is accessible. A WHEELCHAIR LIFT will take you up to the second level so that everyone in your party may stay in the same group. Some ramps at the doorways are short and steep, requiring assistance. There is only one room that is not modified for access. Wheelchair users must remain at the doorway of the music room unless someone is with you that can lift you over two steps. If you notify the ranger guide, the tour will be personalized according to the needs of the individuals in your group. If someone in your party would like to use a wheelchair to get around the grounds at

Scotty's Castle, you may borrow one at the entry kiosk.

The best time to visit Scotty's Castle is in the morning before the tour busses start arriving and the midday sun changes your priorities. Since tickets for the tour are sold only at the ticket window on a first-come-first-served basis, you may have to wait for up to two hours if there is a crowd.

Meanwhile, you can entertain yourself by taking a SELF-GUIDED TOUR of the grounds, or by stopping at the SNACK SHOP for a bite to eat and a cool reprieve from the hot desert air. You may need some help to open the heavy entry door at the snack shop. The VISITOR CENTER, located in the courtyard near the castle, is another cool place to spend some time. There you'll find everything you wanted to know about Death Valley and Scotty's Castle. You may purchase books or gift items and there is a ranger on duty at the INFORMATION STATION who will answer any other questions you have.

On your SELF-GUIDED TOUR, travel surfaces vary from asphalt in the main courtyard area, to packed decomposed granite on the outskirts of the grounds. Mr. Johnson kept his cars in the stable at the end of a long, 550-foot asphalt road (12% max uphill from courtyard). Several of his original cars and equipment are on display in the stable building that is surrounded by packed dirt. With some help, you can visit the mammoth swimming pool or pass by the electrical generating plant and bell tower, both located in the middle of packed desert floor surfaces. Pick up a

map at the visitor center for more detailed exhibit information.

Accessible RESTROOMS are around the back side of the snack bar building about 250 feet from the ticket booth. The sloping (9% max) concrete walkway that leads up to the restroom has several transitions, so be alert. The RESTROOM has a long pivot-transfer stall with low toilet and grab bars, an accessible sink and DRINKING FOUNTAIN. Designated PARKING in front of the castle grounds is shady and about 100 sloping feet downhill from the ticket booth. There are picnic tables in the shade on the lawn next to the parking area if you decide to spend some time waiting near your vehicle.

Camping

Mesquite Spring (FCFS) – Due to a flash flood in 1990 that washed out the access road and much of the campground, Mesquite Spring will not reopen, but rather be relocated to an undetermined place.

Wildrose Area

In the 1870's, the mining industry was in its heyday at Death Valley and especially in the Panamint Mountains. Charcoal was required to process the ores mined from the mountains. Since no natural source existed in the area, charcoal kilns, built by Chinese laborers, made charcoal from piñon pines and junipers harvested close by.

The kilns still stand today one mile beyond the paved portion of Wildrose Canyon Road, seven miles east of Wildrose Campground. They are close enough to the dirt

road to see from the car. Rocky dersert floor that surrounds the kilns precludes wheelchair users from making a closer inspection.

For a detailed history of the kilns, you may purchase the pamphlet, entitled Wildrose Charcoal Kilns, and any of the other pamphlets mentioned, from the Death Valley Natural History Association, PO Box 188, Death Valley, CA, 92328, or from most stores in the valley.

For those who prefer a primitive desert camping experience, the Wildrose area in the southwest section of Death Valley offers small tranquil campgrounds with limited services. The Wildrose park entrance is approximately 39.4 miles north of Trona on Wildrose Canyon Road.

Camping

Because of their altitude, the three campgrounds in the Wildrose area offer a camping flavor unique to Death Valley. The rutted dirt road to two of these campgrounds requires four-wheel drive at times. Piñon pines and other vegetation are more plentiful in this area, and temperatures are milder.

Wildrose (FCFS) – On a creek bank near the Wildrose ranger station, Wildrose Campground is a flat parking area coated with chipped gravel designed for RV's. There are tables and fire rings or BBQ's at each of 30 sites, and water is available. The pit toilets are not accessible, and there is no shade.

Thorndike (FCFS) – Wildrose Canyon Road becomes rough dirt beyond the kilns; four-wheel drive is recommended beyond that point. Sloping dirt campsites on the rolling hills at Thorndike

Campground are not accessible, and there is no water available. Open March through November only.

Mahogany Flat (FCFS) — The rough dirt and gravel of Wildrose Canyon Road continues on its narrow, winding course to an altitude of 8,200 feet. There, perched on a ridge overlooking a broad expanse of Death Valley, is Mahogany Flat Campground. A table and fire ring are provided in the partial shade of piñon pines at each dirt site (some are level). You can park your car next to the table. There is no water nor accessible restroom, only a chemical toilet. Four-wheel drive is required on the road to this campground. It

snows here in the winter! The campground is open March through November only.

Death Valley National Monument

Death Valley, CA 92328
(619) 786-2331

Park Information Available: Park Folder and <u>Death Valley Visitor's Guide</u>, a seasonal newspaper
Location — U.S. 395 passes west of Death Valley and connects with Hwys 178 and 190 to the park. U.S. 95 passes east and connects Hwys 267, 374, and 373 to the park. I-15 passes southeast and connects with Hwy 127 to the park.
Elevation — Badwater 280 feet below sea level; Scotty's Castle 3,000 feet; Mahogany Flat 8,200 feet

ANTELOPE VALLEY CALIFORNIA POPPY RESERVE

In late March and April, after favorable winter and spring rains, the California poppy awakens for a new blooming season on the hillsides west of the city of Lancaster. For four to six weeks, sunshine opens the brilliant orange blossoms of California's state flower, lighting up the hills like a blaze of fire under the azure sky. At the Antelope Valley California Poppy Reserve, you can to stroll in rolling meadows filled with flowers. Scattered amid the dazzling poppy meadows, the dusky lavenders of Blue Dick and zesty yellow of

Take a long accessible walk at the Antelope Valley California Poppy Reserve. *(Photo by John Johnson)*

Checkered Fiddlenecks and Alkali Gold Fields blend with other species to create a springtime spectacle.

The reserve is very accessible to visitors of all abilities and has a WHEELCHAIR to lend on request. A paved walk leads uphill (max 8%) from paved designated PARKING in the packed dirt parking lot. The walk passes by the VISITOR CENTER and ends near a bench at a scenic OVERLOOK in the meadow (total distance - 1,050 feet). Another paved sidewalk takes you to a cozy paved PICNIC AREA shaded by ramadas in a hollow covered with a profusion of colorful blossoms. Other firm, packed dirt trails make loops up and around the hills of the reserve. Though some areas are steep (up to 15%), wheelchair users may wish to explore the fringes of the reserve with a willing assistant.

A stop at the accessible earth-sheltered VISITOR CENTER will enlighten you about the poppy and its place in the natural cycles of the high desert environment. There is a selection of books for sale, and docents are on duty to answer any questions you may have. A fully accessible RESTROOM and accessible DRINKING FOUNTAIN are near the visitor center entrance. The RESTROOM has a lateral-transfer stall, low toilet, and a high sink. There is an additional accessible CHEMICAL TOILET at the foot of the walkway near the designated PARKING.

The flowering season is very short and depends largely on the weather conditions. Be sure to call ahead to the reserve for flower information (805) 724-1180. Other times of the year, grasses blanket the rolling hills of this 1,745-acre reserve. Be aware that there is no public phone at the reserve.

Antelope Valley California Poppy Reserve

15101 West Lancaster Road
Lancaster, CA 93536
(805) 942-0662

Location—Fifteen miles west of Hwy 14 in Lancaster on Lancaster Road, an extension of Avenue I
Elevation—2,800 feet

ANTELOPE VALLEY INDIAN MUSEUM

In 1928, a self-taught artist and Native American artifact collector named Howard Edwards fell in love with the rock formations and desert scenery on Piute Bluff. So he decided to build a home, here in the heart of California's historic Mojave Desert. His unusual house with its seven different roof elevations incorporates the natural rock outcroppings as portions of the walls and floor. Huge Kachina dolls painted on the ceiling panels and drawings on the walls accent the highly decorated interior. When Anthropologist Grace Oliver purchased the home in 1938, she added to it her extensive artifact collection and converted the home to a museum. Forty years later the state purchased the museum.

Today the Antelope Valley Indian Museum houses a broad array of Native American objects displayed in the unusual setting of this distinctive house. The lower section of the museum includes many southwest artifacts, while up a narrow rock passage, displays in the California Hall focus mainly on California Indians.

Four uneven steps access the main entrance to the museum. If you're adventuresome, you could bypass the steps by coming onto the front lawn from the side of the museum near the gift shop. Anyhow, only the foyer is accessible on the lower floor; you'll only have a distant look at many other exhibits from there. Behind the building, a paved ramp leads to a rear door, but rocks and sand hamper wheelchair access near the start of the ramp. Once inside, a wheelchair user could look into the upper exhibit room from a viewing platform. The floor is made of boulders, rendering it inaccessible.

A ½-mile self-guided nature trail that begins near the museum introduces you to the natural habitat and topography of the high desert. Though interesting, the trail is too soft for most wheelchair users.

There is a unisex restroom with accessible features behind the museum. A ramp that leads there begins with a 3-inch lip on the desert sand. After making a sharp turn inside, the stall has a high toilet with grab bars. The museum's packed dirt and sand parking area is downhill from the entrance. The museum is open on Saturdays and Sundays. Docents give tours on Tuesdays and Thursdays by reservation only. If you are a wheelchair user, plan to bring along someone to help.

Antelope Valley Indian Museum

c/o High Desert District
(805) 942-0662

Location—Seventeen miles east of Hwy 14 on Avenue M between 150th and 170th Streets East
Elevation—2,800 feet

SADDLEBACK BUTTE STATE PARK

Located on a granite-topped butte overlooking the broad alluvial bottomland of the Antelope Valley, Saddleback Butte State Park is a fine example of the high desert environment. Besides great views of the desert floor, the park encompasses a parcel of Joshua tree woodland. Here, visitors can learn about the tree's history and unique ecological life cycle. Spring is the most popular time of the year to visit Saddleback Butte, when temperatures are mild, and desert flowers are in bloom. Due to rapid temperature changes on the desert floor, high winds and blowing sand are not uncommon on the butte, so prepare to keep things battened down when you visit.

A hilly self-guided nature trail weaves through rocks and cactus. It is not accessible for wheelchair users, but the trail guide available outside the ranger station is enlightening nonetheless. The ranger station/visitor center has a high step up to the doorway and is open only on weekends during the fall, winter, and spring.

Picnic

Near the ranger station, a community of lean-tos scattered among the chaparral shelter picnic tables and BBQ's from the wind and sun. The desert floor parking and walking surfaces are soft in places.

Camping

A firm dirt and gravel road winds through the park to the campground dotted with Joshua trees and creosote bushes. A lean-to at each site protects a table and BBQ surrounded in gravel, with parking on the desert floor. Wheelchair users may find the way to the campfire center challenging. Soft sand surrounds the seating area and a gravel path is the only access from the campground. There are three accessible _UNISEX REST-ROOMS_ in the campground. To get to the concrete slab at each restroom you must cross some sandy surfaces, and there may be up to a 2-inch transition onto the concrete. The _RESTROOM_ has grab bars and a high toilet; the sinks have push faucet controls; and there is

The Mojave desert is home to the Joshua Tree.   *(Photo courtesy CDPR)*

an accessible _DRINKING FOUNTAIN_ nearby. An RV dump station is provided on your way out of the campground. (FCFS)

Saddleback Butte State Park

17102 Avenue J East
Lancaster, CA 93534
(805) 942-0662

Location — Seventeen miles east of Lancaster (Hwy 14) at Avenue J and 170th Street
Elevation — 2,700 feet

RED ROCK CANYON STATE PARK

Shutterbugs love the rock formations at Red Rock State Park.   _(Photo courtesy CDPR)_

The canyon and scenic desert cliffs of Red Rock Canyon State Park, have been an established route of travel and point of interest for thousands of years. Evidence has it that ancient peoples occupied this area as long as 20,000 years ago. But this point at the southernmost tip of the Sierra Nevada and El Paso ranges lay in the path of the miners who, in the 1870's, flocked to the El Paso range seeking their fortunes. Later, the little town of Ricardo, where the ranger station stands now, became an important stage stop for folks on their way from the Owens Valley to Los Angeles.

More recently, the striated cliffs and unique landscape have drawn movie-makers and photographers to the Mojave Desert. The spectacular rock formations of Red Rock Canyon are a camera buff's dream, especially in the early morning and late afternoon hours when shadows and light create a melange of shapes and colors on the weathered sandstone. After a wet winter, the spring foliage can be especially vibrant. The park

has one main paved road to the ranger station, but there are other primitive roads you may use. These roads, designated by the park, will provide you with vehicle access to **Dove Springs** and **Jawbone Canyon** for more photogenic layouts. Four-wheel drive may be recommended in some of these areas, so check at the ranger station for road conditions.

Visitor Services

Rock and sand surround the modular ranger station that doubles as a visitor center Saturday and Sunday. Five steps lead to the entrance. If you need to stop and chat with a ranger, there are some shade and benches in the patio out front. The visitor center/ranger station is closed in the summer, Labor Day through Memorial Day.

Beyond the ranger station on the park road is a concrete slab with a pit toilet that has lateral transfer to a low seat and no grab bars. There is a 3-inch transition onto

the concrete from a designated _PARKING_ spot on the nearby desert dirt road. Be aware that there are no public telephones in the park.

Camping

Ricardo (FCFS) — For picturesque camping, Ricardo is the place to stay. From your campsite, you can watch the surrounding cliffs change from sienna red to deep chocolate as the day ends. In the morning, you'll wake up to the orange and yellow ocher of the sunrise reflected on the sedimentary sandstone overhead. Campsites lie along a dirt road that winds among the rocks at the foot of the cliffs. Each has a sandy surface with a table and fire ring near the dirt parking place.

Two very accessible designated _CAMPSITES_ are hidden in the shadows of large desert boulders. Pavement covers the surfaces of the extra-wide parking, under the tables with fire rings, around an accessible _DRINKING FOUNTAIN_, and along the path to the accessible PIT

TOILET. Other restrooms in the campground are not accessible. You'll find the campfire center located near the campground entrance. The sandy path from the dirt parking makes access in a wheelchair a challenge.

Red Rock Canyon State Park

RRC Box 26
Cantil, CA 93519
(855) 942-0662
Park Folder Available
Location—Twenty-five miles northeast of Mojave on Hwy 14
Elevation—2,600 feet

PROVIDENCE MOUNTAINS STATE RECREATION AREA

The eastern Mojave Desert, a vast, sun-scorched wilderness, is the setting for 5,900-acres of Providence Mountains State Recreation Area. From park headquarters at an elevation of 4,300, on the eastern slope of Providence Mountains, you overlook some 300 square miles of broad desert valleys filled with creosote bush, cactus, sand dunes, and cinder cones. However, people usually come to explore **Mitchell Caverns Natural Preserve**. Stairs and railings lead visitors into the cool interiors of two caverns; special lighting reveals the intricated limestone formations of El Pakiva and Tecopa

At this time, there are no facilities designed for wheelchair access at Providence Mountains. Loose gravel, steep hills, and stairs preclude travel for most visitors with limited mobility. The six primitive campsites near the park headquarters have no access modifications.

Providence Mountains State Recreation Area

PO Box 1
Essex, CA 92332
(619) 389-2281
Park Folder Available
Location—On Essex Road, 17 miles north of I-40. Forty-five miles west of Needles, 100 miles east of Barstow.
Elevation—4,300 feet

North of Los Angeles

FORT TEJON STATE HISTORIC PARK

In 1854, the United States government established a military outpost at the head of Grapevine Canyon in the Tehachapi Mountains. Documents state that Fort Tejon was founded to protect the Indians of Tejon Reserve. Troups most often served as a police force for the Indian agent and the pioneer population, providing protection for goods transported between outlying areas and Los Angeles. Patrols from the fort ranged as far east as the Colorado River and rode the main supply route, "the Grapevine," between the San Joaquin Valley and Los Angeles. Sometimes, due to the hot climate, the cavalry mounted camels, protecting citizens from bandits and enforcing the law in Southern California.

The restored barracks building and officer's quarters of Fort Tejon lie within the park boundary at the edge of a grassy open area dotted with 400-year-old valley oak trees. On the first Sunday of each month, park docents in period clothing and uniforms demonstrate the lifestyle of the pioneers and service men who worked and lived at Fort

Tejon between 1854 and 1861. On the third weekend of every month from April through October, docents participate in mock Civil War battles carefully recreated for authenticity.

There is a ranger station and small *VISITOR CENTER* with a words-and-pictures display of fort history; designated *PARKING* is close by. From there, a concrete walkway leads gently uphill 300 feet to the inaccessible barracks building and courtyard. Magnificent oak trees near the ranger station shade several picnic tables on a dirt surface. Restrooms, located behind the ranger station at the end of another concrete walkway, are not modified for access. The entry door is very narrow (26 inches) and a long pivot-transfer stall has a low toilet and no grab bars.

Fort Tejon State Historic Park

35251 Fort Tejon Road
Lebec, CA 93243
(805) 248-6692
Location—Forty miles south of Bakersfield and 90 miles north of Los Angeles on I-5
Elevation—3,250 feet

HUNGRY VALLEY STATE VEHICULAR RECREATION AREA

Set in the rolling hills of northern Los Angeles and Ventura Counties, Hungry Valley State Vehicular Recreation Area encompasses 19,000 acres of undeveloped terrain. Off-road enthusiasts bring their four-wheel-drive vehicles, dune buggies, motorcycles, and ATV's for a ride in the scenic washes, challenging runs on rugged badlands, or hill-climbs on the sun-washed bluffs.

Some portions of the park have only primitive camping sites with fire rings and chemical toilets. Otherwise there are no improvements, and water is not available within the park grounds. The best time to visit Hungry Valley is in the fall or spring when weather is mild. In any event, come prepared for weather changes and bring plenty of water with you.

Hungry Valley
State Vehicular Recreation Area

PO Box 1360
Lebec, CA 93243-1360
(805) 248-6447

Park Folder Available
Location — From I-5 at Gorman, one
*   mile north on Peace Valley Road*
Elevation — 3,000-6,000 feet

PYRAMID LAKE STATE RECREATION AREA

North of Los Angeles, 21 miles of narrow canyon walls and dramatic rock strata frame the waterscape of Pyramid Lake. Created in 1973 by the damming of Piru Creek, the lake now engulfs what was once the rugged terrain of a Mexican land grant ranch and gold discovery site. Water from the Plumas National Forest above Lake Oroville in northern California is brought to Pyramid Lake by way of the California Aqueduct System. Water stored here provides drinking and irrigation water, power generation as well as recreation for the Los Angeles area.

Fishing, boating, and personal watercraft riding are popular pastimes at the lake. There is an accessible eight-lane *BOAT LAUNCH* with an accessible *BOAT DOCK* in the day use area at **Emigrant Landing**. In addition, there is wheelchair access to shore fishing in this area. Trout are planted regularly at the lake and join striped bass, largemouth and smallmouth bass, catfish, blue gill, and crappie to challenge both shore and boat fishermen. Accessible *PICNIC AREAS* have a scenic perspective of the cool lake waters and a boardwalk leads to the public docks.

Picnic and Day Use

At the northern tip of the lake, the facilities at **Emigrant Landing** provide access to the lake and day use area. Near parking Lots A, C,

Try and make it to Fort Tejon during one of the living history reenactments, it's a sight to see. *(Photo courtesy CDPR)*

and D, young ash trees shade picnic tables that overlook the lake. Tables and BBQ's are grouped on concrete slabs with ramadas for added shade. All of the parking areas except Lot B are on a level above the lake. Steep paved paths, lead from each lot to the lake level.

Boat-in Day Use—Often visitors pack a picnic lunch in their boats and take it to a spot with a table at one of six boat-in day use areas. There are restrooms at each area, but access from the coarse sand beaches is not provided for wheelchair users except at Spanish Point. Since the lake closes at sunset, camping is not allowed in these or any other shoreline locations.

Spanish Point—The boat-in day use area at Spanish Point is being upgraded to include an accessible VISITOR CENTER with paved PARKING, and a PICNIC AREA with an accessible TABLE and RESTROOM. An off-framp from I-5 to this area is scheduled for completion by the summer of 1992.

Lot A—This is the first parking area you pass as you enter the park. Lot A is the most convenient to shoreline fishing, and accessible PICNIC and RESTROOM facilities. Several designated PARKING places are provided near a PICNIC AREA where pavement connects table groupings with an accessible RESTROOM (grab bars, low toilet, 1-inch door sill). To reach the ranger station or simply for stroll along the lake, a concrete walkway continues as far as the launching ramp at the foot of Lot B.

For fishermen, a paved ACCESS RAMP (less than 8%, 150 feet) will take you to the edge of the water. The ramp is near the entrance to

Lot A where there is designated PARKING. If you would prefer to drive down the short service road and drop off passengers at the bottom of the access ramp, get permission at the entry kiosk. Ramadas shade the picnic tables on concrete slabs, but there is no paving anywhere else near the lake. A RESTROOM near the north end of the parking has no doorway barriers, lateral transfer to a low toilet with grab bars, high sink, and an accessible hand dryer and mirror.

Lot C—Designated PARKING for your vehicle and boat trailer is provided in this lot on the hillside overlooking the boat launching area. A paved area with several shaded tables and a curb cut from a designated PARKING place is the perfect location for an accessible picnic with a view. However, there are no modified tables here. It is a long downhill trip from here to the boat launch.

A snack bar, tackle shop and a low TELEPHONE are located beneath Lot C; a steep (14%) 85-foot asphalt path leads there and to the boat rental and gas dock that are not accessible. A newer accessible restroom and drinking fountain between parking areas C and D has no barriers at the doorway, but there is no walkway to the entry door. You'll have to cross uneven dirt to get there from the picnic areas.

Lot D—Parking Lot D is nearest to the SWIMMING BEACH. Since the parking is higher than the lake level, a steep (10%) asphalt roadway leads downhill to the coarse sand beach 240 feet away. Picnic tables are arranged on the lake side of the lot. The only curb cut

is near the restroom at the end of the parking lot.

The restroom here has a concrete approach with a 1-inch door sill, pivot-transfer stall, high toilet with no grab bars, and high sink. The restroom at the beach level is similar, but the asphalt walkway to get there is a steep (15%) uphill push.

Boat Launch and Dock

If it weren't for the pavement transitions onto the loading dock, the broad concrete boat ramp at the foot of Lot B would be accessible. As it is, most wheelchair users will require some help to manage the dock. Wheelchair access to the loading dock begins at the top of the ramp with a hard right-angle turn over a series of shallow curbing transitions. An accessible RESTROOM close by has a pivot-transfer stall with grab bars, but pavement leading to it has several rough transitions. The designated PARKING places for your vehicle and trailer are provided in Lot C on the level above.

A boardwalk with handrails begins at the base of the loading dock and will take you to the public dock 150 feet away. Just as at the loading dock, there is a difficult transition onto the boardwalk. At the public dock there is a 4-inch-wide gap from the boardwalk to the 20-foot metal gangway with handrails. When you get to the dock at the end of the gangway, there is a 3-inch step. You will need some help to navigate the ramp and dock areas.

Camping

Los Alamos Campground (FCFS) is outside the State Park boundary, 2½ miles west of the day use area. The campground and all other visitor facilities at Pyramid Lake are administered by Pyramid Enterprises, PO Box A, Piru, CA 93040, (805) 521-1319.

Pyramid Lake
State Recreation Area

c/o USDA Forest Service,
Saugus Ranger District
(805) 257-2790

Park Flyer Available
Location — Sixty miles northwest of
downtown Los Angeles on I-5 at
Hungry Valley Road
Elevation — 2,606 feet

CASTAIC LAKE STATE RECREATION AREA

The northern end of the Santa Clarita Valley is home to the largest State Water Project reservoir in Southern California. Located approximately 45 miles northwest of Los Angeles, Castaic Lake is the terminal branch of the California Aqueduct. Water from the Sierra Nevada mountains makes its way down natural channels and 388 miles of canals, eventually arriving at the lake, where it is generated into power for the metropolitan areas and becomes a haven for outdoor recreation.

Castaic Lake State Recreation Area consists of two lakes, the main lake behind the dam and the lagoon below. The park provides visitors with a variety of water sport opportunities. In the upper lake, the reservoir forms a V-shape. The eastern arm is reserved for fishing, sailing, and slow boating while water skiers, personal watercraft riders, and fast boats use the western arm. Near the dam where the two arms converge, jet skiers and sailboarders join in on the watersports. The lake can be especially windy in the afternoon, and at times park officials will close it when winds are considered to be unsafe. Shore fishing is permitted at both upper and lower lakes.

The 80-acre development around the lagoon has more day use facilities than the main lake, but you may find that picnic access is preferable near the boat launches on the lake. In the summer, lifeguards are on duty at four swimming areas on the west shore of the lagoon.

Visitor Center

The Department of Water Resources built the **Castaic Lake Visitor Center** on a hill overlooking the reservoir. Picture windows beginning at a height of 36 inches offer magnificent views of the dam and colorful hillsides surrounding the lake. Diagrams and photos on the walls depict the history of Castaic Dam, and you can see a film about the State Water Project in the accessible *THEATER*. A heavy door with a high handle opens to the fully accessible *RESTROOM* that has lateral transfer to a high toilet with grab bars.

Fishing

Fishing is a popular activity at Castaic Lake. Both lakes are stocked regularly with trout. Anglers also try their luck for large-mouth and smallmouth bass, catfish, or crappie. You may daylight fish in the east arm of the lake, while fishing along the east shoreline at Castaic Lagoon is permitted 24 hours a day. In addition, there are plans to develop an accessible *FISHING AREA* at the day use pier in the lagoon. Or, you can shore fish from the west boat launch when it is not in use.

Boat Launch

East Ramp — The main launch ramp on the eastern shore of Castaic Lake is accessible with help. having two designated *PARKING* places for vehicle and trailer. The park staff will help with launching and trailering, and also will help you over the short steep ramp onto the dock. Concrete pavement and curb cuts lead to a grassy picnic area with tables on pavement where you can watch jet skiers and windsurfers cross the windy lake waters. Grab bars encircle a high toilet in the shallow *RESTROOM* stall nearby.

West Ramp — Only open on weekends and holidays, the launching ramp on the west arm of the lake is much the same as the east ramp. During the week, fishermen can drive directly to the water and cast from the pavement. For a great view of the lake's main section and the backside of the dam, make a stop at a large parking lot and picnic area by the launch ramp. An ample asphalt access ramp leads from designated *PARKING* to a paved path that loops through the area. A few sparse trees shade picnic tables on a flat dirt surface. *RESTROOMS* and an accessible *TELEPHONE* are next to the lifeguard headquarters in the parking lot. Grab bars encircle the low toilet in the shallow restroom stall; there are no other restroom modifications.

Warren M. Dorn Recreation Complex

On the west bank of the lagoon, a gently sloping lawn stretches to the coarse sand of the swimming beach. Concrete walkways with a slope of up to 10% connect the _PARKING_ area to the beach and _RESTROOMS_. Picnic tables under ramadas are clustered in groups on concrete slabs; there are 2- to 4-inch transitions from the surrounding grass. Designated _PARKING_ in each of several lots are not near curb cuts onto lagoon walkways.

At the south end of the lagoon swimming area, you'll find a _SNACK BAR_, _STORE_, _RESTROOM_, and accessible _TELEPHONE_. Two designated _PARKING_ places are provided near a boardwalk access, but a 2-inch lip at the ramp will create a barrier for some. The _RESTROOM_ here has a high toilet in a shallow stall with grab bars and a high sink.

Camping

A new campground on the east shore of the lagoon is scheduled for completion some time in 1992. Paved campsites will lie on the perimeter of a parking area where picnickers and fishermen once parked. Each site is close to the lake and has a BBQ and a table. A packed trail follows the contours of the lake banks, but is steep and slippery in places. Designated _PARKING_ is near weathered paved pathways to each restroom; there are 1- to 2-inch lips at each doorway. The _RESTROOMS_ have heavy doors, shallow stalls with grab bars, a high toilet, and a high sink.

Castaic Lake
State Recreation Area

PO Box 397
Castaic, CA 91310
(805) 257-4050

Park Folder and Newsletter Available
Location—Forty-five miles northwest of Los Angeles on I-5
Elevation—1,535 feet

San Bernardino and Riverside Counties

SECCOMBE LAKE STATE URBAN RECREATION AREA

Somehow the busy city of San Bernardino doesn't seem quite so frantic at Seccombe Lake State Urban Recreation Area. Centered around a pleasant man-made lake, this downtown park provides local residents and visitors with a break from the dynamics of business and traffic. On weekends, families enjoy a lakeside picnic and there is often a game in progress at the athletic fields.

The park is right in the center of Old San Bernardino at the corner of Fifth Street and Sierra Way. Paved or hardened dirt walkways (max 8%) meander through the lake picnic area where the terrain slopes downward toward the waterline. Access ramps with handrails and paved platforms take you to the edge of the lake where waterfowl keep a sharp eye for handouts. Picnic tables, benches, and accessible _DRINKING FOUNTAINS_ are scattered around the lake beside the paths. The walkways continue through the park, leading to playing fields and accessible _RESTROOMS_.

Since there are no curb cuts on the main streets, the best place to park is behind the YMCA on Lugo Avenue. There are a number of designated _PARKING_ spaces and from here you can reach any part of the park on concrete walkways. The _RESTROOM_ in this area has a lateral-transfer stall with a high toilet and grab bars. A _RESTROOM_ near the lake area is similar; both have concrete approaches and heavy doors.

Seccombe Lake
State Urban Recreation Area

Contact County of San Bernardino
(714) 384-5233

Location—On Fifth and Sierra in downtown San Bernardino
Elevation—1,046 feet

SILVERWOOD LAKE STATE RECREATION AREA

Engulfed by the San Bernardino National Forest at an altitude of 3,378 feet, Silverwood Lake is the highest lake in the California Water Project. Besides providing water, electricity, and flood control for surrounding metropolitan areas, the lake offers park-goers a source of recreation close to home.

Besides fishing and water skiing opportunities, you may enjoy family picnicking by the water, accessible _CAMPING_, and a hike or bike along 13 miles of _PAVED TRAILS_ that wander between all of the beach and picnic areas on the southern portion of the lake.

Visitor Services

The **Information Station** for Silverwood Lake State Recreation

Hike/bike trails connect picnic areas, parking, and the beach at Silverwood Lake SRA.

(Photo courtesy CDPR)

Area is housed in a modular unit on the road to the Cleghorn area. It has a 1-inch lip at the top of the access ramp to the doorway. If you take the bike path across the street from the information station parking lot and follow it downhill (8%) for about 250 feet (the path has handrails), you'll find the park *CAMPFIRE CENTER*. There is plenty of paved space for wheelchairs and an accessible *DRINKING FOUNTAIN* and *UNISEX RESTROOM* (open during peak summer season only). For your camping convenience, an RV dump station is provided near the park entrance.

Day Use

At the lakeside picnic areas, you can choose a table in a secluded pocket of shade furnished by black oaks and pine, or a lake view from ramada-shaded tables on rolling lawns. Paved paths to the tables (none modified) are steep in places and will require help. You can reach the most level picnic area on an asphalt path from parking lot #1. Beyond the path, grass descends directly to a swimming beach of coarse sand, where a life-guard is on duty in the summer. *RESTROOMS* at the swimming beach are accessible.

East of the main park entrance, Pilot Rock Road will take you to the **Miller Unit** of Silverwood Lake State Recreation Area. During the spring, snow pack melting off the surrounding mountains finds its way to Miller Canyon Creek. From the overlook at **Devil's Pit** you'll have a bird's-eye-view of rushing whitewater tumbling in a deep ravine that feeds into the lake. To get to the overlook, follow a rutted dirt trail and cross two wooden bridges with up to 2-inch transitions at either end. Dirt parking is about 200 feet from the overlook.

At the end of Pilot Rock Road, paved parking for access to **Serrano Beach** is provided in a sloping lot. An extension of the asphalt bike trail leads to the coarse sand beach, but it is steep (17%) and very weathered. When the lake level is low, there is very little water in this area. An acces-sible *UNISEX RESTROOM* in the park-ing lot has a low shasta toilet with grab bars.

Trails

Besides boating, a favorite pastime at Silverwood Lake is biking. Thir-teen miles of paved *BIKE TRAILS* will take you around most of the southern lake body. Parts of the paved bike trails are also ideal for wheelchair riders. But, because of the hilly terrain (up to 20%) and weathered areas in need of main-tenance, portions of the trail will require some assistance.

If you begin your trip at the visitor center parking lot, you can travel north around the western horn of the southern portion of the lake, or east along the southern shore. The eastbound trail takes you by Mesa Campground, through shady picnic areas, and past a marina to **Miller Canyon** and **Serrano Beach.** In either case, take along a hat, some sun screen, and a bottle of water; there isn't much shade along the way.

Boat Launch

Fishermen, personal water craft riders, and waterskiers launch their boats on the east end of the day use area. Fish habitat abounds in the brushy areas of the lake. Catfish, blue gill, largemouth bass, striped bass, and crappie are the most common seasonal catches; rainbow trout are hooked year round. A designated skiing area on the northern portion of the lake near the dam allows for safety in the day use area where water traf-fic is slow.

There are four designated *PARKING* places in the boat parking lot.

Pavement leads over the curbing to the steep (27%) launching ramp. To reach the marina docks, and a small store, you must descend an equally steep ramp. On your way to the launching ramp, you'll find an accessible *RESTROOM* with a high toilet and grab bars.

The boat launch at Silverwood Lake.
(Photo courtesy CDPR)

Camping

Mesa east—Mesa Campground is divided into two sections by the road leading to Cleghorn day use area. East of the road, campsites #96 through #135 lie around the perimeter of two paved rows of parking, surrounded by curbing. A paved ramp allows access to the tables at designated *SITES* #96, #99 and #100. Each flat site has a table, fire ring, and BBQ on asphalt pavement; all other sites have dirt surfaces and little shade. Opposite the designated *CAMPSITES* is an accessible *UNISEX RESTROOM* with a high toilet with grab bars, an electrical outlet, and an accessible *DRINKING FOUNTAIN*. The adjacent accessible *UNISEX SHOWER* has low controls, grab bars, and a non-retractable seat. Paved paths lead from the campground to the main roads, or to Cleghorn day use area.

Mesa west—The camping area west of Cleghorn Road is a series of six camping loops along an asphalt road surrounded by curbing. Asphalt ramps provide access to designated *SITES* #1, #2, #19, #20, #62, and #70. There is a table on each flat dirt site. Pavement surrounds all three accessible *UNISEX RESTROOMS* in the area. Each has parking nearby, an extra large *SHOWER* with grab bars, low controls, and no seat..

Silverwood Lake
State Recreation Area

Star Route, Box 7A
Hesperia, CA 92345
(619) 389-2303

Park Folder Available
Location— On Hwy 138, 11 miles east
of Cajon Junction at I-5 or 16 miles
from Hesperia on Arrowhead Lake
Road (Hwy 18) to Hwy 138S
Elevation— 3,400 feet

CHINO HILLS STATE PARK

Engulfed by suburban sprawl, over 13,000 acres of primitive wilderness at Chino Hills State Park preserves a last vestige of unspoiled land in southern Los Angeles and Orange Counties. Wildlife such as bobcat, badger, and coyote find haven in protective overgrowth of river habitats enveloped by rolling grass-covered hillsides. Also protected within the park boundary is the largest stand known of native Southern California walnut trees.

Chino Hills State Park will remain undeveloped to protect the existing wildlife. As such, the facilities are not conducive to wheelchair visitors. Thirty miles of trail explore the nooks and crannies of

this peaceful refuge. Equestrians, hikers, and mountain bikers seeking a natural get-away close to home discover that Chino Hills suits them fine. The trails are not suitable for wheelchair users.

After following the three-mile dirt road to the park, you'll come to a small paved area in front of the visitor center where there is a ramp entry and an accessible *CHEMICAL TOILET.* All other surfaces at the park are dirt. Three miles further along a dirt road, hardy campers and their horses stay at nine primitive campsites with adjoining horse corrals.

Chino Hills State Park

PO Box 2163
Chino, CA 91708
(714) 780-6222

Location— Take the 71 Freeway north
from the 91 Freeway Exit on
Pomona-Rincon Road; turn left and
follow the State Park directional
signs. At Soquel Canyon, turn left to
Elinvar, and make another left onto
Sapphire. The park access road is
on the right.
Elevation— 709 feet

CALIFORNIA CITRUS
STATE HISTORIC PARK

Ever since its introduction to the New World by the Spanish, the orange has been a key agricultural product of Southern California. California Citrus State Historic Park spotlights the citrus grower at an actively producing grove in Riverside. Citrus industry history is presented in the accessible *VISITOR CENTER;* programs include an accessible walk through a demonstration grove and packing house at this 150-acre park. The park is still in the development stage, but when it opens in late 1992, wheelchair access will be available at all facilities. Call the park for further information.

California Citrus State Historic Park

1879 Jackson Street
Riverside, CA
(714) 780-6222
Elevation — 920 feet

LAKE PERRIS
STATE RECREATION AREA

Sparkling like a jewel in the Mojave Desert region, Lake Perris is at the end of the California Aqueduct, collecting water that has traveled over 400 miles from northern California. Ringed by scrub-covered hills and small mountains, Perris Valley is also home to an amazing variety of plants and wildlife. A smooth, paved *HIKE/BIKE TRAIL* will bring you closer to the undeveloped areas around the lake where springtime wildflowers flourish after a wet winter and the fringe-toed lizard finds relief from the summer sun in the shade of the sage brush.

This park has something for everyone. It is a favorite among boaters, personal watercraft riders, fishermen, and those who like to picnic or camp near a water playground. Since it is not far from the city of Riverside, the lake attracts suburban families who flock there with jet skies, sailboats, fishing boats, wind surfboards and water wings. There is a water slide complex, miles of trails to ex-plore, and an accessible regional *INDIAN MUSEUM*. Rangers give *CAMPFIRE PROGRAMS* most summer evenings, and offer a variety of other naturalist activities throughout the year.

Most of the park is accessible to wheelchair users. A concessionaire-operated marina offers boat slips, repair, and gas dock. Above the dock is an accessible *SNACK BAR*, and a *GENERAL STORE* that stocks bait, tackle, food, and camping supplies. All of the *RESTROOMS* in the day use area are accessible, and there is plenty of designated *PARKING* near each lake feature. *PICNIC AREAS* are particularly wheelchair-friendly, and designated *CAMPSITES* are available with full hook-ups. Telephones are available in many locations; all are approachable, but too high to reach from a seated position.

Picnic

On weekends, the tables which have shade ramadas and BBQ's are bustling with folks on family outings and get-togethers. Close to the end each school year, the picnic areas of Perris Lake come alive with school children on field trips from the nearby city. Picnicking facilities, designed for heavy use, are paved with concrete around the tables, making them ideal for wheelchair users. Pepper, eucalyptus, cypress, palm and pine trees offer shade to the grassy day use areas. Concrete paths criss-cross the lawns and lead to accessible *RESTROOMS* and *DRINKING FOUNTAINS* in the Perris Beach and Moreno Beach. Designated *PARKING*, available in every parking lot, is located near curb cuts and other park access points.

Store/Snack Bar

At the *MARINA STORE* and *SNACK BAR* located between Perris and Moreno Beaches, you'll be able to stock up on all your needed supplies and grab a bite to eat. The store's narrow aisles are jammed with camping supplies, food, ice cream, water sport equipment, and fishing supplies. The snack bar across the breezeway is also accessible; they serve quick meals including breakfast. You can eat in the dining area, or enjoy a marina view from the veranda.

Marina

The marina rents fishing boats, pontoon boats, patio cruisers, jet skis, and Waverunners. Its staff is experienced in outfitting handicapped watersport enthusiasts. A steep (24%) ramp leads to the boat dock below the store. There is a button labeled "for handicapped assistance" outside the store on the wall. If you don't have someone to help you down the 30-foot ramp, push the button and the marina staff will take you to the floating docks and boat rental area. If you'd like more information about the marina services, call or write Lake Perris Marina, 17801 Lake Perris Drive, Perris, CA 92370, (714) 657-2179.

Boat Launch

Non-motorized boats are welcome to launch off the shallow beach at Sail Cove. From the paved parking in lot #1, the coarse sand beach is only 50 feet away and there is an accessible *RESTROOM* nearby. Parking lots #6, #7, and #8 are designed for boat and trailer parking. There is a steep boat

Sunset over Lake Perris

(Photo courtesy CDPR)

ramp with three loading docks at the foot of each parking lot. Due to the steepness of the ramps, access onto the loading docks is a challenge and not accessible without help.

Trail

A 9-mile *HIKE-AND-BIKE TRAIL* encircles the lake and is paved for all but a short distance at the south end of the dam where the path becomes very steep, rocky, and prohibitive for wheelchairs. On the trail from the day use area, you can explore the eastern rim of the lake bordering the **Upland Game Hunting Area,** and the waterfowl hunting zone on the southeast shore. You are more likely to spot waterfowl, birds of prey, ground squirrels, and rabbits in the early morning or at dusk as they begin and end their day in search of food. In the rainy season between November and April,

wildflowers bloom along the trail and rush to seed before the dry summer season arrives. Take along a hat and plenty of water for your hike. The only developed area along the trail is at **Bernasconi Picnic Area** where there are tables with shade ramadas and an accessible *RESTROOM* and *DRINKING FOUNTAIN*.

Museum

As a bonus to your outing at Lake Perris, you will enjoy a visit to the accessible regional Indian Museum. The museum commemorates Native American culture and lifestyle in the Mojave desert region. Displays in the museum describe the lives of several regional tribes as they lived before, during, and after Hispanic-Anglo colonialization.

All exhibits in the museum are visible from a seated position, including the theater. Designated *PARKING* is provided near the entrance, and there is an accessible *RESTROOM* with a low toilet and grab bars. From this hillside vantage point, there is a marvelous view of the lake. You can take in the view from an accessible *TABLE* on the veranda. However, you will need some help, because there is a steep 23% grade on the pebble-embedded access route to the veranda. Since the museum hours are limited, it is best to check with the ranger or call the park if you plan to visit.

Camping

Luiseno—With its 167 tent sites and 264 RV hook-up sites, the *CAMPGROUND* at Lake Perris is one of the most accessible in the State Park System. Though there is a noticeable lack of shade, each tent site has an asphalt pull-in with a

269

concrete access path to the table and fire ring. Many flat sites are ideal for a wheelchair user. In addition, three designated parking lot style _RV CAMPSITES_ have a ramp over the surrounding curbing to a completely concrete-paved table and BBQ area. There is parking room for two vehicles in the tent sites and for three vehicles in the RV sites.

Every _RESTROOM_ in the campground is fully accessible, has pivot-transfer stalls with grab bars, low hand driers, and mirrors, push-type sink fixtures, and accessible _DRINKING FOUNTAINS_. The _SHOWERS_ in each restroom have an accessible stall with grab bars, a low push-pull control knob, and generous access; there is no seating in the showers. Telephones at each building are too high to reach from a seated position.

Lake Perris State Recreation Area

17801 Lake Perris Drive
Perris, CA 92370
(714) 657-0676

Park Folder Available
_Location—Eleven miles southeast of
    Riverside off Hwy 60 to Morena
    Beach Drive south, or I-215 to
    Ramona Expressway east_
Elevation—1,575 feet

LAKE ELSINORE STATE RECREATION AREA

Over the centuries, Lake Elsinore has been a source of food, refreshment, and recreation for people living in the surrounding countryside. Thousands of years ago, when it was called "The Little Sea," an abundance of fish, game, and edible plants in the valley of the lake provided sustenance for the Pai-ah-che Indians. In the early 19th century, Spaniards claimed the lake and the land around it as Rancho la Laguna, and renamed the lake, Laguna Grande. In 1883, a group of entrepreneurs purchased the land with the intention of creating a resort, deriving its new name of Lake Elsinore after the Danish castle made famous in Shakespeare's _Hamlet_. The town of Elsinore thrived as a health and pleasure resort until the 1950's when the lake nearly ran dry. In 1964, Lake Elsinore was refilled and became Lake Elsinore State Recreation Area.

Nestled between ridges of the Santa Ana Mountains, the lake is subject to the prevailing climate. In wet years, the shallow seven-square-mile lake bed glistens. In times of drought, the surface area recedes significantly, sometimes almost disappearing. Morningtime waters are calm and inviting for water-skiers or fishermen who try their luck for bass, blue gill, catfish, and carp. By afternoon, it seems there is always a breeze, providing sailors and sailboarders a frolic on the choppy lake surface.

You'll find the park entrance at the lake's north shore. In years of light rainfall, this is the last portion of the lake to go dry. A concessionaire operates the boat launch, campground, fishing, and day use areas arranged near the flat shoreline. Development of new homes and businesses is slowly creeping in around the park, but while you're there, the campground seems secluded and roomy. Unfortunately, little at the park is modified for access.

Grassy campsites on the west camping loop at Lake Elsinore

(Photo courtesy CDPR)

Beach

The shoreline is comprised of areas for swimming, jet skiers, fishing, and boat launching. The beach sand is a coarse decomposed granite, and though it appears firm, is quite a challenge to wheel through. Packed decomposed granite also comprises much of the day use parking surface. Picnic tables are scattered through the day use area and onto a sandy point used by jet skiers and motor boats.

There are no accessible restrooms near the beach. Instead, a modular unit with four steps at the entrance houses the main day use restroom. Standard chemical toilets stand at various points on the shore and in the dirt parking area.

Camping

West (FCFS)—In the west campground, most of the grassy sites have a tree for shade. From each asphalt parking area, the table and fire ring are close by and most sites have electrical hook-ups. Unfortunately, the restrooms and shower buildings are not modified for access.

East (FCFS)—The newer east campground is a multiple series of dirt camping loops with grass sites and young trees. Each site has a table and fire ring. Presently, only chemical toilets are available here.

Lake Elsinore State Recreation Area

32040 Riverside Drive
Lake Elsinore, CA 92330
(714) 657-0676

Campground information
(714) 674-3177

Park Flyer Available at kiosk
Location—Twenty-five miles south of
Riverside on Hwy 74 from I-215
Elevation—1,234 feet

Peninsular Range

MOUNT SAN JACINTO STATE WILDERNESS and STATE PARK

Bounded on the south and north by the San Bernardino National Forest, Mount San Jacinto State Park and Wilderness Area covers over 13,000 acres of sub-alpine highlands, granite peaks, and breathtaking views. As Southern California's second highest peak, Mount San Jacinto juts over four other mountain tops that also surpass the 10,000-foot level. The northeast face of the San Jacinto Range plummets 9000 feet to the desert floor in less than six miles, making it one of the sheerest and most spectacular palisades in North America.

The trip to the summit for backpackers and day hikers begins either in Idyllwild from the west, or at the Mountain Tram Station in the east. Many visitors to the mountains never intend to hike to the top, preferring instead to take in the tremendous desert floor vistas from the famous Palm Springs Aerial Tramway. A stay at the mountain station for a snack and a look around the forest will refresh and renew you for your thrilling return trip down the mountain.

While most of the mountains are designated wilderness areas and have hike-in camping only, developed State Park facilities are near the town of Idyllwild. Pine-scented forest encloses two improved campgrounds on Hwy 243. Both are open year round; one has some access modifications.

Tram

Most Palm Springs visitors are familiar with the world famous Palm Springs Aerial Tramway. Rising from Chino Canyon at the north edge of Palm Springs for a vertical ascent of 5,873 feet, the tram is the largest and longest single-lift passenger tramway in the world. Two accessible totally enclosed Swiss-made cars can carry up to eighty passengers. They operate year round to the Mountain Station at the edge of Mount San Jacinto Wilderness. On your 2½-mile trip, you will pass over a succession of plant communities on the cliffs and rugged canyons ranging from arid desert life to the fresh green forest of the high mountains above. You may feel an anxious flutter along the way as your car rumbles over the 200-foot support towers. The most breathtaking part of this 14-minute ride is the magnificent panorama of hundreds of square miles of desert and mountain ranges.

Valley Station is at the end of Tramway Road off SR 111, north of Palm Springs. There is one designated *PARKING* place next to the building. Otherwise, parking lots are terrace down into the canyon and visitors are transported to the station from their vehicles by a shuttle bus that is not accessible. Wheelchair access to the main floor of the station is located on the east end (left side) of the building near the tram terminal. Follow the blue signs on an asphalt service road (10%) for about 110 feet to the diamond-plated metal access ramp with handrails that leads to the tram loading platform. You'll need someone to help you up this very steep (22%) 20-foot ramp.

For an unforgetable ride, take the Palm Springs Aerial Tramway to Mount San Jacinto SP.

(Photo courtesy CDPR)

Those with special boarding passes can board the tram ahead of the other passengers. There are no seats in the car; standing passengers steady themselves on vertical poles and grab railing. If you would prefer to be seated, notify the desk when you purchase your ticket, and the tram operator will provide a chair for you. For wheelchair users, the tram operator attaches a steel access ramp from the boarding area so it is flush with the car floor. If you are seated in the car, viewing through the windows is limited only in the downward direction, so you'll be able to see most of the sights from this vantage point. Be sure to sit near a window. Otherwise, you'll be overwhelmed by the mass of humanity crowded around you on busy weekends.

When you arrive at **Mountain Station**, you will be on the main level of the building. Here you'll find a _GIFT SHOP_, _SNACK BAR_ and restrooms. From the concrete patio on the east side of the building, you'll get a second look at the vastness of the low desert and its surrounding mountains. On the west side of the station, an evergreen forest stands in contrast to the tans and mauves of the desert. From the veranda, you'll have a sweeping view of the Mount San Jacinto State Wilderness. The trail to Long Valley begins here; hikers begin their climb through thickets and stream-fed meadows of the high mountain forests that resemble the Sierras.

To reach the _TICKET OFFICE_, cross the loading platform to the lobby door used by incoming tramway passengers. Once you purchase your ticket, the staff is notified of your boarding time and your special boarding status. They will help you onto the tram through the loading platform door. On holiday weekends there is some-times up to an hour wait, but most of the time you'll be able to board in no more than half an hour. While you're waiting, the station has a spacious lobby area, _GIFT SHOP_, and an accessible _COFFEE SHOP/BAR_ with a terrace overlooking the loading platform. An accessible _RESTROOM_ is on this level.

Other access at the Mountain Station is limited. The restroom stall has a 26-inch-wide door, and offers lateral transfer to a low toilet with a grab bar. The telephone on the main level is not accessible. Because there is a long flight of stairs to either the upper or lower levels, neither are accessible, so you will miss seeing the visitor center, tramway history film, and restaurant. A steep paved trail with handrails leads down the mountainside for ¼ mile to access hiking trails into the wilderness. The only way to get there is from the lower floor.

For a colorful sundown ride, you may purchase a special evening Ride-and-Dine ticket, which includes a dinner from the restaurant at Mountain Station. Though there is no access to the third floor restaurant, the staff will prepare your meal and bring it to you at a table on the main level. For information about hours of operation and time schedules, call the Palm Springs Aerial Tramway at (619) 325-1391.

Camping

Idyllwild—Rolling paved roads wind through the 30-site campground just outside downtown Idyllwild. Outlined in manzanita, 31 pine-studded sites have dirt pull-ins and often slope so that the parking and picnic tables are on different levels. Designated CAMP-SITE #3 is a pull-thru on sloping uneven dirt near an accessible RESTROOM and DRINKING FOUNTAIN. Sloping concrete leads to a very high standard picnic table and very low fire ring in the adjacent dirt. The parking area is not paved, so there is a difficult transi-

tion from the softer dirt surface to the paved site.

From site #3, a 9% sloping path takes you to the restroom building that has a fully accessible UNISEX RESTROOM and accessible SHOWER room, each with a small lip at the doorway. The SHOWER has a retractable seat in the stall, low shower head and controls, and a seat in the drying area. There is no additional parking near the access path to the restroom.

The Idyllwild campground is also home to the park headquarters and ranger station. Rangers at the park headquarters issue day use and overnight camping permits for hikers and help park visitors with their questions. Presently, there are stairs to the entrance of the building, but ramp access to this modular unit is due to be built in 1992. The parking lot is paved and a TELEPHONE nearby is accessible.

Stone Creek—Six miles from park headquarters among a thicket of manzanita, Stone Creek Campground offers a primitive camping experience. A dusty, rutted campground road winds through cedars and pines. There are dirt pull-ins at each sloping campsite. Few sites are level, so camping and parking are not on the same level. Pit toilets located on the hillside are not accessible.

**Mount San Jacinto
State Park and Wilderness**

25905 Highway 243
Idyllwild, CA 92349
(714) 659-2607
Park Folder Available
*Location—Headquarters are in the town
   of Idyllwild*
*Elevation—Park Headquarters 5,400
   feet; Mountain Tram Station 8,516
   feet*

PALOMAR MOUNTAIN STATE PARK

Just west of the world-famous Mount Palomar Observatory lies the beautiful pine and oak woodlands and grassy meadows of Palomar Mountain State Park. High above the valleys of northern San Diego, the park preserves one of the finest evergreen forests in the Peninsular Range. From its crest, you have an awesome view of Riverside and San Diego Counties all the way to the ocean. In spite of fires that devastated a portion of the western slopes, the parklands in the higher altitudes (5,500 feet) remain intact, providing a scenic experience much like the Sierras.

As you share in its recreation opportunities, you're reminded of Palomar Mountain's human history. Accessible CAMPING is on a hillside in Doane Valley where George Doane had his hog and cattle farm in the 1880's. Nearby Doane Pond is just like it must have been back then, but now it is stocked with trout and catfish. You'll find evidence of other early inhabitants of Palomar at Silvercrest Picnic Area, where Luiseno Indians used mortero stones to grind seeds and nuts.

Boucher Lookout

For the most breathtaking view all the way to the ocean, take the park road to Boucher Lookout. At the fire lookout station, there is a small parking lot where you can get out and look around. However, the best view is from your car as you pass around the south side of the parking lot. There are no roadside pull-outs, so watch for vehicles behind you on this one-way road. If you've come on a clear day, you'll be able to see much of the San Diego area and north into Riverside and Orange Counties.

Silvercrest Picnic Area

Hidden among a plethora of oaks and cedar, the Silvercrest Picnic Area is an especially pleasant escape from warm summer sun. A modified _PICNIC TABLE_ near the mortero grinding rock display is at the end of a 350-foot, decomposed granite path that leads from a designated _PARKING_ place. Near the table, the surface becomes soft uneven forest floor covered with acorns and loose twigs. The path continues downhill (8%) to a restroom with a 1½-inch transition to a concrete slab and no accessible stalls.

Doane Pond

Undoubtedly, George Doane ran his livestock on the grassy meadow around Doane Pond. Now, visitors can fish here among the cattails and reeds at the pond. A few picnic tables surrounded by gravel under shade ramadas stand on the perimeter of the pond. It is at the end of a hard-packed decomposed granite trail, about 400 feet from a designated _PARKING_ place. As the trail nears the water, it becomes increasingly steep (up to 12%) and uneven. If you use a wheelchair, you probably will require help to negotiate part of the trail. The restroom near the parking area is not modified for access.

Camping

Doane Valley—Much of this wooded hillside campground is sloping, but in the first camping loop, _THREE SITES_—#4, #6, and #7—are designated and reason-

ably level. At #6 and #7, there are asphalt pull-ins, and pavement covers the surfaces around the table, BBQ, and fire ring. Site #4 is a level paved pull-thru site with sloping roadway at either end of the pull-thru. An accessible DRINKING FOUNTAIN is central to the three sites.

A sloping (7%) asphalt walkway leads down to an accessible _UNISEX RESTROOM/SHOWER_ combination. Make arrangements to obtain the key for the restroom when you check in at the kiosk. A 350-foot paved lighted path (max 9%) to the _AMPHITHEATER_ is across the road from the campsites. There is room for two wheelchairs on the pavement in the seating area. The limited sloping parking provided near both, the path to the _RESTROOM_ and to the _AMPHITHEATER_ is uneven..

Palomar Mountain State Park

Palomar Mountain, CA 92060
(619) 742-3462
Park Folder Available
Location—In northern San Diego County on the west side of Palomar Mountain. From Hwy 76 take either County Road S6 from Rincon Springs (steep and winding), or County Road S7 from Lake Henshaw (a longer but gentler grade).
Elevation—5,161 feet

CUYAMACA RANCHO STATE PARK

The rich variety of terrain at Cuyamaca Rancho State Park surprises many visitors as they ascend from the dry Southern California climate to the forested mountains of the Peninsular Range. Mountain

meadows, streams, chaparral-covered hillsides, and dense stands of conifers and oaks comprise over 24,000 acres at the park, half of which is designated wilderness.

For thousands of years, the ancient Native American tribe of Kumey-a'ay found summer retreat from the hot desert sun in these mountains. They relied on its plentiful water supply and wildlife for survival and named the area, Ah-ha-Kwe-ah-mac, describing it as "the place where it rains." In more modern times, the Mexican government of California settled the region, eliminated the "Indian threat" and created a land grant, calling it Rancho Cuyamaca. In 1860, prospectors discovered gold in the nearby town of Julian. By 1872, the town of Cuyamaca had sprung up around Stonewall Mine, located inside the park, just south of Cuyamaca Lake. As the gold diminished, so went the town. The ownership of the rancho changed hands several times thereafter, and in 1933, the Dyar family sold the rancho to the state. Mr. Dyar's foreman, Harvey Moore, stayed on to become the park's first ranger and was responsible for much the park's first trails and campgrounds.

Both tourists and local San Diegans travel to Cuyamaca Rancho State Park for an all-day picnic, day hike, or just for a drive in the mountains. Over 110 miles of trails invite equestrians and hikers to wander through the wilderness. Campers enjoy oak-shaded _CAMPING_ and _PICNIC AREAS_ that are modified for wheelchair access at both Green Valley and Picacho Campgrounds. For a historical slant on the park, visit the accessible _PARK MUSEUM_ and ranger headquarters, housed in the stone home built in 1923 by the Dyar family.

Visitor Centers

Museum — Words and pictures tell the story of the Kumeya'ay Indians, often referred to as the Diegueno tribe, in the park _MUSEUM_. Built of natural stones, the museum was the home of the last private owner of the rancho, and it retains much of its 1920's charm. Tucked among tall pine trees, you'll find the museum midway in the park on Hwy 79. A large paved _PARKING_ area with a designated place and accessible _RESTROOM_ is about 220 feet from the entrance. The restroom has a shallow stall with grab bars, and a high toilet. There is paved access to both the museum and the restroom. A series of two ramps will take you to the museum doorway where there is a small door sill.

Interpretive Center — A small interpretive center near Paso Picacho Campground displays the plants and animals of the regi.n. A paved parking place is provided, and there are no barriers into the exhibit room.

Trails

The mountain trails at Cuyamaca Rancho State Park are very popular for horseback riders and hikers. Many of the well-established trails that lace the mountains and meadows make use of fire roads. Naturally, because of the changing terrain there are many steep inclines. Also, trail tread can be quite soft where horses leave their hoof prints. If you have someone along to help push, you may be able to manage a hike on a few fire roads. Consult a park ranger for hiking suggestions that fit your needs.

Azalea Glen Loop Trail — Meadow grasses and azaleas thrive in the wide open rolling countryside that bounds the Azalea Glen Loop Trail. This broad, well-traveled trail begins at a spot near the Paso

Cuyamaca Rancho State Park, San Diego's mountain retreat   _(Photo courtesy CDPR)_

275

Picacho Campground entry kiosk. It serpentines along the contours of the hills making gradual inclines and declines for over two miles and then loops back on itself. Comprised mostly of decomposed granite, the trail tread is uneven and a bit soft in places. With some help, you and your wheelchair may be able to tackle all or part of this pleasant trail.

Picnic

Upper Falls — At the southern end of Green Valley Campground, take the easternmost road to Upper Falls Picnic area. There you'll find a paved designated *PARKING* place with a *MODIFIED TABLE* and accessible *DRINKING FOUNTAIN.* Both are set in shade provided by a large stand of oaks. A concrete sidewalk from here leads to an accessible *RESTROOM* nearby.

Lower Falls — Though there is one designated *PARKING* space in this paved day use lot, the picnic tables are not modified, the drinking fountain is not accessible, and the restroom for this area is not retrofitted for access.

Paso Picacho — North of the entry kiosk at Paso Picacho Campground, shady picnic sites are distributed among the trees, next to the day use loop road. A paved pathway leads from designated *PARKING* to two designated *PICNIC SITES* with modified tables that have 29-inch high BBQ's. The nearby restroom is not modified for access, but there are minor access modifications at the entry station *RESTROOM.* The stall at the entry station restroom is not retrofitted except for one grab bar; the doorway is 28 inches wide. A

steep (10%) narrow concrete walkway, takes you to the doorway, where you must execute some tight turns to get in.

Camping

Green Valley — Plenty of oak and pine trees shade each campsite at Green Valley Campground. Asphalt pavement covers the roadways, campsite parking, a paved parking area, and access path to the *AMPHITHEATER.* Though the terrain is hilly, there are many level campsites, each with a table and fire ring on a packed dirt surface.

After entering the campground, you'll find designated *CAMPSITES* in the first camping loop to the right. Though not next to the restroom building, sites #15, #16, #17, and #18 are modified for wheelchair access. From the paved parking place, a concrete walkway leads to the table and accessible *DRINKING FOUNTAIN.* Each camping site and fire ring are on a packed dirt surface next to the paved picnic table area.

Accessible *RESTROOMS* and *SHOWERS* are in the first camping loop and near sites #39 and #40. Each building has a fully accessible *UNISEX RESTROOM* with a high toilet, and a 41" by 41" individual *SHOWER* with a retractable bench and control lever 40 inches from the floor. Both have a paved approach from designated *PARKING* and an accessible *DRINKING FOUNTAIN.*

Paso Picacho — Paved roads twist and turn through the wooded campground at Paso Picacho. Along its western fringes, the rolling grassy hills and meadows

of **Azalea Glen** beckon campers to come and stroll in the sunshine. All of the campsites have paved parking and a table, fire ring and food storage on a firm forest floor surface. None of the sites are designated, but the staff at Cuyamaca considers five of them to be accessible (#55, #59 through #62). Of the five, sites #61 and #62 are the most level and closest to the restroom building.

The *RESTROOM* near these sites has an accessible stall, but the shower is not accessible. The only other accessible *RESTROOM* is near the entry kiosk where you'll also find an RV dump station. The only way to get to the campfire center in the day use area is by a steep (14%) rocky decomposed granite path.

Los Caballos — For horsemen in Cuyamaca, the park also offers great camping facilities along with a network of trails. Horse stalls and corrals are conveniently placed near campsites in the shade of the gently sloping forest. Each site offers a table, fire ring, BBQ, and food storage. The central restroom and shower has a rough asphalt approach and a 30-inch doorway. There are no access modifications in the campground nor at the restrooms.

Cuyamaca Rancho State Park
12551 Hwy 79
Descanso, CA 92016
(619) 765-0755
Park Folder Available
Location — *Thirty miles east of San Diego off I-8, nine miles north on Hwy 79*
Elevation — *Paso Picacho Campground 4,870 feet*

Rock climbers love the formations at Joshua Tree National Monument.

(Photo courtesy NPS)

JOSHUA TREE NATIONAL MONUMENT

The 558,000 acres of Joshua Tree National Monument, preserve a unique portion of the California desert where two contrasting ecosystems meet. In the east, the Colorado Desert, lying below 3,000 feet, is a vast arid region awash with creosote bushes, highlighted with jumping cholla cactus and the spindly branches of the ocotillo reaching for the sun. The higher Mojave region receives more rainfall and is a bit cooler. The Joshua tree, a yucca plant of the agave family, flourishes here in the western portion of the park, along with a wider variety of wildlife. Crossing the transition zone between the Mojave and Colorado Deserts, you'll see an uncommon blend of plants and animals representative of both desert environments.

Joshua Tree also encompasses some interesting and eye-appealing geological formations. Wherever you look, Earth's powerful hand has sculpted colorful shapes and contours unique to the desert. Huge granite boulders and weathered outcroppings make Joshua Tree National Monument a widely recognized haven for rock-climbers of all skill levels.

Since the Monument is not far from Palm Springs, you can easily visit on a day trip from there. Campers who like to spend a little more time enjoying the peaceful surroundings will find some accessible features at two campgrounds.

There are two paved _NATURE_ _TRAILS_ in the high desert and a number of turn-outs along the monument's main road. Interpretive markers at the turn-outs describe plant life, geology, or points of interest along the way. Whether you're staying for a prolonged visit, or just here for the day, you will return home

277

from Joshua Tree National Monument with a new appreciation for the desert.

Visitor Centers

Cottonwood — The small **Cottonwood Visitor Center** has one designated _PARKING_ place and a curb cut to its paved approach. After entering through a heavy door, the office is quite cramped and the desk is very high. Visitors stop here for ranger information and camping registration, and you may purchase the books, posters, and postcards from the park volunteer organization. Restrooms outside the visitor center are not modified for access. Check your _Joshua Tree Journal_ for accessible _RANGER PROGRAMS_ scheduled regularly from October through May. The ranger talks are open to any park visitor. They are held in the morning or evening at the **Cottonwood Campfire Center**. The closest accessible _RESTROOM_ is in the group picnic area on the way to Cottonwood Campground.

A narrow rock-lined path twists through a small garden near the visitor center where markers identify native plants that you'll be seeing on your desert visit. Parts of the hard-packed, 300-foot path are a bit narrow for wheelchair passage. There is a 2-inch transition from the concrete sidewalk at the parking lot to the desert surface.

Oasis — The **Oasis Visitor Center** serves as the main information station and visitor services office. Located outside of the Monument boundary where Utah Trail meets National Monument Drive, the _VISITOR CENTER_ is ¼-mile south of Twentynine Palms Highway (Hwy 62).

Two designated _PARKING_ places have a ramp access to a concrete patio area at the entrance to the visitor center. You are greeted first by a small garden of native plants in the patio, followed by a large points-of-interest map mounted high on an outside wall. Picnic tables are near the visitor center entrance where the paved nature walk begins (see Trails). An accessible _DRINKING FOUNTAIN_ and _RESTROOM_ are also in the patio area. The _RESTROOM_ has a shallow stall with grab bars, and pivot-transfer to a low toilet.

Everyone enjoys the exhibits and book shelves in the building. High contrast graphics and artistically designed artifact displays make this a visually attractive and informative place to explore while finding relief from the sun.

Information Stations

Three additional information stations have maps and directions to help you. They are located at the southern park entrance, Indian Cove Campground, and at Black Rock Canyon.

Indian Cove — Indian Cove is off Hwy 62 between Joshua Tree and Twentynine Palms. Besides offering information, this is the place to pay camping fees for Indian Cove Campground. The office has one designated _PARKING_ place, but you must take a sandy uphill path to reach the entry.

Black Rock Canyon — At the end of Highway 247, east of Yucca Valley, Black Rock Canyon is tucked in the northwest corner of the monument. A concesssionaire operates the _CAMPGROUND_ and _INFORMATION STATION_, but you can

still get most any park information you need. Designated _PARKING_ is at the end of the visitor center building. Follow the rough short ramp to the entry patio where you may need some help with the heavy entry door. There are book sales, informative brochures, and a few exhibits inside. At the information desk, you can arrange for camping at Black Rock. Inside the visitor center, a 10-foot (8%) ramp leads to an accessible _UNISEX-TYPE_ restroom with a low toilet and makeshift grab bar.

Picnic

Cottonwood Group Camping Area — The _GROUP CAMPGROUND_ at the entrance to Cottonwood family campground has concrete pavement around the picnic tables and accessible _RESTROOMS_. There is a curb cut from paved parking to concrete walks leading to groups of tables shaded by ramadas. Since the surfaces are much more accessible than the regular day use area, many wheelchair users prefer to have their picnic here. The accessible _RESTROOM_ nearby has a shallow stall, low toilet, and grab bars. Groups who plan to use this area reserve it in advance. Check with the rangers, and if the campground is not reserved, they will let you to use the tables. Whether you picnic here, or not, these are the only _RESTROOMS_ accessible in the low desert of Joshua Tree National Monument.

Split Rock, Oak Flat — At these two campgrounds, a dirt road leads to a parking area among boulders and other rock formations. This is a good place to pull out and admire the rocks, but be aware that there are no picnic tables and only a chemical toilet in this sandy desert floor area.

Hidden Valley—Boulders shelter picnic tables and BBQ's among Joshua trees across the highway from Hidden Valley Campground. Some desert floor sites are flat, but the pit toilets here are not accessible.

Indian Cove—Picnickers choose Indian Cove for its seclusion, shade, and proximity to rock climbing activities. Here, you'll be able to park very near your chosen picnic table on the desert floor and watch rock climbers scale the massive rock formations common to the high desert of Joshua Tree National Monument. (See Indian Cove Campground for description of facilities.)

Points of Interest

Cholla Cactus Gardens—A narrow, rock-lined path winds through this unusual area where a concentration of bigelow cactus forms a unique garden. A self-guided nature trail begins at a desert floor turn-out and features the native plants and animals of the Colorado Desert. The path has intermittent rocks and is very sandy in places.

Keys View—From its elevation of 5,185 feet, this outstanding overlook point gives you a sweeping view of the valleys, mountains, and deserts at Joshua Tree. From a designated _PARKING_ place, a steep asphalt trail takes you uphill for 150 feet. Unless you use a power chair, you will need a strong assistant for this climb, but the view from the top is well worth the effort.

Keys Desert Queen Ranch Tours—Docents retell the human history of the Mojave Desert region during a tour of the Desert Queen Ranch. Located at a natural spring, the ranch has been home to Native Americans, prospectors and cattlemen, all of whom left their own mark and added their lives to the story of the high desert. During the winter season, docents lead tours of the ranch twice daily. You must be able to walk on soft sand surfaces to see the ranch. It is not accessible for wheelchair users.

The paved Oasis of Mara Nature Walk at Joshua Tree NM is especially nice for wheelchair users. *(Photo courtesy NPS)*

For more information about this and other points of interest at Joshua Tree National Monument, call the Joshua Tree Natural History Association at (619) 367-1488.

Trails

Cap Rock Trail — This 0.4-mile asphalt loop will take you on an informative SELF-GUIDED TOUR of some very interesting rock formations and natural landscape of the Mojave Desert. Interpretive markers describe the geology and plant life along the trail. The weathered paving on this level trail is a bit rough in spots. In the paved lot at the trailhead, there are three designated PARKING places and an accessible PIT TOILET, similar to an accessible chemical toilet. Cap Rock Trail begins directly south of the intersection at the turn-off for Keys View, west of Ryan Campground.

Cholla Cactus Gardens — (See Points of Interest)

Oasis of Mara Nature Walk — A concrete path makes the going easy along this ½-mile SELF-GUIDED NATURE WALK that begins directly behind the Oasis Visitor Center. You should obtain a trail guide to the trail markers in the visitor center; folders at the trailhead are mounted too high to reach easily from a seated position. If someone in your party would be more comfortable using a wheelchair, you may borrow one at the visitor center.

Campground

Camping at Joshua Tree (except Black Rock Canyon) is offered on a first-come-first-served basis. During the cool months from November to April, weekend campers fill the available sites in a hurry, so if you intend to camp, arrive at your chosen campground early in the day.

Cottonwood (FCFS) — Family camping in the low desert at Cottonwood offers two paved loops with pull-in or parallel parking at each desert floor site. There are no designated campsites, but most are flat and have a table and fire ring or BBQ. Parking and a curb cut are provided at each concrete restroom approach. Unfortunately, the stalls are not retrofitted for access. The only accessible RESTROOM is at the group picnic area near the campground entrance.

The CAMPFIRE CENTER is about 300 feet from the parking and restroom at Loop A. A well-lighted smooth paved path leads on a gradual downhill slope (max 9%) to the paved seating area. There is plenty of room for wheelchairs and a fine view of the large picture screen near the fixed benches. For RV'ers, an RV dump station is just outside the campground entrance.

White Tank, Belle (FCFS) — A very uneven dirt road runs through the primitive campsites at both Colorado Desert camping areas. Sites with a table and fire ring are tucked among clusters of boulders on the desert floor; parking is near the table. There are no accessible restrooms in either of these campgrounds.

Jumbo Rocks (FCFS) — These secluded campsites, hidden among giant boulders at Jumbo Rocks, are a favored base camp for rock climbers at the park. A smooth, asphalt road winds through the level campground. Parking is on asphalt near each uneven site where there is a table and fire ring. Transitions onto the dirt surfaces from the parking can be 2 inches or more. One DESIGNATED CAMPSITE has narrow pull-in parking wedged between two boulders. A strip of asphalt bordering the pull-in leads to a very private dirt site in front of the parking. An accessible PIT TOILET, similar to an accessible chemical toilet is also near the parking spot. Like the other sites, this one has a soft coating of sand around the table and fire ring, which makes wheeling difficult.

Ryan (FCFS) — With fewer boulders for shade and more open camping, the sites at Ryan Campground are firmer than those at most other campgrounds. However, roads and campsites are all on the uneven desert floor, and there are no accessible restrooms. This campground is closed in the hot summer months.

Hidden Valley (FCFS) — A rugged asphalt road winds through the campground at Hidden Valley where sites and pull-ins have a desert floor surface. When you first drive into the campground, it does not appear to have any accessible features. If you follow the road along the eastern perimeter where it becomes dirt, you'll find several level sites with smooth desert-floor surfaces. An accessible PIT TOILET, with a narrow concrete walkway approach from the roadway, is across from site #40, but there is a rough transition from the dirt road onto the walkway.

Indian Cove (FCFS) — Climbers and families with active kids camp at Indian Cove for its stacks of boulders and shady protection from the desert sun. Weathered asphalt roads coated with sand wind through the campground. Campsites on the west loop, snuggled into pockets of rocks and boulders, have varying accessibility. Flat campsites on the east loop have parking near the table and fire ring. From your site, you'll be able to watch climbers and climbing schools use the boulders in and around the campground for practice climbs. All sites are hard-packed desert floor with a layer of loose sand over the top. The only restrooms here are chemical toilets and are not accessible.

A huge wall of boulders provides a natual amphitheater for the CAMPFIRE CENTER. A broad hard-packed path with a sandy coating leads from a dirt parking area to the campfire center, 450 feet away. With a maximum slope of up to 13%, most wheelchair users will require help over the irregularities on this lighted path.

Black Rock Canyon—One hundred campsites in the Joshua tree-studded desert offer family camping just inside the Joshua Tree National Monument boundary near Yucca Valley. The desert floor sites have a table and fire ring, but little privacy. At the designated CAMPSITE #101, a weathered asphalt path leads from the paved parking area to a modified table on asphalt; a fire ring is on the desert floor.

Inconveniently, the RESTROOM is quite a distance from the designated camping, but you may park next to the building. A small short ramp leads uphill from the paved designated PARKING to the sidewalk. To get to the restroom entrance, you must cross a battered 1½-inch transition of broken concrete and tile. The RESTROOM has a shallow

stall with grab bars and a high toilet. You can make reservations for this campground by calling MIS-TIX at (800) 365-2267. Black Rock Canyon campground is closed in the hot summer months.

Joshua Tree National Monument

74485 National Monument Drive
Twentynine Palms, CA 92277-3597
(619) 367-7511
Information Available: Park folder; Joshua Tree Journal, seasonal newspaper
Location—South entrance is 25 miles east of Indio off I-10, 140 miles east of Los Angeles.
Elevation—Keys View 5,185 feet; Cottonwood 3,000 feet

INDIO HILLS PALMS

In the heart of the 13,000-acre Coachella Valley Preserve is a spectacular oasis fed by waters seeping along the San Andreas Fault. Over a thousand native California fan palms thrive in the canyons of Indio Hills at this relatively small section of the Colorado Desert. Indio Hills Palms, operated by the Nature Conservancy, encompasses over 2,000 acres, including such species as the Horseshoe, Pushawalla, Biskra and Hidden palm.

Access is limited at the developed visitor's area near Indio Hills Palms by soft desert sand and very uneven surfaces. Palms shade a quaint cabin housing the visitor center and a park official. To reach the cramped interior you must cross a 2- to 4-inch transition from the sandy desert floor into the veranda entry. A nature trail with a marked trail guide follows a narrow, winding path undulating through the trees and among lush greenery that engulfs the springs.

The trail is not accessible for wheelchair users.

To visit the Thousand Palms Oasis, you must park along a dirt access road. The sandy approach to the oasis is rough and rocky. Picnic tables, secreted in alcoves among the palm trees near the springs, are very cozy, but the surfaces leading there are quite uneven. Though actually a part of the Coachella Valley Preserve, many hikers begin their journey into Indio Hills from this point. The only vehicle access to Indio Hills is an unmarked dirt road off Washington Avenue.

For those who wish to recapture the flavor of the old west, a park concessionaire offers covered wagon tours of the Indio Hills desert. If you need help, the staff will lift you into the padded seat in a mule-drawn wagon. On your two-hour trip, your knowledgeable tour guide will help you discover some of the hidden secrets of the living desert, including three oases. For an additional fee, you can hang around the campfire afterwards and enjoy a steak BBQ with entertainment and all the trimmings. For more information call (619) 347-2161.

To find the covered wagon tour, turn north on Ramon Road. A dirt driveway will take you directly to the assembly area. As with the visitor's area, wheeling surfaces are loose, soft sand. There are no special arrangements for wheelchair users.

Indio Hills Palms

c/o Nature Conservancy
(619) 343-1234
Location—Four miles north of Indio, on Thousand Palms Road, 2.1 miles north of Ramon Road
Elevation—600'

SALTON SEA STATE RECREATION AREA

The Salton Sea is a prime example of the powerful force of Nature, and Man's ability to change it. Two moving plates of the earth's surface have been shifting for thousands of years, creating many changes in the topography of the area known as the Salton Trough. Once it was even part of the Gulf of California. Eventually, erosion from the Colorado River cut off this portion, and it dried up. New channels cut by the river periodically refilled the sink. After the water evaporated, deposited minerals created a huge salt field.

It was not until modern society decided to bring water from the river for irrigation that the Salton Sea as we know it came into being. In the late 1800's, the California Development Company built a canal to encourage agriculture. In 1905, spring floods overwhelmed the meager channel and began to fill the depression called the Salton Sink. By the time the water was redirected, a lake had formed that was 45 miles long and 17 miles wide. Since then, it has evaporated to its current level and remains relatively stable. It has a salt content greater than that of the Pacific Ocean.

As a blend of desert and water, the Salton Sea area supports hundreds of bird species. Besides the wading birds like the blue heron or the egret, thousands of migratory geese and ducks arrive here each winter. The best spots for bird watching are in the marshy areas near the fishing jetty, Sneaker Beach, Salt Creek Campground, and north of Mecca Beach.

Visitors also come here for the mild winter weather and fishing opportunities. Depending on the season, you can catch orange-mouth corvina, croaker, sargo, or tilapia at the Salton Sea. Also, this is a popular area for night fishing and one of the few places in the state where night fishing is permitted. A special feature of the park is the fully accessible FISHING AREA at the jetty. CAMPING and RESTROOMS are also accessible, as is the VISITOR CENTER.

Visitor Center

Just south of the park entry kiosk, volunteers offer a friendly greeting and park information at the VISITOR CENTER. Along with book and pamphlet sales, the center features a slide program and interpretive displays on the Salton Sea's unique natural history. In the cooler months, park rangers take visitor's on NATURE WALKS through parts of the park. Call ahead and the ranger will plan a walk designed with your needs in mind.

An accessible RESTROOM is housed in a separate building nearby. Surrounded by smooth concrete, the RESTROOM has a shallow stall with a low toilet and grab bars. There are no other access modifications.

Fishing and Boat Launch

Anglers may fish from anywhere along the State Park's shoreline or take a boat out onto the water. Concrete walkways serve an accessible BOAT LAUNCHING RAMP and dock near the visitor center. Two designated car-and-trailer parking places are provided in the adjacent parking lot.

For shore fishermen, the most accessible FISHING SPOT is at the end of the road from the Los Frijoles campground. Concrete paving covers a flat designated FISHING AREA on a 10-foot bluff at the edge of the water. Safety curbing lines the rim of the low bluff and a ramada provides shade for a nearby table and BBQ. For added convenience, there is an accessible CHEMICAL TOILET nearby.

Picnic

Picnic tables are placed in three scenic locations at the park. North of the entry kiosk, tables are right on the coarse sand at **Sneaker Beach** where bird watching is a favorite pastime. Only dirt parking and inaccessible chemical toilets are nearby. At the visitor center, sea gulls come to beg at your picnic table as the pungent scent of brine permeates the air. You'll have an excellent view of the salty lake from a group of tables at the edge of the paved parking lot. The accessible RESTROOM near the VISITOR CENTER makes this a convenient place to take a break. Picnic tables on the shore at the **Mecca Beach** campground is another good place for bird-watching. You may park on asphalt, but the tables and their shade ramadas stand on a desert floor surface.

Camping

Headquarters — Thirty-eight paved CAMPING SITES (15 with water, sewer and electric hook-ups) suitable for RV's, line a section of the main parking lot near the visitor center. Each pull-thru site has a table and high BBQ. The accessible RESTROOM near the visitor center building is not far away and there is an RV dump station on the southbound road to Los Frijoles camping area.

Los Frijoles — Though Los Frijoles is technically part of the headquarters campground, sites here are much different. Desert floor camping sites line the outer perimeter of a large paved loop. Curbing surrounds the parking areas, blocking wheelchair access to the sites; however, there are gaps in the curbing where it can be bypassed through soft sand. While most of the sites are flat, many have a soft sand surface. Ramadas provide shade for each table, and there are fire rings and food storage at all sites. A weathered asphalt surface surrounds the _RESTROOM_ where there is a 1-inch lip at the doorway. The shallow stall has grab bars and a low toilet; the shower is not accessible.

Mecca Beach — One-and-a-half miles south of park headquarters, Mecca Beach Campground includes 110 campsites with asphalt parking spaces. Tamarisk trees line the parking rows offering some shade to the tables and fire rings on the desert floor. Pavement gently slopes toward the shoreline. A _RESTROOM_ closeby has a shallow stall with grab bars and a low toilet. A narrow 27-inch passageway leads to the stalls in the _SHOWER ROOM_ and seating area. There are no seats in the shower stalls; the controls are 46 inches from the floor, and the shower heads are 66 inches high. You will find an accessible telephone near the campground entrance at the end of a 15-foot flagstone walkway.

Corvina Beach, Salt Creek, and **Bombay Beach** (FCFS) — All three of these campgrounds offer primitive bluff camping on a dirt lot 15 feet above the water's edge. Shore fishermen can cast their lines right from their campsites or launch small boats from the narrow beach below. There is at least one accessible _CHEMICAL TOILET_ at each campground; water is provided either by a central faucet or water tank trailer. Because the ground is quite uneven in places, the ramps to the _CHEMICAL_ toilets sometimes don't meet flush with the ground, making access difficult.

Salton Sea State Recreation Area

PO Box 3166
North Shore, CA 92254-0977
(619) 393-3052
Park Folder Available
Location — Twenty-five miles southeast of Indio on Hwy 111 along 18 miles of the Salton Sea's northeast shore
Elevation — 230 feet

ANZA-BORREGO DESERT STATE PARK

The Anza-Borrego Desert State Park is a huge, wonderful blend of desert life, geology, and Indian history. Like most arid regions, the deserts of southcentral California seem stark and uninviting. You would never believe that the low-lying plains was an ancient sea teeming with life, or that a population of Native Americans once lived in piñon pine-studded hills where they left evidence of their society in creek beds and hillside caves. If you've never visited the desert in spring, you've missed the vibrant colors of the desert floor blooming in life's renewal.

Take the time to listen, and even the silence of the night betrays the movement of nocturnal life guided by the shadows of a desert moon.

As California's first desert state park, the boundaries of Anza-Borrego Desert have grown to include 60,000 acres of badlands, sandstone canyons, rocky hills, and open valleys, making it the largest state park in the contiguous United States. Over one million visitors come to Anza-Borrego each year to share in its tranquil beauty or to find solitude on an obscure park road. The desert attracts nature lovers, hikers, and off-road enthusiasts from all parts of Southern California who come for a change of pace and often leave with a new frame of mind.

To fully appreciate the many facets of this desert jewel, planning is the key. Be sure to pick up a State Park folder and newspaper before visiting the park so you don't miss anything. In addition, most Southern California bookstores have a wealth of information about the Borrego Desert region with topics ranging from wildflowers to ancient history. The best selection, however, is available at the park visitor center. For diverse natural features found only in the nooks and crannies of the desert, off-roaders and backcountry explorers will want to pick up one of many publications about the four-wheel drive roads of the park. Finally, and most importantly, when you plan a trip to the desert, be sure to bring along plenty of water, a sun hat and sunglasses, and a full tank of gas.

Visitor Center

If you are new to the Anza-Borrego region, it is a good idea to make a

283

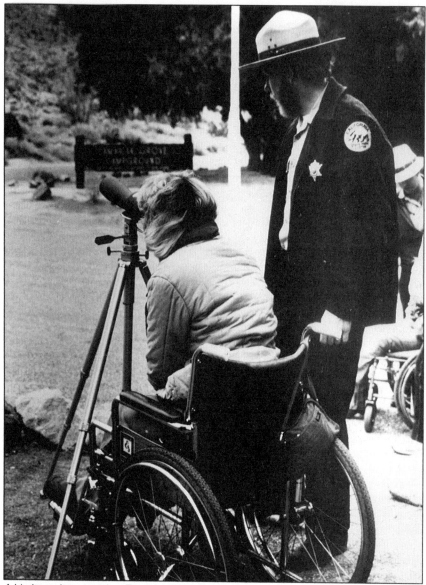
A big-horn sheep watch at Tamarisk Grove Campground   *(Photo courtesy CDPR)*

where the doors are far too heavy to pull open from a seated position. A paved path also leads to an observation deck on the roof of the visitor center. Schematics and descriptions give you a perspective of the surrounding mountain ranges and vistas. Unfortunately, if you are seated your view is limited to a narrow area between a 33-inch rock wall, and railing at 43 inches.

A hard-packed pathway leads off the pavement (1- to 3-inch transitions), where a self-guided nature tour passes a garden area and desert pup fish pond. Ranger-led *NATURE TALKS* originate from the *VISITOR CENTER* and will be adapted to the needs of your group. You may wish to call ahead for arrangements.

The visitor center is located 1.7 miles west of Borrego Springs on Palm Canyon Drive. *RESTROOMS* at the visitor center have very heavy doors with door handles at 48 inches from the ground. The shallow stall has a low toilet with grab bars, standard sinks, and high paper towels. There is an accessible *TELEPHONE* in the foyer.

Campgrounds

Borrego Palm Canyon—By far the most popular and well-used campground is Borrego Palm Canyon. Only one mile up the road from the visitor center, the campground has something to offer most any type of camper, including water, sewer, and electric RV hook-ups. RV camping in pull-ins or pull-thrus is on rough asphalt. Many hard-packed dirt sites have tables with extended ends (designed for a camp stove, but usable for wheelchair access); each has a fire ring on desert floor sur-

stop at the *VISITOR CENTER*. At this subterranean building you'll find a cool desert oasis of information and assistance. An accessible exhibit room displays Indian artifacts discovered in the region, plants and animal samples, and an interesting story of the great earthquake and desert geology. A few of the exhibits may be too high for comfortable viewing from a seated position. You can watch a short

film in the accessible *AUDITORIUM*, and, as mentioned previously, there is an extensive collection of regional-interest books for sale. Knowledgeable park docents are available to help you with any questions you may have or direct you to an appropriate destination.

Pavement leads 250 feet from four paved designated *PARKING* places, to the visitor center entrance

If you decide to explore Anza-Borrego in your vehicle, be sure to have plenty of gas.

(Photo courtesy CDPR)

face. Tent sites are less accessible. Site parking is dirt and nearby restrooms are not accessible. Use the facilities at the picnic area or in the RV section.

In the winter season, rangers offer campfire programs in the AMPHITHEATER at the end of Palm Canyon Road. From the parking lot, a lighted rock-embedded path leads about 300 feet uphill (10%) to the seating area.

New RESTROOM BUILDINGS in the picnic area and near the RV campsites have a fully accessible UNISEX RESTROOM with a low toilet. The SHOWER ROOM has an ample entry area, retractable seats outside and inside the shower; controls are 36 inches high. An accessible TELE-PHONE and DRINKING FOUNTAIN are outside the picnic area restroom building.

Tamarisk Grove—Level campsites, arranged in the midst of a large grove of mature tamarisk trees, have asphalt pull-ins; rocks or berms that define the parking area of each site create a barrier to the table and fire ring on the desert floor nearby. Ramadas shade each table. There is a small ramp entry to the restroom where the shallow stall has no grab bars or other access modifications. If you're driving by the area and wish to stop for a picnic, there are two day use picnic tables and an elevated fire ring near the en-trance. If you're very lucky, you may catch a glimpse of a big horn sheep spending its winter on the ridges north of Tamarisk Grove.

Bow Willow (FCFS)—A 2½-mile dirt road leads to this flat campground. Each site has a table shaded by a ramada and a fire ring on the sandy desert floor. Standard chemical toilets are provided.

Culp Valley, Sheep Canyon, Arroyo Salado, Yaqui Pass, Yaqui Well, Fish Creek, Blair Valley and **Mt. Palm Springs** (FCFS) are all primitive campsites in desert floor clearings. Most have little more than a place to park and a tent site. There is no drinking water available at these locations.

Anza-Borrego Desert State Park

PO Box 299
Borrego Springs, CA 92004-0299
(619) 767-4684

Park Folder and Newspaper Available
Location—Bounded by Interstate 8 to
the south, the park is serviced by
S22, and Hwys 78 and 79.
Elevation—700 feet

OCOTILLO WELLS STATE VEHICULAR RECREATION AREA

Since the end of World War II and the advent of the all-terrain Jeep, off-roading has evolved into an avid pastime for thousands of Americans. At Ocotillo Wells State Vehicular Recreation Area, Southern Californians congregate with all varieties of vehicles designed to explore the sand hills and desert trails of this 14,000-acre park. In your ATV, dune buggy, four-wheel drive, or motorcycle, you'll be able to reach such points of interest as **Blow Sand Hill**, **Devil's Slide**, and **Shell Reef**. Up to 28,000 additional acres are in the acquisition stages and will soon be added to the already spacious desert playground.

To maintain this as a purely off-road vehicle park, improvements are limited to a *PIT TOILET* building on the trail known as Main Street. Camping is permitted anywhere in the area, but there are no other restroom facilities, and water is not available. The popular primitive camping areas have some fire rings and tables. For information or assistance, park headquarters is at the southwest corner of the park off Hwy 78. From a designated *PARKING* place nearby, a ramp access leads to the ranger station and a paved walkway to a fully accessible *UNISEX RESTROOM* (low toilet) in a nearby building. You can pick up food, gas and other supplies at the town of Ocotillo Wells, just across the highway.

Ocotillo Wells
State Vehicular Recreation Area

PO Box 360
Borrego Springs, CA 92004
(619) 767-5391

Park Folder Available
Location—On Hwy 78, 16 to 19 miles
west of Hwy 86
Elevation—700 feet

Off-roaders drive all types of dune buggies and ATV's at Ocotillo Wells SVRA.

(Photo courtesy CDPR)

PICACHO STATE RECREATION AREA

In its heyday in the late 1800's, the town of Picacho (pop. 2,500) was the site a booming stamp mill, processing ore found in the nearby gold mine. The park seems to be cradled by the rugged desert terrain near Picacho Peak and is bounded on one side by the Colorado River. When times were good, paddle-wheelers were a major form of transportation on the river. Now, little remains of the town except a few building foundations and the cemetery.

The area lives on as a retreat for fishermen, boaters, and hikers attracted to Picacho for its natural beauty. Summer temperatures can be quite harsh (up to 120°F), so most visitors prefer to visit from mid-October through April. In spring and fall the native beavers and muskrats share their backwater lakes and tule-lined riverbanks with thousand of ducks, geese, and other migrating waterfowl. Meanwhile, in the backcountry, visitors often spot wild burros and mule deer from the road. Even an occasional bighorn sheep will make an appearance.

Located in the lower Colorado River basin, 25 miles north of Yuma, Arizona, Picacho State Recreation Area is the southeasternmost of the state parks. The unpaved road that leads to this remote park on the river is suitable only for private vehicles and small trailers. All surfaces at the park are desert floor except for a few campsites that use old building foundations. Packed desert dirt roads wind through the campground, day use area and beyond to Taylor Lake, Paddle-wheeler Boat-in camp, and Bear Canyon Falls four-wheel drive trail.

Picnic

From the picnic area overlooking the water, you can watch boaters come and go from the boat launch or with patience, you may spot any one of many birds or animals on the quieter side of the river. The picnic area consists of several tables surrounded by soft sand and shaded by ramadas. Close by is an accessible _CHEMICAL_ _TOILET_ on a concrete slab.

Boat Launch

From Picacho, boaters have access to the 55 miles of the Colorado River from Parker to Imperial Dams. River anglers try their luck for crappie, catfish, sunfish, large-mouth bass, and blue gill. Boats may be launched from several sites at the park including three boat-in camps. Launches have no loading docks and are similar to the primitive concrete ramp near the ranger station.

Camping

Fifty campsites are scattered among feathery Tamarisk trees, ocotillo plants, and mesquite. All are located on the flats were the original town of Picacho once stood. Some surviving paved foundations are incorporated in the campsites. Each site has a table in the shade and a fire ring or a BBQ. A solar shower is central to the campground. It is not accessible, but there is an accessible _CHEMICAL_ _TOILET_ on the desert floor nearby. An RV dump station has been provided as well. (FCFS)

Picacho State Recreation Area
PO Box 1207
Winterhaven, CA 92283
(619) 393-3059
Park Folder Available
Location — Twenty-four miles north of
*   Winterhaven on Picacho Road*
Elevation — 190 feet

The rugged desert at Picacho Mountain

(Photo courtesy CDPR)

"This we know, all things are connected like the blood which unites one family.
All things are connected. Whatever befalls the earth, befalls the sons of earth.
Man did not weave the web of life; he is merely a strand in it.
Whatever he does to the web, he does to himself."

Chief Sealth of the Suquamish Tribe, 1786?-1866. (Seattle is named after him.)

Access Summary

Page		Camping	Campground Restroom	Campground Shower	Lodging	Day Use Restroom	Telephone	Picnic	Trails	Fishing/Pier	Beach Access/Swimming	Boat Launch	Visitor Center/Museum	Stores/Food	RV Dump Station
	A														
46	ADMIRAL WILLIAM STANDLEY STATE REC. AREA								—	—					
72	AHJUMAWI LAVA SPRINGS STATE PARK								—			—	—		
56	ANDERSON MARSH STATE HISTORIC PARK					—		—	a	—					
155	ANDREW MOLERA STATE PARK	a	A						—	—	—				
126	ANGEL ISLAND STATE PARK	a	a			A	A	a	a	a	a		A	A	
58	ANNADEL STATE PARK								—	—	—				
134	AÑO NUEVO STATE RESERVE					C	A	a	A	—	a		a		
257	ANTELOPE VALLEY CALIFORNIA POPPY RESERVE					A	A	A	A				A		
258	ANTELOPE VALLEY INDIAN MUSEUM					a	—	—	—				—		
283	ANZA-BORREGO DESERT STATE PARK	a	A	A		A	A	a	a				A		
65	ARMSTRONG REDWOODS STATE RESERVE					A		A	A				a		
153	ASILOMAR STATE BEACH and CONF. GROUNDS				a				A	—	—				
92	AUBURN STATE RECREATION AREA	—	—		—	—	—	—	—	—	—				
65	AUSTIN CREEK STATE RECREATION AREA	—	a				—	—	—						
38	AZALEA STATE RESERVE								—						
	B														
57	BALE GRIST MILL STATE HISTORIC PARK					A			A				A		
134	BEAN HOLLOW STATE BEACH					a				—	—				
42	BENBOW LAKE STATE RECREATION AREA	A	A			a	—	a	—	a	a	a			
108	BENICIA CAPITOL STATE HISTORIC PARK					—									
108	BENICIA STATE RECREATION AREA	—	—			a		a	A	—	—	—			
198	BETHANY RESERVOIR STATE RECREATION AREA					C		A	a	A		A			
84	BIDWELL MANSION STATE HISTORIC PARK					—	—						a		
84	BIDWELL RIVER PARK	—				C		a	—	a	a	a			
138	BIG BASIN REDWOODS STATE PARK	A	A	A	a	A	A	A	a				a	A	*
168	BODIE STATE HISTORIC PARK					A	—	a	a				a		
237	BOLSA CHICA STATE BEACH	a				A	A	A	A	a	A			a	
248	BORDER FIELD STATE PARK					a		—	a	—	a				
56	BOTHE-NAPA VALLEY STATE PARK	a	A	A		a	A	a	a				a	a	*
107	BRANNAN ISLAND STATE RECREATION AREA	A	a	a		a	A	A	a	a	—	A	a		*
97	BURTON CREEK STATE PARK	—	—												
136	BUTANO STATE PARK	a	a			A	—	—							

A accessible	**a** some access	**C** accessible chemical toilet	**—** not accessible	***** not rated

Page		Camping	Campground Restroom	Campground Shower	Lodging	Day Use Restroom	Telephone	Picnic	Trails	Fishing/Pier	Beach Access/Swimming	Boat Launch	Visitor Center/Museum	Stores/Food	RV Dump Station
	c														
246	CABRILLO NATIONAL MONUMENT					A	A	a	A	—			A	a	
183	CALAVERAS BIG TREES STATE PARK	A	A	A		A	A	a	A	—	—		A		*
267	CALIFORNIA CITRUS STATE HISTORIC PARK					a	a	a	a				a		
106	CALIFORNIA STATE CAPITOL MUSEUM					A	A	a	A				A		
103	CALIFORNIA STATE RAILROAD MUSEUM					A	A								
131	CANDLESTICK POINT STATE RECREATION AREA					A	A	a	A	a					
243	CARDIFF STATE BEACH					A	A			—	a				
241	CARLSBAD STATE BEACH					—		a	A	—	a				
154	CARMEL RIVER STATE BEACH					—				—	—				
199	CARNEGIE STATE VEHICULAR RECREATION AREA														
214	CARPINTERIA STATE BEACH	A	A	A		a	A	a		—	a		a		*
48	CASPAR HEADLANDS STATE BEACH					—				—	—				
48	CASPAR HEADLANDS STATE RESERVE									—					
264	CASTAIC LAKE STATE RECREATION AREA	a	a			A	A	A	a	a	a	a	A	A	
71	CASTLE CRAGS STATE PARK	a	—	A		—	—	a	—	—	—				
137	CASTLE ROCK STATE PARK	—						a	a						
102	CASWELL MEMORIAL STATE PARK	a	—			A	A	a	a	a	a				
160	CAYUCOS STATE BEACH					a				a					
217	CHANNEL ISLANDS NATIONAL PARK					A	A	A	—		—		A		
126	CHINA CAMP STATE PARK	a	A			A	A	a	a	a	a	—	a	a	
267	CHINO HILLS STATE PARK	—	—			C	—		—				a		
213	CHUMASH PAINTED CAVE STATE HISTORIC PARK								—						
89	CLAY PIT STATE VEHICULAR RECREATION AREA					—			—						
54	CLEAR LAKE STATE PARK	A	A	A		A	A	a	a	—	a	a	A		*
206	COLONEL ALLENSWORTH STATE HISTORIC PARK	A	A			A		a					A		*
185	COLUMBIA STATE HISTORIC PARK					A	A	A	a				a	a	
85	COLUSA—SACRAMENTO RIVER STATE REC. AREA	a	a	a		a	—	a	—	a		a			
237	CORONA DEL MAR STATE BEACH					—		—		—	—				
238	CRYSTAL COVE STATE PARK					A	A			—	—	a			
274	CUYAMACA RANCHO STATE PARK	A	A	A		A	a	A	a				A		*

A accessible	**a** some access	**c** accessible chemical toilet	**—** not accessible	***** not rated

		Camping	Campground Restroom	Campground Shower	Lodging	Day Use Restroom	Telephone	Picnic	Trails	Fishing/Pier	Beach Access/Swimming	Boat Launch	Visitor Center/Museum	Stores/Food	RV Dump Station
D,E															
227	DAN BLOCKER STATE BEACH					-					-				
99	D.L. BLISS STATE PARK	A	a	a		A	-	A	-	-	-				*
251	DEATH VALLEY NATIONAL MONUMENT														
252	Furnace Creek	A	A	-	A	a	A	a	A				A	a	*
253	Stovepipe Wells	a	A		A	-	A	-	a					A	*
255	Grapevine					a	A	a	-				A	A	
256	Wildrose	a	-			-	-	-					-		
30	DEL NORTE COAST REDWOODS STATE PARK	a	a	a		a	-	a	-						*
107	DELTA MEADOWS RIVER PARK									-					
167	DEVIL'S POSTPILE NATIONAL MONUMENT	-	-			-	-	-							
233	DOCKWEILER STATE BEACH	A	A	A		A	A	-	A	-	a			a	
230	DOHENY STATE BEACH	A	A	A		A	A	a	A	-	a		A	a	*
96	DONNER MEMORIAL STATE PARK	A	A	A		A	A	a	A	a	a		A		
202	DURHAM FERRY STATE RECREATION AREA	a	A	A		A	-	A	-	-					*
212	EL CAPITAN STATE BEACH														
213	EL PRESIDIO DE SANTA BARBARA ST. HIST. PARK												a		
99	EMERALD BAY STATE PARK	-	-	-		-	-	-	-	-	-	-	-		
215	EMMA WOOD STATE BEACH	a	C			A	-	-		-	-				
91	EMPIRE MINE STATE HISTORIC PARK					A		a	a				A		
F,G															
93	FOLSOM LAKE STATE RECREATION AREA	A	A	a		A	A	A	A	a	A	a	A	A	*
141	THE FOREST OF NISENE MARKS STATE PARK					-		-	-						
38	FORT HUMBOLDT STATE HISTORIC PARK					A		a	A				A		
63	FORT ROSS STATE HISTORIC PARK	-	-			A	A	a	A	-	-		A		
261	FORT TEJON STATE HISTORIC PARK					-		a	a				A		
107	FRANK'S TRACT STATE RECREATION AREA									-					
204	FREMONT FORD STATE RECREATION AREA								-	-					
150	FREMONT PEAK STATE PARK	-	-			a		-	-				a		
154	GARRAPATA STATE PARK								-	-	-				
210	GAVIOTA STATE PARK	a	a	a		a	A	a	-	A	a	a		a	
203	GEORGE J. HATFIELD STATE RECREATION AREA	-	-			-		-	-						

A accessible   **a** some access   **C** accessible chemical toilet   **−** not accessible   ***** not rated

Page		Camping	Campground Restroom	Campground Shower	Lodging	Day Use Restroom	Telephone	Picnic	Trails	Fishing/Pier	Beach Access/Swimming	Boat Launch	Visitor Center/Museum	Stores/Food	RV Dump Station
118	GOLDEN GATE NATIONAL RECREATION AREA														
118	Marin Headlands					A	A	a	a	a	—		A	—	
120	San Francisco Waterfront				A	A	A	A	A	a	a		A	A	
122	Alcatraz					C	—	a	a				a		
123	West Peninsula					A	A	a	a	a	A		a	A	
105	GOVERNOR'S MANSION					a							a		
132	GRAY WHALE COVE STATE BEACH					—					—				
39	GRIZZLY CREEK REDWOODS STATE PARK	A	A	a		a	—	a	a	—	—		A		
101	GROVER HOT SPRINGS STATE PARK	A	A	A		—	—	a	a	—	a				
	H–J														
133	HALF MOON BAY STATE BEACH	a	A			A	—	a	—	—	A				*
35	HARRY A. MERLO STATE RECREATION AREA									—	—	—			
157	HEARST SAN SIMEON STATE HIST. MONUMENT					A	A						A	A	
52	HENDY WOODS STATE PARK	A	A	A		a		—	A	—	—				*
140	HENRY COWELL REDWOODS STATE PARK	a	—			—	—	a	—				A		
202	HENRY W. COE STATE PARK	a	—			—	—	a	—				—		
151	HOLLISTER HILLS STATE VEHICULAR REC AREA	a	A	A		a	—	a	a					a	
35	HUMBOLDT LAGOONS STATE PARK	—	—			a		—		—	—	—	—		
40	HUMBOLDT REDWOODS STATE PARK	a	A	a		A	A	a	A	—	—	—	a		*
261	HUNGRY VALLEY STATE VEHICULAR REC AREA	—	—			—			—						
237	HUNTINGTON STATE BEACH					A	A	A	A	a	A			a	
182	INDIAN GRINDING ROCK STATE HISTORIC PARK	—	—			A	—	a	A				A		
281	INDIO HILLS PALM					—	—	a	—				a		
84	IRVINE – FINCH RIVER ACCESS SITE	—	—			C	—	A		A		A			
59	JACK LONDON STATE HISTORIC PARK					a		a	a				A		
31	JEDEDIAH SMITH REDWOODS STATE PARK	a	a	a		a	—	a	A	—	—		A		*
277	JOSHUA TREE NATIONAL MONUMENT														
	Low Desert	a	—			A		A	a				—		*
	High Desert	A	A			C		a	A				A		
40	JUG HANDLE STATE RESERVE					—		—	a						
157	JULIA PFEIFFER BURNS STATE PARK	—				—	—	a	—				—		

A accessible	**a** some access	**C** accessible chemical toilet	**—** not accessible	***** not rated

Page		Camping	Campground Restroom	Campground Shower	Lodging	Day Use Restroom	Telephone	Picnic	Trails	Fishing/Pier	Beach Access/Swimming	Boat Launch	Visitor Center/Museum	Stores/Food	RV Dump Station
	K,L														
235	KENNETH HAHN STATE RECREATION AREA					a	A	a	A	A					
97	KINGS BEACH STATE RECREATION AREA					a	—	—	—		—				
190	KINGS CANYON NATIONAL PARK														
191	Grant Grove	a	A		a	a	A	a	a				A	A	*
192	Cedar Grove	a	A	—	a	A	—	a	a				a	A	
62	KRUSE RHODODENDRON STATE RESERVE								—						
199	LAKE DEL VALLE STATE RECREATION AREA														
199	East Lake					a	A	A	A	a	a	A		A	
201	West Lake	A	A	A		a	A	a	a	—	a	—	A	A	*
27	LAKES EARL AND TALAWA	—	—			—		—	—	—		—			
270	LAKE ELSINORE STATE RECREATION AREA	a	—	—		—	—	a	a	a	a	—		—	
86	LAKE OROVILLE STATE RECREATION AREA	A	A	A		A	—	A	a	a	a	a	A	a	*
268	LAKE PERRIS STATE RECREATION AREA	A	A	A		A	A	A	A	a	A	a	A	A	*
100	LAKE VALLEY STATE RECREATION AREA														
209	LA PURISIMA MISSION STATE HISTORIC PARK														
80	LASSEN VOLCANIC NATIONAL PARK	A	A	A		A	A	A	A	a	a	a	a	a	*
228	LAS TUNAS STATE BEACH										—				
69	LAVA BEDS NATIONAL MONUMENT	A	a			A	A	a	a				A		
107	LELAND STANFORD MANSION STATE HIST. PARK												—		
221	LEO CARRILLO STATE BEACH	a	A	A		C	A	A	—	—	a			a	*
241	LEUCADIA STATE BEACH										—				
144	LIGHTHOUSE FIELD STATE BEACH					A	A	a	a				—		
38	LITTLE RIVER STATE BEACH									—	—	—			
230	LOS ANGELES STATE/COUNTY ARBORETUM					A	A	a	A				A	A	
229	LOS ENCINOS STATE HISTORIC PARK					A		—					a		
164	LOS OSOS OAKS STATE RESERVE								—						
	M,N														
46	MacKERRICHER STATE PARK	A	A	A		—	—	a	A	—	—				*
53	MAILLIARD REDWOODS STATE RESERVE							—	—						
89	MALAKOFF DIGGINS STATE HISTORIC PARK	a	A			A	—	a	a				a		
226	MALIBU CREEK STATE PARK														
227	MALIBU LAGOON STATE BEACH					a			a				a		

A accessible   **a** some access   **C** accessible chemical toilet   **—** not accessible   ***** not rated

Page		Camping	Campground Restroom	Campground Shower	Lodging	Day Use Restroom	Telephone	Picnic	Trails	Fishing/Pier	Beach Access/Swimming	Boat Launch	Visitor Center/Museum	Stores/Food	RV Dump Station
53	MANCHESTER STATE BEACH	-	-			-	-			-	-				*
233	MANHATTAN STATE BEACH					a	A		A	a	a				
146	MANRESA STATE BEACH					a				-	a			-	
147	MARINA STATE BEACH					a	A		A	-	-			a	
92	MARSHALL GOLD DISCOVERY STATE HIST. PARK					A	A	A	a	a	a		A		
72	McARTHUR—BURNEY FALLS MEM. STATE PARK	a	-	-		A	A	a	a	-	a	a	a	A	*
203	McCONNELL STATE RECREATION AREA	a	A	A			-	-	-	-					
218	McGRATH STATE BEACH	a	a	-			A	-	-	-					*
50	MENDOCINO HEADLANDS STATE PARK					a		-	-	-			a		
188	MILLERTON LAKE STATE RECREATION AREA	A	A	A		A	-	a	a	a	a	-	a		*
169	MONO LAKE TUFA STATE RESERVE					A	A		a		a	-	A		
163	MONTAÑA DE ORO STATE PARK	a	a			a	-	a	a	-					
133	MONTARA STATE BEACH									-	-				
242	MONTEREY STATE BEACH									-	-	-			
148	MONTEREY STATE HISTORIC PARK					A	A						a		
52	MONTGOMERY WOODS STATE RESERVE							-	-						
242	MOONLIGHT STATE BEACH					A	A	a			a		A		
162	MORRO BAY STATE PARK	a	a	-		a	-	a	a	-	-	-	a	-	*
161	MORRO STRAND STATE BEACH	-	-	-		-	-			-	-				
147	MOSS LANDING STATE BEACH														
198	MOUNT DIABLO STATE PARK	-	-			a		A	A				-		
271	MOUNT SAN JACINTO STATE PARK	a	a	a		A	A	a	-				A	A	
116	MOUNT TAMALPAIS STATE PARK	-	A			A	A	a	A	-			-	-	
117	MUIR WOODS NATIONAL MONUMENT					A	A	a	A				A	A	
143	NATURAL BRIDGES STATE BEACH					a		a	A	-	a		A		
144	NEW BRIGHTON STATE BEACH	a	a	-		a	-			-	a				*
	O—R														
286	OCOTILLO WELLS STATE VEHICULAR REC. AREA	-	a			A	-								
102	OLD SACRAMENTO STATE HISTORIC PARK					A	A			a			a	A	
245	OLD TOWN SAN DIEGO STATE HISTORIC PARK					a	A	-					A	a	
129	OLOMPALI STATE HISTORIC PARK														
132	PACIFICA STATE BEACH					-				-	-				
273	PALOMAR MOUNTAIN STATE PARK	A	A	A		-		a	a	a					

A accessible **a** some access **c** accessible chemical toilet **—** not accessible ***** not rated

Page		Camping	Campground Restroom	Campground Shower	Lodging	Day Use Restroom	Telephone	Picnic	Trails	Fishing/Pier	Beach Access/Swimming	Boat Launch	Visitor Center/Museum	Stores/Food	RV Dump Station
235	PAN PACIFIC PARK					A	A	A	A						
36	PATRICK'S POINT STATE PARK	A	A	a		A	—	a	A	—	—		—		
52	PAUL M. DIMMICK WAYSIDE CAMPGROUND	a	—			—	—	—	—						
27	PELICAN STATE BEACH									—	—				
134	PESCADERO STATE BEACH					—			—	—					
61	PETALUMA ADOBE STATE HISTORIC PARK					—		a	a				a		
155	PFEIFFER BIG SUR STATE PARK	A	A	A	—	A	A	—	a	—	—		A	A	*
286	PICACHO STATE RECREATION AREA	a	C	—		C	—	—	—	—		—			*
134	PIGEON POINT LIGHTHOUSE				A		—		a						
152	PINNACLES NATIONAL MONUMENT	a	a			a	A	a	a				A		
236	PIO PICO STATE HISTORIC PARK					—							—		
165	PISMO DUNES STATE VEHICULAR REC. AREA	a	—		a	a	—	a	a	a					
164	PISMO STATE BEACH	A	A	A		A	A	A	A	—	—				*
85	PLUMAS-EUREKA STATE PARK	A	A	a		A	A	A	a	A	—		A		*
227	POINT DUME STATE BEACH					—					a				
154	POINT LOBOS STATE RESERVE					a		a	a						
133	POINT MONTARA LIGHT STATION				A	a	—						a		
218	POINT MUGU STATE PARK	A	A	a		C	—	a	a	—	a				*
111	POINT REYES NATIONAL SEASHORE														
112	Bear Valley	—	—			A	A	a	A				A		
112	Point Reyes					A	A	a	—	—	a		A	A	
113	Tomales Point					A	—	a					a		
113	Other Areas				A	—		a			—				
209	POINT SAL STATE BEACH					—				—	—				
155	POINT SUR STATE HISTORIC PARK					a			a				a		
134	POMPONIO STATE BEACH					—		—			—				
136	PORTOLA STATE BEACH	a	a	a		—	—	a	—				a		
33	PRAIRIE CREEK REDWOODS STATE PARK	a	A	A		a	A	A	A	a	a		A		*
261	PROVIDENCE MOUNTAINS STATE REC. AREA	—	—			—	—		—						
262	PYRAMID LAKE STATE RECREATION AREA					A	A	A	A	a	a	a	A	—	
186	RAILTOWN 1897 STATE HISTORIC PARK					A	—	a					a	a	
233	REDONDO STATE BEACH					A			A		a				
260	RED ROCK CANYON STATE PARK	A	A			a		—	—				—		*

A accessible	**a** some access	**C** accessible chemical toilet	**—** not accessible	***** not rated

Page		Camping	Campground Restroom	Campground Shower	Lodging	Day Use Restroom	Telephone	Picnic	Trails	Fishing/Pier	Beach Access/Swimming	Boat Launch	Visitor Center/Museum	Stores/Food	RV Dump Station
28	REDWOOD NATIONAL PARK				A	A	A	A	A	A	a		A		
211	REFUGIO STATE BEACH														
43	RICHARDSON GROVE STATE PARK	a	A	A		A	−	a	a	−	−		a	a	
233	ROBERT H. MEYER MEMORIAL STATE BEACHES					C	−				−				
56	ROBERT LOUIS STEVENSON STATE PARK							−	−						
129	ROBERT W. CROWN MEMORIAL STATE BEACH					A	A	A	A	A	A		A	A	
237	ROYAL PALMS STATE BEACH					a					−				
48	RUSSIAN GULCH STATE PARK	A	A			−		a	a	−	a				
	S														
259	SADDLEBACK BUTTE STATE PARK	a	A			−		−	−				−		*
147	SALINAS RIVER STATE BEACH					−				−	−				
62	SALT POINT STATE PARK	a	a			a	−	a	−	−	−				*
182	SALTON SEA STATE RECREATION AREA	a	a	a		a	A	a	a	A	a	A	A		*
115	SAMUEL P. TAYLOR STATE PARK	A	a	a		a	A	a	A	−	−				*
132	SAN BRUNO MOUNTAIN STATE PARK					A	A	A	A						
215	SAN BUENAVENTURA STATE BEACH					A	A	a	A	A	a		A		
239	SAN CLEMENTE STATE BEACH	A	A	A		A	−	−		−	a				
242	SAN ELIJO STATE BEACH														
133	SAN GREGORIO STATE BEACH					−		a	−	−	−		−		
149	SAN JUAN BAUTISTA STATE HISTORIC PARK					a	a	a					a		
204	SAN LUIS RESERVOIR STATE REC. AREA														
204	San Luis Reservoir	A	a	a		A	A					a	A		
205	O'Neill Forebay	a	−			a	−	a	a	a	a	a	a		
206	Los Banos Creek Reservoir	a	−		C	a	−	−	−	−					
239	SAN ONOFRE STATE BEACH	A	A	A		A	−		−	−	−				*
244	SAN PASQUAL BATTLEFIELD STATE HIST. PARK					A	A	a	−				A		
160	SAN SIMEON STATE BEACH	A	A	a		a	A	−	−	−	−				*
143	SANTA CRUZ MISSION STATE HISTORIC PARK					a							a		
222	SANTA MONICA MOUNTAINS NATL. REC. AREA	a	a			A	A	a	a				a		
232	SANTA MONICA STATE BEACH					A	A		A		a			a	
230	SANTA SUSANA MOUNTAINS								−						
54	SCHOONER GULCH							−		−	−				
145	SEACLIFF STATE BEACH	a	A	A		a	A	a		a	a		A	A	

A accessible **a** some access **C** accessible chemical toilet **−** not accessible ***** not rated

Page		Camping	Campground Restroom	Campground Shower	Lodging	Day Use Restroom	Telephone	Picnic	Trails	Fishing/Pier	Beach Access/Swimming	Boat Launch	Visitor Center/Museum	Stores/Food	RV Dump Station
265	SECCOMBE LAKE STATE URBAN REC. AREA					A	A	a	A						
190	SEQUOIA NATIONAL PARK														
195	Lodgepole	a	a	A		A	A	a	–	–			A	A	*
195	Giant Forest				A	a	A	–	A					a	
197	Foothills	a	a			A	A	a	–					a	
197	Mineral King	–	–			–	–	–	–					–	
74	SHASTA NATIONAL RECREATION AREA	A	a			A	A	a	–	–	–	a	A	A	
80	SHASTA STATE HISTORIC PARK					–		–	–				a		
248	SILVER STRAND STATE BEACH	a				A	–	A		–	A			a	
265	SILVERWOOD LAKE STATE RECREATION AREA	A	A	A		A	A	A	A	a	a	a	–	a	*
45	SINKYONE WILDERNESS STATE PARK	–	–		–	–	–	–	–	–					
44	SMITHE REDWOODS STATE RESERVE					A	–	–	–	–	–				
64	SONOMA COAST STATE BEACHES	A	a	a		A	–	a	A	–	–				*
60	SONOMA STATE HISTORIC PARK					A	–	a	a				a		
241	SOUTH CARLSBAD STATE BEACH	a	a	–						–	–			–	*
90	SOUTH YUBA RIVER PROJECT	a	C			C	–	A	A	A					
44	STANDISH-HICKEY STATE RECREATION AREA	a	A	A		–		a	–	–	–				
105	STATE INDIAN MUSEUM					a	–						a		
58	SUGARLOAF RIDGE STATE PARK	a	–			–		a	–				A		
98	SUGAR PINE POINT STATE PARK	a	a	–		A	A	a	A	–	–		a		*
146	SUNSET STATE BEACH	a	a	–		–	A			–	–				
104	SUTTER'S FORT STATE HISTORIC PARK					a	–						a		
	T–Z														
97	TAHOE STATE RECREATION AREA	–	–			A		a	–	–	–	–	A		
132	THORTON STATE BEACH						–				–				
114	TOMALES BAY STATE PARK					A	A	a		–	–	A			
229	TOPANGA STATE BEACH					a					–				
227	TOPANGA STATE PARK	–				A	A	–	–						
243	TORREY PINES STATE BEACH					A	A	a		–	a				
243	TORREY PINES STATE RESERVE					a			A		–		a		
37	TRINIDAD STATE BEACH				–	–	–	–							
76	TRINITY NATIONAL RECREATION AREA	a	a	–	–	a	A	a	–	–	–	–		a	A
207	TULE ELK STATE RESERVE					a		a					a		

A accessible	**a** some access	**C** accessible chemical toilet	**–** not accessible	***** not rated

Page		Camping	Campground Restroom	Campground Shower	Lodging	Day Use Restroom	Telephone	Picnic	Trails	Fishing/Pier	Beach Access/Swimming	Boat Launch	Visitor Center/Museum	Stores/Food	RV Dump Station
188	TURLOCK LAKE STATE RESERVE	a	–			A		A	A	a	–	–	A		
144	TWIN LAKES STATE BEACH					–	–	–		–	–			–	
50	VAN DAMME STATE PARK	a	A	A		A		a	A	–	a		A		*
230	VERDUGO MOUNTAINS								–						
100	WASHOE MEADOWS STATE PARK					–			–						
187	WASSAMA ROUNDHOUSE STATE HISTORIC PARK					–		–	a				a		
241	WATTS TOWERS OF SIMON RODIA ST. HIST. PARK					–							a		
79	WEAVERVILLE JOSS HOUSE STATE HIST. PARK					–	–						a		
46	WESTPORT – UNION LANDING STATE BEACH	a	a			a		a		–	a				
77	WHISKEYTOWN NATIONAL RECREATION AREA	a	a	–		A	A	A	A	A	A	A	A	A	*
142	WILDER RANCH STATE PARK					A	A	–	–				a		
83	WILLIAM B. IDE ADOBE STATE HISTORIC PARK					–	a	–	a				a		
159	WM. RANDOLPH HEARST MEM. STATE BEACH					–		a		a	a	–		a	
232	WILL ROGERS STATE BEACH					A	A		A		a				
234	WILL ROGERS STATE HISTORIC PARK					a	–	–	a				a		
85	WOODLAND OPERA HOUSE STATE HIST. PARK					A	–						A		
83	WOODSON BRIDGE STATE RECREATION AREA	a	–	–		–	A	–	–	–					*
171	YOSEMITE NATIONAL PARK														
172	Mather	a	–		–	A	A	a	a		a	a	A	–	
174	Wawona	a	–		A	A	A	A	–				–	–	
175	Glacier Point					A	A	a	A					a	
176	Yosemite Valley	A	A	A	A	A	A	A	A			–	A	A	*
147	ZMUDKOWSKI STATE BEACH					–				–	–	–			

A accessible   **a** some access   **C** accessible chemical toilet   **–** not accessible   ***** not rated

National Park Camping Information

	stay limit	family sites	max. length trailer/ motorhome (in feet)	elevation (in feet)	approx. reservation period	LOCATION AND SPECIAL INFORMATION
DEATH VALLEY Death Valley, CA 92328 Furnace Creek	 14	 130	 37/40	 -178	 10/1-4/30	One half mile west of Furnace Creek Visitor Center. Fresh water, sanitary dump, store, showers and laundry nearby. Pets allowed on leash. No wood gathering. NO HOOK UPS.
JOSHUA TREE 29 Palms, CA 92277 Black Rock Canyon	 14	 100	 35/35	 4000	 10/1-5/31	Five miles south of Yucca Valley off CA 62 on Joshua Lane. Water and flush toilets, campfire programs, hiking. Pets permitted on leash. Two cars per site maximum. NO HOOKUPS.
SEQUOIA-KINGS CANYON Three Rivers, CA 93271 Lodgepole	 14	 250	 30/30	 6750	 5/20-9/2	Twenty-seven miles north of Three Rivers on General's Hwy (CA 198). Store, sanitary dump station, service station, visitor center. Showers and laundry services. Bear habitat food storage regulations strictly enforced. Fishing and horseback riding. Pets permitted.
WHISKEYTOWN Oak Bottom Marina PO Box 197 Whiskeytown, CA 96095 Oak Bottom Tent Sites Oak Bottom RV Sites	 14 14	 100 50	 none/none 36/36	 1220 1220	 5/15-9/4 5/15-9/4	Thirteen miles west of Redding on CA 299. Marina, swimming, boating, fishing, launch ramp, boat rental/fuel, dump station, campground/marina stores, snack bar, interpretive programs. Pets permitted. One vehicle per site in tent sites.
YOSEMITE Box 577 Yosemite NP, CA 95389 Upper Pines Lower River North Pines Lower Pines Upper River	 7 7 7 7 7	 238 138 85 163 124	 35/35 35/35 35/35 35/35 35/35	 4000 4000 4000 4000 4000	 3/15-11/10 3/22-10/26 4/26-10/14 All Year 3/22-10/19	First five campgrounds located in Yosemite Valley. Visitor Center, service station, sanitary dump station, swimming fishing, horseback riding are available. Pets are not allowed in Upper Pines. Upper River does not allow trailers, RV's or electrical generators. Quiet electrical generators may be used sparingly during daylight hours in the other campgrounds. For your convenience and to reduce traffic congestion and pollution in Yosemite Valley, please take advantage of the FREE shuttle bus service.
Hodgdon Meadow	14	10	35/35	4800	5/3-10/27	1/2-mile south of Big Oak Flat Entrance Station, approx. 25 miles northwest of Yosemite Valley. Pets permitted. RV site may not be level. Tent sites have shared parking areas.
Crane Flat	14	141	35/35	6200	5/3-10/27	Eight miles from Big Oak Flat Entrance Station, approx. 17 miles north east of Yosemite Valley. Service station and groceries. RV sites may not be level. Tent sites have shared parking.
Tuolumne Meadows Family Camp Horse Camp	 14 14	 165 4	 35/35 27/30	 8600 8600	 6/21-10/14 6/21-10/14	Eight miles west of Tioga Pass Entrance Station, approx. 55 miles northeast of Yosemite Valley. Facilities include: visitor center, sanitary dump station, fishing, horseback riding, groceries, and gasoline. RV sites may not be level. Tent sites have shared parking. Pets permitted. Horse Camp: 2 vehicles + 1 Horse trailer per site.

Make reservations by calling MISTIX at **1 (800) 365-CAMP** or 365-2267. Be sure to have your VISA, Mastercard or Discovery Card ready. See Introduction, page 25 for further instructions.

FAMILY CAMPING

ABBREVIATIONS

- CD – Coastal Development
- D – Developed Site
- H – Hookup Service
- P – Primitive Site
- SB – State Beach
- SHP – State Historic Park
- SP – State Park
- SRA – State Recreation Area
- SVRA – State Vehicular Recreation Area
- ■ – Wheelchair Accessible Site

PARK & CAMPGROUND	RESERVATION PERIOD	CAMPING DAYS LIMITED JUNE-SEPTEMBER	CAMPING DAYS LIMITED OCTOBER-MAY	CAMPSITES CLASSIFICATION	SHOWERS	MAXIMUM TRAILER LENGTH	MAXIMUM MOTORHOME OR CAMPER LENGTH	CAMPSITE FEE	PEAK SEASON DATES	GENERAL INFORMATION
ANZA-BORREGO DESERT SP										P.O. Box 299, Borrego Springs, CA 92004, (619) 767-5311
• Borrego Canyon (hookup) C6621	All Year	30	30	H	YES	35'	35'	$20	Nov 15-Apr 30	Picnic tables.
• Borrego Palm Canyon C6222	All Year	30	30	D	YES	21'	31'	$12	Nov 15-Apr 30	Ramadas, stoves and picnic tables.
• Tamarisk Grove C6223	All Year	30	30	D	YES	21'	21'	$12	Nov 15-Apr 30	Ramadas, stoves and picnic tables.
• Vern Whitaker Horseman's Camp C6224	All Year	30	30	P	YES	24'	24'	$14	Nov 15-Apr 30	Must have at least one horse/site, maximum 4 horses/corral & site.
BENBOW LAKE SRA ■ C1231	Apr 1-Oct 31	15	15	D	YES	24'	30'	$12	May 1-Sep 30	c/o Eel River District, P.O. Box 100, Weott, CA 95571-0100, (707) 946-2311. Cold showers. Closed when not on reservations.
BIG BASIN REDWOODS SP										21600 Big Basin Way, Boulder Creek, CA 95006-9050, (408) 338-6132.
• Walk-in (tents only) C4061	All Year	15	15	D	YES	—	—	$12	Mar 22-Oct 26	Closed for facilities restoration for all or part of 1991.
• Drive-in C4068	All Year	15	15	D	YES	24'	27'	$12	Mar 22-Oct 26	
• Drive-in (tents only) C4062	All Year	15	15	D	YES	—	—	$12	Mar 22-Oct 26	
• Handicapped ■ C4069	All Year	15	15	D	YES	—	18'	$12	Mar 22-Oct 26	Disabled site only!
BOLSA CHICA SB C5841	All Year	7	15	D	YES	24'	48'	$14	May 24-Sep 2	18331 Enterprise, Huntington Beach 92648, (714) 846-3460. No tents. Self-contained vehicles only. Cold showers. Include towed vehicle in 48' maximum length.
BOTHE-NAPA VALLEY SP ■										3801 St. Helena Hwy. N., Calistoga, CA 94515, (707) 942-4575.
• Ritchie Creek Drive In C2401	All Year	15	15	D	YES	24'	31'	$12	May 1-Sep 30	
BRANNAN ISLAND SRA										17645 Highway 160, Rio Vista, CA 94571, (916) 777-6671.
• Drive In ■ C3141	Mar 1-Oct 31	15	30	D	NO	31'	31'	$12	Mar 1-Oct 31	Berth 35'x10'. Boats over 10' need 2 berths, includes walk-in site.
• Walk In, Boat Berths C3142	Mar 1-Oct 31	15	30	D	YES	—	—	$12	Mar 1-Oct 31	
• Drive In, Boat Berths C3149	Mar 1-Oct 31	15	30	D	YES	31'	31'	$12	Mar 1-Oct 31	
BUTANO SP										P.O. Box 9, Pescadero, CA 94060, (415) 879-0173
• Drive-in C4232	May 1-Sep 2	15	15	D	NO	24'	27'	$12	Mar 22-Oct 26	Very limited extra vehicle parking.
• Walk-in (tents only) C4231	May 1-Sep 2	15	15	D	NO	—	—	$12	Mar 22-Oct 26	
CALAVERAS BIG TREES SP										P.O. Box 120, Arnold, CA 95223, (209) 795-2334.
• North Grove ■ C3062	May 20-Sep 16	15	15	D	YES	30'	30'	$12	May 24-Sep 2	Contact park for winter camping information.
• Oak Hollow C3061	May 20-Sep 16	15	15	D	YES	27'	27'	$12	May 24-Sep 2	
CARPINTERIA SB										c/o Channel Coast Dist., 24 E. Main St., Ventura, CA 93001, (805) 684-2811/654-4611.
• Anacapa/Santa Cruz-35 C5141	All Year	7	15	CD	YES	35'	35'	$14	Mar 15-Sep 29	2 vehicle maximum all sites.
• Anacapa/Santa Cruz-28 C514A	All Year	7	15	CD	YES	—	28'	$14	Mar 15-Sep 29	
• San Miguel (Long Row) C5142	All Year	7	15	H	YES	30'	30'	$18	Mar 15-Sep 29	No tents.
• San Miguel (Inland Hookups) C5148	All Year	7	15	H	YES	21'	21'	$18	Mar 15-Sep 29	No tents.
• San Miguel (Inland) C5146	All Year	7	15	CD	YES	21'	21'	$14	Mar 15-Sep 29	No tents.
• San Miguel (Beach Row) C5143	All Year	7	15	CD	YES	24'	24'	$19	Mar 15-Sep 29	Small tents allowed.
• Santa Rosa (Inland) 24 C5149	All Year	7	15	CD	YES	24'	24'	$18	Mar 15-Sep 29	No tents.
• Santa Rosa (Long Row) C5144	All Year	7	15	H	YES	30'	30'	$18	Mar 15-Sep 29	No tents.
• Santa Rosa (Inland) C5142	All Year	7	15	H	YES	21'	21'	$18	Mar 15-Sep 29	No tents.
• Santa Rosa (Beach Row) C5145	All Year	7	15	H	YES	24'	24'	$23	Mar 15-Sep 29	Small tents allowed.
CASTLE CRAGS SP C1241	May 15-Oct 1	15	30	D	YES	21'	27'	$12	May 15-Oct 1	Castella, CA 96017, (916) 235-2684. May close due to snow.
CASWELL MEMORIAL SP C3161	Mar 15-Sep 15	15	15	D	YES	21'	24'	$12	May 24-Sep 2	28000 S. Austin Road, Ripon, CA 95366, (209) 599-3810. Stanislaus River may be closed seasonally. Contact park for info.
CHINA CAMP SP (Walk-in) C2021	All Year	7	15	P	NO	—	—	$7	Apr 1-Oct 31	East San Pedro Road, San Rafael, CA 94901, (415) 456-1286/456-0766. Tents only. No wheelchair access. Gate locked sunset to 8 AM.
CLEAR LAKE SP ■ C2185	All Year	15	30	D	YES	35'	35'	$12	Apr 1-Oct 31	5300 Soda Bay Rd., Kelseyville, CA 95451, (707) 279-4293.
• Kelsey Creek C2183	All Year	15	30	D	YES	35'	35'	$12	Apr 1-Oct 31	
• Lakeside Premium C2181	All Year	15	30	D	YES	35'	35'	$17	Apr 1-Oct 31	
• Lower & Upper Bayview C2182	Apr 1-Sep 30	15	30	D	YES	21'	21'	$12	Apr 1-Oct 31	
• Cole Creek C2184	Apr 1-Sep 30	15	30	D	YES	24'	24'	$12	Apr 1-Oct 31	
COL. ALLENSWORTH SHP ■ C3411	Mar 15-Sep 8	15	30	D	NO	27'	35'	$12	No Peak	Star Route 1, Box 148, Earlimart, CA 93219, (805) 849-3433.
COLUSA-SACRAMENTO RIVER SRA C1401	Apr 1-Sep 15	15	30	D	YES	24'	27'	$12	May 1-Sep 30	P.O. Box 207, Colusa, CA 95932, (916) 458-4927. May close due to flooding.
CUYAMACA RANCHO SP										12551 Hwy. 79, Descanso, CA 92016, (619) 765-0755.
• Paso Picacho C6183	Mar 29-Oct 31	30	30	D	YES	27'	24'	$12	May 1-Sep 30	No horses allowed at Paso or Green Valley.
• Green Valley ■ C6182	All Year	30	30	D	YES	27'	30'	$12	May 1-Sep 30	Horses at Los Caballos only.
• Los Caballos Horse Camp C6181	May 17-Oct 31	30	30	D	YES	30'	30'	$14	May 1-Sep 30	Horseman only. Four horses only.
DEL NORTE COAST REDWOODS SP C1031	Jun 14-Sep 2	15	30	D	YES	27'	31'	$12	May 24-Sep 2	4241 Kings Valley Road, Crescent City, CA 95531, (707) 464-9533 Closed Sept-Mid June
D.L. BLISS SP C3032	Jun 14-Sep 2	15	CLOSED	D	YES	15'	18'	$12	May 24-Sep 2	P.O. Box 266, Tahoma, CA 95733, (916) 525-7277
• Premium Lakefront C3031	Jun 14-Sep 2	15	CLOSED	D	YES	15'	18'	$17	May 24-Sep 2	Closed Mid September-Mid June
DOHENY SB Inland C6101 ■	All Year	7	15	CD	YES	35'	35'	$14	Mar 1-Nov 30	25300 Harbor Dr., Dana Point, CA 92629, (714) 496-6172. Two vehicle maximum, including trailer, per site. No third vehicle parking available.
• Premium Beachfront C6102	All Year	7	15	CD	YES	35'	35'	$19	Mar 1-Nov 30	
DONNER MEMORIAL SP C3011	May 24-Sep 2	15	CLOSED	D	YES	24'	28'	$12	May 24-Sep 2	P.O. Box 9210, Truckee, CA 95737, (916) 587-3841. Closed Oct 1-May 24. Two vehicle maximum, including trailer, per site.
EL CAPITAN SB C5191	All Year	7	15	CD	YES	27'	30'	$14	Apr 6-Oct 26	#10 Refugio Beach, Goleta, CA 93117, (805) 968-1033. 25 cent cold showers.
EMERALD BAY SP										P.O. Box 266, Tahoma, CA 95733, (916) 541-3030.
• Eagle Point C3131	Jun 14-Sep 2	15	CLOSED	D	YES	18'	21'	$12	May 24-Sep 2	Closed Mid September to Mid June
FOLSOM LAKE SRA										7806 Folsom-Auburn Rd., Folsom, CA 95630, (916) 988-0205. No alcohol or glass on beach.
• Peninsula C3183	May 17-Sep 9	7	30	D	NO	31'	31'	$12	May 24-Sep 2	Remote Campground.
• Negro Bar C3182	Apr 5-Sep 30	7	7	D	YES	31'	31'	$12	May 24-Sep 2	Two vehicle maximum each site, including trailer, at each campground.
• Beals Point ■ C3181	Apr 5-Sep 30	7	7	D	YES	31'	31'	$12	May 24-Sep 2	
GRIZZLY CREEK REDWOODS SP ■ C1101	All Year	15	30	D	YES	24'	30'	$12	May 1-Sep 30	c/o Eel River Dist., P.O. Box 100, Weott, CA 95571, (707) 946-2311
GROVER HOT SPRINGS SP ■ C3221	May 17-Sep 7	15	30	D	YES	24'	27'	$12	May 24-Sep 2	P.O. Box 188, Marklesville, CA 96120, (916) 694-2248. Open for winter camping without showers. Pool and hot springs open 9 a.m.-9 p.m. Use fee $4 Adult, $2 Child each entry.
HALF MOON BAY SB ■ C2775	All Year	7	15	D	NO	27'	27'	$12	May 1-Oct 31	95 Kelly Avenue, Half Moon Bay, CA 94019, (415) 726-6238.
• Perimeter C2771	All Year	7	15	D	NO	21'	21'	$12	May 1-Oct 31	Limited extra vehicle parking in all campgrounds.
• Asphalt Island A C2773	All Year	7	15	D	NO	24'	24'	$12	May 1-Oct 31	No tents.
• Asphalt Island B C2774	All Year	7	15	D	NO	36'	36'	$12	May 1-Oct 31	No tents.
HENDY WOODS SP ■ C1481	May 10-Sep 28	15	30	D	YES	35'	35'	$12	May 3-Sep 28	c/o Mendocino District, P.O. Box 440, Mendocino, CA 95460, (707) 937-5804
HENRY COWELL REDWOODS SP ■ C4181	Mar 15-Oct 15	7	7	D	YES	27'	35'	$14	Mar 22-Oct 26	101 No. Big Trees Park Rd., Felton, CA 95018, (408) 335-4598/438-2396.
HUMBOLDT REDWOODS SP										P.O. Box 100, Weott, CA 95571-0100, (707) 946-2311.
• Burlington C1191	All Year	15	30	D	YES	24'	33'	$12	May 1-Sep 30	
• Hidden Springs C1192	May 17-Sep 30	15	CLOSED	D	YES	24'	33'	$12	May 17-Sep 30	Closed Oct 1-May 17
• Albee Creek C1193	May 17-Sep 30	15	CLOSED	D	YES	24'	33'	$12	May 17-Sep 30	Closed Oct 1-May 17
INDIAN GRINDING ROCK SHP C3731	Mar 1-Sep 2	7	30	D	NO	27'	27'	$12	May 24-Sep 2	14881 Pine Grove-Volcano Road, Pine Grove, CA 95665, (209) 296-7488.
JEDEDIAH SMITH REDWOODS SP C1021 ■	May 20-Sep 2	15	30	D	YES	31'	36'	$12	May 24-Sep 2	4241 Kings Valley Road, Crescent City, CA 95531, (707) 464-9533 or (707) 458-3310.
LAKE OROVILLE SRA										400 Glen Drive, Oroville, CA 95966, (916) 538-2200.
• Bidwell Canyon C1510	Mar 22-Sep 29	30	30	H	YES	31'	40'	$16	May 24-Sep 2	Include boat trailer in total RV length for both campgrounds.
• Loafer Creek ■ C1511	Mar 22-Sep 29	30	CLOSED	D	YES	31'	40'	$12	May 24-Sep 2	Loafer Creek closed during winter. Call park for winter information.
LAKE PERRIS SRA										17801 Lake Perris Drive, Perris, CA 92370, (714) 657-9000
• Luiseno ■ C6652	All Year	15	15	D	YES	31'	31'	$12	May 1-Sep 30	(After hours enter via Moreho Beach Drive) Handicapped site hookups only.
• Hook-up C6651	All Year	15	15	H	YES	31'	31'	$16	May 1-Sep 30	Maximum 2 vehicles in developed sites, and 3 in hookup sites, including trailers.
LEO CARRILLO SB										c/o Santa Monica Mtns. District, 2860A Camino Dos Rios, Newbury Park, CA 91320,
• Canyon C5401	All Year	7	15	CD	YES	31'	31'	$14	Mar 1-Nov 30	(818) 706-1310. May be closed for rehabilitation to July 1991.
MacKERRICHER SP ■ C1461	Mar 22-Oct 13	15	30	D	YES	35'	35'	$12	Mar 22-Oct 13	c/o Mendocino Dist., P.O. Box 440, Mendocino, CA 95460, (707) 937-5804. No additional parking space available.
MALAKOFF DIGGINS SHP C3561	May 1-Sep 15	30	30	D	NO	18'	24'	$12	May 24-Sep 2	23579 N. Bloomfield Road, Nevada City, CA 95959, (916) 265-2740. Trailers/RVs use Tyler Foote Rd. and Cruzon Grade.

FAMILY CAMPING

PARK & CAMPGROUND	RESERVATION PERIOD	CAMPING DAYS LIMITED JUNE-SEPTEMBER	CAMPING DAYS LIMITED OCTOBER-MAY	CAMPSITES CLASSIFICATION	SHOWERS	MAXIMUM TRAILER LENGTH	MAXIMUM MOTORHOME OR CAMPER LENGTH	CAMPSITE FEE	PEAK SEASON DATES	GENERAL INFORMATION
MANRESA SB ■ C4071	Mar 15-Oct 20	7	15	D	YES	—		$14	Apr 6-Oct 26	205 Manresa Beach Rd., La Selva 95076, (408) 761-1795. Walk-in tent sites only!
McARTHUR-BURNEY FALLS MEMORIAL SP C1251	May 1-Sep 30	15	30	D	YES	32'	35'	$12	May 1-Sep 30	Rt. 1, Box 1260, Burney, CA 96013, (916) 335-2777. Two vehicle maximum, including trailers & boat trailers. Include boat trailer length to RV length.
McGRATH SB C5671	All Year	7	15	CD	YES	30'	34'	$14	Mar 15-Sep 29	c/o Channel Coast District, 24 E. Main St., Ventura, CA 93001, (805) 654-4744 or 654-4611. M-F 8 to 5. Limited extra vehicle parking.
MILLERTON LAKE SRA ■ C3781	All Year	15	30	D	YES	31'	31'	$12	May 24-Sep 2	P.O. Box 205, Friant, CA 93626, (209) 822-2332.
MONTANA DE ORO SP C4411	May 24-Sep 2	7	15	P	NO	24'	24'	$7	Apr 6-Oct 26	Pecho Road, Los Osos, CA 93402, (805) 528-0513.
• Hazard Horse Camp	All Year	7	7	P	NO	31'	31'	$7	Apr 6-Oct 26	Maximum 6 horses. Limited corral space. Maximum 4 vehicles per horse camp.
MORRO BAY SP C4432	All Year	7	15	D	YES	31'	31'	$12	Apr 6-Oct 26	c/o Morro Bay SP, Morro Bay, CA 93442, (805) 772-2560.
• Hook-ups C4431	All Year	7	15	H	YES	31'	35'	$16	Apr 6-Oct 26	(Handicapped developed sites only.) (Hook-ups electricity/water only.)
MORRO STRAND SB C4471	May 24-Sep 2	7	15	D	NO	24'	24'	$12	Apr 6-Oct 26	c/o Morro Bay SP, Morro Bay, CA 93442, (805) 772-2560.
MT. DIABLO SP C2031	Oct 1-May 31	30	30	D	NO	20'	24'	$12	May 24-Sep 2	P.O. Box 250, Diablo, CA 94528, (415) 837-2525. All alcoholic beverages prohibited. Fire restrictions 6/1 to 9/30. Contact park information. Park entrance gates closed from sunset to 8:00 a.m. Winding mountain roads. Trailers over 20' not advised.
MT. SAN JACINTO SP										25905 Hwy. 243, P.O. Box 308, Idyllwild, CA 92349, (714) 659-2607
• Idyllwild ■ C6161	All Year	15	30	D	YES	24'	24'	$12	May 24-Sep 2	(North end of town near fire station on Hwy. 243)
• Stone Creek C6162	All Year	15	30	P	NO	24'	24'	$7	May 24-Sep 2	(6 mi. north of Idyllwild on Hwy. 243)
NEW BRIGHTON SB C4081	Mar 15-Nov 30	7	15	CD	YES	36'	36'	$14	Apr 6-Oct 26	1500 Park Avenue, Hwy 1, Capitola, CA 96010, (408) 475-4850
PALOMAR MOUNTAIN SP ■										Palomar Mountain, CA 92060, (619) 742-3462/765-0755
• Doane Valley C6171	Mar 29-Oct 27	30	30	D	YES	21'	21'	$12	May 1-Sep 30	Seasonal trout fishing Nov-Jun
PATRICK'S POINT SP										4150 Patrick's Pt. Dr., Trinidad, CA 95570, (707) 677-3570.
• Agate C1061	May 24-Sep 7	15	30	D	YES	31'	31'	$12	May 24-Sep 2	Two vehicle limit in each campground site.
• Abalone C1063 ■	May 24-Sep 7	15	30	D	YES	31'	31'	$12	May 24-Sep 2	Frequent heavy summer fog.
• Penn Creek C1064	May 24-Sep 7	15	30	D	YES	31'	31'	$12	May 24-Sep 2	
PFEIFFER SIB SUR SP ■ C4481	All Year	7	15	D	YES	27'	32'	$14	Apr 6-Oct 26	Hwy 1, Big Sur, CA 93920, (408) 667-2315. Maximum two licensed vehicles per site.
PISMO DUNES SVRA C2641										Pier Avenue, Oceano, CA 93445, (805) 549-3433.
• Pismo Dunes OHV-Beach	All Year	7	7	P	NO	40'	40'	$5	No Peak	Beach camping (soft sand). Each vehicle entering under own power needs separate reservation.
PISMO SB										Pier Avenue, Oceano, CA 93445, (805) 549-3433.
• North Beach C4461	May 24-Sep 2	7	15	D	NO	31'	36'	$12	Apr 6-Oct 26	Oceano showers not available to North Beach campers.
• Oceano C4462	All Year	7	15	D	YES	18'	31'	$12	Apr 6-Oct 26	
• Oceano (Hook-up) C4463	All Year	7	15	H	YES	31'	36'	$16	Apr 6-Oct 26	Hook-up electricity/water only.
PLUMAS-EUREKA SP										310 Johnsville Road, Blairsden, CA 96103, (916) 836-2380.
• Upper Jamison ■ C3211	Jun 14-Sep 2	15	15	D	YES	24'	30'	$12	Jun 14-Sep 2	All sites are pre-assigned.
• Upper Jamison (walk-in) C3212	Jun 14-Sep 2	15	15	D	YES	—		$12	Jun 14-Sep 2	One vehicle per walk-in site. Maximum walk-in distance 75'.
POINT MUGU SP										c/o Santa Monica Mtns. District, 2860A Camino Dos Rios, Newbury Park, CA 91320,
• Big Sycamore Canyon ■ C5731	All Year	7	15	CD	YES	31'	31'	$12	Mar 1-Sep 30	(818) 706-1310 or (805) 987-3303.
• Thornhill Broom Beach C5732	All Year	7	15	P	NO	31'	31'	$7	Mar 1-Sep 30	Limited extra vehicle parking.
PORTOLA SP C4054 RV	May 3-Oct 26	15	30	D	YES	24'	27'	$12	Mar 22-Oct 26	Star Rt. 2, La Honda, CA 94020, (415) 948-9098 or (408) 335-9145.
PRAIRIE CREEK REDWOODS SP										Orick, CA 95555, (707) 488-2171 or 445-6547.
• Elk Prairie C1041 ■	May 24-Sep 2	15	30	D	YES	24'	27'	$12	May 24-Sep 2	Two vehicle limit including trailer.
REFUGIO SB C5271	Feb 1-Dec 1	7	15	CD	YES	27'	30'	$14	Apr 6-Oct 26	#10 Refugio Beach, Goleta, CA 93117, (805) 968-1033. Subject to closure during rainy season.
RICHARDSON GROVE SP										c/o Eel River District, P.O. Box 100, Weott, CA 95571-0100, (707) 946-2311
• Huckleberry & Madrone C1161	All Year	15	30	D	YES	24'	30'	$12	May 1-Sep 30	
• Oak Flat C1162	Jun 7-Sep 8	15	CLOSED	D	YES	18'	24'	$12	Jun 7-Sep 8	Oak Flat closed Mid Sept.-Mid June
RUSSIAN GULCH SP C1411	Mar 22-Oct 13	15	30	D	YES	24'	27'	$12	Mar 22-Oct 13	c/o Mendocino Dist., P.O. Box 440, Mendocino, CA 95460, (707) 937-5804. No additional parking space available. CAUTION: Narrow roads!
SALTON SEA SRA										P.O. Box 3166, North Shore, CA 92254, (619) 393-3052.
• Headquarters C6231	All Year	30	30	D	YES	30'	30'	$12	No Peak	
• Headquarters (no tents) C6232	All Year	30	30	H	YES	30'	35'	$16	No Peak	One motorhome or trailer per campsite.
SALT POINT SP										25050 Coast Hwy. 1, Jenner, CA 95450, (707) 847-3221/865-2391.
• Woodside C2482	Mar 1-Oct 31	10	10	D	NO	27'	31'	$12	Apr 1-Nov 30	East of Hwy. 1. Two vehicle limit most sites.
• Woodside Walk-in (tents only) C2481	Mar 1-Oct 31	10	10	D	NO	—	—	$12	Apr 1-Nov 30	No dogs. May be closed due to rains. Approx. ½ mile hike to campsite.
• Gerstle Cove C2489	Mar 1-Oct 31	10	10	D	NO	27'	31'	$12	Apr 1-Nov 30	
SAMUEL P. TAYLOR SP ■ C2331	Mar 25-Sep 15	7	7	D	YES	24'	27'	$12	Apr 1-Oct 31	P.O. Box 251, Lagunitas, CA 94938, (415) 488-9897
SAN CLEMENTE SB C6111	All Year	7	15	CD	YES	24'	28'	$14	Mar 1-Nov 30	3030 Avenida del Presidente, San Clemente, CA 92672, (714) 492-3156.
• Hook-ups C6112	All Year	7	15	H	YES	30'	30'	$18	Mar 1-Nov 30	One trailer or RV per campsite.
SAN ELIJO SB ■										2680 Carlsbad Blvd., Carlsbad, CA 92008, (619) 753-5091
• Premium Beachfront C6541	Feb 1-Nov 30	7	15	CD	YES	35'	35'	$19	Mar 1-Nov 30	Two licensed vehicles per site (trailer considered as a vehicle).
• Inland C6542	Feb 1-Nov 30	7	15	CD	YES	35'	35'	$14	Mar 1-Nov 30	
SAN LUIS RESERVOIR SRA ■										31426 W. Hwy. 152, Santa Nella, CA 95322, (209) 826-1196.
• Basalt C3331	Mar 15-Sep 15	15	30	D	YES	30'	30'	$12	May 24-Sep 2	
SAN ONOFRE SB C6631	All Year	15	30	CD	YES	30'	30'	$14	Mar 1-Nov 30	c/o Pendleton Coast District, 3030 Avenida del Presidente, San Clemente, CA 92672, (714) 492-4872. Outdoor/cold showers.
SAN SIMEON SB ■										P.O. Box 8, San Simeon, CA 93452, (805) 927-4509/927-2068
• San Simeon Creek C4871	Mar 15-Sep 30	10	30	D	YES	35'	35'	$12	Apr 6-Oct 26	One trailer per site at San Simeon Creek.
• Washburn C4872	Mar 15-Sep 30	10	30	P	NO	21'	31'	$7	Apr 6-Oct 26	San Simeon Creek facilities not available to Washburn campers.
SEACLIFF SB C4091										State Park Drive, Aptos, CA 95003, (408) 688-3222/688-3241
• Premium Beachfront	All Year	7	7	H	YES	36'	40'	$23	Apr 6-Oct 26	No tents! Subject to storm evacuation.
SILVERWOOD LAKE SRA										Star Route 7A, Hesperia, CA 92345, (619) 389-2303
• Mesa C5921	All Year	10	30	D	YES	31'	34'	$12	May 1-Sep 30	All visitors must wait in line.
SONOMA COAST SB										Bodega Bay, CA 94923, (707) 875-3483/865-2391.
• Bodega Dunes ■ C2091	All Year	10	30	D	YES	31'	31'	$12	Apr 1-Nov 30	Two vehicle limit all sites. Limited parking.
• Wrights Beach Premium C2092	All Year	10	30	D	NO	27'	27'	$17	Apr 1-Nov 30	
SOUTH CARLSBAD SB ■										2680 Carlsbad Blvd., Carlsbad, CA 92008, (619) 438-3143.
• Premium Beachfront C6522	All Year	7	15	CD	YES	35'	35'	$19	Mar 1-Nov 30	No extra vehicles parking! Two vehicles per site strictly enforced!
• Inland C6522	All Year	7	15	CD	YES	35'	35'	$14	Mar 1-Nov 30	Trailer is considered a vehicle.
STANDISH-HICKEY SRA ■										c/o Eel River District, P.O. Box 100, Weott, CA 95571-0100, (707) 946-2311
• Hickey Rock Creek C1171	All Year	15	30	D	YES	24'	27'	$12	May 1-Sep 30	
• Redwood (Lower) C1172	Jun 7-Sep 8	15	CLOSED	D	YES	—	18'	$12	May 1-Sep 30	No trailers. Redwood closed Sep 10-Jun 7.
SUGARLOAF RIDGE SP C2471	All Year	15	15	D	NO	24'	27'	$12	May 3-Sep 2	2605 Adobe Canyon Road, Kenwood, CA 96452-9004, (707) 833-5712, (707) 938-1519. One mile steep narrow winding road.
SUGAR PINE POINT SP C3391	Jun 14-Sep 2	15	30	D	YES	24'	30'	$12	May 24-Sep 2	P.O. Drawer D, Tahoma, CA 95733, (916) 525-7982. Showers closed in winter.
SUNSET SB C4101	Mar 15-Oct 20	7	15	CD	YES	31'	31'	$14	Mar 15-Nov 30	201 Sunset Beach Road, Watsonville, CA 95076, (408) 724-1266.
TAHOE SRA										P.O. Box 583, Tahoe City, CA 95730, (916) 525-7982
• Lakeside C3021	May 24-Sep 2	15	CLOSED	D	YES	24'	28'	$12	May 24-Sep 2	2 vehicle limit/site (including trailers).
• Hillside (tents only) C3022	May 24-Sep 2	15	CLOSED	D	YES	—	—	$12	May 24-Sep 2	2 vehicle limit/site. Closed Oct.-Mid May
TURLOCK LAKE SRA C3111	Mar 15-Sep 15	15	15	D	YES	24'	27'	$12	May 24-Sep 2	22600 Lake Road, La Grange, CA 95329, (209) 874-2008/874-2056.
VAN DAMME SP C1421	Mar 22-Oct 13	15	30	D	YES	35'	35'	$12	Mar 22-Oct 13	c/o Mendocino Dist., P.O. Box 440, Mendocino, CA 95460, (707) 937-5804. No extra parking available.
WOODSON BRIDGE SRA C1291	May 1-Sep 30	15	30	D	YES	31'	31'	$12	May 1-Sep 30	25340 South Avenue, Corning, CA 96021, (916) 839-2112.

Appendix D — Access Organizations

Environmental Traveling Companions

Fort Mason Center Bldg. C
San Francisco, CA 94123
(415) 474-7662

Offers outdoor and environmental education programs for people with special needs, including river rafting and a kayak trip to Angel Island State Park

Green Pastures, Inc.

Contact Jeff Marks
730 Cornelia Court
Mountain View, CA 94040
(415) 965-2333

A group home for disabled children providing a home-like environment to love and challenge each child to reach his/her full God-given potential

Dr. Louis Levy

4961 Edgerton Avenue
Encino, CA 91436
(818) 567-3155

Information regarding Ritter Rings, access mats for soft or uneven surfaces.

National Handicap Sports

Berkeley — (415) 642-8342

Fresno — Regional office
(209) 252-6126

Los Angeles Chapter
"The Unwreckables"
Contact Linda Fryback
PO Box 3064
Redondo Beach, CA 90277
(213) 374-6775

A mostly adult group with all types of disabilities. Sponsors monthly ski trips to Mammoth, waterskiing, kayaking, and camping trips.

Northern California Chapter
5926 Illinois Avenue
Orangevale, CA 95662
(916) 989-0402

Large membership sponsoring a wide range of accessible activities including the Summer Games sports, and Tahoe Handicap Ski School in Alpine Meadows December — April

Orange County Chapter
Contact Janet Beutner
531 Heather Avenue
La Habra, CA 90631
(213) 697-0351

Family-oriented activities

San Diego Chapter
San Diego Adventures
Contact Charlene Rawls
3169 Linlow Street
San Diego, CA 92015
(619) 582-3871

Began as a ski group; now includes accessible waterskiing trips.

Truckee Chapter
Operation Challenge
PO Box 9780
Truckee, CA 96162
(916) 582-0520

Sponsors accessible weekend summer campouts at Donner Lake.

**Sequoya Challenge/CIMIN
(Calif. Institute of Man in Nature)**

Contact John Olmstead
PO Box 1026
Nevada City, CA 95959
(916) 272-3823

Sponsors a number of projects to provide accessible trails in the parks and forests of California including the South Yuba River Project.

Sierra Club- Angeles District

Contact Pepi Feinblatt
3550 West 6th Street, Suite 321
Los Angeles, CA 90020
(213) 387-4287

Recreational Outdoor Activities for the Disabled (R.O.A.D.) — Inner City Outings Committee sponsors accessible outdoors adventures in the San Gabriel and Santa Monica Mountains area.

Telephone Pioneers of America

Contact Clyde Wright
2180 Fall Trail Road
Placerville, CA 95667
(916) 622-5654

A service organization of retired Pacific Bell employees. One of many contributions is to assist the state in constructing docks, paths and drinking fountains for the physically impaired.

Whole Access, Inc.

Contact Phyllis Cangemi
517 Lincoln Avenue
Redwood City, CA 94061
(415) 363-2647

A non-profit organization that works to make parks and nature experiences accessible to people of all abilities. Provides education, training and technical consulting to planners, designers and managers of park and open space facilities.

The Wilderness Institute

Contact Brad Childs.
28118 Agoura Road
Agoura Hills, CA 91301
(818) 991-7327

Sponsors accessible outings in the Santa Monica Mountains area and other activities such as skiing, river rafting and rock climbing.

State Park District Offices

The following list of district offices only includes those referred to in the text. This is not a complete list. Send correspondence to: California Department of Parks and Recreation, c/o district office listed below.

USDA - Forest Service
Saugus Ranger District
(Pyramid Lake SRA)
30800 Bouquet Canyon Road
Saugus, CA 91350
(805) 296-9710

Big Sur District
Big Sur, CA 93920
(408) 667-2315

Cascade District
PO Box 2430
Shasta, CA 96087
(916) 225-2065

Channel Coast District
24 East Main Street
Ventura, CA 93001
(805) 654-4611

Clear Lake District
5300 Soda Bay Road
Kelseyville, CA 95451
(707) 279-2267

Diablo District
4180 Treat Boulevard, Suite D
Concorde, CA 94518
(415) 687-1800

East Bay Regional Park District
11500 Skyline Boulevard
Oakland, CA 94619-2443
(510) 531-9300 Ext. 2200

Eel River District
1600 Highway 101
Garberville, CA 95440
(707) 247 3378

(Photo courtesy CDPR)

Four Rivers District
31426 West Highway 152
Santa Nella, CA 95322
(209) 826-1196

Frontera District
3990 Old Town Avenue, Suite 300-C
San Diego, CA 94937
(619) 238-3195 or 631-3195

Gaviota District
#10 Refugio Beach Road
Goleta, CA 93117
(805) 567-5013 or 968-1411

Klamath District
4150 Patrick's Point Drive
Trinidad, CA 95570
(707) 677-3570 or 445-6547

Marin District
1255-A East San Fancisco Boulevard
San Rafael, CA 94901
(415) 456-1286

Mendocino District
PO Box 440
Mendocino, CA 95460
(707) 937-5804

Napa District
3801 St. Helena Highway North
Calistoga, CA 94515
(707) 942-5370

Pajaro Coast District
101 Madeline Drive
Aptos, CA 95003
(408) 688-3241

Russian River District
PO Box 123
Duncan Mills, CA 95450
(707) 865-2391

San Diego Coast District
2680 Carlsbad Boulevard
Carlsbad, CA 92008
(619) 729-8947

San Joaquin Valley District
PO Box 205
Friant, CA 93626
(209) 822-2661

San Luis Obispo Coast District
3220 S. Hiquera, Suite 311
San Luis Obispo, CA 93401
(805) 549-3312

San Mateo Coast District
95 Kelly Avenue
Half Moon Bay, CA 94109
(415) 726-6238

Santa Cruz Mountains District
101 North Big Trees Park Road
Felton,. CA 95018
(408) 335-7077

Sonoma District
20 Spain Street East
Sonoma, CA 95476
(707) 938-1519

Glossary

ACCESSIBLE — Any feature described that is reasonably available to a wheelchair user with or without the assistance of another person. Any barriers or special considerations are specified in the description of each feature.

☐ **Campsite** — Ample room for wheelchair to manouver and no obstacles impeding travel from the vehicle to the table and tent site. Preferably, surfaces are paved or hardened, there is an accessible picnic table, and an accessible restroom is within easy wheeling distance.

☐ **Chemical toilet** — A portable toilet that is specially designed for wheelchair users. A shallow entry ramp leads to a wide doorway. With the door closed, there is enough room inside to allow pivot transfer onto a raised seat. Grab bars are provided.

☐ **Dock** — Loading dock at a lake or beach that has a smooth approach with less than 1-inch transition onto the dock itself. Unless otherwise mentioned, assistance is recommended when using accessible docks. There are usually no railing or wheel stops in these areas and slopes to the docks are usually steeper than 5%.

☐ **Drinking fountain** — The standard accessible fountain found in most parks extends out from a pedestal at a height of no less than 30" and has room for access from a sitting position.

☐ **Grade** — Inclines of 0% to 3% are considered accessible without assistance; 3% to 6% grades require more of a push but are still accessible. Inclines of over 6% are defined as being steep enough to need assistance.

☐ **Picnic Table** — A table with a seating area suitable for a wheelchair user. See PICNIC TABLE.

☐ **Restroom** — Doorways are a minimum 27" wide with no barriers such as lips or fixtures. Restroom stalls must have at least a 30" entry and grab bars must be affixed to the walls. High toilet seats and transfer type are mentioned when necessary.

☐ **Shower** — The shower stall and approach are ample for wheelchair passage, controls for the shower head are within reach of a person in a seated position (less than 48" from the floor), and grab bars are afixed to the walls. Other features of an accessible shower may be: a retractable seat in the stall, drying area with a bench, and a lowered or hand-held shower head.

☐ **Sink** — A specially designed sink that allows for easy water control and provides knee room for a wheelchair user.

☐ **Telephone** — The coin slot on a public telephone is no more than 54" from the floor and there are no barriers in front of phone such as curbing or soft wheeling surface.

☐ **Trail** — Trails are described as being accessible with or without help. For the purposes of *California Parks Access*, a trail is accessible if it has a grade of no more than 6%, the trail tread is firm and even, and there are no physical barriers (roots, steps). A trail that requires assistance may have inclines of more than 6%, soft or irregular trail tread, and/or small obsticles, but is still broad enough for wheelchair travel.

☐ **Water Spigot** — An outdoor hose bib for drawing drinking water. Usually found near a campsite with no barriers and high enough to reach from a seated position. Often, the on-off control is a long lever.

AMPHITHEATER — An outdoor gathering place, usually in a clearing near the campground. There is usually simple seating and a stage. Sometimes the surface is paved, but most often it is natural. Can be used synonymously with Campfire Center.

ADOBE — A building made of large natural clay blocks. Often associated with Mexican architecture.

APPROACH — A surface leading to a given park feature.

ATV — All-terrain vehicle. Motorized 3- or 4-wheel vehicle like a motorcycle, that is designed to ride off-road.

BBQ — A box-shaped metal fire container with a grate for cooking usually on a pedestal at varying heights.

BOARDWALK — A pathway defined by a succession of lateral wooden boards providing firm access to a given destination.

Telephone Pioneers of America have built many boardwalks and accessible trails in California's parks.

(Photo courtesy Telephone Pioneers of Americal)

BOAT-IN CAMPING — A campsite reached by a body of water where a slip, mooring or beach area is provided for your boat.

CALIFORNIA DEPARTMENT OF PARKS AND RECREATION (CDPR) — The department of the California government responsible for the administration of all the State Parks, Recreation Areas, Beaches and Monuments.

CAMPFIRE CENTER — Can be used synonymously with Amphitheater. An area usually in the campground, with seating, a stage and large campfire ring where rangers and naturalist groups offer programs for campers and/or park visitors. Often during the evening program, the ranger will build a traditional campfire.

CONCRETE BBQ — A ground-level box-shaped fire container made of concrete with a grate for cooking purposes.

DAY USE AREA — Part of a park that is only open for use during daylight hours. Camping is not allowed in day use areas.

DESIGNATED — Any parking place, campsite, restroom, or other park feature that is specifically marked for use by a "handicapped" person. Because a feature is designated, does not necessarily mean that it is accessible without assistance or even that there are modifications to enhance access. These discrepencies are noted when applicable.

DIAGONAL TRANSFER — Transfer to another seat requiring less than a 180° turn of the body.

DOCENT — A volunteer from the community that serves as an adjunct to the staff at a State or National Park. A docent can act as tour guide, ticket taker, information officer or in any other capacity that is helpful to the park and its visitors. Docents are organized in associations that serve a specific park or parks and raise money for park improvements through book and gift sales and fund raisers.

ELEVATION — Listings of elevation are given for the accessible roads or features of the individual parks, not necessarily the highest elevation in the park. When a range is given, it indicates that places of interest are located at more than one general altitude.

ENROUTE CAMPING — An area designated solely for overnight camping. Usually, vehicles must be self-contained and there may or may not be restroom facilities. All enroute camping is delineated with small caps whether or not there are accessible features. It is assumed that the user will be in a self-contained vehicle. Enroute camping must be vacated by 9 a.m.

FCFS — First-come-first-served; campgrounds labeled "(FCFS)" cannot be reserved. If you wish to stay in a FCFS campground, you must arrive early enough to find a vacant campsite.

FLAT — See LEVEL

FOOD STORAGE — Usually an upright wooden box with doors that open on the side. The box can be used for storage of food and supplies and can sometimes be locked. The box is usually placed on or near the table at a campsite to protect food from scavenging animals.

FULLY ACCESSIBLE — Meets the Uniform Federal Access Standard (UFAS) requirements for accessibility. Under normal circumstances, this would mean that the average user would not require assistance to access this feature. In the case of a restroom, fully accessible includes a lateral-transfer stall.

GRADE — A measurement of incline. *California Parks Access* uses %; incline can also be measured as a ration such as 1:50 (i.e. one foot increase in altitude for every fifty

feet of distance traveled), or in degrees (where 90° is straight up.)

HIGH SINK — A standard sink that has been raised to allow knee room for a wheelchair user. The controls may or may not be modified.

HIGH TOILET — The height of the toilet is between 17 and 20 inches making transfer easier from a wheelchair. Fully accessible restrooms have high toilets unless otherwise noted.

KIOSK — A small booth at the entry of a park or campground where an attendent collects fees or provides information. Most business at the kiosk can be done from your vehicle.

LATERAL TRANSFER — Transfer to another seat in a sideways motion requiring little or no twisting of the body. Often aided by the use of grab bars.

LEVEL — A surface with no more than a 3% gradient change. Same as FLAT.

LIP — An abrupt change in height of a surface. Is sometimes referred to as a transition.

LOW TOILET — The top of the toilet seat is lower than 17 inches. Unless otherwise mentioned, all restrooms have low toilets. Where there are low toilets in otherwise accessible restrooms, it will be so noted.

MODIFIED — Describes an object or structure that can accomodate a wheelchair user.

NATIONAL MONUMENT (NM) — A parcel of federal land set aside by presidential decree not requiring congressional approval. Land at a National Monument is intended to

preserve at least one national significant resource.

NATIONAL PARK SERVICE (NPS) — A branch of the United States Department of Agriculture responsible for National Parks, Monuments and Recreation Areas.

NATIONAL RECREATION AREA (NRA) — Lands and waters set aside for recreational use by an act of Congress. Many times they include bodies of water impounded by dams. National Recreation Areas are administered by the NPS or by other agencies such as the National Forest Service or the United States Department of Agriculture.

NATIONAL PARK (NP) — Usually contains a variety of natural and historic resources in a large expanse of land. National Parks can only be created by an act of Congress.

PICNIC TABLE — Most picnic tables are of three main types. The traditional type is made of lumber; wooden seats on either side are attached to the wooden table legs. Another table has a wooden top and seat, but the base and legs are made of metal piping. The third type is made of formed concrete. None of these tables are considered accessible unless they have been modified, but many times there may be room at the end of the tables to pull up a chair.

☐ **Modified** — Any picnic table that has been changed or built specially for wheelchair access. A seat may be removed for a side approach to the table, or the end of the table top could be longer than standard.

☐ **Extended end** — The table top of a standard picnic table has been built longer to provide a wheelchair user with access to the side and/or end of the table.

PIVOT TRANSFER — Transfer from a wheelchair to another seat requiring up to a 180° turn of the body.

PRIMITIVE — Describes park features having little improvements.

☐ **Boat ramp** — A sloping surface leading into a body of water used for launching small water craft. Usually dirt but sometimes paved, there are normally no docks, walkways or any other improvements nearby.

☐ **Camping** — Places reserved for camping within the park with few improvements. There is usually a table at each site, a chemical toilet and a water source nearby.

PARKING — Any place where vehicles may be left unoccupied. Parking surfaces in the parks varies from sloping dirt to smooth extra-wide designated places.

PAVED — Describes a surface covered with a firm protective material such as concrete or asphalt. Unless specifically noted, a paved area can consist of either by asphalt or concrete.

RETROFITTED — Describes any change or modification made to an already existing structure providing improved access for wheelchair users. Can be used synonymously with MODIFIED.

RV DUMP STATION — Facility for the disposal of sewage from the holding tank in a recreational vehicle.

SHALLOW STALL — A restroom or changing stall that is not long enough to accomodate a wheelchair with the privacy door closed.

SILL — The framing around a door creating a lip.

STALL — An area in a restroom or changing room with partition walls.

STATE URBAN RECREATION AREA (SURA) — A recreation area located within the metropolitan development of a major city.

STATE RECREATION AREA (SRA) — Area providing multiple outdoor recreational opportunities to meet other than purely local needs. These areas are selected for having terrain capable of withstanding extensive human impact and for their proximity to large centers of population, major routes of travel, or proven recreational resources such as man-made or natural bodies of water.

STATE BEACH (SB) — Areas fronting on the ocean or bays, designed to provide swimming, boating, fishing and other beach-oriented recreational opportunities.

STATE VEHICULAR RECREATION AREA (SVRA) — Areas where topographical features and associated recreational vehicle opportunites are the primary values. Such areas are chosen to insure that no substantial natural values are lost and that adjoining properties do not incur adverse effects.

STATE PARK (SP) — Major areas with outstanding scenic, natural, cultural, and/or ecological values, preserving the most significant examples of California's landscape.

STATE HISTORIC PARK (SHP) — Areas established primarily to preserve objects of historical interest and places commemorating important persons or historical events. Public facilities are limited to those necessary for the safety, comfort and enjoyment of visitors, such as access, parking water, sanitation, interpretation and picnicking.

STATE RESERVE (SR) — An area embracing outstanding natural or scenic characteristics, where native ecological associations, unique flora or fauna, and geological features are preserved in a condition of undisturbed integrety. Improvements are strictly limited to the minumum day use facilities necessary for public enjoyment and education. State Reserves may be either terrestrial or underwater.

STATE WILDERNESS — Areas where the earth and its community of life are untrammeled by Man, where the land retains its primeval character and influence. No permanent improvements or human habitations are permitted in a wilderness area.

TENT CABIN — A small, framed structure with canvas top and sides, a door, and a hard floor.

TOILET — Using the toilet as a trash receptacle costs us all money.

At Pismo Dunes SVRA, you can drive and camp right on the beach. The authors visited California's parks in their camper van conversion by Sportsmobile West of Fresno, California, available with wheelchair adaptations.

Please do not place anything other than toilet paper and human waste in the toilets. Where waste collection is made, solid items clog the vacuum system. In composting units, things such as diapers, trash and even heavy paper goods must be separated from the rest of the materials before biological breakdown can occur.

☐ **Chemical** — A portable toilet structure usually made of plastic. Waste is stored with a chemical disinfectant and deodorizer in a holding area below the toilet and collected when necessary.

☐ **Composting** — Permanent or temporary structure with a waterless toilet system. Waste is stored and enzymatically decomposed in a holding area below the toilet. Unlike the pit toilet, these toilets have less odors and do not attract as many flies.

☐ **Flush** — Any toilet that uses water to drain the bowl into a sewer or septic system. The flush mechanism can be on the tank, as in standard home models; on the pipe behind seat, as with most commercial toilets; mounted on the wall or floor; and sometimes on the end of a chain.

☐ **Pit** — Most commonly referred to as "outhouse." Usually permanent structures with a toilet seat. Waste is stored in a holding area below the toilet and collected when necessary.

☐ **Shasta** — A permanent structure with a waterless toilet and holding area below. Solid wastes are then separated from liquid to decompose. Due to the unpredictable efficiency of the shasta system, many of these units are being used now as composting or pit toilets.

☐ **Vault** — A term used synonymously with composting.

TRAIL TREAD — The walking surface of a footpath or other walkway. Trail treads may be rough, smooth, uneven, gravelly, etc.

TRAILHEAD — A place to access a trail often near parking or other developed area.

TRANSITION — The change in elevation of a walking surface where two surfaces do not meet flush. Often found when a dirt surface abuts a paved area.

UNEVEN — Describes an unreliable wheeling surface often requiring help to cross. Not smooth. Uneven surfaces can consist of dirt, grass or weathered pavement. Small ruts or depressions can catch front casters or make for an uncomfortable ride.

WAYSIDE CAMPGROUNDS — Relatively small areas suitable for overnight camping and offering convenient access to major highways.

YOUTH HOSTEL — Originally, youth hostels were dormitory-like facilities for young traveling people. Often housed in historic buildings, hostels provide a bed, bathroom, and communal eating facility in exchange for a nominal fee and cooperative clean-up. All ages of travelers are welcome, now, but "youth" hostels still retain their name.

"Everyone needs beauty as well as bread, places to play in and pray where nature may heal and cheer and give strength to body and soul alike."

John Muir

ORDER FORM

If you are borrowing this book, why not get a copy of your own? *California Parks Access* **is also a great gift idea for a friend or loved one. Here's how you order...**

TELEPHONE ORDERS: Call *TOLL FREE* 1-800-735-3805. Have your MasterCard or VISA ready

FAX ORDERS: Dial 1-619-738-0282

POSTAL ORDERS: Send to Cougar Pass Publishing Company

P.O. Box 463060A

Escondido, CA 92046-3060

Send me _____ copies of *California Parks Access: A Complete Guide to the State*

and National Parks for Visitors with Limited Mobility – $19.95 each $_____

(Allow 3 weeks for delivery)

California residents add 8.25% sales tax ($1.65 per copy) $_____

Add $3.50 shipping for first copy ordered $_____

Add $ .50 shipping for each additional copy ordered $_____

For rush orders add $2.00 shipping per copy ordered $_____

TOTAL $_____

Name _____

Street address _____

City _____ State _____ Zip _____

Daytime Phone (   ) _____

☐ Check or Money Order enclosed
☐ Please charge my MasterCard
☐ Please charge my VISA

Account Number _____

Signature _____ Exp. Date _____

Call TOLL FREE and order now!